A Terry Teachout Reader

A
Terry Teachout
Reader

❦

YALE UNIVERSITY PRESS

NEW HAVEN AND LONDON

Set in Postscript Galliard type by Keystone Typesetting, Inc.
Printed in the United States of America by Vail-Ballou Press.

Library of Congress Cataloging-in-Publication Data
Teachout, Terry.
A Terry Teachout reader.
         p.   cm.
Includes index.
ISBN 0-300-09894-4 (alk. paper)
1. Arts, American — 20th century. I. Title: Reader. II. Title.
NX504.T43 2004
700′.973 — dc22   2003016561

A catalogue record for this book is available from the British
Library.

The paper in this book meets the guidelines for permanence
and durability of the Committee on Production Guidelines
for Book Longevity of the Council on Library Resources.

10 9 8 7 6 5 4 3 2 1

To Laura Demanski,
the sister I wanted

If it was priggish for an older generation of reviewers to be ashamed of what they enjoyed and to feel they had to be contemptuous of popular entertainment, it's even more priggish for a new movie generation to be so proud of what they enjoy that they use their education to try to place trash within the acceptable academic tradition.

— PAULINE KAEL, "Trash, Art, and the Movies"

We spoke of the union of the advanced with the popular, the closing of the gulf between art and accessibility, high and low, as once in a certain sense it had been brought about by the romantic movement, literary and musical. But after that had followed a new and deeper cleavage between the good and the easy, the worthwhile and the entertaining, the advanced and the generally enjoyable, which has become the destiny of art. Was it sentimentality to say that music — and she stood for them all — demanded with growing consciousness to step out of her dignified isolation, to find common ground without becoming common, and to speak a language which even the musically untaught could understand, as it understood the Wolf's Glen and the Jungfernkranz and Wagner?

— THOMAS MANN, *Doctor Faustus*

Contents

PART THREE / DOWN TO THE CROSSROADS

PART FOUR / POST-POSTMODERN

Introduction: Across the Great Divide

I WROTE MY FIRST NEWSPAPER REVIEW IN 1977, THE YEAR Elvis Presley died and *Star Wars* was released, a quarter of a century ago — an eternity, measured by the hectic clock of daily journalism, and a fairly long time by just about anybody else's standards. It never occurred to me that I had found my life's work: I was an undergraduate in need of pocket money, pleased to be paid to go to mediocre concerts and write about them. Nor did it occur to me that America was about to change beyond my imagining. I was twenty-one, young enough to know I knew everything (not a bad attitude for a fledgling critic, either, so long as he grows out of it). Still, it is strange to contemplate what the world looked like as I made my way to the city room of the *Kansas City Star* to clack out my copy on an IBM Selectric typewriter. The *Star* already had a mainframe computer, but I didn't use it that night, and a decade would pass before I bought my first PC. In fact, I didn't even own an electric typewriter. I wrote my first magazine pieces on a big black Royal manual (one guitar-playing wag referred to it as my "acoustic typewriter"), corrected them with Liquid Paper, and mailed them to my editors. I had no fax, no e-mail, no VCR, no compact discs, no iPod. Nobody did. If you wanted to watch *M*A*S*H* or *Laverne & Shirley,* you stayed home on Tuesday nights.

I have a good many friends who are a good deal younger than I, and insofar as possible I try not to waste their time telling them what things were like when I was their age. I sometimes feel the temptation to live in the past, but one can truly live only in the moment, and the last thing I want to do is end up like the pathetic narrator of "Hey Nineteen," the Steely Dan song about a no-longer-young baby boomer who tries to tell his teenaged girlfriend about Aretha Franklin but discovers that "she don't remember / The Queen of Soul," subsequently realizing that "we got nothing in common / No, we can't talk at all." On the whole, I prefer to hear about the world they live in, though sometimes their stories make me shiver.

This, however, is a book, not a conversation. Moreover, it is a particular kind of book, a collection of some of the essays, articles, and reviews I have published in the course of the past decade and a half—that is, since I moved to New York, bought a home computer, and set up shop as a critic-for-hire (or, as an unfriendly colleague once described me, a "freelance philistine"). During that time, the world of my childhood disappeared, and America crossed a great cultural and technological divide. Now that we are firmly ensconced in the twenty-first century, I believe that a selection of the pieces I wrote between then and now may have some value as a chronicle, a road map of how we got from there to here, and what we lost— and gained—in the process.

So perhaps it is worth pausing to ask: what did *there* look like? How did it feel to grow up on the far side of the chasm, back in the days of the Beatles, the Berlin Wall, and black-and-white TV sets that only brought in three channels?

REVISITING THESE PIECES REMINDS ME, ABOVE ALL, THAT I grew up in the Age of the Middlebrow, that earnest, self-improving fellow who watched prime-time documentaries and read the Book of the Month. That was me, in spades. I was born in a small Missouri town in 1956, the year Dwight Eisenhower was reelected by a landslide, and as far back as I can remember, I was eager to learn what was going on beyond the city limits of that small town, out in the great world of art and culture. Not that we were hopelessly at sea—we had a Little Theater and a Community Concerts series—but my home was hundreds of miles from the nearest museum, and it wasn't until I went to college that I saw my first live performance of a ballet. Nevertheless, I already knew a little something about people like Willem de Kooning and Jerome Robbins, thanks to *Life* and *The Ed Sullivan Show,* and what little I knew made me want to know more.

Ours is essentially a popular culture, and as this book makes clear, I have never thought otherwise. Virtually from the start of my career, I wrote about TV, movies, and pop music of all kinds. They were part of the air I breathed. But in the democratic culture of postwar America, there was also unfettered access to what Matthew Arnold so famously called "the best that has been thought and said in the world." Just as important, there was no *contempt* for it. To be sure, there have always been Americans who, in Robert Warshow's words, "have no real stake at all in respectable culture. These are the open enemies of culture, despising indiscriminately a painting by Picasso and a painting by Maxfield Parrish, . . . readers of pulp magazines and comic books, potential book-burners, unhappy patrons of astrologers and communicants of lunatic sects, the hopelessly alienated and outclassed who can enjoy perhaps not even Andy Hardy but only Bela Lugosi." What Warshow did not envision in 1946 was that some of them would become professors of cultural studies, but that's another story; when I was a boy, most Americans who didn't care for high art still held it in a kind of puzzled respect. I doubt that Ed Sullivan cared much for Maria Callas or Edward Villella, but that didn't stop him from putting them on his show, along with Louis Armstrong and the original cast of *West Side Story* (not to mention Jackie Mason and Señor Wences). In the Sixties, all was grist for the middlebrow mill.

Intellectuals of the *Partisan Review* stripe were for the most part deeply suspicious of middlebrows, having beheld the effects of Popular Front Stalinism on American art. They feared, not unreasonably, that any broaching of the dam separating high art from pop culture would lead inexorably to the watering down of the former by the latter. As Dwight Macdonald observed in "Masscult & Midcult," the 1960 essay that did so much to shape the way we think about middlebrow culture, *Life* was given to publishing "nine color pages of Renoir paintings followed by a picture of a roller-skating horse." To those who argued that such juxtapositions had the effect of introducing Renoir to people who might otherwise have known only about roller-skating horses, he replied, "Somehow these scramblings together seem to work all one way, degrading the serious rather than elevating the frivolous. . . . that roller-skating horse comes along, and the final impression is that both Renoir and the horse were talented."

That was funny—sort of—but it could have been written only by someone who lived in a place where high art was on tap twenty-four hours a day, seven days a week. In southeast Missouri, it mostly came on TV or in the mailbox, and I was glad to get it, roller-skating horses and all. Just as city dwellers can't understand what it meant for the residents of a rural town to wake up one day and find themselves within driving distance of a Wal-Mart, so are they incapable of properly appreciating the true significance of middlebrow culture. For all its flaws, it nurtured at least two generations' worth of Americans who, like me, went on to become full-fledged highbrows—but highbrows who, while accepting the existence of a hierarchy of values in art, never lost sight of the value of popular culture.

The truth is that one cannot fully appreciate *any* kind of American art without acknowledging the extent to which so much of the best of it springs from our popular culture. Clement Greenberg, the first critic to single out the middlebrow as a threat to the integrity of high art, once referred to "the American mind" as typified by "its positivism, its unwillingness to speculate, its eagerness for quick results, and its optimism." But just as he underestimated the benign effects of middlebrow aspiration, so did he fail to realize that those traits might themselves serve as the basis for a characteristically American style in art, one that would amalgamate high, middle, and low, thereby ennobling popular culture even as it popularized serious culture. It was a tricky balancing act, and artists as diverse as Leonard Bernstein and John Marquand sometimes found it hard to keep from slipping into the slough of pandering. But it was possible, and time and again I find myself returning to the work of those artists who spoke in the crisply empirical, immediately accessible tone of voice now acknowledged by the whole world as all-American. Louis Armstrong, Budd Boetticher, Willa Cather, Raymond Chandler, Aaron Copland, Duke Ellington, Chuck Jones, Bill Monroe, Fairfield Porter, Dawn Powell, Frank Sinatra, Stephen Sondheim, Paul Taylor, Tom Wolfe: surely these and others like them rank high among our exemplary figures, the ones whose work is indelibly stamped "Made in U.S.A."

Even so, Greenberg had a point when he warned that "it is middlebrow, not lowbrow, culture that does most nowadays to cut the social ground from under high culture. . . . And since the socially powerful amateur, whether he be few or many, still controls our kind of culture, the middlebrow level tends to become its crucial one, where the fate of the whole of our culture may be decided." That is pretty much what happened, but in a way Greenberg could not have anticipated when he published "The Plight of Our Culture" in *Commentary* a half-century ago. For the middlebrow culture whose long-term influence he feared was a *common* culture, based on the existence of widely shared values, and it is now splintered beyond hope of repair. Under the middlebrow regime, as I explain elsewhere in these pages, ordinary Americans were exposed to a wide range of cultural options from which they could pick and choose at will. They still do so, but without the preliminary exposure to the unfamiliar that once made their choices potentially more adventurous. The rise of digital information technology, with its unique capacity for niche marketing, has replaced such demographically broad-based instruments of middlebrow self-education as *The Ed Sullivan Show* with a new regime of seemingly infinite cultural choice. Instead of three TV networks, we have a hundred channels, each "narrowcasting" to a separate sliver of the viewing public, just as today's corporations market new products not to the American people as a whole but to carefully balanced combinations of "lifestyle clusters" whose members are known to prefer gourmet coffee to Coca-Cola, or BMWs to Dodge pickups.

The information age offers something for anybody: *Survivor* for simpletons, *The Sopranos* for sophisticates. The problem is that it offers nothing for everybody. By maximizing and facilitating cultural choice, information-age capitalism fused with identity politics to bring about the disintegration of the middlebrow common culture of my youth. It also led to what V. S. Naipaul has called the "proletarianization" of popular culture. Long before the emergence of what is inexplicably known as reality TV, I wrote that television was the best possible argument against the free market. That was a joke, but a serious one: although I believe in markets, I know how frightfully they coarsened American culture once their efficiency began to be heightened by digital technology. In such monstrous spectacles as the short, unhappy career of David Helfgott, a schizophrenic pianist from Australia whose handlers paraded him before American concertgoers and TV audiences in 1997 in order to take further advantage of the commercial success of an exploitative movie based on his life, we beheld the final corruption of the middlebrow ideal.

WHAT VANISHED FROM AMERICAN CRITICAL DISCOURSE around the same time was the willingness to make value judgments — to take Duke Ellington seriously while simultaneously acknowledging that Aaron Copland was the greater composer. In its place, we got postmodernism, which not only denied that either man was great, but rejected the very idea of greatness itself.

Taken literally, postmodernism means nothing more than that which came after modernism, and by the Sixties the modern movement in art, for all its epochal significance, was nearing the end of its run. Not that all modernists had ceased to do major work (a few, such as Paul Taylor and Helen Frankenthaler, are doing it to this day), but the movement, as movements will do, had degenerated into a rigid ideology whose spokesmen habitually drew false conclusions from false premises. Those were the days when abstract painting, atonal music, and plotless dance were being presented as historically inevitable, a quasi-Marxist argument whose makers not infrequently sought to quash dissent, also *à la* Marx. It was time for a change, but the one that came would prove reminiscent of H. L. Mencken's definition of democracy as "the theory that the common people know what they want, and deserve to get it good and hard."

For all the reams of fuzzy prose that have been penned on the subject of postmodernism, its initiating premise is straightforward: postmodernists disbelieve in truth and beauty, claiming instead that nothing is good, true, or beautiful in and of itself. Rather, "goodness," "truth," "beauty," and "quality" are constructs imposed by the powerful on the powerless for political purposes. Hence there can be no great art and no great artists (except, of course, for Marcel Duchamp, the patron saint of postmodernism and its own exemplary figure). Shakespeare? Beethoven? Cézanne? Mere capitalist tools, used to anesthetize the masses and prop up the decadent ruling classes of the West. Under the aspect of postmodernism, randomness was as good as order, noise as good as music, and all artistic statements were created equal, though those made by the nominally powerless were more equal than others.

As a theory, postmodernism is so patently absurd as to need no refuting — save by the immediate experience of great art — but its practical consequences have not been altogether negative. For one thing, it put a long-overdue end to the stifling late-modernist monopoly. Precisely because of its indifference to "quality," postmodernism also encouraged the mixing of dissimilar styles, an approach well suited to American artists, who have always had a knack for melting down unlikely combinations of cultural ingredients into such shiny new alloys as jazz and modern dance. It gave tradition-loving artists room to maneuver, especially those classical composers who still believed in the natural law of tonality, which had long since been declared anathema by the avant-garde. From time to time, postmodernism even spawned a genius like Merce Cunningham who was capable of extracting high art from the anti-aesthetic of Duchamp. Most of the time, though, audiences were expected to make do with the resoundingly empty gestures of conceptual art and minimalist music, in which theory replaced content. (I have more than once had occasion to cite Hugh Kenner's definition of conceptual art as that which, once described, need not be experienced.) In the whole history of art, no major theoretical movement has produced more theory and less art than postmodernism. Ultimately, it amounted to little more than a set of attitudes, foremost among them the marginalization of the idea of beauty and its replacement with the sniggering, fearful Irony Lite that was the hallmark of American culture in the Nineties.

Therein lay the great divide that separated middlebrow America from postmodern America. It was, at bottom, a loss of nerve. We lost the courage of our aesthetic and cultural convictions, the willingness to say, with Clement Greenberg, that "in the long run there are only two kinds of art: the good and the bad. This difference cuts across all other differences in art. At the same time, it makes all art one. . . . the experience of art is the same in kind or order despite all differences in works of art themselves." By choosing instead to embrace absolute relativism, postmodernism made possible the paradoxical rise of a new generation of cultural totalitarians so secure in their belief that the personal is political that they dismissed any art they could not reduce to a laundry list of self-righteous platitudes. Thus did the Stalinist philistinism of the Thirties, the stridently drab decade of *The Cradle Will Rock* and *The Grapes of Wrath,* return with a vengeance in the Eighties and Nineties, though in a sense it had never really gone away, philistinism being an inevitable by-product of zealotry in all its forms. The world has always been full of people like Flo Whittaker, that agonizingly earnest character from Randall Jarrell's *Pictures from an Institution* who "couldn't bear to read old novels, novels written before the last fifty or sixty years. I asked, 'Why is that?' She answered: 'I get too upset at the status of women in those times. It was so *degrading*.'" The difference between Jarrell's world and ours is that nowadays, people like Flo run things — museums, foundations, English departments — though encouraging signs of rebellion have lately been seen in the academy, with critics like Dave Hickey even daring to put in the occasional good word for beauty.

We have been too quick to stuff Stalinism down the memory hole, and so I have made it part of my job as a critic to show that what we now call political correctness is rooted, wittingly or not, in the soil of that "low dishonest decade" of which we heard so much immediately after September 11, 2001, when W. H. Auden's "September 1, 1939" crackled across the Internet like a *samizdat* newsletter. It was bracing in those desperate days to open a piece of e-mail and find Auden's prescient lines, though I remember thinking that another of his poems might have been more to the point: *Either we serve the Unconditional / Or some Hitlerian monster will supply / An iron convention to do evil by.*

ON THE SUNDAY AFTER THE WORLD TRADE CENTER CRUMBLED into dust, I flew over the southern tip of Manhattan, transfixed by the insane spectacle far below me, gaping in dumb wonder at the black hole in my adopted home. Did postmodernism abruptly come to an end that week, the way Virginia Woolf claimed that "on or about December 1910 human character changed"? I doubt it, but *something* changed, and we are only just starting to realize it.

Sitting in a McDonald's on New York's Upper West Side four months later, I was surprised to hear Diana Krall's recording of "The Look of Love." What was surprising was that it was playing on the radio. It was, after all, an old-fashioned romantic ballad, beautifully sung by a jazz musician and no less beautifully arranged by Claus Ogerman, who used to work with Frank Sinatra and João Gilberto before becoming a full-time classical composer. Such records had vanished from the airwaves decades ago. What was this one doing playing in a fast-food joint? The answer is simple: it was a hit. At the time, *The Look of Love* was the eighth biggest-selling CD on amazon.com — and not just among jazz albums, but *all* albums. This success could not be written off as a mere exercise in salesmanship. Yes, Krall had been skillfully marketed, but the fact remains that huge numbers of ordinary listeners, many of them raised on rock, were and are happily paying to hear a jazz singer perform ballads from the Great American Songbook.

Is Diana Krall's popularity a fluke? Or is it a sign of a cultural sea change? I'm not fond of trend-sniffing, but it seemed to me at the time, and still does, that September 11 may well have brought an end to the unthinking acceptance of postmodern relativism. On that never-to-be-forgotten morning, Americans awakened to the crudest possible reminder that some things aren't a matter of opinion. You can't explain away three thousand freshly slaughtered corpses. Outside of the pseudo-intellectual lunatic fringe, few tried, and those who dared to defend the indefensible were promptly relegated to the margins of respectable society. All at once, my fashion-obsessed Manhattan neighborhood was awash in fear and bedecked with flags, and the word *evil* reentered the vocabulary of a generation of educated innocents who thought there was no such thing.

Something similar happened when, a few days later, musicians in New York and elsewhere began giving memorial concerts to which the public flocked. What did we come to hear? Yo-Yo Ma played Bach at Carnegie Hall; Placido Domingo sang Verdi at the Metropolitan Opera House; Kurt Masur and the New York Philharmonic broadcast Brahms's *German Requiem* to the entire country over PBS. And did anybody complain because the Met performed *Otello* instead of *Moses und Aron* or *Einstein on the Beach*? To ask the question is to know the answer. "One greatly needs beauty when death is so close," old King Arkel sings in *Pelléas et Mélisande*. Never before had I understood the meaning of those words. What we wanted in our time of need was beauty, and we never doubted for a moment that such a thing existed. Nor did we seek it in order to be "healed." Art isn't therapy, just as beauty is more like bread than medicine: we need it not merely to feel better but to live, though it can also serve as balm for scarred souls. Of all the countless performances I attended in the anxious days and weeks following September 11, I particularly remember the night I saw Ballet Tech dance Eliot Feld's *The Jig Is Up*. I'd seen it at least a dozen times before, but as I watched it yet again, I found myself reveling in its unity. All the parts of *The Jig Is Up*—steps, music, structure, lighting, costumes—fit together like the pieces of a perfectly tooled puzzle, and that was what made it so satisfying in a time of turmoil. If anything about a masterpiece can "heal" us, it is just this kind of organic wholeness, which reminds us of the hidden presence of superworldly order amid the seeming chaos of our wounded world.

No less impressive to me has been the willingness of a few independent-minded American filmmakers to engage directly—and beautifully—with the problem of postmodern relativism. One encounters it, for instance, in Terry Zwigoff's *Ghost World,* the poignant story of two disaffected teenagers trapped in a grubby pop-culture hell of strip malls, convenience stores, and round-the-clock Muzak, set adrift on the sea of relativity by their barely visible baby-boomer parents. Or Kenneth Lonergan's *You Can Count on Me,* in which we meet Terry, an immature small-town drifter, and Sammy, his stay-at-home older sister, orphaned in childhood and desperately lonely as young adults, deeply flawed but not without virtue, seeking to make their way in a world that no longer has much to offer in the way of certainty. Revealingly, Lonergan himself plays the role of a Methodist minister so afraid of being "judgmental" that he is reluctant to assure Sammy that the adulterous affair in which she is engaged is endangering her immortal soul. ("Well, it's a sin," he says, "but we don't tend to focus on that aspect of it, right off the bat.")

I don't want to sound too optimistic. The beauty-haters may be in temporary retreat, but they still have two things going for them, tenure and patience, and even though they don't believe in anything, they disbelieve in it passionately. The good news is that their nihilism is no longer fashionable, at least not in the way it was when I wrote most of the pieces in this book. Indeed, I believe that at some point in the Nineties, we quietly entered a period for which no one has yet come up with a better word than post-postmodernism, and in the next-to-last section I consider some of its manifestations. If I am right, the period of time covered by these essays will be remembered as an interlude, a time of transition — the end of the postmodern moment — and my guess is that the key figure in that transition will turn out to have been Mark Morris, for which reason I have included two of my pieces about him. "Going a Lot to the Mark Morris Dance Group" tracks the evolution of my opinion of his choreography, which at first glance I took to be quintessentially postmodern. I changed my mind, although I also think Morris changed his ways. Whatever the case, the best of his dances, in particular the masterly *V* and *L'Allegro, il Penseroso ed il Moderato,* now seem to me to have that emotional directness without which no art can be truly great.

Like so many artists who have been touched by postmodernism, Morris continues to defy ready categorization, and I expect that the fluidity of idiom typical of his work will turn out to be the one enduring legacy of the postmodern moment. "Boundaryless" polystylism, for example, is now very much the thing in contemporary popular music. To name only a few of its practitioners, the songwriters David Cantor and Adam Guettel, the cabaret singer Mary Foster Conklin, the jazz musicians Julia Dollison, Ethan Iverson, Pat Metheny, and Luciana Souza, the klezmer clarinetist David Krakauer, the classical-soprano-turned-Broadway-diva Audra McDonald, the bluegrass band Nickel Creek, and the big-band composer Maria Schneider are all making music that is, in Duke Ellington's useful phrase, beyond category. Nor is such rampant hybridizing limited to the field of pop music. What mixed-media pigeonhole, for instance, can accommodate the "comix" of Daniel Clowes (the creator of *Ghost World*) and the "picture stories" of Ben Katchor? From Morris's dance-driven operatic productions to Susan Stroman's part-danced, part-acted *Contact,* a Broadway "musical" in which nobody sings, American theatergoers also find themselves delighted by works of art whose genre cannot be easily defined. Were the puppeteer Basil Twist's fanciful, visually rich "stagings" of Igor Stravinsky's *Petrushka* and Hector Berlioz's *Symphonie fantastique* puppet shows or ballets? And what about Robert Weiss's adaptation of *The Kreutzer Sonata,* in which the dancers of Carolina Ballet were joined by two actors for an intensely compelling version of the Tolstoy novella, accompanied by the music of Beethoven and Janáček? Was it a ballet or a play? Or do such distinctions simply not matter anymore?

What does matter, again and at last, is the quest for beauty, and a growing number of post-postmodern artists use that word without encasing it in the protective quotation marks of irony. "Trying to compose beautiful things, I say what I mean and mean what I say," explains Paul Moravec, a member of the group of American classical composers that I have dubbed the New Tonalists. "The irony in my work is not glibly postmodern, but rather the essence of making audible the experience of fundamental paradox and ambiguity." Osama bin Laden and his cronies, the ones who banned music from Afghanistan, would scarcely have approved of such talk. For them, as for every other zealot who murders in the name of a false god, earthly beauty was a mere illusion, a distraction from the One True Cause. But if September 11 taught us anything, it was that beauty is real — as real as evil — and worth fighting for.

"TO APPRECIATE TWO OF THE ARTS IN A DISCERNING MANNER is not unusual," Anthony Powell once observed. "Where three are claimed, more often than not, grasp of the third shows signs of strain." I write about all the arts, but I would never claim to grasp them with equal discernment. As an intellectual, I am strictly homemade, and at no time in my life have I stretched a canvas, stood at a barre, or taken a course in political philosophy. I became a utility outfielder by accident. A musician by training and experience, I started out writing about classical music, then jazz, after which I found myself reviewing books about an increasingly wide variety of nonmusical subjects. In time, it seemed natural to write about whatever interested me, but I am all too aware that when I discuss any art form other than music, it is as a more or less well-informed amateur, not a practitioner. The only claim I would make for myself is that because I chose not to remain a specialist, I thereby acquired a feel for the unity of the arts that has had its own value. Looking at the dance taught me to see paintings, just as reading the letters of Flannery O'Connor gave me a clearer perspective on the place of tonality in twentieth-century music, even though she happened to be tone-deaf.

The present book is not an exact reflection of my cultural interests. With a few exceptions, I have omitted profiles, performance reviews, and purely journalistic articles. I like writing profiles and regard them as a species of criticism, but they didn't seem to sit well alongside my essays, so I mostly left them out. I began to write regularly about theater and the visual arts after the period covered by this book, so I have little to say about them here save in passing, just as there are artists I love about whom I have never had occasion to write, or have yet to write anything good enough to keep. Be that as it may, these pieces are not unrepresentative of my tastes, insofar as they have to do with American art and artists, America now being the home of virtually everything significant about Western culture. Europe died in 1945, or maybe 1939—you pick the date. Perhaps it gave up the ghost when George Balanchine crossed the Atlantic and made *Serenade* on a roomful of American dancers, or when Jackson Pollock first took a can of paint in hand and dribbled its contents all over a canvas. In any case, the West, such as it is, lives here, for which reason I have chosen to include in the present collection only my writings about the American scene, despite the fact that I have also written with enthusiasm about European artists ranging from Dmitri Shostakovich to Patrick O'Brian.

I should add, too, that a few of these essays have been reworked. Anyone perverse enough to wonder exactly what I have done to them will get no help from me. Like every journalist, I write on the fly, and I have sought to improve after the fact certain pieces that were written too hastily. Where I have changed my mind, I have (usually) changed my words, and in some cases I have folded material from one piece into another one, rather than reprint both and court redundancy. Back when I was an editor, I used to tell writers that they could "fix it in the book." I have tried to take my own advice.

Finally, I have made a point of including four pieces that stirred up a certain amount of controversy on their original publication. "Tolstoy's Contraption" attracted the attention of Saul Bellow and Tom Wolfe, both of whom begged to differ with me, while "Louis Armstrong, Eminent Victorian," "The Color of Jazz," and "(Over)praising Duke

Ellington" were even more widely discussed, sometimes angrily and sometimes sympathetically. It is nice to be disagreed with — sometimes.

A TERRY TEACHOUT READER WAS HARRY HASKELL'S DOING, and he saw it through the press with due diligence and uncommon care, seconded by Phillip King, for which I could not be more grateful. Paul Taylor asked me to write "Notes Toward the Definition of Paul Taylor," originally published as the foreword to the second edition of *Private Domain*, his autobiography. The other pieces were assigned by newspaper and magazine editors, and special thanks go to those editors who commissioned most of them, invariably making the most (and best) of them: Michael Anderson, Adam Bellow, Jody Bottum, Erich Eichman, Joseph Epstein, Eric Gibson, Adam Goodheart, Annette Grant, Mike Hale, Caroline Herron, Deal Hudson, David Klinghoffer, Neal Kozodoy, Charles McGrath, Michael Potemra, Fletcher Roberts, and Steve Smith. I also want to tip my hat to Chilton Williamson, Jr., who bought my very first magazine piece, and many more, when he was back-of-the-book editor of *National Review*. None of them are included here — I got better later — but I doubt that any of the pieces I have chosen to preserve in this book would have been written had it not been for his faith and encouragement.

Anita Finkel, founder and editor of the late, lamented *New Dance Review,* would have had plenty to say about this book had she lived to see it. I bless her memory, and the memories of four other departed friends and teachers, John Haskins, Samuel Lipman, Neil McCaffrey, and Viola Statler. Myra Unger, who never doubted that I would grow up to be a critic, *did* live to see it. Blessings on her, too.

The five pieces in the last section are not part of the implicit narrative I have outlined, though they relate to it. I have included them for mainly personal reasons, in particular "My Friend Nancy," a reminiscence of Nancy LaMott, the cabaret singer whose untimely death in 1995 deprived her of the chance to play what surely would have been a major role in the restoration of beauty. In addition to admiring Nancy's singing, I loved her with all my heart, and though she was the furthest thing from an intellectual, I like to think she would have been amused to find herself in such high-toned company.

PART ONE ~ AMERICAN WAYFARERS

Far from Ohio: Dawn Powell

EVERY DECADE OR SO, SOMEBODY WRITES AN ESSAY about Dawn Powell, and a few hundred more people discover her work, and are grateful. And that's it. Few American novelists have been so lavishly praised by so many high-powered critics to so little effect. Diana Trilling, writing in 1942, called Powell "our best answer to the familiar question, 'Who really says the funny things for which Dorothy Parker gets credit?' "; Edmund Wilson, writing in 1962, judged her to be "quite on a level with . . . Anthony Powell, Evelyn Waugh and Muriel Spark"; Gore Vidal, writing in 1987, said she "should have been as widely read as, say, Hemingway or the early Fitzgerald." No such luck. Dawn Powell remains today what she was a half-century ago: a fine and important writer adored by a handful of lucky readers in the know and ignored by everybody else.

Interestingly, Powell has yet to be taken up by the tenure-haunted injustice collectors who live to exhume Unfairly Neglected Women Writers and add them, by *force majeure* if necessary, to the canon they affect to despise. It says much about the mind-set of the pesto-and-phallocentrism crowd that the person who may end up being chiefly responsible for bringing about a Powell revival is, of all things, a mere journalist. Tim Page, a music critic lately of *New York Newsday* and now of the *Washington Post,* has been collecting Powell first editions (there are no Powell second editions) for years. What started out as a hobby has become an industry. Page is at work on the first biography of Powell, and he edited *Dawn Powell at Her Best,* an omnibus volume that attracted wide and favorable critical notice. Now Steerforth Press, publisher of *Dawn Powell at Her Best,* has brought out two "new" Powell books. The first is a much-needed paperback reissue of Powell's 1944 novel, *My Home Is Far Away,* with an introduction by Page. The second is one of the outstanding literary finds of the last quarter-century: Powell's diaries, which cover the last thirty-four years of her life (she died in 1965) and whose existence was not generally known until Page prepared them for publication.

Powell actually began keeping a diary in 1925, shortly after she moved to Greenwich Village, the scene of most of her later novels, but the entries were sporadic and fragmentary. It was not until 1931 that she embarked on a serious diary. The first sentence — "The tragedy of people who once were glamorous, now trying in mediocre stations to modestly refer to their pasts" — announces its nature: it would be a writer's notebook, concerned less with earthshaking events and true confessions than with the raw material of what later became her novels. This is not to say that the diaries are lacking in gossip value. In fact, the book is full of cruelly funny vignettes, some as short as a single steel-tipped line. Here, for example, is Powell on Clifford Odets: "Later he talked of the Odets Plays, the audience joy over Odets Plays, as if Odets, the genius, was quite apart from Odets, the 'modest' citizen." And admirers of Powell's novels will be glad to learn something about the life and character of the woman who wrote them. It takes a special kind of toughness to keep on writing for four decades without any great material success; to read Powell's diaries is to learn just how tough their author really was.

Powell was born in 1897 in Mount Gilead, Ohio, deep in the heart of the Babbitt belt. The idyll of her small-town childhood was brought to a harsh end by the death of her mother in 1903. Her father, a ne'er-do-well traveling salesman, subsequently married a joyless puritan, and Powell soon ran away: first to the home of a maternal aunt, then to college, and finally, in 1918, to New York. Within three years, she had married a drunk named Joseph Gousha and given birth to a son who suffered from cerebral palsy and schizophrenia. By the Thirties, husband and wife had settled into a bizarre ménage à trois with Coburn (Coby) Gilman, a witty, self-destructive magazine executive with whom Powell appears to have been deeply in love; he and the still-married couple lived in a Ninth Street duplex with separate entrances.

That all this turned Powell into an unsparing satirist is hardly a surprise. But it took a decade of hard work before she found herself. Five of her first six novels are set in Ohio, and they are an odd amalgam of harshness and pathos, rather like a cross between Theodore Dreiser and Sinclair Lewis, only well written. Not until 1936 did Powell shift her sights to her new milieu, publishing *Turn, Magic Wheel*, a glittering comedy of manners in which her mature self comes instantaneously into focus from the first page onward. " 'Satire,' " she wrote in her diary that year, "is the technical word for writing of people as they are; 'romantic,' the other extreme of people as they are to themselves — but both of these are the truth." That is Powell in a nutshell: like her heroines, she believes in love, even though she knows better.

In her novels, Powell is cold-eyed and confident; in her diaries, the mask sometimes slips, and she reveals the debilitating effects of writing brilliantly and selling poorly. She is vain ("In *Turn, Magic Wheel,* I believe firmly that I have the perfect New York story") and self-pitying ("It's too horrible a life, waking up to the jabbering of a noisy maniac, a dreadful future for all of us to face — 10,000 days of hopeless work to pay for hopeless treatments"). Saddest of all, she is forever scheming to sell out and win commercial success, at which she has no more luck than Henry James's Ralph Limbert, the hapless hero of "The Next Time," whose books become ever more subtle the harder he tries to water them down.

But just when the reader is starting to tire of Powell's understandable unhappiness, her wit flares up irresistibly. "Wits," she wrote in 1939, "are never happy people. The anguish that has scraped their nerves and left them raw to every flicker of life is the base of wit. . . . True wit should break a good man's heart." There is much heartbreak in these diaries, and more mirth; it is possible to read them solely for their historical interest (Powell writes vividly of close friends like John Latouche and John Dos Passos), but it is wiser to read them for pleasure. From the long set pieces to the flashing one-liners ("Never give a guest Dexedrine after sundown"), *The Diaries of Dawn Powell* is a book in a thousand, a rowdy chronicle of life in the city its author loved beyond compare.

First-timers, though, would perhaps do better to start not with the diaries but with *Dawn Powell at Her Best,* which contains both *Turn, Magic Wheel* and *Dance Night* (1930), among the best of the Ohio novels, or *The Locusts Have No King* (1948), a New York novel in which she balances satire and romance with crafty virtuosity. And those who already know the half-dozen Powell books currently available in paperback (including *The Locusts Have No King*) will most definitely want to read *My Home Is Far Away,* the long-unavailable novel in which she tells the story of her Ohio childhood. Powell discussed the technical basis of *My Home Is Far Away* in a 1943 diary entry: "At the beginning, it is written as for a child — words, images, etc., are on the table level of their eyes; everyone is good to the three sisters, their pleasures are simple, their parents good. As they grow, the manner of writing changes — the knowledge of cruelty, divorce, disillusionment, betrayal — the anguish of adolescence, of not being wanted, of struggle for survival." It is an ambitious plan, and one perfectly realized in this remarkable novel, one of the permanent masterpieces of childhood, comparable with *David Copperfield, What Maisie Knew* and the early reminiscences of Colette.

Reading *My Home Is Far Away,* one inevitably wonders why Powell never found an audience. The most likely reason is that her books are devoid of the dogged earnestness that has always been for most Americans the only sure sign of true art. Like all satirists, Powell was in deadly earnest, but she never saw any reason to be tiresome about it. Her touch was light, her tone whip-smart, a pair of attributes that confused even so shrewd a critic as Diana Trilling, who gave *The Locusts Have No King* a mixed review to which Powell replied in her diary, "Gist of criticisms (Diana Trilling, etc.) of my novel is if they had my automobile they wouldn't visit my folks, they'd visit *theirs*." Trilling is nobody's fool, but she went to see the wrong family. Dawn Powell was one of America's best novelists, and if there is any justice — a proposition at which she would doubtless have laughed wildly — she will soon receive her due.

New York Times Book Review 1995

Father Babbitt's Flock

A MAN OF ONE BOOK IS EASY TO FIGURE. SO IS A MAN OF many books. It is the man of a few good books who is hard to pin down. By the age of forty-five, J. F. Powers had written a grand total of three books: *Prince of Darkness,* published in 1947; *The Presence of Grace,* published in 1956; and *Morte d'Urban,* published in 1962. Yet his gifts were acknowledged by critics ranging from Evelyn Waugh to Gore Vidal, and he was regularly mentioned in tandem with Flannery O'Connor as one of the most promising young Catholic writers in America. When *Morte d'Urban,* Powers's first novel, won the National Book Award in 1963, F. W. Dupee, another critical admirer, rightly remarked that its author enjoyed "an inconspicuous fame."

That fame trailed off to next to nothing in the succeeding quarter century, during which Powers published only one other book, a slender collection of prose sketches and work in progress called *Look How the Fish Live.* No selected essays, no collected letters, no regular appearances on the campus lecture circuit, no groaning casebooks of close readings appeared in the wake of *Morte d'Urban.* Powers allowed his reputation, such as it was, to be sustained solely by four books, published roughly a decade apart. Not surprisingly, he soon became a ghostly figure.

Why has Powers published so little? Back in 1963, he told Pete Hamill that his modest output up to that time was due in part to the fact that he earned his living as a teacher. "I usually teach creative writing courses," he said, "and I read the damned things, the stories, and sometimes I wish that I had that story, because I could do something with it. As a result, I don't do my own work." As for his long silence since *Morte d'Urban,* he explained it to a *New York Times* reporter as follows:

> My wife was sick for a long time before she died. That was part of it. And basically I'm lazy. But I was [also] somewhat despairing after *Morte d'Urban,* which sold only 25,000 copies in seven printings. I could not get the publisher to print enough. A couple of months after *Morte d'Urban* won the National Book Award, it went out of print. They let it run out.

But Powers, though silent, was not forgotten, as the publication of his second novel, *Wheat That Springeth Green,* proved. Profiles and interviews suddenly began appearing in a variety of respectable venues as the word began to get around that Powers, at the age of seventy-one, finally had a new book coming out. The reviews were universally favorable, and a second National Book Award nomination followed in due course. The lackluster reputation of a half-remembered writer had somehow regained its old patina. For once, a cautionary tale of the literary life had a happy — and well-deserved — ending.

THE LONG ROAD THAT LED TO *WHEAT THAT SPRINGETH GREEN* began in Jacksonville, Illinois, where James Farl Powers was born in 1917. His father was a plant manager for the Swift Packing Company. "My first serious writer," Powers says, "was Sinclair Lewis. . . . [H]e said things about people, about society, about institutions that I hadn't realized were being thought or said or printed. Lewis made me realize that I was not so odd or strange or out of it as I thought."
A child of the Great Depression, Powers attended night classes at Northwestern University but could not afford to stay long enough to get a degree. After a frustrating search for employment, he went to work in a Chicago bookstore. "Finally," he said in 1963, "I began to think, maybe *I'm* a writer. Maybe that's what I should do. It was mostly anger. Anger at not being able to get a job; anger at the plight of the Negro; anger at other things I was just beginning to see." A conscientious objector, he spent thirteen months in a Minnesota prison during World War II. By 1943, he had settled in Minnesota and had published three prose sketches in the *Catholic Worker.* In that same year, he began

contributing to *Accent,* the prestigious University of Illinois quarterly that, three years later, bought Flannery O'Connor's first published story.

The second story Powers sold to *Accent* was "Lions, Harts, Leaping Does," a sensitively written tale of a dying priest. The stylistic sureness of "Lions, Harts, Leaping Does," which would eventually become one of the most widely anthologized of modern American short stories, came as a surprise to the editors. As they later recalled in the introduction to *Accent: An Anthology 1940–60:*

> Once in the early 1940s the editors somewhat reluctantly (and after heavy blue-penciling and "improving" — which the author, surprisingly, agreed to) printed a story based on the already hackneyed subject of Negro jazz musicians in a city night club. A few months later the same author submitted a second story so extraordinarily different in theme and superior in writing that the editors could hardly believe it came out of the same typewriter.

Powers met and married Betty Wahl in 1946 and began to teach creative writing at St. John's University in Collegeville, Minnesota. A year later, he published *Prince of Darkness,* his first collection of short stories. The book received good reviews, and he was spotted as an up-and-coming Catholic writer by no less an expert than Evelyn Waugh. "The book is Catholic," Waugh said in his review of the English edition of *Prince of Darkness.* "Mr. Powers has a full philosophy with which to oppose the follies of his age and nation." Many of Waugh's non-Catholic readers, of course, would have viewed these remarks as sufficient reason to ignore J. F. Powers altogether. In the late Forties, literary critics commonly assumed that an openly Catholic writer was necessarily engaged in narrow propagandizing for the Faith. The situation was particularly oppressive in the United States, where the native Catholic tradition was still decidedly anti-intellectual. "You probably have not imagined what it is to write as a Catholic," Flannery O'Connor wrote to Carl Hartman in 1954, "knowing that most of the people who read you will think what you believe is utter rubbish. . . . I have read people (Orwell) who say Catholics can't write novels on acct. of being Catholics."

O'Connor sidestepped this problem by eliminating Catholic characters from her stories altogether. Powers's solution was more direct and, in a way, more subtle: he started writing about priests. Powers never attended a seminary and, by his own account, never wanted to be a priest ("I didn't want a life of having to deal with everybody. Every old woman, every drunk or wife of a drunk, the constant traffic of people which is the priest's work"). But all the best stories in *Prince of Darkness* deal with the daily lives of Roman Catholic priests and their parishioners. Powers's specialty, moreover, is not merely the priesthood per se but the priesthood as practiced in the cities and small towns of Minnesota and the Midwest. For the most part, his clerics are paunchy, irritable types more concerned with the size of last week's collection than the state of their souls.

"This country is decidedly a specialist's country," Powers said in 1963, "and I think it's happened to me. I know that sounds like I'm a gall bladder man, but it does happen." But he gets all there is to be gotten out of his particular literary specialty. His clerical tales are meticulous sketches of a distinctive part of the American scene. They are also very funny. Powers's comic sense is something which could not reasonably have been expected from the creator of the dying priest of "Lions, Harts, Leaping Does." Unlike the saintly Father Didymus, most of the other priests in *Prince of Darkness* are Babbitts in reversed collars, transplanted from Zenith, Ohio, to Minnesota with a slight change of occupation along the way. Their sermons and small talk are recorded with a flawless ear, their environment described with a cool and acerbic eye. In the title story from *Prince of Darkness,* for example, Ernest "Boomer" Burner, a frustrated curate who yearns for a church of his own, observes one of his more flamboyant parishioners:

> Mr. Tracy shed his shabby anonymity for Father Burner, and grew executive markings. He became the one and only Thomas Nash Tracy— T.N.T. . . . His company's advertising smothered the town and country; everybody knew the slogan "T.N.T. Spells Security." He figured in any financial drive undertaken by the diocese, was caught by photographers in orphanages, and sat at the heavy end of the table at communion breakfasts. Hundreds of nuns, thanks to his thoughtfulness, ate

capon on Christmas Day, and a few priests of the right sort received baskets of scotch. He was a B.C.L., a Big Catholic Layman, and now Father Burner could see why.

By concentrating on the secular aspects of the priestly life, Powers avoided the parochialism that had long been the curse of Catholic fiction writers. His tone was even sufficiently urbane for him to publish in the *New Yorker* — a magazine where the blunter, more grotesque parables of Flannery O'Connor were misunderstood and unwelcome. This lightness of touch, coupled with an absence of the more obvious kinds of pietistic sentimentality, misled some commentators into thinking that Powers's choice of subject matter had nothing to do with his spiritual convictions. "Mr. Powers," Peter De Vries went so far as to suggest in his introduction to a 1963 collection of Powers's short stories about priests, "does not seem to me a religious writer at all. He is undoubtedly a religious man, but that is something else entirely."

J. F. Powers is certainly a religious man, but he is quite clearly a religious (or, if you prefer, spiritual) writer as well. His stories invariably revolve around a single question: how is it that ordinary people, with all their commonplace failings, can do the work of God? Powers approaches this simple but intriguing paradox from a dozen different angles, and the fundamental incongruity that it implies is the source of his richest humor. In "Prince of Darkness," Father Burner, through desultory indulgence in the seven deadly sins, is actually transformed into a devil — the most petty and preposterous of devils, to be sure, but one in whom the transformation is so complete that the reader is even allowed to catch a fleeting glance of diabolic features ("Father Burner, applying a cloven foot to the pedal, gave it the gas").

HAVING FOUND HIS MÉTIER, POWERS HAD THE WIT TO STICK with it. He wrote slowly and carefully, producing an occasional story about secular characters but generally remaining loyal to the dryly comic tone and idiosyncratic subject matter that had served him so well.

Powers's second story collection, *The Presence of Grace,* was more consistent in quality than *Prince of Darkness* but lacked the high points of the earlier volume. ("I agree with you that nothing in this present collection of Powers equals the best in the first," Flannery O'Connor wrote to a friend in 1956. "However, who am I to be saying that in public?") Two of the stories that originally appeared in the *New Yorker,* "Death of a Favorite" and "Defection of a Favorite," made use of a rectory cat as narrator, a Saki-like device which Powers carried off with ease and charm but which is an unconvincing departure from his customary acerbity.

The Presence of Grace, though engaging, suggested that the formula that had brought Powers so much success in *Prince of Darkness* might be reaching a point of diminishing returns. This suspicion was laid to rest with the publication in 1962 of his first novel, *Morte d'Urban.* Installments of the novel, which took Powers more than six years to complete, appeared at intervals in various American magazines between 1956 and 1962, and some critics suggested that it was not a true novel but a succession of short stories unconvincingly stitched together. They were wrong. *Morte d'Urban* is sectional, even picaresque, in its approach, but it holds together brilliantly — so brilliantly, in fact, as to add up to one of the most impressive comic novels written by an American.

Father Urban, "fifty-four, tall and handsome but a trifle loose in the jowls and red of eye," is the quintessential Powers priest. Having drifted into the priesthood without any obvious vocation, he treats it precisely as he would any other job: with one eye firmly fixed on the main chance. The star preacher of the Clementines, a midwestern order that "labored under the curse of mediocrity," the peripatetic Father Urban, whose thoroughly modern mottos are "Be a winner" and "You may be right," ministers to his flock with hearty sermons and after-dinner speeches:

> [Father Urban] was true to his vow of poverty — to the spirit, though, rather than the letter. For someone in his position, it could not very well be otherwise. Always, after an accounting at the Novitiate, there would be a surplus: not Mass stipends, which had to be turned in and processed, but personal gifts from grateful laymen and understanding pastors, fives, tens, and twenties literally forgotten among Father Urban's effects or prudently held out because traveling first-class cost so much more than a tight-fisted bursar could be expected to make allowances for without losing respect for himself and his job.

Morte d'Urban begins when the Father Provincial of the Order of Saint Clement, sensing that his star preacher has grown too big for his collar, assigns him to a rundown retreat in the wilds of Minnesota. Father Urban promptly puts his go-getting energies to work and turns the monastery into a four-star lay retreat complete with a beautifully tended golf course. The building of this elaborate institution is used as the occasion for an equally elaborate *tour d'horizon* of small-town life in Minnesota in which Powers divides his satirical potshots between the foibles of the Catholic Church and the vulgarities of middle-class America in the age of Eisenhower.

Father Urban's comeback takes a sharp turn for the worse when he is hit on the head with a stray golf ball, a physical jolt that is accompanied by his belated recognition of the moral deficiencies of Billy Cosgrove, the arrogant Catholic tycoon whom Urban has previously seen as his greatest "catch" ("I happen to know that the Dalmatians are making a play for this man"). He loses his nerve and becomes fearful and uncertain. This being precisely the right state of mind for a new Father Provincial of the Order of Saint Clement's, Father Urban is promptly tapped for the post. But he renounces his worldly ways in the very moment of his triumph—though whether the "death" of the old Father Urban is the product of inward contemplation or a delayed effect of concussion by golf ball is deliberately left vague.

The fate of Father Urban offers ample opportunity for excesses of religious sentiment, and it is to Powers's credit that he avoids them completely. We are invited, if it suits us, to dismiss Father Urban's "conversion," but the author himself clearly regards it with the utmost seriousness. It is Powers's sense of literary grace that allows him to leave the question unresolved, and he handles with similar reticence the subtle references to the Arthurian legend around which *Morte d'Urban* is built. The tone of *Morte d'Urban* is predominantly comic; Powers's larger purpose is expressed as a discreet undertone of spirituality that gives unexpected resonance to a genuinely touching book.

MORTE D'URBAN WAS A HARD ACT TO FOLLOW, AND POWERS, AS it turned out, would have a good deal of trouble following it. To be sure, he announced that he was embarked on a new novel, two long chapters of which subsequently appeared in the *New Yorker*. He also published a scattering of stories and sketches in other magazines. But his novel remained incomplete, and he made the ultimate gesture of futility in 1975 by publishing a story collection, *Look How the Fish Live,* which contained "Bill" and "Priestly Fellowship," the two chapters of his unfinished novel. Despite their high quality, the rest of *Look How the Fish Live* had a sketchy, unpolished air, and the book received mixed reviews.

After spending a decade living with his family in Dublin, Powers returned to Saint John's University to teach writing and care for his dying wife. His byline became less and less common, and he did nothing to compensate for its growing rarity. The Hogarth Press reissued his books in paperback in England, but they remained out of print in America. His admirers gradually and reluctantly concluded that the rich comic talent that was on display in *Morte d'Urban* had simply dried up. Then Powers brought out *Wheat That Springeth Green,* in which "Bill" and "Priestly Fellowship" at last found their proper place in yet another comic novel about a middle-aged priest. In *Wheat That Springeth Green,* however, the underlying premise of *Morte d'Urban* is reversed. Father Urban was a secular man who ultimately attained sanctity; Joe Hackett, the hero of *Wheat That Springeth Green,* enters the priesthood and, initially obsessed with sanctity, is gradually coarsened by the grinding pressures of everyday parish life.

Wheat That Springeth Green is not as finished an artistic product as *Morte d'Urban*. The old J. F. Powers attacked the vulgarization of the church in America through satire and indirection. *Wheat That Springeth Green* makes the same points in the same way, but Joe Hackett is also allowed to do more than a little complaining of his own, in the course of which one hears a crotchety authorial voice that the younger Powers would have taken care to avoid. ("We used to stand out in the crowd," Joe says of the Catholic Church. "We had quality control. We were the higher-priced spread. No more.") In addition, the charges of slackness wrongly leveled at *Morte d'Urban* are far more applicable to *Wheat That Springeth Green*. The great set pieces of *Morte d'Urban* gain added strength from their context in the complete novel. But the seams that join "Bill" and "Priestly Fellowship" to the rest of *Wheat That Springeth Green* are perhaps too visible to the naked eye.

In the end, *Wheat That Springeth Green* is likely to strike the reader familiar with Powers's other books as not quite necessary — a trope on *Morte d'Urban,* so to speak, rather than the product of a fresh and fully independent artistic conception. But Powers has not lost his sharp eye for the absurdities of priestly life in a secular society. (What other novelist could extract laughs from a hair shirt?) And if the best parts of *Wheat That Springeth Green* are the chapters which originally appeared in *Look How the Fish Live,* it is still satisfying to see how ingeniously Powers has developed them.

"Some of the new book," Powers said in a recent interview, "might be a little too subtle for a lot of people. It's not the kind of thing I'll clean up on." No doubt. He is precisely the kind of minor master whom most American readers (and many American critics) do not understand very well. But within the comparatively narrow framework of what he has tried to do, he is at his best quite nearly perfect. One need not be a skeptic to appreciate his wit; one need not be religious to appreciate his spirituality. And the smallness of his output is redeemed by its exceptional quality. To have written a dozen first-rate short stories and a comic novel comparable to *Cakes and Ale* or *Black Mischief* requires no apology. It is an unalloyed pleasure to have him back, and one hopes that *Wheat That Springeth Green* will not be his last word on the splendors and miseries of the Roman Catholic Church in Minnesota.

New Criterion 1989

The Conversion of Tom Wolfe

Tom wolfe's second novel is the story of a conversion. It is, of course, many other things as well — a deeply knowing fable of race and class in the New South, a caustic morality play about the unintended consequences of capitalism, a cautionary tale of the sexual revolution and its aftermath — but it is impossible to read *A Man in Full* without recognizing that the central event in this densely packed, superlatively vigorous book is the journey of Charlie Croker, real-estate developer and plantation owner, from unreflective unbelief to the realization that there is more to life than the aggressive pursuit of his fleshly desires.

Or so, at any rate, I would have thought. But as I read the reviews of *A Man in Full,* I noticed that what had seemed perfectly obvious to me was obscure to most critics. Needless to say, there are plenty of secular readers who are as insensitive to the spiritual aspect of a contemporary novel as a color-blind man is incapable of fully appreciating a painting. But even some conservative reviewers who were evidently predisposed to like *A Man in Full* failed to fix on its religious dimension or dismissed it as trivial, even though the climax occurs when Charlie makes a lengthy, articulate, and spectacularly public profession of his newfound faith.

One possible impediment to understanding *A Man in Full* is its sheer eventfulness. Not since the days of Trollope and Balzac has a novelist of significance (and the author of *A Man in Full* and *The Bonfire of the Vanities* must now be counted a very significant novelist indeed) sought to fill so vast a canvas with so detailed a portrait of urban life in all its proliferating complexity. Wolfe could easily have spun any one of his narrative threads into a full-length novel; instead, he has woven them together, and the resulting tapestry is wondrous to behold. Yet it is precisely this richness that may well have kept some readers from seeing his point. Not until halfway through *A Man in Full* does he introduce the theme that will resonate throughout its final chapters, and by then the plot has already picked up so much speed that it's easy to overlook this new development.

It doesn't help, either, that the "religion" to which Charlie is converted is not Christianity in any of its myriad varieties, but Stoicism, the pagan doctrine of self-control expounded by Epictetus and Marcus Aurelius. We now think of Stoicism less as a religion than a philosophy, yet Charlie Croker embraces it as his gospel, as can be seen from the "sermon" he preaches to a hostile audience of Atlanta journalists and politicos at the end of *A Man in Full:*

> You think if only you can acquire *enough* worldly goods, *enough* recognition, *enough* eminence, you will be free, there'll be nothing more to worry about, and instead you become a bigger and bigger slave to how you think others are judging you. . . . The Manager has given every person a spark from His own divinity, and no one can take that away from you, not even the Manager himself, and from that spark comes your character. Everything else is temporary and worthless in the long run, including your body. What is the human body? It's a clever piece a crockery containing a quart a blood. And it's not even yours! One day you're gonna have to give it back! And where are your possessions then? They're gonna be picked over by one bunch a buzzards or another. What man's ever been remembered as great because of the possessions he devoted his life to 'cumulating? I can't think of any. So why don't we pay more attention to the one precious thing we possess, the spark the Manager has placed in our souls?

Those few critics who took Charlie's sermon at face value seemed surprised that Tom Wolfe, the great chronicler of modern materialism, should have produced a novel whose principal character is a sixty-year-old real-estate mogul who suddenly discovers the perils of wealth. But it's not so hard to see why a sixty-eight-year-old author who recently suffered a heart attack would have become preoccupied with the problem of life's meaning. Neither is it difficult to understand Wolfe's fascination with Stoicism, for it is a doctrine that has always appealed to intelligent men who lack the gift of faith but nonetheless hunger for a morally challenging rule of life.

For my part, I found it more surprising that even though *A Man in Full* is set in Atlanta, Christianity plays no part whatsoever in the lives of its characters. The South, as Flannery O'Connor so memorably put it, is Christ-haunted: it is a place where people not only go to church but dream of hell. But not these people. Except for Charlie Croker and Conrad Hensley, the escaped convict who introduces him to the writings of the Stoic philosophers, not a single major character — not even Roger White II, the upwardly mobile black attorney whose father was pastor of the Beloved Covenant Church — believes in anything other than the importance of his own ambitions. Surely it is no coincidence that the only minister in *A Man in Full* is a political operator, and the only scene set in a church is a political rally.

Wolfe is, of course, a consummate reporter, and if he were telling us that the New South has turned its collective back on that old-time religion, I'd be inclined to believe him. But I suspect that the absence of Christianity from *A Man in Full* says more about Wolfe's own interests than about the South as a whole. The only genuinely religious man to figure prominently in any of his past books, after all, is John Glenn, whose starchy Presbyterianism served as a comic foil to the religious indifference of his fellow astronauts in *The Right Stuff*. More to Wolfe's taste, I suspect, is the hustling Reverend Bacon of *The Bonfire of the Vanities,* a scalding satire of New York in the Eighties from which moral coordinates are conspicuously missing. (I wonder, too, what particular churches Wolfe visited in the course of researching *A Man in Full*. It's not hard to imagine a soft-spoken, white-suited son of Virginia recoiling from some of the more exotic species of religious enthusiasm found in the Bible Belt.)

Yet there is no getting around the fact that once he embraces Stoicism, Charlie Croker longs irresistibly to "shed all the shabby baggage of this life" and "become a vessel of the divine." That is the language of conversion, and it is, I think, very much to the point that in the epilogue, Wolfe shows Roger White and Wes Jordan, the black mayor of

Atlanta, shaking their heads in puzzlement over the news that Charlie has renounced his earthly goods and become an itinerant evangelist. This last touch is so subtle that it has been generally misunderstood by reviewers, who seem to think that by consigning him to so ignominious a fate, Wolfe is somehow making fun of religion. Far from it. Nothing could be more fitting than that Roger and Mayor Jordan, who put their trust not in God but politics, should think that Charlie has lost his mind: to the worldly man, all faith is mad.

Indeed, Charlie turns out to be so good a preacher that Fox signs him to do a weekly TV series, *The Stoic's Hour*. That's funny, though not in quite the way Wolfe thinks, since the very idea of a Stoic evangelist is a contradiction in terms. Stripped of its pagan trappings, Stoicism amounts to little more than a gentleman's code, and such codes, though they may capture the imaginations of isolated individuals, are by definition incapable of speaking to all men in all conditions; even in its heyday, Stoicism was never sufficiently compelling to engage more than a tiny band of middle-class intellectuals, or to halt the long slide of the Roman Empire into decadence and despair. Civilizations are built on revelations, not books of etiquette.

Still, it is far better to be a Stoic than to believe in nothing at all, just as it is a remarkable development — one I readily confess to not having foreseen — for America's supreme critic of manners to have moved so decisively beyond the coolly detached satire of *The Bonfire of the Vanities*. Brilliant though *Bonfire* was, this book is so much more morally comprehending that it inevitably leaves one wondering what lies in store for Tom Wolfe. I can't imagine what he will choose as the subject of his third novel, but no doubt we will all someday be reading it with delight, and marveling at how far its author has traveled since *A Man in Full*.

Crisis 1999

Merce Cunningham: Pale Horse, Pale Rider

"I SEE THE SHAMAN IS IN RESIDENCE TONIGHT," A SKEPTICAL-sounding balletomane remarked drily after looking over the program of a performance by the Merce Cunningham Dance Company during its last City Center season. Translation: Merce Cunningham was dancing in *Enter*, thus allowing veteran Merce-watchers to engage in the umpteenth annual discussion of whether or not his increasingly wobbly onstage appearances still have some artistic validity. Merce-watchers always argue about his cameos (I like them), just as they continue to debate the merits of the organized sound that accompanies his dances. But these are family arguments, amiable pseudo-quarrels hardly more serious than the yearly wrangle over whether Aunt Suzy should put more sage in the dressing next Thanksgiving. No minds are changed, and nothing is at stake. At least in New York, there is rarely anyone in attendance at a performance of the Cunningham company who doesn't already know he'll like what he sees.

Those who venture into City Center unwittingly are generally driven from it quickly, most often by one of the high-voltage electronic scores Cunningham likes to deploy from time to time. This time around there were two, for *Sounddance* and *CRWDSPCR*, and a handful of people stalked out of every performance I saw of both dances. Yet this, too, is considered part of the Merce Cunningham experience. You don't have to wander very far at intermission to hear Cunningham fans chattering happily, even complacently, about how Merce can still drive the Philistines out of the theater, even at the ripe old age of seventy-five. It occurred to me — not for the first time — that there is something unattractive about the attitudes implicit in such talk. Snobbishness is a venial sin, but it tends also to be a two-way proposition. In the case of Merce Cunningham, it's hard to spend much time watching his company on stage without getting the feeling that somebody up there is intensely interested in cultivating the perception that the genius of Merce is simply not accessible to every Tom, Dick, or Harry who stumbles in off Fifty-fifth Street.

On one level, of course, this is perfectly true: Merce Cunningham is not Bob Fosse. But it is also true that most of the great geniuses of art have sought, and ultimately won, a popular following. This is most especially true of George Balanchine, the choreographer to whom Cunningham is most often compared. There was a time when Balanchine was widely viewed as difficult — not difficult as Shakespeare is difficult, but as Joyce is difficult. Yet Balanchine wanted to please the largest possible audience — on his own terms, to be sure, but those terms were far more generous than was commonly supposed in, say, 1940. New York City Ballet is the institutional embodiment of that desire, a place where tens of thousands of people come every year to see *Agon* and *Concerto Barocco* and *The Four Temperaments* and *The Nutcracker* and *Slaughter on Tenth Avenue*. It offers masterpieces to suit every taste, including the common. Merce Cunningham, by contrast, has made little or no impression on those people for whom dance is an occasional entertainment rather than a central concern. Just prior to the company's City Center season, Mikhail Baryshnikov's White Oak Dance Project danced Cunningham's *Signals* at the New York State Theater. It was clear to the most casual eavesdropper that the house was full of people who had no idea who Merce Cunningham was (and who, at evening's end, were firmly resolved to keep it that way). The interesting thing is not that he has failed to reach a general audience but that, as far as I can see, he doesn't want to. Perhaps I do him an injustice; it may be that in his secret heart, Merce would like his company to perform in sold-out arenas. But the fact remains that the atmosphere of a Cunningham season is not just serious but esoteric — cultic, if you like.

I took three Cunningham first-timers to City Center this year, and questioned them afterward. To a woman, they were mystified by the monolithic repertory: three dances a night, all plotless, all structureless, all fitted out with impenetrably gnomic titles. John Martin's famously idiotic line about *Symphony in C* — "Balanchine has once again given us that ballet of his, this time for some inscrutable reason to the Bizet symphony" — not infrequently comes to mind when I see a Cunningham premiere. Similarly, the company is full of good dancers, but it is impossible for a novice to tell them apart. The dancers are listed alphabetically, both in the company roster and for every individual dance. There are no photos in the program, or in the lobby. Even when specific dancers are featured, as Alan Good and Jenifer Weaver were in *Beach Birds,* it's anybody's guess who they are. The printed slip identifying the cast of *Sounddance* in order of appearance had the feel of a last-minute concession, as if Cunningham had to be strapped down and tortured before finally giving permission to put it in the program. As it happens, this approach does rough justice to far too many of Cunningham's dancers, most of whom are individual only in the sense that identical twins have different fingerprints. There isn't a woman in Paul Taylor's company I wouldn't recognize on the street. Not so Merce's troupe. Night after night, the curtain goes up on a stageful of pretty-but-not-too-pretty WASPs. (Even the company's lone black dancer seems white in retrospect.) Fine as the overall level of the dancing was this season, there were only two company members, Good and Weaver, who made strongly individual impressions.

Cunningham's style of presentation reminds me of the way Walt Disney used to do the credits for his animated features. Every artist who worked on the picture, no matter how briefly, got screen credit — in small print, at the end of the last reel. Needless to say, you came away remembering only one name. Anyone who knows anything about Merce Cunningham knows that the studied facelessness of his ensemble is a reflection of his larger philosophy of Eastern egolessness. But anyone who knows anything about history knows that those who claim to be egoless usually have the biggest egos of all. I suppose it doesn't really matter. Merce is a genius — we all know that. But there is something just a little bit pat about his wanting to have it both ways.

THIS IS ONLY ONE OF THE MANY ELEMENTS OF THE CUN-ningham aesthetic in which theory and practice seem out of kilter. To spend an evening with the Merce Cunningham Dance Company is to leaf through a fat scrapbook of twentieth-century nonsense. As we look at the self-consciously alphabetical listing of dancers, we are reminded of the communal ideals of the Sixties, the decade in which the props were kicked out — perhaps permanently — from under Western culture. As the curtain goes up, we find ourselves face to face with two of the most absurdly rigid theories ever foisted upon a dance audience: the idea that dance and music ought to take place simultaneously but not synchronously, and the idea that large choreographic structures can be meaningfully determined by rolling dice. As the "orchestra" starts to play, we are confronted by the ghost of John Cage, the man whose hare-brained notions probably did more to damage Western music than any-one since Schoenberg. (Fifty years from now, Cunningham's dances will keep Cage's music alive in exactly the same way *La Bayadère* keeps the music of Minkus alive.) And then we forget the theories, and are enthralled. The superficial foolishnesses recede quickly into the back-ground; even the music becomes unimportant, a distant clatter one quickly learns to tune out. The dances are all that matter. Of all the lessons Merce Cunningham teaches us, this is the most important one: theory is meaningless to a genius.

I don't mean to deprecate the power of theory to carry even the finest artist across slack stretches of inspiration. It is absurd to suggest that Balanchine ever played it safe for one instant in his creative life, but it is certainly true that he did his high-wire acts over a safety net. Two nets, in fact: the twin disciplines of classical ballet and classical music. Not that these disciplines can make bad steps good, but when you submit to them, you're betting with the house, not against it. Cunningham al-ways works without a net, and always bets against the house. He does not rely on music, on a libretto, or a strong scenic conception, or the structural conventions of classical ballet, to give shelter to his dances. He makes steps and strings them together according to a method of his own devising. Under normal circumstances, only one aspect of his dances is predetermined: there will usually be three of them on a pro-gram, meaning that they must last somewhere between twenty and forty minutes. After that, all bets are off.

That Cunningham's method works at all, much less that it works so often, is an extraordinary tribute to his fertility. He is, in fact, so fertile that we have thereby been deprived of a clear understanding of the growth of his art. For the last decade or so, the Cunningham company has mostly performed new and newish dances. As a result, those who started watching Cunningham after about 1980 are inescapably limited in their knowledge of how Merce got from there to here. Though there are books to read, some of which are illuminating, the most important book, a *catalogue raisonée* of Cunningham's dances, has not yet been written. Until David Vaughan finally does for Cunningham what he did for Frederick Ashton, we are forced to rely primarily on the films Cunningham has been making since 1973. Sadly, Cunningham's films tell us little about the first half of his career. The earliest of his dances to have been filmed in its entirety is *Septet* (1953). There is nothing earlier, and not all that much later—he didn't get serious about filming his work until the late 1970s. But this season, in addition to having access to Cunningham's complete filmed oeuvre, New York dancegoers were able to augment their sketchy knowledge of Cunningham's middle period with two rare and supremely important revivals: *Signals* (1970), danced by White Oak, and *Sounddance* (1975), danced by the Cunningham company. For Merce's younger fans, it was catch-up time.

The most valuable of Cunningham's films from the period before he began to work with director Charles Atlas is the beautifully legible *Septet* shot in 1964 by Hakki Seppala for a Finnish TV broadcast. To see it is to see the Merce that might have been—a conventional Cunningham. Though the body language of *Septet* is as idiosyncratic as anything the Cunningham company dances today, the tone of the dance is startlingly "normal." It isn't just that *Septet* derives its structure (and counts) from a piece of music, Erik Satie's *Three Pieces in the Form of a Pear.* It's the style, the cheery atmosphere of accessibility, that startles. The Finnish audience laughs happily at the handshake scene, and even goes so far as to applaud one especially virtuosic combination. Don't they know this is modern dance?

Septet came at the end of a long string of works, most of them to Cage's pre-chance music for prepared piano, which one gathers from contemporary accounts to have been more or less problematic. Had Cunningham continued to work in the vein of *Septet,* we would doubtless now see it his "breakthrough" work, in much the same way that

Aureole was Paul Taylor's breakthrough work—the point at which his creative conception stabilized, allowing the audience to begin the long process of catching up with his imagination. In Taylor's case, that process culminated thirteen years later in *Esplanade,* the dance that made him popular. But Cunningham treated *Septet* as an end, not a beginning. Starting in 1953, he abandoned conventional music and the dance structures that arise from it, opting instead for structures determined in part by the use of chance operations.

The film of *Crises* (1960), shot at a 1962 rehearsal, shows how quickly Cunningham sloughed off convention. The music, by Conlon Nancarrow, takes place in the same time frame as the choreography, but does not generate it. (Nor could it: Nancarrow's player-piano etudes are based on irrational rhythmic relationships that make *Le Sacre du printemps* look like freshman algebra.) Hence the dance, convincing from point to point, seems somewhat aimless when viewed as a whole. This is a problem that Cunningham has never consistently managed to solve, except by claiming that it isn't a problem. But it is, at least for the audience. By abandoning both tonal music and what Vaughan calls "the usual principles governing dance structure—cause and effect, conflict and resolution, building to a climax," Cunningham tears down the signposts that allow the viewers of a dance to orient themselves in time—to know, among other homely but relevant things, that a dance is almost over. (One gets the feeling that a great many Cunningham dances end when the alarm clock goes off.)

The only thing missing from *Crises* is the Dadaist scenic element that Cunningham had begun to incorporate into his work in the late Fifties. This aspect of middle-period Cunningham we know more by description (and from some of the earlier films) than anything else, though *Signals,* with its stick and chairs, gave a hint of what it was like to see the Cunningham company in the days when its members used to dance *around* the set pieces created by Robert Rauschenberg and his associates. Once again, theory comes into play, in this case Cunningham's celebrated theory of "multiplicity of centers." As the choreographer explained to Jacqueline Lesschaeve in *The Dancer and The Dance:* "The three arts don't come from a single idea which the dance demonstrates, the music supports, and the decor illustrates, but rather they are three separate elements each central to itself." And once again, theory and practice diverge: Cunningham has not kept in his active repertory any of the dances that make use of elaborate set pieces like Andy Warhol's helium-filled pillows of *RainForest* or Jasper Johns's Duchamp-inspired decor for *Walkaround Time.* His sets are now for the most part purely decorative backdrops. In late Cunningham, the steps are the thing.

THE "NEW" CUNNINGHAM — THE ONLY ONE TODAY'S AUDI-ences can know in any kind of detail — makes two kind of dances. One kind is pure: no plot, no concept, no metaphors, nothing but steps in time. This is the Cunningham of *CRWDSPCR,* the more impressive of the two new works danced at City Center this season; this, too, is the Cunningham that novices, however fascinated, tend to find intimidating. And not just novices, either. *CRWDSPCR* is a very exciting dance, but it is also a very busy dance, one that I found impossible to grasp on first viewing (and far from easy to grasp when I went back a second time).

The other Merce Cunningham is the maker of *Sounddance* and *Beach Birds* (1991), to my mind the highlights of the company's current repertory. *Sounddance* is, on its surface, a quintessential specimen of the Bad Cunningham, the one who accompanies his dances with earsplitting music and crams in so many steps that you get a headache trying to tease them apart. But *Sounddance,* far from being inaccessible, is actually as close as Cunningham has come to making a crowd-pleasing applause machine. The reason is simple: *Sounddance* has an immediately intelligible structure. The dancers make their entrances, one by one, through the "door" in the center of the canvas backdrop; they exit, in a different order, through the same "door." Regardless of what happens in between, the twin bookends of those marvelously individual entrances and exits are what make *Sounddance* add up.

Nor is this structure purely arbitrary. Cunningham has furnished us with a clue, an epigraph from *Finnegans Wake:* "In the beginning was the sounddance." It is a very open-ended clue, and only a crudely literal mind would leap to the simplest explanation, that *Sounddance* is "about" the life cycle. It is no more about the life cycle than *The Four Temperaments* is about astrology. But the controlling visual metaphor of the dance is bound to evoke varyingly sophisticated mental images of that kind. This gives *Sounddance* an expressive force that transcends the sum total of its steps. Even David Tudor's score contributes significantly to the overall effect. Its sheer loudness is very much in keeping with the highly charged energy of the onstage action. Random though the correlation of music and dance necessarily is, the final impression left by *Sounddance* is congruent and convincing — even theatrical.

Many of the same things could be said about *Beach Birds*. Like *Sounddance,* it is dominated by a frankly theatrical concept: Cunningham's steps and Marsha Skinner's costumes clearly suggest that we are viewing a colony of water birds. And though the structure is less conventional than that of *Sounddance* (there is never any sense that one choreographic event need necessarily follow another), *Beach Birds* rests unequivocally on a dramatic fulcrum: a man comes on stage, plucks a woman from the ensemble, and dances with her. For Balanchine, this is standard operating procedure; for Cunningham, it is wildly heterodox. Cunningham rarely places a pas de deux at the center of his dances, and even more rarely charges it with romantic implications: "You see a man and a woman dancing together, or being together, it doesn't have to be thought of this way, but you make a gesture which can suddenly make it intimate, and you don't have to *decide* that this is an intimate gesture, but you do something, and it becomes so." But it is hard to view the *Beach Birds* pas de deux as other than romantic, an impression strengthened by a viewing of *Beach Birds for Camera* (1992), Cunningham's latest and most satisfying film.

Beach Birds for Camera is the first film in which Cunningham and his current director-collaborator Elliot Caplan have completely solved the vexing problem of "where" a dance film takes place. Most of Cunningham's films are shot in his New York studio, and no attempt is made to conceal the fact that we are watching dancers in a studio, or to create the illusion of stage space. Looking at the earlier films, one felt that Cunningham took this line because he didn't have the money to do anything else; the results usually seem cheesy and, occasionally, coy. But *Beach Birds for Camera* was filmed in two different locations, a dance studio and a sound stage. We are carefully distanced from the former by the subtle use of soft focus, translucent light, and handsomely grainy black-and-white cinematography. Then, just as Alan Good begins to dance with Victoria Finlayson, the film abruptly changes locales — and switches to color.

This jolting transition is obviously intended to mark off the main structural event of the dance. But it also reinforces the romantic atmosphere of the pas de deux. It is as if Good, entering into a sexless community of bird-dancers, carries with him the charge of sexuality that brings Finlayson to life (i.e., living color). The climactic phrase of their mating dance, so memorable on stage, becomes almost unbearably intense on film: Finlayson slowly spreads her slender arms over Good and brushes the back of his bowed head with her face. It is an oddly solemn act of tenderness, almost a benediction. Then Good turns to look at her, a gesture of utmost simplicity that nonetheless makes the remainder of *Beach Birds,* lovely though it is, seem like an afterthought. The whole film is wonderfully intimate — Cage's all-but-silent score leaves plenty of room to hear the dancers move and breathe and grunt — but the pas de deux, mostly shot in close-up, raises this intimacy to an unexpectedly high level.

In the black-and-white section of *Beach Birds for Camera,* we also get a brief but memorable glimpse of Jenifer Weaver, by far the most interesting of Cunningham's new crop of female dancers. Weaver lacks the austerely athletic beauty of Finlayson. Seen at rest (as we see her briefly in *Touchbase*), she makes no special impression. Her hair is lank, her face plain and sober. But as soon as she starts to move, she seizes the eye. Her large feet strike and pierce the stage; her legs become taut with certainty; her face radiates the ecstasy of action. She is a *big* dancer — the only woman in the company of whom this can be said — and she makes out of the *Beach Birds* pas de deux, which she now performs on stage, something so bold that the first time I saw *Beach Birds for Camera,* Finlayson actually looked a bit wan by comparison.

Though that impression gave way on successive viewings, it reminded me of the thing about Cunningham's dances I find least appealing: they have a way of seeming pale, even safe, when viewed in bulk. This may sound like a bizarre thing to say about a man who at the age of seventy-five can still make people run screaming from City Center. But the Cunningham aesthetic is one of renunciation: renunciation of conventional structure, conventional music, even the conventional effect of distinctively individual dancers. Renunciation is a religious act, a means of putting temptation behind you. Yet it is precisely because dances like *Beach Birds* and *Sounddance* yield to temptation — because they incorporate theatrical effects about which Cunningham usually seems dubious — that they make much of the company's current repertory look flat.

"Grace," says Cunningham in an oft-quoted remark, "comes when the energy for the given situation is full and there is no excess." This is a beautiful aphorism, and a revealing one. Cunningham's excesses are invariably ones of energy, not passion. The opening tableau of *CRWDSPCR*, an explosion of complex movement enacted by a stageful of seemingly frenzied dancers, is a deliberate act of excess — there is simply too much to see. But other kinds of excess are rigorously shunned. Try to imagine a *vulgar* Cunningham dance. It is impossible precisely because Cunningham never risks vulgarity, or exhibitionism, or sentimentality. To praise this restraint as a manifestation of his classicism is to confuse form with content. Cunningham's classicism is an act of concealment. It is supremely characteristic of the Cunningham aesthetic that his dancers almost never smile on stage.

The remarkable thing about Merce Cunningham is not that his aesthetic should occasionally fail to satisfy, but that it works as well as it does. I can't imagine him as my desert-island choreographer any more than I can imagine going on a macrobiotic diet. But if I could have three choreographers for my desert-island company, I suspect he would be one of them. There is no doubt in my mind that he would be a better artist (and a more popular one) if he were more willing to embrace than renounce. Still, this sort of criticism is valid only at the very highest level of achievement. I wish he were warmer, but I love him as he is.

New Dance Review 1994

Notes Toward the Definition of Paul Taylor

CHOREOGRAPHERS, LIKE COMPOSERS AND PAINTERS, are not much given to formal reminiscence. Fewer than a dozen important dancemakers have left behind full-length autobiographies, of which Paul Taylor's *Private Domain* is among the best. It would have been surprising had Taylor written a dull book, for he is a walking history of dance in postwar America. Born in 1930, he appeared in the premiere of George Balanchine's *Episodes* and danced with the companies of Merce Cunningham and Martha Graham before striking out on his own, and the hundred-odd dances he has made to date comprise one of the most sustained and significant bodies of work yet produced by a modern-dance choreographer. Even if it were less well written, Taylor's autobiography would thus be of interest solely for the insights it affords into his oeuvre. But *Private Domain* is more than just the chronicle of a career — it is also a memoir of real literary distinction. That a novice author should have produced so stylish a book without the aid of a ghostwriter is hard enough to believe; that he wrote it in between making such dances as *Roses, Last Look,* and *Syzygy* is little short of astonishing.

Though *Private Domain* will obviously be of special interest to those who are already familiar with Taylor's dances, one need not have seen any of them to appreciate his grimly amusing tales of a dancer's life, of which this snapshot from his company's 1961 tour of Italy is typical:

> Always sapping our energy are the stages to mop and the costumes to wash, mend, and pack. Our bare feet need constant desplintering and bandaging. Our theaters and hotels are crummy. . . . But I guess it's the press interviews that bother me most. Sponsors insist that I do

them to help ticket sales. At one of them a long-haired aesthete asks, "Signore . . . er, um, Taylor, is it? . . . with *Junction* have we not strayed a bit too far from the music?"

"Yeah, yeah," I answer, winningly. "But too far ain't far enough."

"I see," he answers, unimpressed. "*Signore,* our readers are fascinated by the mysterious wellsprings of creativity. How would you define the esemplastic power of the poetic imagination?"

"Come again?"

"Your creative juice, from whence does it come?"

"Oh, I getcha. You mean sperm. Gosh, you know, the usual place."

In Siena my clenched jaws ached.

Such vignettes remind us that Taylor's singular achievement as a choreographer has been to siphon the angst out of modern dance without simultaneously removing the seriousness. Even when his subject matter is shocking, his tone invariably remains light and effortless, which is why the heavy emotional weather of his darker dances never becomes oppressive. A case in point is *Company B,* in which stark images of battlefield carnage are played off against the relentlessly cheery singing of the Andrews Sisters. As the curtain rises, a dozen young men and women start to move about the dance floor to the strains of "Bei Mir Bist du Schön." Then you suddenly catch sight of a man lying motionless at their feet. The man vanishes and the music plays on, but the picture of his prone body sticks in your mind like a thorn. The juxtaposition is meant to startle—and it does. Yet *Company B* is no simple-minded sermon about pacifism, for its maker is not a simple-minded man. It is, rather, an attempt by a great artist to shed new light on the oldest truth known to humankind: in the midst of life is death. "Speaking of death," Taylor once told me in unnervingly good-humored tones, "I think somebody ought to count the number of my pieces that somehow can connect up with death and disintegration! But I don't think of death as a terrifying monster. It's just another of nature's ways." And so it is portrayed in *Company B:* war is terrible, but it is something human beings do, and will always do. Soldiers die and lovers mourn them, and the rest of the world keeps on dancing.

To view *Company B* in the larger context of the modern dance movement as a whole suggests the extent of Taylor's departures from its stern orthodoxies. Martha Graham and her contemporaries believed that by moving in a manner unencumbered by the conventions of classical technique, they would achieve both aesthetic and personal (including sexual) liberation. Graham in particular preached that credo with near-religious fervor, thereby charging her work with the power of an idea — but also cutting her off from large areas of human experience and a wealth of choreographic possibilities. Small wonder that the dances she made during the second half of her career were not about men and women of flesh and blood, but mythological figures. The whole point of Taylor's richly varied repertory, by contrast, has been to portray human experience in the fullness of its complexity. Choreographed in 1991, *Company B* is all of a piece with his earlier dances, in which the opposing polarities of man's divided self — dark/light, male/female, primitive/civilized, innocent/knowing — are put on stage and set in motion, there to collide with one another, sometimes fatally and sometimes comically. Just as it is no coincidence that Graham's most famous dances are based on myth, so it is wholly characteristic of Taylor that his most disturbing dances are funny. He has taken modern dance and stood it on its head, lightening its ponderous textures with wit and using comedy (which is tragedy inverted) to illuminate the blackest recesses of the soul.

Dualistic symbolism often implies a specifically religious vision, but Taylor's dualism is more Blakean than conventionally religious, especially in its deep-seated ambivalence toward love and lust. In such "classical" dances as *Aureole, Airs,* and *Arden Court,* the music is preromantic, the atmosphere joyous and civilized, the dancing lyrical and plotless — and the displays of sexuality mostly muted or undeveloped. These are dances of innocence, not experience. Conversely, Taylor never allows the viewer to assume for very long that human desire is nothing more than a simple matter of mutual gratification by consenting adults. In *Piazzolla Caldera,* set in a smoky nightclub situated on the outskirts of hell, seven men and five women dance together with a brittle, self-conscious physicality that has the ragged edge of barely controlled violence; no sooner has the curtain gone up than one senses that their casual couplings will lead to unintended consequences of the direst kind.

All these aspects of Paul Taylor's work are touched upon in *Private Domain,* though it is sometimes necessary to read between the lines in order to catch his drift. The wry account of his increasingly uneasy tenure as a member of Martha Graham's company, for instance, doubles as a searching critique of her self-absorbed aesthetic. (His passing remark that the choreographer of *Clytemnestra* and *Phaedra* "views us men onstage as giant dildos" says more about her later dances than a dozen well-worded essays.) And it is impossible to read Taylor's harrowing description of a week of debauchery in Liverpool—a tale told with a sharp eye for the absurd and no trace of self-pity—without realizing that behind the brutal candor of *Piazzolla Caldera* lies a lifetime of hard-won knowledge.

Private Domain also has much to say about its author's oft-remarked willingness to reexamine traditions long thought alien to modern dance. Taylor's relationship to ballet, as he makes clear in this book, has always been problematic at best. Yet it is worth noting that, in addition to dancing for Graham and Cunningham, he learned three Balanchine roles (one was Apollo) and was subsequently asked to join New York City Ballet, an offer he declined with thanks but which surely left its mark on his subsequent output. Whatever now-forgotten critic first described Taylor's dances of innocence as "barefoot *ballets blancs*" summed them up shrewdly: no modern choreographer has been more frequently drawn to eighteenth-century music, and none has done more to reconcile the earthy language of modern dance with the airy grace of classical ballet.

This aspect of Taylor's style was, of course, an even more radical departure from the rules of an art form that had long prided itself on being an insider's game. The smaller and unhappier the crowd, the greater the integrity—or so the early practitioners of modern dance affected to think. Taylor eventually came to know better, and it is fascinating to learn what was going through his mind during the making of *Aureole,* his first popular success:

> At this time—'62—modern dance [was] still keeping its distance from lyricism, "pure" or unexpressionistic kinds of dance, and reassuringly melodic music. . . . *Aureole* had been child's play compared with others

that I had to dig for, grapple with, and slave over, ones that had a more developed craft to them but weren't as popular. It was impossible to know if it would continue to be appreciated; yet for all its success, perhaps because of it, *Aureole* filled me with resentment. I was wary of it. It caused me to see a time coming when a choice would have to be made — to remain on the comfortably safe side of the doorway to success, or to pass through it and into a tougher and lot less familiar place.

Significantly, *Private Domain* ends in 1974, on the day that Taylor, having been forced from the stage by illness, begins work on *Esplanade*, the dance that would become his company's signature piece. In the quarter-century since then, he has become truly successful, more so than any other modern-dance choreographer, without compromising in the least his bleak vision of the human predicament. Each viewing of his greatest dances — among them *Aureole, Big Bertha, Esplanade, Cloven Kingdom, Le Sacre du Printemps (The Rehearsal), Sunset, A Musical Offering, Speaking in Tongues, Company B,* and *Piazzolla Caldera* — strips away yet another layer of charm and brings their dark secrets that much closer to the surface.

I once asked Taylor whether he thought his dances would survive him. "I don't know if they'll last," he replied. "I try to make them to last. They're not made to be seen one time." Having looked at them repeatedly, both on stage and on videotape, I've come to believe that they are likely to last a very long time indeed. I am fully as confident about the prospects for *Private Domain,* which to my mind ranks with Hector Berlioz's *Memoirs* as the finest autobiography to be written by a major practitioner of a nonverbal art form. By turns frank and fey, naggingly elusive and breathtakingly direct, *Private Domain* is an invaluable companion to the dances whose genesis it recounts, and I have no doubt that it will last as long as they do.

Foreword to *Private Domain* 1999

Stephen Sondheim's Unsettled Scores

F OUR DECADES AFTER *A FUNNY THING HAPPENED ON the Way to the Forum* opened, the jury is still out on Stephen Sondheim. He's a cold fish. *No — he's full of passion and rue.* His lyrics are brittle and heartless. *No — they're brilliantly perceptive.* He can't write a good tune to save his life. *No — he's the most original musical-comedy composer since Leonard Bernstein.* He's too smart for Broadway. *Well . . .*

Nancy LaMott used to introduce Sondheim's songs on stage by wryly complaining that except for "Send in the Clowns," she couldn't sing any of them more than twenty-five miles outside New York. But even in his supposedly sophisticated hometown, he plays to a smallish audience of admirers and cultists (there's a difference), not even the most devoted of whom can explain away the awkward fact that his shows lose money. It doesn't matter how good the reviews are: ordinary theatergoers just don't warm to him, and it isn't likely that they'll change their minds now that the Great White Way has become a Disney theme park.

What is it about Sondheim's work that leaves so many people shrugging their shoulders? It's not that his melodies are overcomplicated (even Madonna finally learned how "Sooner or Later" goes), or that his subject matter is particularly recherché (though *Pacific Overtures,* in which he explored the cultural implications of Commodore Perry's 1853 visit to Japan, definitely stretched the boundaries of the musical to their limits). The real problem is undoubtedly that while traditional musical comedy seeks to reassure its audiences that love conquers all, Sondheim's shows preach a very different sermon. Some of his endings are happy, some not, but all are tinged with the naggingly bittersweet flavor of doubt. Ambivalence, he says, is his "favorite thing to write about, because it's the way I feel, and I think the way most people feel." Perhaps, but it's not the way most people want to feel as they drive home to Scarsdale, having just blown $200 on a pair of tickets. They demand certainty, and Stephen Sondheim won't give it to them.

For those who hold that the best test of an artist's worth is the power of his work to get itself accepted in the competition of the market, that would seem to be the end of it. But of course it isn't, not by a long shot. Sondheim may not go over big in the mass marketplace, but neither does Verdi, at least not by comparison with Andrew Lloyd Webber. Therein lies one of the main reasons why his shows stir up controversy: the wrong people go to see them. Though the composer of *Passion* has long since outlived and outgrown the commercial theater that gave him his start, he continues to present his increasingly complex work there, and thus is judged by its increasingly coarse standards. Were he writing for, say, New York City Opera, a different set of standards would automatically come into play— perhaps no more relevant, but at least more accommodating.

To be sure, Sondheim has never written anything specifically for New York City Opera. But two of his musicals, *A Little Night Music* and *Sweeney Todd,* have been staged there, as well as in other such venues. The New York Philharmonic, for example, has performed and recorded *Sweeney Todd* in concert, and the show was also presented at Washington's Eisenhower Opera House as part of the Kennedy Center's Sondheim Celebration. Shortly thereafter, Chicago's Lyric Opera took *Sweeney Todd* into its repertoire, hiring Bryn Terfel to sing the title role, and London's Royal Opera House announced plans to follow suit. In explaining the latter decision, musical director Antonio Pappano said he wanted to "open the windows," adding, "I am not interested in this old argument about what is opera and what is musical theater. Often it's so intense and serious here, but it is O.K. for this opera house to have fun, too."

The defensiveness of Pappano's tone says more about Covent Garden in particular than the state of opera in general. Indeed, few American theatergoers would be likely to suppose that the best way for an opera company to show off its populist sentiments is to produce

Sweeney Todd, or any other Sondheim show. To the contrary, Sondheim is widely viewed as a coterie artist, and while most drama critics admire his work, there are plenty of dissenters. (Mark Steyn has called him "the man who knows more than anyone else about musicals except how to write one where you don't notice how much he knows.") At the same time, Broadway itself is now far less hospitable to musically challenging scores, and in recent years a growing percentage of the new musicals opening in New York have been "jukebox" shows, such as *Contact, Mamma Mia!* and *Movin' Out,* whose undemanding "scores" are pieced together from preexisting pop songs. It's hard to think of a single memorable song of the past half-dozen years that was first heard on a Broadway stage.

Given all this, you can't help but wonder whether certain of Sondheim's shows might belong in opera houses rather than on Broadway. Sondheim himself makes no secret of thinking otherwise. He even affects not to like opera, and has never written a work specifically intended for opera-house production. Still, the alacrity with which *Sweeney Todd* and *A Little Night Music* are being taken up by major companies raises the question of whether they might really have been, all along, modern operas in disguise.

THIS QUESTION CANNOT BE ANSWERED WITHOUT FIRST AT-tempting to define two famously slippery terms. *Tristan und Isolde,* for instance, is definitely an opera and *Annie Get Your Gun* no less definitely a musical, if only because *Annie Get Your Gun* is a play with spoken dialogue into which simple closed-form songs have been interpolated, whereas *Tristan* is a quasi-symphonic work in which every word is sung. Not that this broad-gauge distinction holds true in all cases. *Carmen,* a French *opera-comique,* and *The Magic Flute,* a German *Singspiel,* both contain spoken dialogue and simple, song-like arias. In that respect, both works would seem to have more in common with *Annie Get Your Gun* than *Tristan,* and it is worth noting that Oscar Hammerstein II rewrote the libretto of *Carmen* and successfully brought it to Broadway in 1943 as *Carmen Jones.* Similarly, Michael John LaChiusa, a Broadway composer who contends that his stage works are musicals rather than operas, considers *The Magic Flute,* which ranks among the highest and most profound expressions of the operatic ideal, to be a "prototype" for the modern musical.

Yet *Carmen* and *The Magic Flute,* different though they are from *Tristan,* also have something essential in common with it: they are *scores,* unified musico-dramatic structures whose separate parts serve a larger theatrical end. By contrast, nearly all the songs in *Annie Get Your Gun* are free-standing entities that can be sung on their own without reference to the show and its plot. And while the arias of Bizet and Mozart are fully as hummable as Irving Berlin's songs, they aspire, like the music of Wagner, to a far higher level of technical sophistication and—lest we forget—emotional intensity. Not all musicals are comedies, but very few are tragedies.

In addition, opera differs from musical comedy in that its theatrical effects are almost always nonverbal in origin. An opera libretto is a dramatic situation brought to life by music. Its words are sung (or spoken) by the performers, but their literary quality is irrelevant. All that matters is the quality of the music and the plausibility of the situation it illustrates. Even in an opera-comique or Singspiel, the performers usually spend much more time singing than speaking. In a musical, most of the book is spoken, so it must be engaging enough in its own right to hold the audience's attention. Moreover, musical-comedy singing is more conversational in style than operatic singing, meaning that the words of a song must be as memorable as its music (though their relative importance will vary from song to song in a given score). This is why relatively few operagoers know the words to the *Liebestod,* whereas most theatergoers know the lyrics to all their favorite show tunes.

Where do Sondheim's musicals rank on this continuum? *A Funny Thing Happened on the Way to the Forum* (1962), *Anyone Can Whistle* (1964), *Company* (1970), and *Follies* (1971), the first four Broadway shows for which he wrote both words and music, are all essentially non-operatic in structure. Instead, they are book-driven, and the songs and ensembles, though distinctive in style, are nonetheless rooted in the conventional musical-comedy practice that Sondheim learned from his youthful apprenticeship with Oscar Hammerstein II. Even so, two things set these works well apart from other musicals of the Sixties and

Seventies. The first is Sondheim's compositional technique. Unlike most of the American songwriters who preceded him, he had extensive classical training—he studied with the avant-garde composer Milton Babbitt—and was strongly influenced by the harmonic usages of the French impressionists. As a result, his songs are typically based on undulating chordal figurations over which he superimposes melodies painstakingly built up out of short, angular motivic fragments.* Listeners familiar with the music of Debussy and Ravel, or with modern jazz, will hear nothing abstruse in this approach, but anyone whose knowledge of music is limited to the ballads of such Broadway composers as Berlin or Richard Rodgers, with their long, seemingly self-generated melodic lines, will likely find Sondheim's songs to be insufficiently tuneful.

No less individual are his lyrics, and the sentiments they express. Though Sondheim's virtuosity is not without precedent (few of his elaborate rhymes would sound out of place in a lyric by Ira Gershwin or Cole Porter), his ambivalence toward love is all but unique in American songwriting. Even Lorenz Hart, that most disillusioned of lyricists, left no doubt of his fervent, even desperate longing for the state about which he wrote with such self-lacerating wit. Not so Sondheim, whose best songs are more often than not written from the point of view of an inhibited, alienated man unable to open himself up to the prospect of romantic love. Sometimes, as in "Being Alive," the finale of *Company,* he suggests that true love necessarily entails a near-intolerable sacrifice of personal autonomy: "Someone to need you too much, / Someone to know you too well, / Someone to pull you up short, / To put you through hell." At other times, as in the title song of *Anyone Can Whistle,* he portrays it as desirable but impossible: "It's all so simple: / Relax, let go, let fly. / So someone tell me, why / Can't I?"

In their unsettling fusion of yearning and ambivalence, these songs

---

* In addition to being his most popular song, "Send in the Clowns," from *A Little Night Music,* is a perfect example of Sondheim's tendency to construct even the most lyrical of his melodies out of these motivic building blocks— here, the four-note cell to which the first and second lines ("Isn't it rich? / Are we a pair?") are both sung.

constitute a near-complete break with the romantic optimism of the American musical-comedy tradition. In his next show, *A Little Night Music,* Sondheim moved still further away from that tradition, composing an operetta-like musical about the narrowing horizons of middle age. Though it is a bittersweet comedy with a happy ending à la *Der Rosenkavalier* (from which Sondheim quotes directly in "A Weekend in the Country," the brilliantly constructed first-act finale), *A Little Night Music* is ultimately no less bleak in its view of romantic possibility than its immediate predecessors, *Company* and *Follies.* It is, however, far more musically elaborate and demanding than any of Sondheim's previous shows, so much so as to approach in places the complexity of a full-scale opera. Two things, however, prevent it from attaining true operatic status. One is the vocal writing, two of the show's leading roles having been originally intended for performance by nonsinging actresses. The other is the large amount of spoken dialogue, which many opera singers are unable to negotiate effectively. Still, it was obvious that Sondheim was interested in moving beyond the narrow expressive compass of the old-fashioned Broadway musical, and in his next show he would do so decisively.

THE OPENING OF *SWEENEY TODD* IS ONE OF SONDHEIM'S MOST spectacular dramatic coups. An organ fills the theater with sober, Bach-like sounds. The ugly shriek of a factory whistle cleaves the air, and as its echo dies away, the orchestra begins murmuring nervously. Then, one by one, the members of the chorus emerge from the darkness, each singing a single ominous sentence:

> Attend the tale of Sweeney Todd.
> His skin was pale and his eye was odd.
> He shaved the faces of gentlemen
> Who never thereafter were heard of again.
> He trod a path that few have trod,
> Did Sweeney Todd,
> The Demon Barber of Fleet Street.

So begins his macabre musical version of Christopher Bond's play about a demented barber who slits his clients' throats, then uses their flesh as filling for the tastiest meat pies in London. By his own account, Sondheim's immediate reaction upon seeing the play for the first time was to wonder whether it might serve as "the basis of a good operatic piece." John Dexter, who had long been encouraging Sondheim to write "a through-composed piece" and knew his way around an opera stage, replied unhesitatingly that it would be "perfect." Six years later, *Sweeney Todd*, billed as "a musical thriller," opened at Broadway's Uris Theater, where it ran for 558 performances, 434 more than the original production of *Porgy and Bess*. The question of what Sondheim and librettist Hugh Wheeler had written thus seemed to have been answered more or less straightforwardly: *Sweeney Todd* was a musical, and a hit at that.

But just as *Porgy and Bess* defied such casual categorization, so did *Sweeney Todd* refuse to fit into any known theatrical pigeonhole. If it was a musical, then it was one that broke nearly all the rules of the game. Yes, it was funny, but in a manner so black as to recall Jonathan Swift at his most ferocious, with a pinch of Bertolt Brecht thrown in for good measure. Nor did Sondheim and Wheeler spare their audiences anything in the way of shock: *Sweeney Todd* ends with a stageful of dead bodies and dazed survivors. The score, as Sondheim had promised Dexter, was "through-composed," with a minimum of spoken dialogue and a maximum of richly expansive music greater in force and intensity than anything that had ever before been heard on a Broadway stage. No previous musical, not even the similarly operatic *Porgy* or Leonard Bernstein's *West Side Story* (for which Sondheim had written the lyrics), had pushed so hard against the outer limits of the genre.

Yet for all its self-evident sophistication, the sources of *Sweeney Todd* were as popular as a bag of popcorn. Bond's original play was a modernized version of a nineteenth-century melodrama that had once played in theaters all over England. Sondheim had gone to see it because it was the closest thing he could find to the eyeball-gouging spectacles that had once been presented by Paris's Théâtre du Grand Guignol, the long-popular company that specialized in one-act horror plays written for the sole purpose of scaring tourists. (The prop masters of the Grand Guignol had ten different recipes for stage blood.) And once he started writing the score to *Sweeney Todd*, Sondheim found himself drawn to the music of Bernard Herrmann, the film composer whose scores for such thrillers as Alfred Hitchcock's *Vertigo* and John Brahm's *Hangover Square* are at once lushly romantic and deeply unsettling. "It's an open secret," he has written, "that the music for *Sweeney* is in homage to Herrmann's harmonic language."

All this notwithstanding, *Sweeney Todd* is deeply rooted in a style of music drama more characteristic of the opera house than of Broadway or Hollywood. Just as its tightly knit ensembles and Debussyan harmonies ("The Ballad of Sweeney Todd" contains near-verbatim quotations from *La Mer* and *Nuages*) speak of a wider musical awareness, so do its theatrical methods imply a seriousness of purpose alien to the musical-comedy idiom of Sondheim's youth. It is not merely the lurid subject matter that sets it apart, though that alone would have been sufficient to put *Sweeney Todd* far outside the ambit of conventional musical comedy. Still, major characters had died violent deaths in other musicals. What was unique to *Sweeney Todd* was the savage irony with which Sondheim killed them off. The first-act finale, "A Little Priest," is a rollicking waltz whose lyrics pay sardonic homage to the social utility of cannibalism: "The history of the world, my sweet, / Is who gets eaten and who gets to eat." The show's most tender ballad, "Not While I'm Around," is sung by Toby, an unsuspecting street urchin, to Mrs. Lovett, an amoral monster who at that very moment is scheming to have the boy killed.

Most disturbing of all is "Epiphany," an overtly operatic mad scene in which Sweeney dedicates himself to the sacred cause of mass murder. Wracked with grief over the death of Lucy, his wife, he comes to the horrific conclusion that "we all deserve to die" and vows to bring that about by slashing the throats of his customers, one by one:

> I will have vengeance,
> I will have salvation! . . .
> And my Lucy lies in ashes
> And I'll never see my girl again,
> But the work waits,
> I'm alive at last
> And I'm full of joy!

Nor is the blackness of Sondheim's "comedy" merely cynical. Sweeney is a genuinely tragic figure, a man driven mad by his longing for revenge, not just on those individuals who have wronged him but on an entire society poisoned by hypocrisy: "Swing your razor wide, Sweeney! / Hold it to the skies! / Freely flows the blood of those / Who moralize!" Yet as he looks into the abyss and laughs, he fails to see that the dark and vengeful god whom he serves must in time lead him to kill not only the wicked, but the innocent—and, in the end, even those whom he loves most.

Such emotional extremism is the stuff of grand opera, of *Rigoletto* and *Otello* and *Don Giovanni,* and a few of those who saw *Sweeney Todd* in 1979 knew as much. On opening night, the veteran theater critic Harold Clurman spotted Schuyler Chapin, then the general manager of the Metropolitan Opera, in the lobby of the Uris Theater. As Chapin later reported, "He came charging across the lobby at me and said, 'Why didn't you put this on at the Met?' And I replied, 'I would have put it on like a shot, if I'd had the opportunity.' And I would have. There would have been screams and yells and I wouldn't have given a damn. Because it is an opera. A modern American opera."

Once again, Sondheim affects to differ with this appraisal. For him, *Sweeney Todd* is "not an opera" but, rather, "a black operetta in feeling and form." The distinction is finicky, and not fully convincing: if *Sweeney Todd* is something other than an opera, then what is *Carmen*?* In any case, such distinctions have grown less relevant now that the rampant hybridizing of postmodern polystylism has come to dominate art forms of all kinds. Regardless of whether *Sweeney Todd* is a true opera, it is without doubt one of the twentieth century's most powerful and thought-provoking pieces of musical theater.

* A more compelling objection to *Sweeney Todd*'s acceptance as an opera is that it was orchestrated not by the composer but by Jonathan Tunick, who has scored most of Sondheim's Broadway shows. Sondheim's inability to write directly for the orchestra is a major limitation of his work. Not only is much of his "orchestral" writing too obviously pianistic in origin, but the fact that he allows the instrumental colors and textures of his music to be supplied by other hands means that he cannot be given full credit for its creation.

NEVER AGAIN WOULD SONDHEIM WRITE A WORK SO FRANKLY operatic in style and scale as *Sweeney Todd,* though two of his later shows, *Sunday in the Park with George* (1984) and *Passion* (1994), make similar use of operatic techniques and might also benefit from opera-house production. His continuing reluctance to give up on Broadway is undoubtedly rooted in his dislike of the old-fashioned operatic production style of his youth, with its enervating emphasis on singing over drama. In addition, he seems to feel both that his talents are too good for musical shows and that the shows themselves are not good enough. "I'm serious," he has said, "but I'm serious in an art [form] that is barely worth being called one. There's a case to be made for 'Am I wasting my time in the long run?'"

The first of these objections, though, is puzzling, since there are any number of medium-sized American opera companies in which theatrically serious productions are mounted not by chance but as a matter of course. Foremost among them is New York City Opera, whose artistic director, Paul Kellogg, intends to make Sondheim's shows a regular part of that company's repertoire. As for the second, it may make more sense to say instead that Sondheim's best work is too serious in tone to appeal to the same mass audience that flocks to such latter-day Broadway hits as *The Producers* or *Hairspray.* If this is so, then his shows will flourish only to the extent that adventurous opera companies take them into their repertories (festival-style undertakings such as the Kennedy Center's Sondheim Celebration being by definition exceptional), and some of them are hopelessly ill-suited to opera-house production. While *Sweeney Todd* and *A Little Night Music* have long since proved their viability, a show like *Company,* with its extended dialogue scenes and pop-flavored songs, is no more operatic than *Annie Get Your Gun* or *Guys and Dolls,* and would sound no less absurd if performed by classically trained singers in a large house.

As for his more musically ambitious scores, Sondheim himself may have predicted their eventual fate in observing pithily that "when [Gian Carlo Menotti's] *The Medium* and *The Telephone* were done on Broadway, they were Broadway musicals; when they were done in opera houses, they were operas." In recalling the short-lived vogue of the Thirties and Forties for Broadway productions of such then-new operas as *The Medium* and Virgil Thomson's *Four Saints in Three Acts* (a vogue distantly echoed in the Baz Luhrmann–directed version of Puccini's *La Bohème* currently running on Broadway), he reminds us that his are not the only important musical-theater works that have initially presented problems of definition. Time was when *The Magic Flute* played to purely popular Viennese audiences, but now it is securely ensconced in the repertoire of every major opera house in the world. Should *Sunday in the Park with George* and *Passion* be successfully taken up by opera houses, then they, too, will become operas, and Sondheim will be recognized as one of the notable opera composers of the twentieth century, whether he likes it or not.

For the moment, though, we are left with just two Sondheim "operas," and the first, *A Little Night Music,* is problematic not only because of its heavy reliance on spoken dialogue but because of its characteristically ambivalent tone. The emotional power of comic opera—indeed, of all "serious" comedy—arises when the dramatic conflicts driving the plot are resolved through romantic reconciliation. The sense of restored unity this reconciliation produces in the viewer is what makes the "happy endings" of comic operas such as Mozart's *Marriage of Figaro* or Verdi's *Falstaff* seem earned rather than imposed. The light-hearted ending of *A Little Night Music,* by contrast, is at odds with the anti-romantic sentiments expressed in such songs, compelling in themselves, as "Every Day a Little Death" or "The Miller's Son":

> It's a very short fetch
> From the push and the whoop
> To the squint and the stoop and the mumble.
> It's not much of a stretch
> To the cribs and the croup
> And the bosoms that droop and go dry.

After such knowledge, what reconciliation?

Sweeney Todd, by contrast, does not pretend to be a comedy (despite the fact that much of it is bitingly funny). Here, at last, Sondheim accepts the tragic implications of his worldview and produces a score whose "operatic" anguish and violence—not to mention its operatic scope and largeness of gesture—are consistent with it. For this reason,

I'm increasingly inclined to think that it makes its strongest effect when sung and played by classically trained artists capable of rising to its near-operatic musical challenges. Heard under such circumstances, it is easier to recognize as a work that, for all its deep roots in musical comedy, can hold its own without apology in the operatic repertoire. One might well hesitate to compare it with such modern masterpieces as, say, Benjamin Britten's *Peter Grimes,* Leoš Janáček's *Makropoulos Case,* or Francis Poulenc's *Dialogues of the Carmelites,* but I have no doubt that *Sweeney Todd* is the most successful of all American operas, better than *Four Saints in Three Acts* or Aaron Copland's *The Tender Land* or — yes — *Porgy and Bess.*

Commentary 2003

What Randolph Scott Knew

I F YOU LONG TO MEET ODD PEOPLE, IT'S HARD TO TOP
Manhattanites who go to movies on weekdays. To be sure, I am
among their number, but at least I have an excuse: I *write* about
movies. The viewers I have in mind are the pure-hearted obsessives,
overwhelmingly male and uniformly unattractive, who flock to revival
houses on sunny spring afternoons to take in the latest week-long tribute to Alexander Dovzhenko, Ida Lupino, or maybe Edgar G. Ulmer —
it scarcely matters, since the same folks show up every time, no matter
what's showing.

Rarely are such proceedings invaded by those with lives, but innocent strangers have been known on occasion to wander into an art
house just for fun. Not long ago, I was flabbergasted to see a gaggle of
so-I'm-like-duh teenagers in attendance at a screening of Jean Renoir's
The Rules of the Game, though I soon realized that they were merely
film-studies students doing their homework. A few weeks later, I went
to the opening of a Budd Boetticher festival presented by the Film
Society of Lincoln Center, and was equally astonished to find myself
seated behind an intense-looking man who'd brought along a pair of
small children. Wondering how a fellow who bore all the familiar stig-
mata of film geekery could ever have forgotten himself long enough to
father two cute kids, I tuned in on their pre-show chatter. Would they
be lisping about aspect ratios or dye-transfer processes? Far from it. No
sooner had I started listening than I overheard a snatch of conversation
so appropriate to the occasion that I scribbled it down in my notebook:

CHILD #1 *(firmly):* "Two wrongs don't make a right!"

CHILD #2 *(smugly):* "Oh, yes, they do!"

The children didn't know it, but the conundrum about which they were arguing was the subject of the movie their father had brought them to see. *Ride Lonesome,* originally released in 1959, is a B Western directed by Boetticher and starring Randolph Scott. Unlike such better-remembered films as *Shane, Rio Bravo,* and *The Searchers,* it is known only to a small but stalwart band of critics and buffs who regard it as a minor masterpiece. As a rule, fanatics are not to be trusted on any subject whatsoever, least of all one that falls within the compass of their obsessions — but every once in a while, they're right.

IN CERTAIN WAYS, HOLLYWOOD TODAY IS JUST LIKE IT WAS A half-century ago. It's a company town, a plantation devoted to the manufacture of cultural commodities designed to please the largest possible number of people. Then as now, nearly all of the films produced there fit neatly into the pigeonholes of a limited number of highly stylized genres: gangster movies, costume dramas, romantic comedies, Westerns.

The main difference between then and now is that in the old days, such films were mass-produced on the assembly lines of the major studios. Americans of all ages went to the movies at least once a week, and they expected to see something different every time they went. Hence the studio system, which ground out product fast enough to meet the omnivorous demand. Except for the occasional *Gone With the Wind,* the modern Spielberg-style "event" movies that now dominate Hollywood filmmaking didn't exist. You went to the movies not to see *Spider-Man* or *Lord of the Rings,* but simply to see a show. If the show in question was a Western or a mystery, that was good; if it starred John Wayne or Robert Mitchum, that was better. But nobody went out of his way to see a Wayne Western directed by Howard Hawks, much less a Mitchum mystery directed by Jacques Tourneur. You took what you got, and if what you got happened to be *Red River* or *Out of the Past,* then you got lucky.

That's why so many of the best films made in Hollywood in the Forties and Fifties were Westerns and mysteries. Precisely because they *were* commodities, their makers tended to be ignored by the front office. So long as your last picture turned a profit, however small, you got to make another one. If the movies in which you specialized were low-budget genre pieces for which demand was more or less constant, all that mattered was that you stay more or less within the accepted conventions of the genre, and the conventions of the Western and the mystery happened to be wonderfully well-suited to the artful telling of serious stories that were both entertaining and cheap to produce. The art, of course, was optional, and most such movies were as forgettable as a *Law and Order* rerun, but some of them were as good—and as serious—as a movie can be.

Randolph Scott didn't set out to make serious movies. A dignified upper-middle-class gent from North Carolina, he went to Hollywood on a whim in 1928, caught the eye of a talent scout, and within a couple of years was churning out Zane Grey Westerns by the score. As it happens, Scott also had a knack for light comedy—he appeared in two Fred Astaire–Ginger Rogers movies, *Roberta* and *Follow the Fleet*—and there seems no obvious reason why he became typecast as the white-hatted good guy who rode a horse. Had the breaks fallen differently, he might well have evolved into an all-American version of Cary Grant, with whom he shared a bachelor pad in the Thirties, a living arrangement that caused rumor-mongers to whisper that the two men were lovers. (The rumor circulates to this day, though Scott denied it and no one has proved him wrong.)

After 1947, though, Scott started making Westerns exclusively, and for several years they ranked among the highest-grossing movies in America. Most filmgoers under the age of sixty are puzzled by the scene in Mel Brooks's *Blazing Saddles* in which Black Bart attempts to persuade the craven townspeople of Rock Ridge to stand up to the evil Hedley Lamarr by telling them, "You'd do it for Randolph Scott." To this they respond in unison, *"Randolph Scott!"* then doff their hats reverently—an accurate indication of how closely identified Scott was with the Western genre. He always played the same character, a lanky, dryly amusing cowboy with a Virginian accent who spoke only when spoken to and shot only when shot at, and you could take it for granted that he'd do the right thing in any given situation. If he'd been younger and prettier, he would have been too good to be true, but Scott was no dresser's dummy: he had a thin-lipped mouth and a hawk-like profile, and wasn't afraid to act his age on screen. Nobody in Hollywood, not even John Wayne, looked more believable in a Stetson.

On two occasions, in *Coroner Creek* (1948) and *Hangman's Knot* (1952), Scott wriggled out of his good-guy straitjacket to deliver cold-eyed, unsettlingly harsh performances that showed what he could do when he gave himself the chance, but otherwise he stuck to predictable B-plus oaters whose profits he shrewdly invested in the oil business. ("My outlook is purely mercenary," he told an interviewer.) Eventually, Scott's indifference caught up with him. Though he was at least as popular as John Wayne, Wayne consistently picked better directors and scripts, and by the mid-Fifties, Scott was slipping into bottom-of-the-bill obscurity just as his younger competitor was becoming the most beloved American actor of his time.

Ironically, it was Wayne who turned Scott's career around. The two men had worked together twice in the Forties, but didn't quite get along. In 1955, Wayne read a script called "Seven Men from Now" by a novice writer named Burt Kennedy, bought it for his production company, Batjac, and hired Budd Boetticher, an all-but-unknown journey-man director, to put it on the screen. Wayne was already committed to filming *The Searchers,* so when Boetticher asked him whom he wanted to play the lead, he casually replied, "Let's use Randolph Scott. He's through." Boetticher and Scott went on to make five more films to-gether (plus *Westbound,* a forgotten potboiler that Boetticher directed simply to keep the collaboration going). *The Tall T* (1957), *Decision at Sundown* (1957), *Buchanan Rides Alone* (1958), *Ride Lonesome* (1959), and *Comanche Station* (1960), all co-produced by Scott and his partner Harry Joe Brown, run about seventy-five minutes each, the length of a typical B movie, and were shot quickly on location in the barren, rock-strewn hills of Lone Pine, California. The casts were kept small and star-free to hold down costs still further, and Scott and Brown cut other corners whenever they could. *Ride Lonesome* and *Comanche Station,* for example, contain no interior scenes whatsoever.

The clean, spare look of the Boetticher-Scott films is mirrored in their no-nonsense scripts. *Ride Lonesome* and *Comanche Station,* both written by Kennedy, are for all intents and purposes the same movie as

Seven Men from Now — the basic plot mechanism is recycled from film to film, along with a few choice snippets of dialogue — while *Decision at Sundown* and *The Tall T,* the former doctored by Kennedy and the latter adapted by him from a novel by Elmore Leonard, arise from different situations but develop in similar ways. More often than not, Scott plays the part of a solitary, vengeful drifter who is searching for a man who has wronged him, usually by murdering his wife. In the course of his travels, he meets an unhappily married woman, to whom he is powerfully and illicitly attracted, and a villain who is charming and courageous — a hero gone bad, in other words. The villain proves to be looking for the same man as Scott, but their interests are in conflict, forcing them into a climactic showdown.

What sounds repetitive on paper proves miraculously varied in practice. Just as Degas never tired of the ballet dancers he painted time and again, so does Boetticher come up with ever-fresh ways to frame his players among the sun-scorched rocks of Lone Pine, finding painfully austere beauty in that least seductive of landscapes. Though he was never obvious about it, Boetticher was among the most visually imaginative of Western directors. I once had the opportunity to ask him if his feel for composition had been shaped by the paintings of such artists as Albert Bierstadt and Frederic Remington, to which he replied that while he liked their work, Renoir and Toulouse-Lautrec had meant even more to him. (I could see how much he enjoyed telling me that, too.) Similarly, Burt Kennedy makes a virtue out of necessity by letting Scott and his engaging enemies spend most of their time talking instead of fighting. He gives the best lines to the not-entirely-bad guys — Lee Marvin in *Seven Men from Now,* Richard Boone in *The Tall T,* Pernell Roberts in *Ride Lonesome,* Claude Akins in *Comanche Station* — and it is Roberts, not Scott, who gets the line that could stand as the motto of all six films, "There are some things a man just can't ride around."

Scott was secure enough to let his colleagues do the talking, knowing that his gritty, hard-faced on-screen presence would speak for itself. The dashing young leading man of the Thirties now looked as though he'd been carved from a stump, and every word he spoke reeked of disillusion. Yet he continually found himself forced to make moral choices that were always clear but rarely easy. What Scott *should* do at any given moment is never in doubt, but we also understand that doing it will not make him "happy" in any conventional sense of the word: he must do the right thing for its own sake, not in the hope of any immediate reward. Significantly, he sees the potential for redemption in the men he kills, slaying them reluctantly and only after giving them a fair chance to change their ways. Sometimes the woman's weak husband dies in the crossfire, thus freeing her to fall in love with Scott, but in *Ride Lonesome* and *Comanche Station,* the best and most characteristic films of the series, he discharges his stern duty and rides off into the sunset without looking back, alone again and likely to remain so.

This was and is an unusual approach to the Western, whose moral ambiguities generally prove on closer inspection to be superficial. John Wayne, for instance, usually played strong men with tainted pasts who nevertheless knew the right thing to do. (This is what makes *Red River* and *The Searchers* Wayne's most morally interesting movies. In both cases, he knows what to do—kill Montgomery Clift and Natalie Wood—but it's the *wrong* thing.) Conversely, the "adult" Westerns that followed in the wake of Sam Peckinpah's *The Wild Bunch,* the most influential Western of the postwar era, tend to be nihilistic. The heroes are villains, the villains heroes, and everyone in sight is corrupt beyond hope of redemption. Redemption, on the other hand, is the whole point of the Boetticher-Scott films. It is what Scott is seeking, and what he hopes to offer to the warped half-heroes whom he meets on his endless pilgrimage. And though Boetticher shies away from overt religious symbolism—the cross-like hanging tree in *Ride Lonesome* is a rare exception—it is hard to fathom Scott's old-fashioned integrity without supposing that he believes in something beyond his own iron will. Why else would he insist on preserving his honor at the cost of his happiness?

This message rings truer still as we look back on a century that might have been designed for the sole purpose of dramatizing the truth of Dostoyevsky's terrible warning, "If there is no God, then anything is permitted, even cannibalism." I doubt that Randolph Scott ever got around to reading *The Brothers Karamazov,* but he and Boetticher knew by instinct that in a world without laws or lawmen, every man must choose between the integrity of the old-fashioned cowboy and the moral cannibalism of his self-willed enemies.

THOUGH COMPARATIVELY FEW CRITICS ARE MORE THAN vaguely familiar with the Boetticher-Scott films, they have always had their fervent admirers, both here and abroad. André Bazin called *Seven Men from Now* "the most intelligent Western I know, while being at the same time the least intellectual, the most subtle and least aestheticizing, the simplest and finest example of the form." But when Boetticher died, only one of them, *Comanche Station,* was available on videocassette, and so far as I know there are no plans to release any of the others. Nor are they likely ever to become cable-TV fodder, for they are at once too spare and concentrated to please the contemporary shoot-'em-up audience and too morally aware for the comfort of postmodernists.

Fortunately, all six films can be seen with reasonable regularity in art houses and on museum film series, where movie lovers continue to stumble onto them in much the same way that the novels of Dawn Powell keep on being rediscovered four decades after their author's demise. What's more, some of Randolph Scott's original fans are still alive and well. I stood behind two of them in the popcorn line at Lincoln Center's Walter Reade Theater, a pair of silver-haired dowagers whom you'd never have taken for Western fans. Colin Powell had said something flaccid about Yasser Arafat that morning, and the women were grumbling about how weak-willed he was. "That's why I'm here today," the first one proclaimed without a trace of irony. "At least *Randolph Scott* always knew what to do." The other one nodded her head in emphatic agreement. No doubt stranger scenes have taken place in Manhattan since September 11, but that one was strange enough for me.

I like what André Bazin said about *Seven Men from Now,* but I like what the first old lady said about Randolph Scott even more: he always knew what to do, and whether he liked it or not, he did it. Midway through *The Tall T,* Richard Boone tries to explain to Scott why he became an outlaw. "I'm gonna have me a place someday," he says. "I thought about it, I thought about it a lot. A man should have somethin' of his own, somethin' to belong to, to be proud of."

"And you think you'll get it this way?" Scott asks.

"Sometimes you don't have a choice," Boone answers.

"Don't you?"

That's what Randolph Scott and Budd Boetticher knew: everybody has a choice. And that is why it is good to watch their movies at a time when America is struggling to deliver itself from the evil in which its citizens have long been taught to disbelieve. Without preaching or hectoring, Boetticher and Scott remind us that there is a difference between hard choices and meaningless ones, between the uneasy honesty of moral ambiguity and the slick-walled abyss of moral relativism. I can't think of a better reason to go to the movies on a pretty spring day.

Weekly Standard 2002

That Wascally Pwofessor

SELF-CONSCIOUSNESS IS THE CURSE OF A HIGH CULTURE with shallow roots. That's why American popular art at its not-infrequent best is so much better than, say, your average first novel by a promising young American writer (especially one who went to graduate school). Yes, the market often squashes art down to its lowest common denominator, and you end up with gangsta rap or professional football. But every once in a while, it also creates a working environment whose narrow confines mysteriously free the artist from what W. H. Auden called "the fetters of Self," and then you end up with Fred Astaire — or Chuck Jones.

For those not in the know, Chuck Jones is the creator of Wile E. Coyote and the Road Runner, and if that doesn't impress you, go talk to Professor Hugh Kenner, whose book *Chuck Jones: A Flurry of Drawings* is a monograph in the new "Portraits of American Genius" series from the University of California Press. Kenner knows a thing or two about art, and when he compares Jones to Buster Keaton, lesser folk would do well to listen up.

Chuck Jones was the most imaginative of the half-dozen men who directed cartoons for Warner Bros. between 1930, when the first Looney Tunes cartoon was released, and 1963, when Warner stopped producing animated shorts. In addition to directing the Road Runner and Pepé Le Pew series (as well as dozens of superior one-shot cartoons), he was mainly responsible for the definitive versions of Bugs Bunny and Daffy Duck. It was his inspired notion to make Bugs an urbane boulevardier who went ballistic only in response to intolerable provocation and, conversely, to turn Daffy into a walking id, a twitching mass of terror, vanity, and greed who, in Jones's words, "rushes in and fears to tread at the same time."

Jones had plenty of competition throughout the Forties and Fifties, not only at his own studio but at MGM, where Tex Avery was cranking out six-minute exercises in surrealist slapstick that remain watchable to this day. But it is Chuck Jones's best cartoons, among them "Duck Amuck," "One Froggy Evening," "What's Opera, Doc?" and "Rabbit Seasoning," that have lodged most firmly in the collective consciousness of the baby-boom generation, and rightly so. Says Professor Kenner: "Should you ever face the solemn task of preserving just one six-minute instance from the unthinkable thousands of hours of animated footage that's accumulated since — oh, since 1914, you'd not go wrong in selecting 'a Jones.'" The high quality of the Warner shorts owed much to the fact that they were created not by posterity-conscious "artists" but by craftsmen on tight budgets who were left alone by the front office as long as they hit their deadlines: "Like the 60,000-word novel, the six-minute cartoon derives its tautness from an economy imposed by commerce, not art. Art can work within that economy . . . the Warner system, albeit by inadvertence, guaranteed a niche where miracles could happen: where 'Art,' an overused word, is fitfully applicable."

Chuck Jones brought to this peculiar trade a stiff dose of what can only be described as classicism. The Road Runner cartoons, for instance, were all made according to self-imposed rules of the utmost strictness: "When the Coyote fell off [the cliff], I knew he had to go exactly 18 frames into the distance and then disappear for 14 frames before he hit." That may seem like a lot of brainwork for so unassuming a product. So it was — which is why Jones's cartoons have been playing on TV every Saturday morning for the last quarter-century. They haven't dated, and they hold up.

Dozens of books, some of them good, have been written about Chuck Jones and his contemporaries. What makes this one special is that it is the work of a first-rate critic, a man experienced in the subtle art of seeing. Here, to take one particularly choice example, is Hugh Kenner on Jones's greatest creation:

The Road Runner saga, all four-plus hours of it, relies on just one theme, seemingly inexhaustible. That is Wile E. Coyote's persistence in pursuit of what was once a potential snack and has long since mutated into an ideal conquest. The viewer of a new installment has seen all of it before and yet seen none of it before. The setting is always an idealized American Southwest, paradise of bluffs and canyons and vast spaces. Trucks or freight trains intrude sparingly, their human denizens never visible. Also mail brings wares of the Acme Company, which invariably malfunction. (But not grossly; no, subtly. The defect that sends the Coyote yet one more time off the cliff is as minute as the programming error that can cost NASA yet another satellite.)

That Kenner should have devoted such well-chosen words to Wile E. Coyote will doubtless exasperate more than a few stalwart defenders of high culture. But there is a big difference between what he has to say about Wile E. Coyote and what most academics have to say about anything at all: he has no ideological axe to grind. Nowhere does he refer to cartoons as texts, suggest that "Bully for Bugs" is every bit as good as *The Wings of the Dove,* or complain that "Ali Baba Bunny" privileges grey rabbits over black ducks. Instead, Hugh Kenner simply takes Chuck Jones's 204 Looney Tunes and Merrie Melodies at their proper value — as artful pieces of comic craftsmanship — and explains why they make him laugh. The result is a balanced and illuminating exercise in critical appreciation that is not only the best thing ever written about Hollywood animation but one of the best things ever written about any aspect of American popular culture. This is exactly the sort of book somebody ought to write about Raymond Chandler or Johnny Mercer or *Cheers:* shrewd, stylish, and very much to the point. Not unlike a Chuck Jones cartoon, in other words.

National Review 1994

Louis Armstrong, Eminent Victorian

MY FAVORITE LOUIS ARMSTRONG ANECDOTE CON-
cerns his audience with Pope Paul VI. The Holy Father, so
the story goes, asked Armstrong if he and his wife had any
children. "No, Daddy," the trumpeter cheerfully replied, "but we're still
wailing." Though it seems unlikely that Armstrong said anything quite
like that, it is the sort of thing one would have wanted him to say, and
the two men did in fact meet at the Vatican in 1968—which is, of
course, the real point of the story. They were photographed together,
and an unmistakable glint of pleasure can be seen on the Pope's tired,
worn face; as for Armstrong, he looks blissful. Perhaps he was thinking
about how far he had come from New Orleans, where he was born in
direst poverty in 1901, the bastard child of a fifteen-year-old whore who
had no idea that her son would become the most celebrated American
musician of the century.

Armstrong's celebrity cannot be separated from his artistry. It is central to his place in the history of jazz, which is harder to explain than is
commonly understood. He did not invent jazz, nor was he its first
important figure, and it is not even quite right to call him the first
great jazz soloist (Sidney Bechet preceded him, and Bix Beiderbecke
emerged as a major soloist at the same time as Armstrong, almost to the
month). Instead, he became the first great *influence* in jazz—the player
other players copied—and one reason he cast so long a shadow is that
he was as great a personality as he was a musician. He really did perform
with everyone from Bessie Smith to Leonard Bernstein; he really did
smoke marijuana virtually every day of his adult life; he really did write
the finest of all jazz memoirs, unassisted by a ghostwriter; he really did

end his concerts (some of them, anyway) by playing 250 or more high Cs, capped with a high F; he really was adored (no lesser word is strong enough) by all who knew him. Is it any wonder so many of his contemporaries longed to play the way he played and sing the way he sang?

Yet Armstrong's personality was not as wholly benign as one might have supposed from the stove-like warmth of his yard-wide smile. Benny Goodman once made the mistake of high-hatting him at the start of a joint concert tour, and was soon reduced to feigning a heart attack to escape the trumpeter's wrath. Nor did he hesitate to speak his mind, loudly and publicly, whenever he thought it appropriate. In the most celebrated of his oubursts, triggered by Dwight Eisenhower's initial unwillingness to force Orval Faubus to desegregate the public schools of Little Rock, he informed an astonished reporter that the President of the United States had "no guts" and that "the government can go to hell." Popular entertainers, especially black ones, didn't make a habit of saying things like that in 1957.

All this is part of the Armstrong legend, and thus fairly well known — but there was more to Armstrong than the legend. The same man who told off Eisenhower, for example, scrawled another set of fighting words onto a grade-school notepad as he lay in a Manhattan hospital room in 1969. As always with Armstrong, the syntax was homemade, but the meaning was as clear as a high note:

> Negroes *never* did stick together and they *never* will. They hold too much *malice — Jealousy* deep down in their heart for the *few* Negroes who *tries.* . . . they know within themselves that they're doing the wrong things, but expects *everybody* just because he is a *Negro* to give up everything he has *struggled* for in life such as a *decent* family — a *living,* a *plain* life — the *respect.* . . . And the *Negro* who *can't see* these *foolish* moves from some *over Educated fools'* moves — then *right* away he is *called* a *White* Folks *Nigger.* Believe it — the White Folks did *everything that's decent* for *me.* I wish that I can *boast* these *same* words for *Niggers.*

You will not find this scorching jeremiad in *Louis Armstrong: An Extravagant Life,* Laurence Bergreen's 1997 biography. Instead, it is paraphrased — gingerly. Gary Giddins's invaluable *Satchmo,* published in 1988, mentioned it only in passing, though Giddins quoted extensively from the remainder of the document in which it appears, a seventy-seven-page autobiographical manuscript now in the possession of the Louis Armstrong House and Archives at Queens College. Not until 1999 did it finally see print, first in Joshua Berrett's *Louis Armstrong Companion,* then in Thomas Brothers's *Louis Armstrong, in His Own Words: Selected Writings.*

Brothers's volume, amazingly enough, was the first book devoted solely to Armstrong's own writings (and it was far from complete — the uncollected letters could easily fill another volume). Most jazz fans are at least vaguely aware that he did quite a bit of writing, including dozens of magazine and newspaper articles, hundreds of letters, and *Satchmo: My Life in New Orleans,* his 1954 autobiography. Few, though, seem to grasp their unique significance. Many jazz musicians have published autobiographies, but nearly all of them were actually "written" by collaborators. Armstrong, by contrast, is one of a handful of jazz musicians, and the only major one, to have left behind a substantial body of writing in which his thoughts are presented in wholly or essentially unmediated form.

Granted that serious jazz scholarship is a comparatively young field, it is still odd that so many scholars and critics have been so slow — if not positively reluctant — to grapple with the sometimes uncomfortable implications of what Armstrong wrote about his life and work, which does not always mesh neatly with his public image. One who has done so is Dan Morgenstern, who wrote the introduction to the 1986 paperback reissue of *Satchmo: My Life in New Orleans.* In it, he shrewdly observed that while Armstrong "doesn't pass judgment on the 'gamblers, hustlers, cheap pimps, thieves [and] prostitutes' among whom he was raised, it is clear throughout this book that his values, from a very early age on, differ from theirs. . . . He was different from most of them, and the key difference was character."

AGAIN, MOST PEOPLE KNOW IN A GENERAL WAY THAT LOUIS Armstrong grew up poor, but the devil is in the details. Born in the poorest quarter of New Orleans, he was abandoned at birth by his natural father and sentenced at the age of eleven to the Colored Waif's Home, an orphanage-like reform school, for the crime of firing a revolver into the air to celebrate the Fourth of July. It was the first time his name appeared in print, and by all rights it should have been the last, save perhaps for a final entry on a police blotter; instead, he wrote himself indelibly into the history of Western music. Yet his genius alone was not powerful enough to pull him out of the gutter. That took something more, and he knew it.

Why did Armstrong spend so much of his spare time hunched over a typewriter? Partly because he was a gregarious soul who loved to send lively letters to his friends, but also because he thought he had something important to say. Armstrong's autobiographical writings "can be seen as a series of moral lessons," Bergreen argues, and, like Morgenstern, he got it right on the nose. Having been born desperately poor, Armstrong worked desperately hard, first as a boy and then as a man, much like Ragged Dick, Horatio Alger's plucky bootblack, whose burning desire to "grow up 'spectable" propelled him into the ranks of the middle class. Self-discipline, self-improvement, self-reliance: these were his lifelong watchwords, and no Alger hero could have improved on his iron determination to get ahead in the world. Once he did so, he felt an obligation to tell others how to do the same thing. "I don't want anyone to feel I'm posing as a plaster saint," he wrote in *Satchmo*. "Like everyone I have my faults, but I always have believed in making an honest living. I was determined to play my horn against all odds, and I had to sacrifice a whole lot of pleasure to do so."

This aspect of Armstrong is no longer fashionable, to put it mildly, and even in his lifetime, long before the nineteenth-century work ethic of individual responsibility and deferred gratification had become politically controversial, progressive-minded intellectuals were starting to have trouble with it. Around the time that Armstrong was sent to the Colored Waif's Home, George Bernard Shaw was writing *Pygmalion,* in which Eliza Doolittle's father savagely mocks the then-accepted distinction between the "deserving" and "undeserving" poor: "I dont need less than a deserving man: I need more. I dont eat less hearty than him; and I drink a lot more. . . . What is middle class morality? Just an excuse for never giving me anything." A true child of his time, Armstrong would have found such talk absurd at best, pernicious at worst. To be sure, he smoked marijuana every day and cheated happily on all four of his wives, but when it came to poverty, he was a perfect Victorian, certain that work was the only path to freedom and that those unwilling to follow it earned their dire fate. "The *Negroes* always wanted *pity,*" he recalled in his 1969 reminiscence of life in New Orleans. "They did that in place of going to work . . . they were in an alley or in the street corner shooting dice for nickels and dimes, etc. (mere pittances) trying to win the little money from his Soul Brothers who might be gambling off the money [they] should take home to feed their starving children or pay their small rents, or very important needs, etc." The note of anger — of contempt — is unmistakable.

In a review of *Louis Armstrong, in His Own Words* and *The Louis Armstrong Companion,* Brian Harker, an assistant professor of music at Brigham Young University, remarked that Armstrong was "a product of turn-of-the-century African American ideology, especially that of Booker T. Washington. Like Washington, Armstrong was an accommodationist, determined to play — and win — by the rules of the white majority." This is true as far as it goes, but it overlooks the fact that most jazz musicians, black and white alike, come from middle-class backgrounds, while most of those who are born poor strive mightily — and, more often than not, successfully — to join the ranks of the middle class. Anyone who doubts that Armstrong filled the latter bill need only visit his home, located some seven blocks from Shea Stadium in a shabby but respectable part of Queens. It is a modest three-story frame house whose elaborate interior is uncannily reminiscent of Graceland, Elvis Presley's gaudy Memphis mansion. From the Jetsons-style kitchen-of-the-future to the silver wallpaper and golden faucets of the master bathroom, the Armstrong house looks exactly like what it is: the residence of a poor southern boy who grew up and made good.

Unlike Graceland, though, it is neither oppressive nor embarrassing. As one stands in Armstrong's smallish study (whose decorations include, among other things, a portrait of the trumpeter painted by Tony Bennett), it is impossible not to be touched to the heart by the aspiration that is visible wherever you look. This, you sense, was the home of a *working* man, one bursting with a pride that came not from what he had but from what he did. The American dream has had no more loyal exemplar. "I never want to be anything more than I am, what I don't have I don't need," he wrote. "My home with Lucille [his fourth wife] is good, but you don't see me in no big estates and yachts, that ain't gonna play your horn for you. When the guys come from taking a walk around the estate they ain't got no breath to blow that horn." Is it any wonder that it enraged him to be branded an Uncle Tom? As far as he was concerned, working hard was not "acting white": it was acting human. Therein lay the ultimate meaning of his epic journey from squalor to immortality: his great and generous art spoke to all men in all conditions, and helped make them whole.

ARMSTRONG'S OWN MORAL WHOLENESS WAS CAUGHT IN THE words his mother spoke to him on her deathbed in 1927: "Son, carry on. You're a good boy. You treat everybody right, and everybody white and colored loves you. You have a good heart. You can't miss." Thirty-seven years later, I saw him for the first time, singing "Hello, Dolly" on *The Ed Sullivan Show*. I didn't know who the old man with the ear-to-ear smile was, but I can remember my mother calling me into the living room and saying, "This man won't be around forever. Someday you'll be glad you saw him." That was in 1964, back when the public schools in my hometown were still segregated, two decades after a black man was dragged from our city jail, hauled through the streets at the end of a rope, and set afire. Yet even in a place where such a monstrous evil had once been wrought, white people came to love Louis Armstrong — and, just as important, to respect him — not merely for the beauty of the music he made but also for the self-evident goodness of the man who made it.

That great smile, then, was no game face, donned to please the paying customers: it told the truth about the man who wore it, a man who did not repine but returned love for hatred and sought salvation through work. "I think I had a beautiful life," he said not long before his death in 1971. "I didn't wish for anything I couldn't get, and I got pretty near everything I wanted because I worked for it." It would be hard to imagine a more suitable epitaph for jazz's most eminent Victorian.

New York Times 2001

Bill Monroe and His Discontents

I ONCE MET BILL MONROE, THE CREATOR OF BLUEGRASS music, backstage at the Grand Ole Opry in Nashville. He stood six feet tall and looked at least seven, and his expressionless face might have been carved from a stump of petrified wood. He wore a white Stetson hat and a sky-blue suit with a pin in each lapel — one was an enamel American flag, the other an evangelical Christian emblem — and everyone in earshot called him *"Mister* Monroe." Never were italics more audible.

Such stiff-necked dignity went out of fashion long ago, but it was common enough in country people of Monroe's poverty-scarred generation (he turned eighteen two weeks before Black Tuesday in 1929), along with an iron reserve still more rarely encountered in our flabby, confessional age. Nobody ever complains in Monroe's songs, though there is usually plenty to complain about, while bluegrass itself is no less contradictory in its blending of seemingly incompatible styles and themes. It is at once lively and bluesy, hopeful and tragic, fabulously virtuosic and as plain as a cast-iron skillet. And while it often sounds like folk music, it is in point of fact the highly sophisticated invention of one prodigiously gifted man.

Jelly Roll Morton did not invent jazz, nor did Jerome Kern invent musical comedy, but there would be no bluegrass without Bill Monroe. You can hear it starting to take shape in the very first recordings he made with his brother Charlie in 1936; his lickety-split mandolin solos and hard-bitten, high-flying tenor harmonies were already recognizable. Ten years later, he walked into a Chicago recording studio with a new band featuring Lester Flatt on guitar and Earl Scruggs on banjo, and all at once the thing was done. What the Blue Grass Boys were playing in 1946 is the same music Alison Krauss and Rhonda Vincent play today, a music whose shadow extends over much more of American popular culture than is generally realized. One of the songs Monroe cut that day was his own "Blue Moon of Kentucky," which would be re-recorded eight years later in a revved-up rockabilly version by a then-unknown Monroe fan named Elvis Presley.

This tale has been told many times, most notably in Neil V. Rosenberg's magisterial *Bluegrass: A History,* but the story of Monroe's stormy life had yet to be recounted in detail before the publication of *Can't You Hear Me Callin'?* Richard D. Smith has produced a carefully researched biography based on interviews with many of the surviving key figures of the early days of bluegrass. It is factually reliable, musically knowledgeable, adequately written, and appropriately frank (especially as regards Monroe's chronic extramarital philandering), and I cannot imagine its being bettered for a long time to come.

William Smith Monroe was the eighth and last child of a timber farming family from Jerusalem Ridge, Kentucky, whose hard-working members had little time left over for love. "For many years," he later told a friend, "I had nobody to play with or nobody to work under. You just had to kindly grow up. Just like a little dog outside, tryin' to make his own way, trying to make out the best way he can." By the time he was sixteen, he had lost both parents and went to live with his Uncle Pen, an amateur fiddler who introduced him to the square-dance tunes whose stamping rhythms would eventually be absorbed into the language of bluegrass. In 1929, he moved to Chicago to work at an oil refinery, part of the great migration of ambitious young men from the South; it was there that he and Charlie Monroe began performing professionally, becoming a full-time duet act in 1933.

The Monroe Brothers' music was a homemade amalgam of "old-timey" ballads and white gospel songs, lightly brushed with jazz and the blues and enlivened by a daredevil energy all their own. When the brothers went their separate ways, Monroe put together a four-piece band called the Blue Grass Boys and auditioned for the Grand Ole Opry, winning a place on the weekly radio show in 1939. Though the group's galloping style was an instant hit with Southern audiences,

Monroe continued to tinker with it for another seven years; Scruggs's syncopated three-finger banjo picking turned out to be the missing ingredient, and once he joined the band in 1946, no more tinkering was necessary.

Younger musicians began copying the Blue Grass Boys almost immediately, and when Flatt and Scruggs left in 1948 to start their own band, the Foggy Mountain Boys, they played, logically enough, in exactly the same style. Instead of finding such imitation flattering, the famously hot-tempered Monroe was enraged by it, and grew angrier still as the more shrewdly managed Foggy Mountain Boys found wider popular success. It was not until the folk revival of the early 1960s that he won recognition as the "father" of what had come to be known generically as bluegrass. By that time, he was working with younger, bettereducated musicians, many of them urban northerners, and though they treated him as a living legend, he found it hard to view his new colleagues as anything other than objects of suspicion.

Success made Monroe more approachable, but he remained essentially solitary to the end of his long life (he died in 1996), never fully capable of trusting anyone else's good intentions, and his loneliness was writ large in his music. He sang of love gone wrong in a harsh, stoic wail, the cry of a strong man in agony who cannot quite manage to keep his pain to himself. This intensely inward quality — what fans of bluegrass call its "high lonesome sound" — coexists uneasily with the joyous sound of fleet-fingered pickers sprinting wildly to the finish line. It is this delicate balance that gives bluegrass its double-edged character, and it was Bill Monroe who first struck it.

Does that make him "the most broadly talented and broadly influential figure in American popular music history," as Smith asserts? That covers a lot of ground, as does the incautious claim that he can be "ranked with Duke Ellington, Louis Armstrong, Charles Ives, and Hank Williams as a true giant of American music." For all its emotional intensity, bluegrass is far narrower in expressive scope than the jazz that influenced it, and I suspect most unbiased observers would thus be reluctant to rank Monroe with Armstrong and Ellington as a musical innovator. Even so, the invention of bluegrass was without doubt an important cultural event, very probably significant enough to justify calling its inventor a musical giant. If so, that would explain Bill Monroe's lifelong melancholy as well as anything that happened to him in childhood: giants are always lonesome.

New York Times Book Review 2000

Citizen Sinatra

THE BEST PICTURE EVER TAKEN OF FRANK SINATRA WAS shot from behind. It shows him walking out of the studio alone at the end of a recording session, sharply dressed in topcoat and snap-brim hat, shoulders bent with exhaustion. If a picture is worth a thousand words, this one rates a whole novel, preferably by Raymond Chandler. Pete Hamill once said it would take "some combination of Balzac and Raymond Chandler" to do Sinatra justice, and the solitary man in the picture could indeed just as easily be Philip Marlowe at the bitter end of *The Big Sleep*, making ready to go once more down the mean streets of Los Angeles. The only thing missing is the face—and, of course, the voice.

Not that we need much prompting to recall either one. Frank Sinatra is the fixed star in the crowded sky of American popular culture, a hot-blooded senior citizen who has jumped triumphantly across the chasm of time into the chilly age of cyberspace, synthesizers, and reflexive irony. "Frank Sinatra—THE Diva!!" started by a California opera buff, was one of the most popular message threads on the Compuserve Music/Arts Forum this summer; four books about Sinatra have just been published, and Carnegie Hall recently devoted three consecutive evenings to a stirring celebration of his life and work. Even Generation X, which revels in admiring nobody, has paid him his due. "Teen Angst," a song by the alternative-rock group Cracker, contains the following quatrain: "What the world needs now is a new Frank Sinatra / So I can get you in bed / What the world needs now is another folk singer / Like I need a hole in my head."

Yet the face of Frank Sinatra is still turned from us, as much by default as by choice. He is the great missed opportunity of American letters. No musician seems ever to have interviewed him at length; no first-rate book has been written about his life. Instead of a novel, we got a trashy tell-all biography. Kitty Kelley, the author of *His Way: The Unauthorized Biography of Frank Sinatra* (1986), rummaged through steaming heaps of Las Vegas garbage and found everything—except the sled called Rosebud. And most other chronicles of his life and work have been hopelessly superficial. (A case in point is Lew Irwin's *Sinatra: The Pictorial Biography,* which devotes fifteen pages to Sinatra's movies of the Fifties and a page and a half to his recordings of the same decade. The disproportion is breathtaking even for a celebrity journalist, though the evocative photographs chosen by Irwin, the publisher and editor of the entertainment industry newsletter *Studio Briefing,* partly offset the predictability of his text.)

For the most part, we have done better by the artist than the man. It stands to reason; he is, after all, a more familiar type. That bruised, acrid romanticism is forever turning up in our novels and movies. It is the underside of the coin of masculine fantasy in America: heads John Wayne, tails Humphrey Bogart. And in adapting the Bogart persona to his own artistic ends, Sinatra fused it with a natural musicality of the highest order. There was never anything incongruous about his recording with the Hollywood String Quartet, or conducting the music of Alec Wilder. For all his undeniable theatrical gifts, Frank Sinatra was first and foremost a musician, a protean interpreter who took the best popular songs of his time and etched his versions of their words in our memories, making them inseparable from the sound of his burnt-umber voice.

It is this aspect of Sinatra that Will Friedwald analyzes with unexpected acuity in *Sinatra! The Song Is You,* a musical biography whose subject is not Sinatra's life but his recordings. I say unexpected because Friedwald's last book, *Jazz Singing,* reeked of excessive self-regard, and *Sinatra! The Song Is You* is frequently marred by the same bratty cleverness. When Friedwald says that Milt Bernhart's trombone solo on "I've Got You Under My Skin" sounds like the work of "one of Stan Kenton's girdled nails-on-chalkboard brassmen who has somehow quantum-leaped smack into the middle of an otherwise smooth-groove, pat-your-foot Basie chart," the temptation to snap *Sinatra! The Song Is You* shut and drop it in the nearest wastebasket is all but overwhelming.

Fortunately, Friedwald has mostly managed to stay on track this time around. Much of his commentary is alert and perceptive, and even more valuable is the wealth of pointed reminiscence drawn from interviews he has done with musicians who worked closely with Sinatra. "I've never heard of a book like that," Al Viola, the singer's longtime guitarist, told Friedwald, "a book on Frank where they talked to guys like me. The people that were really there with him, sweating it out. That's the one book on Frank that hasn't been written. And I think that's the soul of his music." Viola is quite right, and the results, if uneven, are also remarkable: *Sinatra! The Song Is You* is the most important book published about Frank Sinatra to date.

Still, Friedwald's narrowness of focus, though it contributes to his book's quality, inevitably tells only half the tale. Frank Sinatra is not just the Voice, that disembodied wraith who materializes out of the mist when a microphone is placed in his hand; our interest in him has always been a combination of unfeigned love of his exquisite singing and unwilling fascination with his coarse public image. *The Frank Sinatra Reader*, an exemplary collection of essays, articles, and book excerpts edited by Steven Petkov and Leonard Mustazza, goes a long way toward filling in the blanks. Most of the best pieces written about Sinatra since 1944 are included in this wide-ranging anthology, some famous (Gay Talese's "Frank Sinatra Has a Cold") and some familiar only to aficionados (Neil McCaffrey's "I Remember Frankeee"), and all very much worth reading.

But even *The Frank Sinatra Reader*, fine as it is, generally draws the line well this side of absolute candor. Much as Sinatra's admirers would wish it otherwise (most of them, anyway), there is no getting around the fact that the same man who recorded with the Hollywood String Quartet also kept company with thugs like Sam Giancana. He is a double man, an artist and a brute; combine his two faces and you get an American icon, mysterious and troubling and complete.

What made Sinatra Sinatra? A dominating mother, a passive father, a scrawny boy who was sensitive about his looks and had an artistic streak: it sounds almost like *Tea and Sympathy,* or the libretto of an Antony Tudor ballet. Even minus the mob, it would have been the perfect recipe for a double man — especially where women were concerned.

Sinatra's are so central to his image that they even find their way into Nancy Sinatra's *Frank Sinatra: An American Legend,* a lavishly appointed scrapbook destined for the coffee tables of avid fans. Her tone is for the most part naive to the point of disingenuousness: "As reports about Nazi atrocities against Jews began to filter back from Europe . . . Dad felt he had to do something about racial and ethnic discrimination, so he had 100 copies of a special medallion made. On one side was a St. Christopher medal, on the other a Star of David." But amid the acres of carefully sanitized, uniformly unrevealing anecdotes that make up the text of her book, she has taken care to include not only angry excerpts from the memoirs of her father's ex-wife, Ava Gardner, and his ex-fiancée, Lauren Bacall, but also her own sad account of how she came to terms with his incessant philandering.

The full story, of course, is in the records, and it is, as Friedwald reminds us, a tale of multiple personalities: Sinatra the wide-eyed romantic, Sinatra the brashly swinging (i.e., callous) lover, Sinatra the wrist-slitting quarter-to-three "saloon singer." Add them up and you get a man incapable of coming to terms with women as they really are, whose psychobiography is an angry gloss scrawled in the margins of the history of feminism. If anything about Frank Sinatra's life is interesting, it is this; much more interesting than all the my-pal-Vito horror stories, sickening though they are. Though it is impossible to reduce him to a formula (what Theory of Sinatra could explain away the astonishing fact that he married Mia Farrow?), his recordings can nonetheless be understood as a musical setting of Freud's great question: what do women want?

It is a question he has never stopped asking, and that is why his anguish and confusion continue to speak to us. Whenever I listen to the harrowing ballad albums of Sinatra's early maturity — *In the Wee Small Hours, Where Are You? Only the Lonely* — I think of T. S. Eliot's line: "The notion of some infinitely gentle / Infinitely suffering thing." I think, too, of Philip Marlowe, who in *The Long Goodbye* tore up the bed in which he slept with Linda Loring, incapable to the last of accepting his own need for women, yet equally incapable of turning his back on them.

AND NOW THAT HE IS AT THE END OF HIS PERFORMING CA-reer, one last purifying paradox has come into view: it is the women, not the men, who are carrying on his art. Sinatra was so overwhelming an influence on the male singers of his own day that he washed most of them out. It stands to reason that women could not imitate him in so literal a way; try to imagine a feminine version of Frank Sinatra and the mind shudders to an immediate halt. Yet the most impressive cabaret singers of the baby-boom generation are all women, and in the finest of them, Nancy LaMott and Wesla Whitfield, one hears the essence of Sinatra miraculously abstracted from its masculine context: the same richly detailed readings of lyrics, the same high tension between ideal-ism and despair. Whatever these singers may think of Sinatra as a per-son, it is clear that they are capable of peeling away the outward skin of crudity to heed the tender message of the artist within.

It is this tenderness, often thwarted but always present, that makes Frank Sinatra so essentially American a figure. We have always been a nation of hopeless romantics, and we sense that the lonely man in the topcoat and hat is one of us, only more so. One would prefer him to have been, in Raymond Chandler's words, a man "who is not himself mean, who is neither tarnished nor afraid . . . a man of honor, by instinct, by inevitability, without thought of it, and certainly without saying it." But when the last standing ovation has died away and the fully comprehending biography is finally written, we will be left with something in which conventional notions of honor play no part: the records, those haunting testaments of passion and fear that arise from and explain his life — and, perhaps, justify it as well.

New York Times Book Review 1995

PART TWO ～ MIDCULTISTS

Seven Hundred Pretty Good Books

The Good, the True, the Beautiful:
Those are the things that pay!
— Lewis Carroll

MOST AUTHORS CAN CONTEMPLATE THE PROSPECT OF making a lot of money with breathtaking equanimity. George Santayana, for instance, had no difficulty in grasping the news that *The Last Puritan* had been picked as a Main Selection of the Book-of-the-Month Club. "Of course it is gratifying to have this sudden boost," he wrote to a friend in 1935, "but someone must have it, apparently, every month, and really it's not extravagant to think that *The Last Puritan,* which is a major work and original in some respects, should have been chosen to be one of the twelve in one year."

But what was to Santayana cause for detached, perhaps even smug, self-congratulation provoked in John P. Marquand an oddly splenetic outburst. When his 1943 novel *So Little Time* was chosen as a Book of the Month, Marquand wrote to his son John, Jr.:

> This, as you may know, is one of the things which we boys in our profession strive for, and I am told that I am peculiarly honored since I am one of the few novelists who have had two novels selected by this august money-making organization, and nearly the only one who has had two in succession. Aside from this I am not deeply moved. I think the Book-of-the-Month Club is a racket that is spoiling the general sale of books by concentrating on the few that it sends to its customers. It is really another of these organizations which exploits our writers as do agents and the publishers themselves, as well as the damn movies.

The difference between Marquand's exasperation and Santayana's detachment was probably more a matter of self-confidence than anything else. Marquand, for years a highly paid contributor of slick short stories to the *Saturday Evening Post,* had been struggling since the publication of *The Late George Apley* to gain recognition as a serious novelist. ("I have never understood," he wrote, "why a sinner is not allowed at least to attempt reformation in the American World of Letters.") He deserved it — Marquand was a sharp-eyed observer of American manners whose two best books, *Apley* and *Point of No Return,* are unquestionably ripe for revival — but his efforts succeeded only in cementing the admiration of newspaper reviewers, the affection of millions of American readers, and the respect of the editorial board of the Book-of-the-Month Club.

For a frustrated highbrow like Marquand, the approval of the Book-of-the-Month Club was sheerest gall. The orthodox view of the BOMC as America's caretaker of middlebrow literary taste was neatly summed up three decades ago by Dwight Macdonald, who observed in "Masscult & Midcult" that "Midcult is the Book-of-the-Month Club, which since 1926 has been supplying its members with reading matter of which the best that can be said is that it could be worse, i.e., they get John Hersey instead of Gene Stratton Porter." Nor was this elaborate disdain a mere affectation of Macdonald's. When Norman Podhoretz was an undergraduate whiz at Columbia in the late Forties, envious but socially tonier peers gleefully predicted that he would become another Clifton Fadiman when he grew up. Fadiman, who also started out as an undergraduate whiz at Columbia, ended up reviewing books for the *New Yorker,* starring on the popular radio show *Information, Please,* and joining the BOMC panel of judges. The insult was apparently considered definitive by its wielders. If the Book-of-the-Month Club had been around in 1922, George Follansbee Babbitt would surely have been a charter member.

Blackballed by the American World of Letters, Marquand finally succumbed to the blandishments of the Book-of-the-Month Club — in spades. Not only did he accept without further protest the fifty thousand dollars the selection of *So Little Time* added to his 1943 royalty statement, he also accepted an invitation to become one of the club's judges, the ultimate Midcult literary sinecure. Marquand kept the job, which paid him twenty thousand a year, for the rest of his life, and whatever pleasures it afforded him, he knew that it had defined him more firmly than ever.

WERE THE HIGHBROWS RIGHT ABOUT THE BOOK-OF-THE-Month Club? More than seven hundred books have been chosen as Main Selections in the six decades during which the club has been doing business, and it is, after all, worth remembering that *The Last Puritan* did indeed make the cut. So did *Nineteen Eighty-Four, Doctor Faustus, A Preface to Morals, The Catcher in the Rye, The Gulag Archipelago, In Cold Blood,* and *Seven Gothic Tales,* none of them quite the thing for perusing on hot summer nights in Zenith, Ohio.

The quality of these titles alone suggests that there might just be more to the Book-of-the-Month Club than meets the highbrow eye. Such is the case made by Al Silverman, chairman of the BOMC and editor of *The Book of the Month: Sixty Years of Books in American Life,* a celebratory miscellany of articles originally published in *The Book-of-the-Month Club News,* a monthly magazine that describes the club's current selections, alternates, and dividends. Silverman's ostensible purpose is to mark the sixtieth anniversary of the founding of the Book-of-the-Month Club. But one quickly realizes that this miscellany has a message. Silverman, it seems, earnestly wishes to convince the reader that the BOMC, far from being a mere middlebrow business venture, has in fact been an institution central to the American literary life.

That Silverman takes the Book-of-the-Month Club seriously is evident in his choice of epigraph for *The Book of the Month,* a generous slice of Milton's "Areopagitica." That he means to place the BOMC in the mainstream of American literature is equally evident in his opening paragraph: "Harry Scherman picked a good time to start a book club. It was 1926 and Hemingway was posing for a photograph with Joyce, Eliot, and Pound at Sylvia Beach's bookstore in Paris." But the full scope of his intentions is revealed when he explains that the purpose of *The Book of the Month* is to "tell a story of the social history of the past six decades as seen through books," adding that "I wanted to know more about the club's past because that way I would know a little more about *our* past as a country." (Shades of Charlie Wilson and General Motors.)

Cynics will doubtless respond that the real purpose of *The Book of the Month* is to provide advertising for what John Marquand, who knew the value of a dollar, succinctly described as a "money-making organization." But Silverman, it turns out, is at least partly right. Not that *The Book of the Month* has any particular literary value. Though a great many distinguished authors who have contributed to the pages of *The Book-of-the-Month Club News* turn up in the pages of this volume, their contributions tend to run to what Joseph Epstein calls "blurbissimo." The best piece of writing in *The Book of the Month,* ironically, is a droll letter that highbrow radio comedian Fred Allen sent to the BOMC in response to a request for a review of a novel by an old Allen jokewriter named Herman Wouk.

Still, *The Book of the Month* does contain the raw material for an exercise in social history that, if not quite as broad as the one promised by Al Silverman, is nonetheless intriguing. This is the story of the club itself, a tale that George Santayana, chronicler of America's genteel tradition and author of two Main Selections of the Book-of-the-Month Club, would have appreciated to the fullest. And though Silverman devotes too much space to corporate puffery and not nearly enough to hard facts, his book gives the reader a clear sense of the important role the club has played in what William Shirer, a favorite author of BOMC members, might have described as the rise and fall of American literature since World War I.

The idea of a mail-order book club had apparently been floating around for a good many years before Harry Scherman got the notion to start one in 1926. Subscription libraries in the United States go back to the days of Benjamin Franklin. The German *Volksverband der Bücherfreunde* (People's Union of Book Lovers) published and distributed books at a discount as a response to the postwar hyperinflation. But the Book-of-the-Month Club sprang up as a result of an entirely different problem: the poor distribution of books outside America's major cities. In 1930 there was one bookstore for every thirty thousand Americans. Thirty-two percent of Americans had no direct access to any bookstores whatsoever. Shorter working hours, higher literacy rates, and rural electrification had combined to increase the number of potential readers of books and magazines. A huge, untapped market was waiting for the right kind of businessman to come along.

The Twenties may have been the decade of Hemingway, Joyce, Eliot, and Pound, but they were also the age of what Al Silverman adroitly describes as "entrepreneurs of the word." *Reader's Digest* was founded in 1922, *Time* in 1923, the *New Yorker* in 1925. These business ventures, like the men who founded them, were as characteristic of the Twenties as bathtub gin. DeWitt Wallace, Henry Luce, and Harold Ross were all classic specimens of the Great American Culture Salesman, half genius and half rube, a type that seemingly came in with Coolidge and went out with Pearl Harbor. Wallace was once described by a colleague as having a "strictly average" mind that "completely reflects the mentality of his readers." Though he boasted of his "passable" Latin and Greek, Harry Scherman was clearly cut from the same bolt. His business philosophy was straight out of the pages of Dale Carnegie or Elbert Hubbard — or, for that matter, *Reader's Digest* itself:

> If you are to deal with or think about the American people en masse, you can trust them as you trust yourself. You can trust their consuming curiosity about all the quirks and subtleties of human existence; you can trust their fascination with every colorful aspect of history; you can trust their immediate response to good humor and gaiety, but also to the most serious thought; you can trust their gracious open-mindedness, forever seeking new light upon their troubled but wonderful world.

A man who can say such things without cracking a smile is doomed to become a millionaire, and Harry Scherman did not disappoint. Recognizing that there was a fortune to be made in mail-order books, he devised an ingenious subscription system in which club members were required to purchase a fixed number of titles a year and were automatically sent a Main Selection each month. Scherman then added a stiff jolt of very special old snake oil. He decided that the Main Selection would be chosen by an all-star editorial board, which met regularly to have lunch and select the "Book of the Month": Henry Seidel Canby,

Dorothy Canfield Fisher, Christopher Morley, Heywood Broun, and William Allen White.

The result, a typically American combination of steak and sizzle, caught on with amazing speed. Starting out with 4,750 members, the Book-of-the-Month Club expanded to 46,539 within eight months. By 1929, 110,588 people were members of the club, which was well on its way to becoming a fixed star of American popular culture. People told jokes about the Book-of-the-Month Club. Novelists satirized it. Other entrepreneurs imitated it, using Scherman's basic subscription principle to sell everything from fruit to phonograph records. There was even a highbrow equivalent of the BOMC, the Reader's Subscription, whose editorial board consisted of Jacques Barzun, Lionel Trilling, and W. H. Auden.

The club's initial selling point was convenience. (The BOMC's first advertising slogan was "Handed to You by the Postman, the New Books You Intend to Read.") But the all-star board made the Book-of-the-Month Club a household word. The purpose of the board, Scherman later said, was "to set up some kind of authority so that the subscribers would feel that there was some reason for buying a group of books. We had to establish indispensable confidence with publishers and readers." By giving his editorial board absolute freedom to pick the Main Selection each month, Scherman gave to the Book-of-the-Month Club a patina of independence and literary respectability; by choosing as panelists five conservatively minded writers who were already in the business of attracting large audiences, he ensured that the Main Selections would never be so *recherché* as to scare off an excessive number of subscribers.

Dorothy Canfield Fisher anchored the first BOMC panel to the literary center as rigidly as Scherman could possibly have wished. Though her own novels are forgotten today, her aesthetic standards are suggested by a 1946 exchange of letters reprinted in *The Book of the Month*. To an unhappy BOMC member complaining that the current Main Selection depicted "a group of people whose entire conversation is made up of talk of sleeping with each other, and such dirty stuff," Miss Canfield stalwartly replied:

Three of the five members of the Editorial Board . . . are of Quaker background. That is, I think you will agree, a guarantee of our sober, careful upbringing in our youth, and of our recognition of moral values during our adult life. . . . I am repelled as you are by what seems to me the overemphasis laid in modern novels on sex-relations. But I feel that if there is in our American twentieth-century life as it is lived by large numbers of people, in actual reality, such an overemphasis, with its resultant misery and dreariness, it would be ostrich-like for our serious novel writers to ignore it.

What squalid fancy of the editorial board, one wonders, could Miss Canfield possibly have been defending? *The Company She Keeps*? *Memoirs of Hecate County*? *Other Voices, Other Rooms*? None of the above. It was a best-selling novel about the advertising business called *The Hucksters*. One wonders what poor Miss Canfield, who died in 1958, would have made of the sex relations overemphasized in such later Main Selections as *The World According to Garp*.

Even more central to the success of that first panel were Henry Seidel Canby and Christopher Morley, the best-known literary popularizers of their day. Both men achieved a modest immortality by being on the receiving ends of two of the wickedest parodies imaginable, Morley a brutal 1938 Edmund Wilson spoof called "The Pleasures of Literature" ("With how sure an expectation of solace, amid the turmoil and perplexities of our time, do I turn, when the fires of evening are lit, to my silent companions of the library!") and Canby an even more savage character sketch in Randall Jarrell's *Pictures from an Institution*:

He was a prominent literary critic: he had a column of criticism, every week except the last two weeks in August, in the best-known literary weekly; he was a director of a club that picked books for readers who didn't know what to read . . . during the school year he would lecture to colleges, and when the school year was over he would make commencement addresses to them or get honorary degrees from them; he was the chief reader of a publishing house, he was one of the vice-presidents of the American branch of the Académie Française; you saw one-act plays by him, if you fell among anthologies of one-act plays; he even wrote informal essays.

Scherman's first panel, as Richard Rovere noted in the *American Mercury,* "carried the stamp of culture without being too frighteningly highbrow." The Main Selections they picked out from the thousands of titles submitted to the BOMC each year attracted herds of loyal, trusting subscribers. (Up to 50 percent of the club's members were taking the Main Selection as late as 1948.) And as the original board members died or retired, Scherman continued to display an impeccable sense of middlebrow literary taste in choosing their replacements. John P. Marquand, who came aboard in 1944 and remained until his death in 1960, was in many ways the quintessential board member of the Book-of-the-Month Club. The country's most consistently popular author throughout the Forties and Fifties, he was unfailingly sensitive to the need to offer the widest possible variety of books to the club's members. Reporting to his fellow board members in 1947 on a novel by Thomas Costain, Marquand noted: "It seems to me about time that we gave the customers something with entertainment value, and never mind the art and implications." After reading *Intruder in the Dust,* he told board member Amy Loveman that the book "really would be easier to read if [Faulkner] adopted a few printer's conventions, but perhaps its being hard to read makes it great literature."

Despite a penchant for highbrow-baiting, Marquand was just as capable of pushing a book like Peter De Vries's *The Tents of Wickedness* or Francis Steegmuller's translation of *Madame Bovary,* and his recommendations were generally as solid and reliable as was his own writing. Judges like Marquand and Clifton Fadiman, for all their literary sophistication and intelligence, were sufficiently aloof from the more upsetting crosscurrents of modernism to ensure that each month's Main Selection would be respectable enough to keep the business side of the BOMC humming.

NO COMPLETE LISTING OF THE CLUB'S SEVEN HUNDRED-ODD Main Selections is currently available to the general public, making it difficult to analyze changes in the quality and character of the club's offerings over the years. But *The Book of the Month* provides an informative, if unsystematic, overview of the club's offerings throughout its sixty-year history, and one of the most striking things about Silverman's running commentary is the candor with which he confesses the failings of the selection process.

Leafing at random through *The Book of the Month*, one runs across sentence after sentence like these: "For some unfathomable reason, *All the King's Men* by Robert Penn Warren was not picked as a Selection of the Club." "No Faulkner novel became a book of the month until his last book, a minor work called *The Reivers*, perhaps because one judge confessed that he always giggled when reading Faulkner." "Thus *The Sun Also Rises* did not become *the* Book of the Month." "No F. Scott Fitzgerald work ever became a Book of the Month." "It is somewhat disconcerting to note that Saul Bellow's first BOMC Selection came late in 1975." "But it wasn't until 1979, with *The Ghost Writer*, that a Roth book became a Club Selection."

What caused these embarrassing oversights? One suspects that a good deal of blame can be laid on the board's use of the principle of concurrence in choosing Main Selections. "The old Quakers in their business meetings," Canby explained, "never voted. If the majority could not persuade the minority to concur, the proposal was dropped." Conventional balloting having failed to work in the BOMC's early years, Canby persuaded the board to use concurrence instead. As a result, a lot of books were dropped over the years because they failed to accord with the sensibilities of one or the other of the five judges. John Marquand claimed that *Intruder in the Dust* was passed over as a Main Selection because it made one of the judges "nervous." And when Amy Loveman agreed to concur in the selection of Robert Ruark's *Something of Value*, she insisted on being allowed to publish the following starchy dissent in *The Book-of-the-Month Club News*:

> This is an absorbing book, but many readers will find it a shocking one, as I did, and that is the reason I did not approve of its selection. It is not shocking in the ordinary sense of the word, for it contains no obscenity and no deliberate attempt at sensationalism, but shocking by sheer weight of its facts.

Even when the board managed to pick a book of undeniable seriousness, strange things sometimes happened in the course of the selection process. Books were read and considered six months or more prior to publication, and it was not uncommon for the board to suggest revisions to the author. For the most part these suggestions were made to novice authors. But the editorial board actually dared to suggest to George Orwell that *Nineteen Eighty-Four* would benefit from two cuts, the appendix on Newspeak and the thirty-page "Theory and Practice of Oligarchical Collectivism." Orwell declined ("I really cannot allow my work to be mucked about beyond a certain point," he told his American publisher) and the board, to its credit, backed down.

George Orwell scored twice, the first time with *Animal Farm*. James Michener, on the other hand, has racked up ten Main Selections since 1947, making him the all-time fiction champ of the Book-of-the-Month Club. Five to one sounds about right. "Because no permanent contribution to world literature has been published in the month of May," Canby asked rhetorically, "is a critic therefore stopped from recommending somebody's good and readable novel?" This question could have easily served as the credo of the BOMC editorial board. Some of the board's selections were first-rate, some frankly trashy, most comfortably middle-of-the-road. Charles Lee cites the following "distinguished selections" in his introduction to *The Hidden Public: The Story of the Book-of-the-Month Club,* written with the full cooperation of the club, and his list would seem to be as representative of its period as any: *All Quiet on the Western Front, Gone with the Wind, The Good Earth, John Brown's Body, Life with Father, Kristin Lavransdatter, Revolt in the Desert, The Rise of American Civilization, Elmer Gantry, The Last Puritan, Darkness at Noon, Animal Farm, Anthony Adverse, Benjamin Franklin, The Nazarene, The Gathering Storm, The Old Man and the Sea, Andersonville,* and *By Love Possessed.*

Confronted with so bewildering a hodgepodge of titles, the reader is likely to grope for *some* sort of meaningful ordering principle. Such groping is in vain. Canby claimed that his sole purpose in selecting books was "the passing on of sound values to others." Fadiman speaks of "my own direct, uncomplicated, eager interest in a book." The judges explained in the very first issue of *The Book-of-the-Month Club News* that their object had been "not to deliver an ultimatum as to the 'best' book each month, but to find a book that will appeal most winningly and forcibly to widely differing tastes." William Allen White broke down those tastes in 1940 as follows: 20 percent "who will accept subtlety in literature, who like stylists, who do not mind 'dirt,' who quickly fall in with new literary fashions"; 20 percent "who have made good but have not had much education, who like the looks of the books on their living-room tables, who intend to read but never get around to it"; and 60 percent "solid professional people — doctors, school principals, and so on." If there is a better definition of middlebrow taste, I haven't heard it.

Highbrow opinions of the Book-of-the-Month Club, not surprisingly, have varied wildly. When Charles Lee sent Malcolm Cowley a list of the club's Main Selections from 1926 to 1953 and invited comment, Cowley pointed out that Faulkner, Proust, Joyce, Kafka, Gide, Pirandello, Rilke, Lorca, D. H. Lawrence, Dos Passos, Yeats, Eliot, Mauriac, Conrad Aiken, Valéry, Claudel, and Colette were among the important authors of the day who were missing. (Proust and Colette eventually made it as alternates.) Still, Cowley's overall opinion of the club was one of "very qualified praise."

Dwight Macdonald, on the other hand, was convinced that middlebrow institutions like the Book-of-the-Month Club had a dangerous and destructive effect on American culture:

> Up to about 1750, art and thought were pretty much the exclusive province of an educated minority. Now that the masses — that is, everybody — are getting into the act and making the scene, the problem of vulgarization has become acute. I see only two logical solutions: (a) an attempt to integrate the masses into high culture; or (b) a contrary attempt to define two cultures, one for the masses and the other for the classes. I am for the latter.

Macdonald saw the Book-of-the-Month Club, like the novels of John Marquand or the plays of Thornton Wilder, as a flagrant example of Midcult, a consciously commercial attempt to bridge the gap between Masscult and High Culture. He was convinced that Midcult undermines and vulgarizes the values of High Culture and makes it easier for the barbaric minions of Masscult to storm the gates. And he argued forcefully that Midcult values, "instead of being transitional — 'the price of progress' — may now themselves become a debased, permanent standard."

As an indictment of mass culture as a whole, this argument carries a good deal of weight. As an indictment of the Book-of-the-Month Club in particular, it doesn't wash. Al Silverman himself makes the case for Midcult in *The Book of the Month,* although not very well:

> In his challenging essay "Masscult and Midcult," Dwight Macdonald criticized the Book-of-the-Month Club for what he felt was its tendency to water down and vulgarize high culture. . . . Harry Scherman was a pragmatist, and a populist, when it came to reading. He understood that there would always be that gulf between Macdonald's High Culture and popular culture, but he also felt that the two sometimes merged and, anyway, that a bridge existed between the two and that people could walk back and forth as they chose.

A more convincing argument, however, is implicit in this earnest but naive rebuttal of "Masscult & Midcult." Harry Scherman, like DeWitt Wallace and Henry Luce, proposed to make a lot of money by improving people's minds, and he took both sides of the equation seriously. The purpose of the Book-of-the-Month Club, as Scherman saw it, was to bring an unprecedentedly wide selection of books into as many homes as possible. "In the late nineties or early nineteen hundreds," he wrote in 1928,

> conditions were probably at their worst. That was the day of the real best seller, when half a dozen books sold up to half a million copies each, when the general reading population *all* read the same five or six books — and very few others — when 2,000 copies was a good sale for a serious nonfiction book, and 300,000 moderate distribution for a popular milk-and-water novel. That is standardization — and we had it.

To judge by those goals, Scherman succeeded brilliantly, selling books to the masses that almost certainly would not have reached them otherwise. Many of those books were good. And a good book, as Carl Van Doren once said, "is not made less good or less useful by being put promptly into the hands of many readers." One suspects that even

George Santayana would have agreed. Surely the forty thousand copies of *The Last Puritan* sold to the members of the Book-of-the-Month Club more than adequately define the club's very real place in the American literary life.

WHAT HAS THE PASSING OF TIME DONE TO HARRY SCHERMAN'S radiant vision of a more literate America? Up until a few years ago, it still made perfect sense. I should know, for I was once a member of the Book-of-the-Month Club, and my memories of it are wholly benign. I joined the club as a high-school senior for the very good reason that there wasn't a decent bookstore much closer than a day's drive from my hometown. During the two years I belonged, I purchased at least three Main Selections that have remained on my bookshelves to this day: William Manchester's *American Caesar,* Tom Wolfe's *The Right Stuff,* and Anthony Burgess's *Earthly Powers.* I bought my fair share of alternates and dividends, too, among them a very nice set of Evelyn Waugh's early novels and a Nabokov package that contained *Lolita, Speak, Memory,* and *Pale Fire.* It's hard to get much more highbrow than that.

But times have changed back where I come from. Now there are a couple of surprisingly good bookstores thirty miles from my old front door. The spread of chain bookstores throughout the small towns and rural areas that once provided the BOMC with its staunchest customers has revolutionized the publishing business. It has also deprived the Book-of-the-Month Club of one of its chief reasons for existing. Fred Smith, then BOMC publicity director, noted in 1948 that "we do more than half of our business in cities where the publishers do less than 20 percent of theirs. Where publishers do 90 percent of their business, we do something over 40 percent. . . . This would indicate that our business is directly related to book distribution, that the vast majority of our members are people who have no readily available retail source of books." Those words have an ominous ring today.

Moreover, the drawing power of the Book-of-the-Month Club editorial board has been on the wane for years. John Marquand was probably the last panelist widely known to the general reading public. Today's editorial board consists of veterans Clifton Fadiman and John K. Hutchens; novelists Mordecai Richler and Wilfrid Sheed; and David

McCullough and Gloria Norris, both of whom started out as members of the BOMC staff before being promoted to the board. Good judges all, no doubt, but one has to wonder exactly what they add to the appeal of the club out in the boondocks. Not that the Book-of-the-Month Club is to blame. Literary celebrity just isn't what it used to be. What public figure of today, literary or otherwise, could possibly wield an authority equivalent to that once exercised by the likes of Canby or Marquand? John Updike? William F. Buckley, Jr.? James Clavell? Bill Cosby? Phil Donahue? A grim little party game suggests itself.

In any event, the literary scene today shows no sign of having been influenced for the better by Harry Scherman's democratic plans for the bookbuying future. "We thought that we might be able to create a new kind of audience for good reading," Henry Seidel Canby said in 1947, "and we did." Maybe so. But though more people are indeed buying more books, the books they are buying are for the most part trashier than ever. Publishing has become an impossibly big business, and the margin for error at the major houses has become so narrow as to squeeze out almost anything that can't be sold by the truckload.

The current issue of *People,* which is lying on my desk as I write this paragraph, contains an article about a woman named Sally Beauman whose first novel, *Destiny,* was recently signed by Bantam Books for a record-breaking one-million-dollar advance. Stephen Rubin, Bantam's editorial director, describes Miss Beauman as follows: "This is a woman who not only understands the elements of a blockbuster, but she can write as well. There is elegance in *Destiny,* along with intelligence, energy, and sex." One week before the official publication date, *Destiny* appeared at the number six spot on the *New York Times* bestseller list.

When I read this cautionary tale, I immediately thought of an indelible remark Diana Trilling made in her review of John P. Marquand's 1946 novel *B. F.'s Daughter:*

> Without transcending the high-grade commodity level, he has done a great deal to raise our standards of what a literary commodity can be. Without urging us to regard his novels as "important," he has done more than any writer of our time to close the dangerous gap between important and popular fiction.

Well, Mrs. Trilling, that gap is yawning again. There are no more Marquands, and if there were their books probably wouldn't sell. Their closest equivalents are such pandering sexual politicians as John Irving and E. L. Doctorow. The comparison between Marquand's popular but artistically serious novels and the fifth-rate throwaway tracts of his successors illustrates with grisly accuracy the deterioration that has taken place in American literature over the last couple of decades. But there is still a Book-of-the-Month Club, fumbling along in its well-meaning, idealistic way, bringing pretty good books to the prairies year after year. To be sure, the pickings are slimmer these days. Where once the BOMC could offer its readers *The Heart of the Matter* and *Brideshead Revisited* and *The Last Hurrah,* they now get . . . *And Ladies of the Club* and *The Accidental Tourist* and *The Cider House Rules.* And publishers are increasingly less willing to cut deals with the BOMC when they can dump millions of copies of a piece of garbage like *Destiny* directly into the chain bookstores without wasting time and money on middlemen.

Still, one shouldn't blame the BOMC for the declining quality of the books it has to sell. No doubt the judges are patiently making do with the likes of John Irving in the secret hope that another John Marquand will finally come along. "Optimists as always," Al Silverman writes in *The Book of the Month,* "all of us who work for the Club today are looking for more for tomorrow. We are joined together to find, among the 5,000 submissions we get from publishers every year, the book that will bring us wonder and joy or help us understand this fragmented age." The current hoopla at the BOMC involves the board's decision to offer an art book as the Main Selection for the first time ever. The book in question is *Andrew Wyeth: The Helga Pictures,* and the BOMC has ordered up a special edition. It's comforting to note that whatever the long-term prospects of the Book-of-the-Month Club, America's literate middlebrows continue to be suckers for the right kind of pitch.

Me, I'm not a member anymore. There are enough good bookstores in New York to suit my tastes. But I wish the Book-of-the-Month Club well. Its old-fashioned goals remain every bit as brave and foolish as Dwight Macdonald's chilly vision of a society where "the masses have their Masscult" while "the few who care about good writing, painting, music, architecture, philosophy, etc., have their High Culture," not to mention a good deal more humane. If Clifton Fadiman and company ever find themselves in need of a new board member, they can write to me. I know a good lost cause when I see one.

New Criterion 1987

Sentimental Journey

I F SALES EQUAL SUCCESS, THE POSTHUMOUS CAREER OF John Steinbeck is one of the most spectacular success stories in the annals of modern American literature. A quarter-century after his death in 1968 at the age of sixty-six, all of his novels remain in print, selling more than 700,000 copies each year. Yet Steinbeck gets even less respect today than during his lifetime, when he was generally regarded by serious critics as a well-meaning middlebrow. Perhaps the kindest thing ever said about him by an intellectual came from Edmund Wilson, who wrote in 1940 that "there remains behind the journalism, the theatricalism and the tricks . . . a mind which does seem first-rate in its unpanicky scrutiny of life." As left-handed compliments go, that one deserves some sort of prize.

Jay Parini argues in his new biography that Steinbeck got a raw deal. "A number of influential critics thought his writing had generally declined since the publication of *The Grapes of Wrath,* in 1939, and they banished Steinbeck to the swollen ranks of the second-rate and half-forgotten," Parini writes. "When he received the Nobel Prize in 1962, the decision of the Swedish Academy was ridiculed in America by a few well-known academic critics and a handful of journalists who refused to believe that a writer with a popular following could be any good." Unfortunately, the case against Steinbeck isn't quite that simple, and Parini's seeming unawareness of this fact is the only blot on an otherwise excellent book.

John Steinbeck: A Biography runs rings around its immediate predecessor, *The True Adventures of John Steinbeck, Writer* (1984), by Jackson J. Benson, which at 1,116 pages is as elephantine as its title is arch.

Parini, by contrast, wraps things up in just under 500 pages of text, a length nicely suited to the life of a man who married three women and published nearly thirty books. Not that Steinbeck's story has much to offer in the way of high drama: it was for the most part the usual depressing tale of serial monogamy interspersed with heavy drinking. Still, Parini lays out the facts with clarity and sympathy, and anyone curious as to precisely how famous American novelists earn the money to pay their liquor bills will find the resulting narrative of more than passing interest.

The trouble with *John Steinbeck* is that its author sincerely believes his subject was a major novelist and spends far too much time trying to prove the point. Whenever Parini strays from the straight and narrow path of biography and starts playing critic, his book grinds to a halt amid clouds of dusty prose: "The heroes (and they are always male) are seen in the later work (especially in *Viva Zapata! East of Eden, Travels With Charley* and *The Winter of Our Discontent*) as separate integers within the larger context of the group and the environment as a whole." As for the critical judgments themselves, suffice it to say that there must be something wrong with the ear of a novelist and professor of English who can cite without the slightest flicker of irony Steinbeck's description of a character in *Cannery Row* as "concupiscent as a rabbit and as gentle as hell."

To his credit, Parini's admiration for Steinbeck's work has not stopped him from placing in evidence numerous exhibits for the prosecution, among the most damning of which is a remark made by Edith Mirrielees, Steinbeck's creative-writing teacher at Stanford University, who told a later student how "she tried to curb his sentimental side. That was his Achilles' heel." Indeed it was, and Steinbeck never overcame it. His style, a clunky blend of hypermasculine sentimentality and Hemingwayesque faux simplicity, is at times almost eerily reminiscent of the simile-happy hard-boiled mystery novelists of the 1930s. (Here is my favorite bad line from *The Grapes of Wrath:* "Ma looked down at her hands, lying together like tired lovers in her lap.") But while Raymond Chandler and Dashiell Hammett scrupulously avoided mounting the soapbox, Steinbeck camped out on top of his, most notably in *The*

Grapes of Wrath: "I'll be ever'where—wherever you look. Wherever they's a fight so hungry people can eat, I'll be there. Wherever they's a cop beatin' up a guy, I'll be there. . . . An' when our folks eat the stuff they raise an' live in the houses they build—why, I'll be there." Small wonder Steinbeck spent the rest of his career trying *not* to write another *Grapes of Wrath*. Rarely has an author so completely revealed himself in a single book, for better or worse.

His flaws notwithstanding, Steinbeck continues to sell by the carload, something that cannot be said of any number of superior novelists who made a comparable stir in their day. It is not hard to see why. For all his sentimentality and derivativeness, Steinbeck knew how to tell a story. The sheer narrative sweep of his best books is undeniable, and admirable. It is no surprise that most of Steinbeck's novels were made into movies or plays and were usually improved in the process: Hollywood kept the plots and cut the sermons.

Steinbeck is also one of the most teachable of American novelists. Parini recalls how a junior high school teacher steered him to *Of Mice and Men:* "She led me to his long shelf of books, where I have lingered happily for many decades." It is a charming story, and an illuminating one. *Of Mice and Men* and *The Grapes of Wrath* are novels with training wheels—ideal preparation for the greater challenges posed by better writers. Their combination of juicy plots, crudely obvious symbolism, and good liberal politics is as irresistible to teenagers as it is to teachers. (One wonders exactly how many of the 50,000 copies of *The Grapes of Wrath* sold in this country annually are bought by readers over the age of twenty-one.)

Steinbeck's work, as Parini suggests, may well be ripe for a critical revival. The market for utilitarian art with a maudlin streak is at least as large today as it was in his heyday, and though he was hardly a cookie-cutter ideologue (he loathed Communism and supported the Vietnam War), Steinbeck was in every other way a child of the Thirties, that painfully earnest decade of proletarian fiction, Socialist Realism and art as a weapon. In 1940, the year *The Grapes of Wrath* won the Pulitzer for fiction, Steinbeck's fellow prizewinners included Carl Sandburg (for *Abraham Lincoln: The War Years*) and William Saroyan (for *The Time of*

Your Life). "While in the past I have sometimes been dubious about Pulitzer choices," Steinbeck told a friend, "I am pleased and flattered to be chosen in a year when Sandburg and Saroyan were chosen. It is good company." He certainly knew a peer when he saw one.

New York Times 1995

Norman Mailer: Forgotten but Not Gone

WHY IS NORMAN MAILER STILL FAMOUS? HE HASN'T written a good book since *The Executioner's Song*. Except for *The Naked and the Dead*, none of his novels continues to be read, and his magazine journalism long ago curdled into self-parody. I've never met anyone under the age of forty who took him seriously. Yet Random House, which so far as I know is not a charitable institution, is celebrating his seventy-fifth birthday by bringing out a 1,200-page anthology of his writing, chosen by the master himself. That's a pretty fancy birthday present, especially given the fact that it will surely wind up on the remainder tables by year's end.

Mailer has been writing badly for so long that it is easy to forget that a great many intelligent people once took him almost as seriously as he took himself. (Trivia question: Who called him "one of the few postwar American writers in whom it is possible to detect the presence of qualities that powerfully suggest a major novelist in the making"? Answer: Norman Podhoretz, writing in 1959.) And *The Time of Our Time* contains ample proof that for all his faults, the young Mailer really did have talent to burn. He could blather on for page after page about existential anguish, then snap into focus and toss off the kind of brilliantly exact description that made his colleagues sweat with envy. Here is Truman Capote, pinned down in one perfect sentence: " 'I didn't want to do this show,' he said in a dry little voice that seemed to issue from an unmoistened reed in his nostril."

The trouble with Mailer was that he was drunk on ideas, a deadly tipple for woolly-minded pseudo-intellectuals. Sensing instinctively that liberalism had run its course, he made the mistake of assuming that radicalism was the only way out, and complicated matters still further by opting for a romantic radicalism rooted in sexual mysticism. As a result, his style grew bloated and slack, especially on the increasingly frequent occasions when he grappled with imperfectly digested philosophical concepts:

> It is on this bleak scene that a phenomenon has appeared: the American existentialist — the hipster, the man who knows that if our collective condition is to live with instant death by atomic war, relatively quick death by the State as *l'univers concentrationnaire,* or with a slow death by conformity with every creative and rebellious instinct stifled (at what damage to the mind and the heart and the liver and the nerves no research foundation for cancer will discover in a hurry), if the fate of twentieth-century man is to live with death from adolescence to premature senescence, why then the only life-giving answer is to accept the terms of death, to live with death as immediate danger, to divorce oneself from society, to exist without roots, to set out on that uncharted journey into the rebellious imperatives of the self.

Yet Mailer had little choice but to write about ideas, for he had little else about which to write. The publication in 1948 of *The Naked and the Dead* left him "prominent and empty" at the age of twenty-five, and he spent the rest of his youth and early middle age living in the glare of renown, making it impossible for him to accumulate the private experience out of which good novels are spun. He wrote interestingly about his problem in *Advertisements for Myself* ("My farewell to an average man's experience was too abrupt. . . . I was a node in a new electronic landscape of celebrity, personality, and status"), but that was a trick that could be brought off only once: from then on, it would be ideas or nothing.

It was thus inevitable that he would turn to journalism, which supplies the gifted but unformed writer with pre-set subjects on which to hone his style. Unfortunately, his celebrity made it impossible for him to undergo the normal period of apprenticeship: he was thrown in at the deep end, and his self-indulgent flounderings were mistaken for originality. To be sure, *The Presidential Papers, The Armies of the Night, Miami and the Siege of Chicago,* and *Of a Fire on the Moon* are not without their bright spots, and "The Liberal Party," the chapter of *The Armies of the Night* in which Mailer describes a visit to a party thrown by "an attractive liberal couple," is a minor masterpiece of social observation:

> Conservative professors tend to have a private income, so their homes show the flowering of their taste, the articulation of their hobbies, collections adhere to their cabinets and odd statements of whim stand up in the nooks; but liberal instructors, liberal assistant professors, and liberal associate professors are usually poor and programmatic, so secretly they despise the arts of home adornment. . . . the artist on the wall is a friend of the host, has the right political ideas, and will talk about literature so well, you might think you were being addressed by Maxim Gorky.

But even at his best, Mailer was addicted to navel-gazing, and his insistence on placing himself on stage alongside his subjects, though initially refreshing, ultimately proved disastrous. It is no coincidence that the two most successful pieces of book-length reportage to come out of the Sixties, Truman Capote's *In Cold Blood* and Tom Wolfe's *The Right Stuff,* scrupulously avoid the self-aggrandizement that was Mailer's journalistic trademark (or that *The Executioner's Song,* by far Mailer's strongest piece of journalism, is also one of the few nonfiction books he has written in which he does not figure as a major character).

So what is it about this seventy-five-year-old has-been that continues to make aging editors weak in the knees? The answer, I think, is that he is to literature what the Kennedys are to politics, a living, breathing relic of the vanished era of high hopes. Even though he was already washed up as a novelist by 1960, Mailer had retooled himself as a middlebrow journalist just in time to bang the drum for JFK. Talk about sucker bait: Mailer had spent the Fifties bemoaning the "partially totalitarian society" that was America under Dwight Eisenhower, and along came a handsome young Democratic philosopher-king, a glamorous millionaire who wrote books (or at least signed them), flattered susceptible authors (including Mailer), and hung out with the likes of Frank Sinatra and Marilyn Monroe. All at once the joint was jumping, and everything seemed possible, from racial equality to free love: "Yes, this candidate for all his record, his good, sound, conventional liberal record, has a patina of that other life, the second American life, the long electric night with the fires of neon leading down the highway to the murmur of jazz."

Appropriately enough, Mailer became the chief chronicler of the Sixties, the high-priced hired gun for whom magazine editors with money to burn sent whenever they wanted to put the seal of literary seriousness on political conventions or moon shots. He was the first American novelist since Ernest Hemingway to be widely known by name to people who didn't read books, and it begins to look as if he'll be the last one. (Has David Letterman *ever* interviewed a novelist?) But like so many quondam revolutionaries, he proved unwilling to ride the train to the end of the line, revealing himself in *The Prisoner of Sex* (1971) to be unalterably opposed to the woman's-liberation movement, an irretrievable blunder that brought to an abrupt end his quarter-century-long run as the golden boy of American letters.

At this point, a better writer might have finally gotten down to business and produced the memorable novels everybody had long expected Mailer to write. Certainly he had no shortage of ambition. "I am imprisoned with a perception that will settle for nothing less than making a revolution in the consciousness of our time," he announced at the age of thirty-six, adding that his writings "will have the deepest influence of any work being done by an American novelist in these years." Alas, his post-1971 output, *The Executioner's Song* excepted, is noteworthy only for its flaccid awfulness. *Ancient Evenings, Tough Guys Don't Dance, The Gospel According to the Son* . . . need I say more? Not since Sinclair Lewis has an author of note ground out so dreary a string of flops.

No doubt Mailer, like Kennedy, will never lack for bootlickers, at least while his generation is still alive. It's hard to accept that a once-promising writer has become a burnt-out case, especially when the memory of his promise is part of your own lost youth. Who would have guessed in 1960 that the first literary star of the electronic age would end his days as a nostalgia act, the Glenn Miller of Camelot? Once again, Jack Kennedy got it wrong. Life *is* fair — all you have to do is give it time.

National Review 1998

Real Cool Killers

THE LIBRARY OF AMERICA, A NONPROFIT PUBLISHER whose dust jackets declare it to be "dedicated to preserving America's best and most significant writing in handsome, enduring volumes," has brought out *Crime Novels: American Noir*, a pair of volumes containing eleven examples of what has lately come to be called "noir fiction," after the cinematic genre of the Forties known as film noir. No such fancy name was applied to these short novels when they first appeared in paperback, bedecked with cheesy cover art and tumescent blurbs promising their semiliterate purchasers the cheapest of thrills. Forty years ago, Jim Thompson's *The Killer Inside Me* and Charles Willeford's *Pick-Up* were smut; now they belong to the ages.

Arrant relativism? Well, yes, and then some. But while the noir novelists scarcely deserve to be ranked among America's best and most significant writers, their harsh tales are infinitely more readable than the chokingly tedious output of a thousand American writers of impeccably correct reputation, and I venture to guess that people will still be turning the pages of James M. Cain's *The Postman Always Rings Twice* and Cornell Woolrich's *I Married a Dead Man* long after the likes of Toni Morrison and Allan Gurganus are remembered only by aging professors of literary theory who wonder why nobody signs up for their classes any more.

Noir fiction is not the same as the "hard-boiled" detective stories of Raymond Chandler and his progeny. Most hard-boiled novels are installments in a series featuring a recurring hero who beneath his cynical exterior is actually an idealistic knight errant; most noir novels are one-offs whose desperate protagonists either die in the last chapter or wish they had. (Only two of the books reprinted here, Patricia Highsmith's *The Talented Mr. Ripley* and Chester Himes's *The Real Cool Killers,* are series novels.) The difference is crucial. Chandler's novels are powerful expressions of his loathing for the moral corruption of modern American life, but they also presuppose the existence of honorable men who can rise above that corruption. In the nihilistic world of noir, by contrast, everyone is tainted, and every human act — including the act of love — leads but to the grave.

This bleak vision is as confining as the flat, sour prose in which most noir novels are written, but its narrowness is the source of its underlying strength: noir fiction never, ever goes soft at the end. Similarly, the noir novelists consistently refused to indulge in the easy political point-making that such lesser contemporaries as John Steinbeck found irresistible. While some of their books, most notably Edward Anderson's *Thieves Like Us,* can certainly be read as critiques of the American class system, social commentary always took a back seat to action. Yet it was precisely because they did not play the blame game that the noir novelists made a far more telling critique of American individualism: rarely has the corrosive loneliness of urban life been more memorably portrayed than in their best work. (Predictably but appropriately, a painting by Edward Hopper, the poet of American alienation, is reproduced on the dust jacket of the first volume.)

Robert Polito, Jim Thompson's biographer, has chosen the novels, edited the texts, and supplied the pithy notes that are, here as always, among the most useful features of the Library of America's well-made volumes. His picks are consistently sound, and they serve as a welcome reminder that not all noir fiction is set in Los Angeles on a rainy night in 1946. I was especially pleased by the inclusion of William Lindsay Gresham's *Nightmare Alley,* the horrific story of a carnival shill turned spiritualist minister, and Kenneth Fearing's *The Big Clock,* by far the cleverest of the many novels that purport to tell what it was like to work for *Time* in the days of Henry Luce:

> The [story] conference went on, like all those that had gone before, and, unless some tremendous miracle intervened, like many hundreds sure to follow. . . . Down the hall, in Sydney's office, there was a win-

dow out of which an almost forgotten associate editor had long ago jumped. I occasionally wondered whether he had done so after some conference such as this. Just picked up his notes and walked down the corridor to his own room, opened the window, and then stepped out.

The flap copy calls these eleven novels "underground classics." In fact, some were best-sellers and attracted the notice of leading critics (Edmund Wilson wrote about *The Postman Always Rings Twice* and Horace McCoy's *They Shoot Horses, Don't They?*), and eight were made into films, not a few of which were both financially and artistically successful (François Truffaut, no less, turned David Goodis's *Down There* into *Shoot the Piano Player*). I mention this because of the persistent notion that Americans are reluctant to acknowledge their collective shortcomings and strangenesses. The truth is that we like nothing better. From *Scarface* to *L.A. Confidential,* movies that show us at our seediest have invariably cleaned up at the box office. The only thing we refuse to admit is that all of us are like that, or secretly wish we were. Such is the latter-day shame of the intellectuals: self-loathing just doesn't sell, except to them.

National Review 1997

Crosby Major, Crosby Minor

FOR VIRTUALLY ANY AMERICAN OVER THE AGE OF SIXTY, Bing Crosby's name is likely to evoke a wide range of memories. Though he was by far the best-known popular singer of the pre-rock era, Crosby was also a full-fledged movie star who won a best-actor Oscar for *Going My Way* (1944) and easily held his own opposite the likes of Fred Astaire and Bob Hope in such lighter fare as *Holiday Inn* (1942) and *The Road to Morocco* (1942). His radio shows were no less successful, and with the arrival of TV in the Fifties, his face became as familiar a fixture in American homes as was his easygoing bass-baritone voice.

But Crosby's fame did not long survive his death in 1977. Indeed, it is now difficult to find anyone under the age of forty who knows anything specific about him other than that he recorded Irving Berlin's "White Christmas." By and large, his work is available only on hard-to-find CDs released by independent European labels, while most of his films are long forgotten. And although several other artists of his generation — Louis Armstrong, Duke Ellington, and Benny Goodman among them — continue to be widely recognized as key figures in American music, Crosby tends increasingly to be overlooked by critics and journalists. He was, for instance, omitted entirely from Ken Burns's ten-part PBS series *Jazz,* and he is mentioned only in passing in Geoffrey C. Ward's companion volume to the series.

How could so bright a star have dimmed so fast? Was there less to Bing Crosby than met the ear? Gary Giddins thinks not, and in *Bing Crosby: A Pocketful of Dreams,* the first installment of a two-volume biography, he makes the case for Crosby in unprecedentedly rich and rewarding detail. Though certain chapters could have been trimmed to useful effect (many readers will feel, for example, that far too much space is devoted to Crosby's less important films), the book as a whole is both finely written and thoroughly engrossing. Still, in telling the story of how Crosby became "a phenomenon in the cultural life of the United States," *A Pocketful of Dreams* occasionally dwells on the phenomenon at the expense of the artist. Giddins is not himself a musician, trained or otherwise; for all his evident appreciation of Crosby's singing, he lacks the technical knowledge needed to explain fully what he is hearing. And though his discussion of the posthumous decline in Crosby's reputation is plausible as far as it goes, he is similarly unable to supply a completely adequate *musical* explanation for why "the most influential and successful popular performer in the first half of the twentieth century" should have faded into semi-obscurity a mere quarter-century after his death.

BORN IN 1903 IN TACOMA, WASHINGTON, HARRY LILLIS Crosby, Jr., was the fourth of seven children of a charming but lazy bookkeeper and a cold, manipulative woman who demanded that, unlike their ne'er-do-well father, her children get ahead in the world. The Crosbys moved to Spokane in 1905, and Bing (he acquired his nickname because of his liking for *The Bingville Bugle,* a humorous newspaper supplement of the time) spent eight years attending the Jesuit-run Gonzaga High School and University, where he received a Catholic-style classical education, doing well at both Greek and Latin.

Crosby's background explains much about the complicated man he became. The happy-go-lucky "regular guy" who bantered amiably on screen with Bob Hope and Dorothy Lamour was in real life highly intelligent and well-read (in a Fifties interview, he casually mentioned having recently read novels by James Gould Cozzens, John P. Marquand, and Evelyn Waugh). He remained a practicing Catholic his whole life long and would always be modest to a fault about his musical gifts. But he was also an acutely self-aware artist with an unrelenting will, who from adolescence onward hid his vaulting ambitions behind an iron mask of affability.

One observer who saw through Crosby's facade was the clarinetist and bandleader Artie Shaw, who watched him up close in the radio studios:

> Bing was never a matinee idol. He developed a screen personality that worked because it was based on who he wanted to be — casual, relaxed. But it was a tense sort of relaxing because you knew he was working at it. Bing wasn't Bing any more than Bogart was Bogart.

For all the warmth of Crosby's public personality, his family and friends found him distant and enigmatic. According to his younger brother Bob, a singer who fronted one of the best big bands of the swing era, he "built a cellophane bag and sealed himself inside and didn't let anyone inside because [people] knew he was shy and that he couldn't say no." Apparently as a way of coping with his anxieties, he went on periodic alcoholic binges, a habit that would soon put his reputation — as well as his voice — at risk, though he finally brought it under control.

Crosby's academic education came to an abrupt halt when he fell in love with popular music. Though his only training was a handful of singing lessons he had taken as a teenager, he had great natural ability and a quick and retentive musical memory, making it possible for him to learn new songs easily even though he could not read music. His rise to stardom was astonishingly fast: he quit school in 1924 to sing professionally, and within two years he had joined the Paul Whiteman Orchestra, the first full-time singer ever to be hired by a major dance band.

Contrary to widespread critical belief, the Whiteman band was one of the most musically advanced ensembles of the Twenties. In it, Crosby worked side by side with such innovative artists as the cornetist Bix Beiderbecke, the bassist Steve Brown, the guitarist Eddie Lang, and the arranger Bill Challis. He also began to listen closely to the playing and singing of Louis Armstrong, the most important figure in early jazz, whose rhythmic forcefulness and flexibility were then having an incalculably large impact on other young jazz musicians (and who in turn would later emulate Crosby's distinctive ballad style).

While Crosby's singing reflected all these influences, the overall effect was wholly individual: nobody sounded quite like him. It helped that the voice itself was inimitable, a resonant, virile-sounding baritone with a range of nearly two octaves, from low G to high F, and a warm, attractively husky timbre that Armstrong likened to "gold being poured out of a cup."* But it was what Crosby *did* with his voice that made him stand out. Prior to the Twenties, American popular singing was theatrical in style: singers had to make themselves heard over pit orchestras without benefit of amplification, a circumstance that forced them to employ vocal techniques not unlike those of opera singers. As it happens, Crosby's voice was naturally large enough to have permitted him to sing that way: Kitty Carlisle, an actress with classical vocal training, heard him in person for the first time in 1934 and was startled by "his technique, his effortlessness, the fact that his voice was so much bigger and more available for, really, operatic roles than [what] you saw at the movies."

Instead, he chose another path. With the coming of electrical recording in 1925, small-voiced, effete-sounding tenors had briefly become fashionable. But Crosby swept them away with a style that was forthrightly masculine yet intimate in scale. Thanks to his canny use of the microphone, he could sing as if he were speaking—and not to a large audience, either, but to just one person at a time.

MUSICALLY, CROSBY COMBINED ARMSTRONG'S INFALLIBLE swing with Beiderbecke's lyricism. Such early 78 sides as "I'm Coming, Virginia" (1927), "Ol' Man River" (1928), and "Make Believe" (1928) show him to have been astonishingly light on his rhythmic feet, more so than any singer of the period besides Armstrong. He reworked melodies with the self-assurance of a master improviser, adding ornaments and altering rhythms as his fancy dictated, and his "scat" singing (the made-up nonsense syllables popularized by Armstrong), heard to especially good advantage on the electrifying version of "St. Louis

---

*The mutual admiration of the two men, who worked together frequently in radio and motion pictures, was both genuine and endearing. Crosby called Armstrong "the beginning and the end of music in America," while Armstrong's praise for Crosby was no less emphatic. "The man was a *Natural Genius* the day he was born. Ever since Bing first opened his mouth, he was the *Boss of All Singers* and Still is."

Blues" he recorded with Duke Ellington's band in 1932, was wonderfully bold. The young Bing Crosby was, in short, a jazz singer, arguably the first one after Louis Armstrong, and without question one of the best who ever lived. He was also, as Giddins correctly points out, "the first great ballad singer in jazz. . . . His sound had little precedent: rich, strong, masculine, and clean."

By 1931, Crosby had left the Whiteman band and the Rhythm Boys, the vocal trio with which he had been featured during his years with Whiteman, and embarked on a solo career. In that year he began to appear in short subjects directed by Mack Sennett, the king of movie slapstick, thereby revealing himself to be a natural comedian, and was hired by CBS to star in his own radio show, *Fifteen Minutes with Bing Crosby*. Crosby's movies and radio appearances advertised his recordings, which began to sell in vast quantities, and within two years he was so successful that he was able to stop performing in public altogether. Between 1933 and 1975, the only crowds he sang for were the studio audiences invited to watch his radio shows. Dozens of other pop singers based their styles on his, among them Russ Columbo, Perry Como, Bob Eberle, Billy Eckstine, Dick Haymes, and Dean Martin. "All the singers tried to be Crosbys," one of them wryly admitted. "You were either a high Crosby or a low Crosby." At the age of thirty, Bing Crosby had become (in Duke Ellington's words) "the biggest thing, ever."

But the ultimate basis for Crosby's superstardom — his voice — was proving to be perilously fragile. He had long had problems with laryngitis (an attack of which forced him to postpone his highly publicized network radio debut for two days), and many of the records he was making in the late Twenties and early Thirties reveal a hoarseness in the upper register that, though part of his appeal, was also an unmistakable sign of strain.

Late in 1931, a doctor warned Crosby that he had developed a node on one of his vocal cords, thus rendering him particularly susceptible to laryngitis. Surgery was impossible: it might alter the quality of his voice unpredictably and permanently. The only treatment was complete vocal rest, but, Crosby having just reached the peak of his early stardom, that, too, was out of the question. He kept on singing — and drinking to excess, thereby doing further damage. According to Giddins, Crosby's difficulties cured themselves over time. But to listeners familiar with the long-term consequences of faulty vocal technique, his records tell a different story. Though his natural tessitura was that of a low baritone, he had an upper extension that he used freely, casually tossing off high Es and Fs. But because he had no formal training, he never learned how to negotiate safely the "break" leading to his upper register, and a combination of overwork, drink, and flawed technique gradually weakened that part of his voice.

Crosby's 1931 recording of Hoagy Carmichael's "Stardust" provides a dramatic illustration of the risks he was taking. It is one of his most famous recordings, and deservedly so: his youthful ballad style, vibrant and robust, is heard here in all its golden glory. But he is also audibly hoarse, and he sings the repeated high Es of the chorus in a wide-open, "uncovered" voice that any competent teacher would immediately have spotted as a recipe for disaster.

Predictably, Crosby had another vocal crisis in 1932, and was told to "rest and don't even answer the phone — don't talk, don't do anything." Instead, he took a ten-day break, then resumed his busy schedule. Giddins mentions this episode in passing, apparently not realizing that it marked a turning point in the singer's career, the moment when he began irreversibly to "lose his top." Though he continued to sing full-voiced high Fs on record as late as 1935, they became fewer and farther between, and songs that he might once have performed in the key of F, such as "June in January" and "With Every Breath I Take" (both 1934), were transposed down a full step, to E flat. Nor was the change limited to his upper register: by 1935, his voice had grown darker in timbre and heavier in texture from top to bottom. As Crosby lost his high notes and settled into a less demanding bass-baritone range, he also changed his style. Not only did he abandon the jazzy scat singing of his young years, he seemed almost to lose interest in jazz itself. Though he was always capable of unlimbering for such frisky novelties as Johnny Mercer's "I'm an Old Cowhand" (1936) and "Bob White (Whatcha Gonna Swing Tonight?)" (1937, with Connie Boswell), he now concentrated on ballads, which he sang with a quiet warmth well suited to his deeper range.

By this time, Crosby was recording for Decca, a new label whose chief producer, Jack Kapp, had encouraged him to explore a repertoire better suited to the tastes of "the masses." Kapp assured Crosby that by shunning "'hot' songs" and concentrating instead on a wide-ranging mixture of contemporary ballads, prewar standards (like "I Love You Truly" and "Let Me Call You Sweetheart"), collaborations with other popular Decca artists like the Andrews Sisters, and ethnic novelties ranging from country to Hawaiian music, he could attain a degree of popularity "as great as ever enjoyed by any singer in this country. You have in your grasp," Kapp added, invoking the name of the astonishingly successful Irish tenor, "the opportunity to be the John McCormack of this generation." Crosby unhesitatingly took Kapp's advice, and the results were just as predicted. By the Forties, he was more than a pop singer, more than a movie star. Instead, he became, as Giddins rightly says, a member of the family: "No other pop icon has ever been so thoroughly, lovingly *liked* — liked and trusted. . . . His was the voice of the nation, the cannily informal personification of hometown decency — friendly, unassuming, melodious, irrefutably American."

BUT CROSBY PAID A HIGH PRICE FOR ALLOWING JACK KAPP TO turn him into the musical equivalent of a Norman Rockwell *Saturday Evening Post* cover. Jazz is not an absolute value, and the fact that Crosby's new style was less explicitly "jazzy" did not necessarily make it less good. (Nat Cole, for example, became a better singer when he gave up jazz piano to concentrate on ballads.) The problem with the new Crosby was that his singing had become less vital, less compelling, less *interesting*. It was as though the loss of his high notes had also robbed him of his sense of musical adventure, his ability to surprise and delight the ear. The decline was not inexorable, and he would continue to make occasional memorable recordings well into the Forties. For the most part, though, he was now singing — figuratively as well as literally — in a lower key.

Gary Giddins has mixed feelings about Crosby's change of style. "What his singing forfeited in muscularity," Giddins argues, "it gained in poignancy. . . . Bing in the mid-Thirties was the most quietly assured male pop singer alive." Yet he also admits that there was more to it than that:

[I]n singling out McCormack as a career template and encouraging Bing to deflect hot songs, [Kapp] hoped to remake him as a smoother, less mannered, ultimately less expressive singer, a kind of musical comfort food. . . . [Crosby] was now on the verge of reinventing common-denominator aesthetics, creating a national popular music that pleased everyone. The cost, in the opinion of many observers, was encroaching blandness.

The strengths and weaknesses of the new Crosby can be heard in the great ballads he recorded during World War II. "What's New?" (Johnny Burke and Bob Haggart, 1939), "Skylark" (Johnny Mercer and Hoagy Carmichael, 1942), "It Could Happen to You" (Burke and Jimmy Van Heusen, 1943), "Long Ago and Far Away" (Ira Gershwin and Jerome Kern, 1944), and "Out of This World" (Harold Arlen and Mercer, 1944) rank high among the outstanding love songs of the decade, and Crosby sang them all with taste and sensitivity. But his interpretations seem almost detached, lacking the energy and ardor one might reasonably expect from a comparatively young man. To hear them is to be put in mind of Father O'Malley, the amiable priest Crosby played in the 1944 movie *Going My Way*. Like the good father himself, Bing Crosby in the Forties sounded pleasant, engaging, humorous — and celibate.

By the Fifties, a new generation of Americans was transferring its musical loyalties to a very different kind of singer. Frank Sinatra started out as a "high Crosby," but quickly developed into something more: singing with the big band of Tommy Dorsey, he brought to the ballads of the Forties a vulnerability that teenagers found irresistible. Like Crosby, he weathered a vocal crisis from which he emerged with a lower, darker voice, but it made him more rather than less interesting. The Sinatra of the Fifties sang with a sharp edge of sexuality and aggression, while his youthful vulnerability deepened into a quality bordering at times on outright despair.

Sinatra's emotional candor stands in stark contrast to the impenetrable reserve of Crosby, who once famously told the lyricist Johnny Burke not to write songs for him that contained the phrase "I love you." Unlike Sinatra, he was never a confessional artist, and the intensity he brought to his early recordings of ballads like "Stardust" was musical rather than dramatic. (To put it another way, he sang songs, not monologues.) Revealingly, he preferred the middle-of-the-road backing of John Scott Trotter's studio orchestras to the harder-swinging, harmonically sophisticated arrangements that Nelson Riddle created for such classic Sinatra albums as *Songs for Swingin' Lovers* and *Only the Lonely.*

The Fifties continue to be portrayed in the media as a decade of mindless conformity, but they were actually a time of considerable cultural volatility, nowhere more so than in popular music and jazz. While the comforting sound of Crosby's balladry remained reassuring to many Americans, others were looking for something more emotionally challenging, and Sinatra's confessionalism, like the deceptively "cool" jazz of the trumpeter Miles Davis, suited their mood perfectly.

TO THE END OF HIS LIFE, CROSBY CONTINUED TO MAKE RECords and appear on radio and TV, and he never lost his ability to swing. ("Bing had the beat, the absolute best time," said the drummer Jake Hanna. "You just followed him and he carried you right along.") But his way of making music had become unfashionable, and because the middle-aged Crosby was the only one whom younger listeners knew, they came to see him as a symbol of everything they held in contempt. As Giddins puts it:

> He was known to [the postwar generation] as a faded and not especially compelling celebrity, a square old man who made orange-juice commercials and appeared with his much younger family on Christmas telecasts that the baby boomers never watched. . . . They would have been amazed to learn how advanced, savvy, and forceful a musician he had been in his prime.

Fortunately, the other Bing Crosby—the greater Crosby—lives again in the first half of *A Pocketful of Dreams,* and on the best of the hundreds of records he made between 1927 and 1936. "As far as I am concerned," Crosby said in 1960, "with the exception of a phonograph record or two, I don't think I have done anything that's really outstanding or great or marvelous or anything that deserves any superlatives." In fact, he was a nonpareil jazz singer who has been unfairly written out of the history of the music he helped to shape, as well as a balladeer of magical sensitivity and irresistible vitality. In helping to restore him to life, and despite certain deficiencies in musical understanding, Gary Giddins has done an inestimable service to American music.

Commentary 2001

That Nice Elvis Boy

LL SLOPES ARE SLIPPERY. FORTY YEARS AGO, COLUM-
nists and clergymen were tearing their hair over Elvis Presley,
whose televised hip-swiveling was contemptuously compared
by the *New York Times* to "the repertoire of the blonde bombshells of
the burlesque runway"; today, MTV pumps gangsta rap and heavy
metal into the homes of millions of teenage suburbanites, and nobody,
least of all the *Times*, hoists an eyebrow. As for Elvis, I caught him on
the Disney Channel just the other night, looking (and sounding) as
innocent as Jo Stafford. The French, as usual, were wrong: the more
things change, the worse they get.

Peter Guralnick's *Last Train to Memphis: The Rise of Elvis Presley*, the
first installment of a two-volume biography of the founding father of
rock and roll, seeks to strip away four decades of celebrity and show the
young Elvis as he was: "I wanted to rescue Elvis Presley from the dreary
bondage of myth, from the oppressive aftershock of cultural significance." Not altogether surprisingly, Guralnick's Elvis comes out looking very much like the Elvis still beloved of countless middle-aged
Southerners, the soft-spoken young man who adored his parents, said
"sir" and "ma'am," and spoke unabashedly to suspicious big-city journalists of his religious beliefs: "My Bible tells me that what he sows he
will also reap, and if I'm sowing evil and wickedness it will catch up
with me. I'm right sure of that, sir, and I don't think I'm bad for people.
If I did think I was bad for people, I would go back to driving a truck,
and I really mean this."

Guralnick's book is an oddity: a perfectly serious, even scholarly
biography of a rock star. Thorough but not pedantic, stylish but not

overheated, *Last Train to Memphis* is easily the best thing I've read about the early years of rock, not least because its author takes for granted the significance of his subject. Instead of battering the reader with roll-over-Beethoven comparisons, Guralnick simply assumes that Elvis Presley was a man whose story is worth telling, and goes about telling it with considerable grace and sensitivity. Unusually for a non-Southerner, he has a real feel for the texture of Southern life, and painstakingly avoids condescension, even about religious matters. The keynote of this excellent book, indeed, is sympathy:

> I don't know if I ever thought about the real Elvis Presley until I was driving down McLemore Avenue in South Memphis one day in 1983, past the old Stax studio, with a friend named Rose Clayton. Rose, a native Memphian, pointed out a drugstore where Elvis's cousin used to work. Elvis used to hang out there, she said; he would sit at the soda fountain, drumming his fingers on the countertop. "Poor baby," said Rose, and something went off in my head. This wasn't *"Elvis Presley"*; this was a kid hanging out at a soda fountain in South Memphis, someone who could be observed, just like you or me, daydreaming, listening to the jukebox, drinking a milk shake, waiting for his cousin to get off work. "Poor baby."

It's impossible to understand Elvis Presley without understanding the dizzying speed with which the kid at the soda fountain became the most famous man in America. Born in 1935 to a white-trash family in Mississippi, Presley cut his first record in 1954, made his first network TV appearance in 1956, and began on his first movie eight months later. Raw talent is not enough to explain that kind of instant success, though the talent was definitely there: Presley had a rich, resonant voice and natural acting abilities that impressed everyone who encountered him when he first came to Hollywood. Said Walter Matthau, who co-starred in *King Creole*, Presley's fourth movie: "I almost hesitate, I creep up to the sentence, 'He was an instinctive actor.' Because that almost is a derogation of his talents. . . . he was quite bright, too. He was very intelligent. Also, he was intelligent enough to understand what a character was and how to play the character simply by being himself *through* the means of the story."

No one should have been surprised that Elvis Presley could act. A painfully shy boy who only came to life behind his guitar, Presley carefully cultivated the young-punk image that enraged his elders: "I don't know anything about Hollywood, but I know you can't be sexy if you smile. You can't be a rebel if you grin." But his contemporaries saw through the half-sullen, half-ebullient exterior to the vulnerable boy-man within. So did Sam Phillips, the producer of Presley's first recordings: "He tried not to show it, but he felt so *inferior*. He reminded me of a black man in that way; his insecurity was so *markedly* like that of a black person." It is this insecurity that comes through vividly in the surviving films of Presley's youthful public appearances, and to which his audiences responded so powerfully. Small wonder teenage girls flocked to him. For all his frank sexuality, it was their budding maternal urges to which he spoke most directly, then as now.

Last Train to Memphis ends in 1958 on the day Private Elvis Presley gloomily boarded a troop ship for Germany to join the Third Armored Division, certain his fans would forget him by the end of his two-year hitch. Instead, he forgot himself, spending the remaining nineteen years of his life plumbing the depths of personal and artistic squalor. I was raised in a small town whose only movie house showed Presley's pictures regularly, and I remember, a couple of years before his death, my father making, apropos of nothing, the following remark: "I never cared much for Elvis back in the Fifties. But he changed. He grew up. He started giving the people good, clean entertainment." The story of Elvis Presley is the story of a cocky, musically daring young man who walked into Sam Phillips's recording studio to cut "That's All Right" and "Blue Moon of Kentucky" and who, two decades later, had turned into a puffy, jump-suited self-parody who supplied hard-eyed Las Vegas gamblers with good, clean entertainment. It is also the story of the people who loved him more in the second half of his career than in the first half, and who loved him best of all after he died. It is a great story—gripping, touching, ultimately tragic. For fame and fortune overwhelmed Presley, and he collapsed under the weight of his fans' expectations. His records and movies became synonymous with shoddiness; supermarket tabloids reveled in tales of his drug-sodden carousing.

Buried beneath the rubble of renown was the real Elvis, the mama's boy from the Memphis housing projects who liked everything from gospel to Mario Lanza and whose unaffected sweetness of character won over no less hard-boiled a customer than Ed Sullivan: "I wanted to say to Elvis Presley and the country that this is a real decent, fine boy . . . we want to say that we've never had a pleasanter experience on our show with a big name than we've had with you." Poor baby, indeed.

National Review 1995

High Anxiety: Martha Graham

E VER SINCE SHE FINALLY STOPPED DANCING IN 1969, AN event greeted by a sigh of collective relief whose echoes are audible to this day, Martha Graham has existed in a world beyond criticism. Most of what gets written about her consists of variations on a theme set forth concisely in the Martha Graham Dance Company's stock biography of its founder: "Martha Graham was recognized as a primal force from the beginning of her career. She has been compared to Picasso and Stravinsky because of her unquestionable dominance of her art. Choreographers and dancers acknowledge that Martha Graham made the single most significant contribution to dance in this century with her original movement technique and her monumental body of dance works." Even for a canned bio, that's laying it on pretty thick. And such genuine criticism of Graham as manages to make its way into print tends to reflect one of two standard approaches, both of which have the unintended consequence of derailing thoughtful discussion of the actual merits of her dances.

The orthodox view of Martha Graham, pared to essentials, goes something like this:

Martha Graham is one of the greatest choreographers of the twentieth century. She made her most significant dances in the Forties and early Fifties. Her work subsequently went into decline, and she failed to maintain her seminal dances in representative condition; in addition, the dancers who joined her company from the Sixties on performed them in an anachronistic, ballet-influenced style that distorted their true character. Nevertheless, those who saw Graham's middle-period dances at the time of their premieres agree that they were masterpieces, and there is no reason to doubt this judgment, even though it can no longer be verified at first hand.

In recent years, a revisionist position has begun to attract support among a growing minority of dance critics:

> Martha Graham is one of the greatest choreographers of the twentieth century. She made her most significant dances in the Thirties, just before she entered the psychological-cum-mythic phase for which she is best known. Few of these dances have survived, and fewer still are performed regularly by the Graham company. Nevertheless, those who saw them agree that they were masterpieces, and there is no reason to doubt this judgment, even though it can no longer be verified at first hand.

While these two approaches to Graham are dissimilar in content, they are structurally identical, reducing in the end to the same slogan: *You had to be there.* Though they attend its performances, Graham's most assiduous acolytes seem to feel that the real presence of her genius is somehow missing from the Martha Graham Dance Company as presently constituted. Yet few question the assumption that Graham *was* a genius, even though it is widely believed that this fact can no longer be deduced from looking at her works as they are currently staged. It's as if Graham's significance must be treated as a postulate in a theorem — or an article of faith — rather than a hypothesis subject to the continuing test of critical observation and revaluation.

That great dances can vanish without trace is a given. That ostensibly accurate stagings of great dances can bear no real resemblance to the works we read about in history books and contemporary reviews is also a given. (Does anybody really think *Les Biches* now looks anything like it did in 1924?) That a great repertory can vanish before our eyes is a trickier proposition. Something of the kind is certainly happening at New York City Ballet, where numerous Balanchine masterpieces are in shockingly bad shape. Yet it is possible for first-time dancegoers to see *The Four Temperaments* or *Stravinsky Violin Concerto* and come away dazzled, and I know few balletomanes who would seriously argue that those dazzled novitiates didn't really see what they thought they saw.

The detail may be fuzzy, the style wrong or confused, but the evidence of our eyes still tells us that George Balanchine was an indisputably great choreographer.

Should one similarly trust one's eyes when looking at the Martha Graham Dance Company? For those in attendance at "Radical Graham," a two-week festival of Graham's early- and middle-period dances held at the Brooklyn Academy of Music, the question was inescapable, and troublesome. For all Graham's historical importance, her work will survive only as long as it can hold an audience. Older dancegoers are entitled to prefer their memories to "Radical Graham," but the rest of us must choose between blind faith and open eyes. Fortunately, it is now possible for balletomanes who started looking at the dance long after Graham retired from the stage to make up their own minds on the basis of reliable evidence. "Radical Graham" was itself a major contribution to the debate: it was, incredibly, the first full-scale retrospective of Graham's work ever presented. In addition, our knowledge of the evolution of the Graham company style was augmented last year by a PBS *American Masters* documentary on Graham that made extensive use of rare archival film. To look at this film, and at the broadcast version of *Appalachian Spring* made for television in 1959 by Nathan Kroll, is to be left with little doubt that the essence of Graham's key works is coming through clearly and intelligibly on stage.

It's necessary, of course, to allow for the effects of bad dancing. I saw an *Appalachian Spring* at BAM that was as bad as any performance of anything I've ever seen. But it wasn't so bad as to be unrecognizable. This is not to say that the company's style is the same today as it was in 1944, or that it is possible to recreate the effect of a Graham concert of the Thirties. But the Graham company, for all its obvious weaknesses (not to mention its equally obvious strengths, foremost among which are the consistently compelling dancing of Christine Dakin and Terese Capucilli), does seem to me capable of performing Martha Graham's dances in a way that allows modern audiences to disentangle the choreography from the legends that surround its maker, and to draw meaningful conclusions about its quality.

THE MUCH-BALLYHOOED CONCEIT OF "RADICAL GRAHAM"
was that it showed off Graham at her most "modern" (BAM presented
the company as the first event of its Next Wave Festival), and more
than a few dance journalists happily snapped at the bait, filing stories
asserting that Graham is as fresh as yesterday's paint. This is, of course,
nonsense. Graham is as much a period piece as any of her modern-
dance contemporaries. The only difference is that her pieces are still
danced by the company she founded, and are still thought to have a
continuing claim on our attention fifty years and more after their
premieres.

Though I've long felt that Graham's dances have aged poorly, this
opinion was based on a comparatively small sample of her work. Prior
to the opening of "Radical Graham," I had seen nothing older than *El
Penitente* (1940), and my acquaintance with the other dances of the
Forties was spotty. For me as for countless other New York dancegoers,
"Radical Graham" offered a crash course in early Graham. Repertory
for the festival included complete performances of *Heretic* (1929),
Lamentation (1930), *Primitive Mysteries* (1931), *Satyric Festival Song*
(1932), *Celebration* (1934), and *Deep Song* (1937), as well as three
excerpts from *Chronicle* (1936). Having seen a working rehearsal of
Chronicle, I think it safe to say that the last section, "Prelude to Action,"
should have been billed as "after Graham" rather than by her, and the
same is probably true of *Satyric Festival Song.* But the other dances,
most of which were restaged or reconstructed during Graham's lifetime, clearly added up to a representative cross-section of her work
from the Thirties.

The thing that struck me most forcibly about these early dances was
their crudity. *Heretic,* made when Graham was a month short of her
thirty-fifth birthday, is a repetitious piece of ensemble movement comparable in subtlety to a *New Masses* cartoon. I can't imagine how anyone
could ever have been impressed by this leaf from a juvenile sketchbook.
Yet John Martin, who reviewed the premiere for the *New York Times,*
called it "strikingly original and glowing with vitality," and Agnes de
Mille, a woman admittedly given to overstatement, claimed she found
herself "uttering dry sobs" the first time she saw it. That George

Balanchine already had *Apollo, Prodigal Son, The Seven Deadly Sins, Serenade, Le Baiser de la Fée,* and *Jeu de Cartes* under his belt by the time he was thirty-five is a reminder of the extent to which American dance critics of the time were ignorant of the expressive possibilities of the medium they covered. While Graham's other ensemble works of the Thirties are more ambitious than *Heretic,* none of them, not even *Celebration,* suggests anything more than a rudimentary grasp of the principles of group composition. The ensembles are usually simple to the point of naivete. As for *Lamentation* and *Deep Song,* I confess to being left cold by their claustrophobic earnestness and utter lack of design. Whatever impression these much-admired solos made in the Thirties, they now seem the very essence of everything pretentious and embarrassing about first-generation modern dance.

That Martha Graham should have gone from *Celebration* and *Deep Song* to *Appalachian Spring* (1944) and *Cave of the Heart* (1946) in the course of a decade is one of the most spectacular cases of late blooming in the history of modern art. Whether or not one finds their angst-ridden content sympathetic, the dance dramas of Graham's major phase are brilliantly accomplished exercises in total theater, a true synthesis of movement, music, and decor. But the dramatic sophistication of these works contained the seeds of its own decadence, which blossomed the moment Graham was no longer able to hold the stage through dancing alone. Unwilling to stop performing as her powers declined, she gradually began to replace her earlier works with new dances in which she substituted theatrical effects for movement. The results can best be gauged simply by looking at a chronology of Graham's work. Rightly or wrongly, she is primarily remembered today for the eleven surviving dances she made during the Forties. By contrast, the dances she made during the last four decades of her life were by most accounts a virtually unbroken string of unwitting self-parodies.

Why, then, is Martha Graham treated with such cloying reverence? Is it simply a matter of respect for the honored dead? Or is there something about her work that continues to engage the imagination of audiences? Certainly the crowds that flocked to "Radical Graham" were large and enthusiastic—and young, or at least youngish. What is it about Graham's dances that speaks to these people? One important aspect of her enduring appeal has nothing whatsoever to do with the artistic merits of her work: Martha Graham is an icon of feminism, a "strong woman" who invented a choreographic language of her own without recourse to the assistance or patronage of men. It is not necessary to understand dance, or even like it very much, in order to respond to the Graham oeuvre — and to first-generation modern dance in general — as an embodiment of proto-feminist ideals. Indeed, the atmosphere at several of the "Radical Graham" performances I attended smacked more of a consciousness-raising seminar than a dance recital; not surprisingly, the works that were received most warmly were the ensemble pieces of the Thirties, *Celebration* in particular.

The trouble is that the Graham legend is, here as elsewhere, sharply at variance with reality. Those who admire the Graham of the Forties must grapple with the fact that she achieved artistic maturity only after adding men to her company and beginning to explore a subject matter in which women not infrequently realize themselves through their relationships with men. It is fascinating to read of the loathing with which Graham's all-female troupe greeted the arrival in 1938 of Erick Hawkins, the company's first male dancer. One would like to know whether these early acolytes responded with comparable dismay to dances like *Dark Meadow* (1946), an inadvertent comedy in one act that grows increasingly more preposterous with the introduction of each ooh-you-big-strong-man phallic symbol.

No less attractive to modern audiences is the tone of Graham's work: sincere, humorless, and, above all, self-obsessed. (Nothing sums up Martha Graham better than the fact that she liked to speak of herself, presumably with a straight face, as "doom eager.") When Arlene Croce emptied both barrels at practitioners of "victim art" in the *New Yorker,* she suggested that their work was an outgrowth of the proletarian art of the Thirties. But it also descends in a direct line from Graham's dances of the Forties, most of which present her as a beleaguered yet ultimately triumphant "victim" of life itself — the equivalent, as it were, of a *Donahue* guest. One of the valuable things about "Radical Graham" was the way in which it dramatized the essential shallowness of Graham's interest in politics. A dance like *Deep Song* may ostensibly have been motivated by the Spanish Civil War, but it is not in any meaningful way a political statement. In tone and technique, *Deep Song* is all but indistinguishable from the later Graham of *Deaths and Entrances* (1943) and *Errand into the Maze* (1947), the lapel-clutching monomaniac whose sole and only subject is How She Came Through. A work like Bill T. Jones's *Still/Here* could hardly have existed without the example of Graham, the original high priestess of the choreographic cult of Self.

Small wonder that Graham suddenly got big after World War II. Her high-strung, tightly-wound brand of dance drama was a near-perfect epitome of New York in the Forties, the same decade that brought us Arthur Miller and Tennessee Williams, the Doug and Wendy Whiner of Broadway. (If Hollywood had decided to film *The Martha Graham Story,* surely Ida Lupino would have been the star.) Small wonder, too, that it becomes so tiresome in large doses. Few choreographers have been so relentlessly uniform in tone as was Martha Graham in her major phase. I have always thought that Graham's greatest mistake was to refuse permission for her dances to be performed on mixed bills by other companies. To watch *Cave of the Heart* or *Appalachian Spring* in isolation is to see a woman of the theater at work. It is when one sees three Graham dances in a row — or twenty, as was the case with "Radical Graham" — that the limitations of the underlying style become oppressive.

These limitations include not merely the numbing uniformity of tone but the vaunted Graham technique itself. Even the silliest dances of Graham's middle period contain passages of genuinely elegant choreographic design. But the movement vocabulary is too restricted, and restrictive, to maintain visual interest over long spans of time. Edwin Denby, one of Graham's earliest admirers, summed up with exceptional clarity the inherent problems of the Graham technique in a 1944 essay:

> Judging by what I look for in ballet, Miss Graham's gesture lacks a way of opening up completely, and her use of dance rhythm seems to me fragmentary. It does not rise in a long, sustained line and come to a conclusion. I find she uses the stage space the way the realistic theater does, as an accidental segment of a place, not the way the poetic theater uses the stage, as a space complete in itself. And I do not feel the advantage to dancing in these qualities of her style.

The truth is that Graham's "technique" was not so much a true technique as a canon of individual quirks. Its ultimate effect was not to liberate, as does the gravity-defying technique of classical ballet, but to constrict. In dance as in life, those who seek to escape from the prison of the past by making up their own rules almost always find themselves trapped in the cramped cell of personal idiosyncrasy. It is a lesson as old as Goethe: *Only in limitation is mastery revealed, / And law alone can give us freedom.*

In a way, the remarkable thing about Martha Graham is not that she failed in her Whitmanesque attempt to forge a new kind of dance, but that she left behind as much of value as she did. Perhaps a half-dozen of her best works are theatrical creations of the first rank (though one might usefully think of them less as dance than as early specimens of performance art), with another half-dozen or so worthy of occasional showings. That may not sound like much, but Antony Tudor's reputation rests on an even smaller body of work and still seems fairly secure. What is far more questionable is the need for a company whose sole reason for existing is to perform those half-dozen dances over and over again. You can count on the fingers of one hand the number of modern-dance choreographers whose work is diverse enough to feed a full-time company. That Martha Graham was one of them is a proposition that can only be seriously entertained by those who care more about legends than steps.

New Dance Review 1995

Choreography by Jerome Robbins

ORE THAN HALF A CENTURY AGO, IN 1944, THE CUR-
tain went up on *Fancy Free*, the first ballet by a twenty-five-
year-old dancer from New York named Jerome Robbins.
There had never been anything quite like it. At a time when classical
dance in America was still dominated by foreign-born performers, choreographers, and impresarios, *Fancy Free* dealt with a contemporary
American subject (three sailors on shore leave in Manhattan), featured the jazz-flavored music of a contemporary American composer
(Leonard Bernstein, fresh from his conducting debut with the New
York Philharmonic), and made convincingly idiomatic use of the steps
of American popular dance.

The premiere of *Fancy Free*, which received twenty-five curtain calls,
made Robbins a star overnight. Eight months later, he and Bernstein
joined forces again for *On the Town*, a musical, based loosely on the
same ballet, which ran for 463 performances and was filmed by MGM.
Within a few years, Robbins had become both the most powerful
musical-comedy director on Broadway and the most famous ballet choreographer in America. In 1969, he left Broadway to become co-ballet
master-in-chief of George Balanchine's New York City Ballet, where he
remains active to this day. His latest ballet was premiered in January,
and a revival of *West Side Story* incorporating his original dances is now
touring the East Coast.

Robbins's name is often linked with that of Bernstein, and indeed the
two had much in common beyond the shared triumphs of their youth.
Like Bernstein, Robbins was Jewish, homosexual, and involved in radical politics, going so far as to join a Communist group during World

War II. (In 1953, six years after having broken with the party, he named the members of the group to the House Un-American Activities Committee.) Both men moved freely between the worlds of high and popular culture; both also regularly produced "serious" works that were dismissed by many critics as shallow and pretentious. And both, despite their critics, were vastly successful with audiences of all kinds: no American artists working in the field of high culture have been better known to the public at large. But Robbins's fame, unlike that of his flamboyant collaborator, is based solely on his work, not his life. He rehearses behind closed doors and rarely gives interviews; no book has yet been written about him, and while he is known to be a demanding taskmaster, dancers' memoirs have typically been circumspect in commenting on his character. He has never discussed his homosexuality publicly, or commented on his still-controversial decision to "name names."

Critics have long been sharply divided over Robbins. Some, including most notably Arlene Croce, believe him to have been at his best on Broadway and in such lighter dances as *Fancy Free* and *Afternoon of a Faun* (1953). For these critics, his more ambitious later efforts, like *Dances at a Gathering* (1969) and *The Goldberg Variations* (1971), while not without interest, cannot bear serious comparison to the ballets of his colleague George Balanchine, the foremost choreographer of the twentieth century. Yet Robbins also has his staunch supporters, among them Clive Barnes, who has called him "the greatest American-born classicist."

Which — if either — of these views is correct?

THE DIRECTOR OF *WEST SIDE STORY* WAS BORN JEROME RABInowitz in New York in 1918, the second child of parents who had come to America to escape the pogroms of Russia and Poland. After growing up in New Jersey, and spending a year as a chemistry major at New York University, Robbins dropped out of college to study dance and acting. Between 1937 and 1940 he appeared in the choruses of four Broadway musicals and performed summers at Camp Tamiment, a socialist-owned resort in Pennsylvania's Pocono Mountains, alongside the comedians Imogene Coca and Danny Kaye.

In 1940 Robbins joined Ballet Theater (now American Ballet Theater). There he studied with Eugene Loring, who had collaborated with Aaron Copland in 1938 on *Billy the Kid*, among the first ballets on an American theme, and with the English-born choreographer Antony Tudor, famed for such "psychological" dances as *Pillar of Fire* and *Undertow*. He also learned the title role of *Petrushka* from Michel Fokine, who had originated that famous ballet for Serge Diaghilev's Ballets Russes. Robbins's appearances as Petrushka in 1943 were favorably noticed by critics, clearing the way the following year for him to choreograph a dance of his own in which he could also star. The result was *Fancy Free*.

From the first entrance of the three sailors, who come cartwheeling on stage to the sound of four rim shots on a snare drum, *Fancy Free* offered a synthesis of ballet and popular dance that was astonishingly self-assured — especially for a twenty-five-year-old novice — and that, a half-century later, remains as fresh and vital as Leonard Bernstein's superb score. At the same time, *Fancy Free* was very much a *theater* piece: the story is told through pantomime, and each of the performers is clearly differentiated as a character. This was a quality not normally found in classical dance, where dramatic characterization is typically subordinated to the sweep and flow of un-self-conscious, directly presented movement. But pure dance classicism had gone to seed by the mid-Forties, and was sorely in need of renewal. Balanchine, as it happens, was then engaged in just such an undertaking, but Robbins had yet to dance in any of his neoclassical ballets; his own imaginative world was still circumscribed by the angst-ridden dance drama of Tudor and the decadent "classicism" of the Russian émigrés who dominated Ballet Theater. Robbins's straightforward theatricality thus came as a breath of fresh air, and few were inclined at the time to reflect on its possible limitations.

During the next decade and a half, Robbins made a dozen more ballets, ranging from the high-strung *Age of Anxiety* (1950, music by Bernstein), described by the choreographer as "a ritual in which four people exercise their illusions in their search for security . . . an attempt to see what life is about," to *The Concert* (1956, music by Chopin), a brilliantly effective set of comic sketches that illustrate the idle fantasies going through the minds of various people attending a piano recital. While some of these dances had more or less explicit libretti—most notoriously *The Cage* (1951, music by Stravinsky), which tells the story of a tribe of insectlike women who kill the men with whom they mate—others dispensed altogether with plot, a tendency seen as early as Robbins's second ballet, *Interplay* (1945, music by Morton Gould), and further encouraged by his first encounter and subsequent close association with Balanchine, the reigning master of "abstract" ballet.

In 1948, Robbins saw a New York City Ballet performance of Balanchine's *Symphony in C,* then as now one of the company's signature pieces. He wrote to the older choreographer, and Balanchine, already an admirer, immediately hired him as a dancer and choreographer, appointing him associate artistic director the following year. By his own account, Robbins was deeply impressed by Balanchine's ability to fill his plotless ballets with "the most extraordinary encounters and events"—so much so, indeed, that in testifying before HUAC in 1953, he claimed to have broken with the Communist party in part because its repudiation of "bourgeois formalism" in art was incompatible with Balanchine's neoclassical style. Yet Robbins also remained uncomfortable with pure classicism, and it is significant that not long before he joined NYCB he had attended the Actors Studio, then run by the director Elia Kazan. There he had studied "the Method," whereby actors (his fellow students included Marlon Brando and Montgomery Clift) were taught to analyze in psychological and sociological terms the characters they portrayed. From then on, Robbins would use Method-derived techniques in working with dancers.

It is thus no coincidence that Robbins's ballets, even the plotless ones, typically emphasize situation over movement. A characteristic example from the Fifties is *Afternoon of a Faun,* a pas de deux set in a dance studio with a boy and girl staring mutely into the studio mirror as they dance together, preoccupied more with the beauty of their individual bodies than with the possibility of mutual attraction. In describing *Faun,* Robbins himself has invoked imagery more typical of a theatrical director than of a choreographer: "I always thought the girl had just washed her hair and just had on new toe shoes and a new clean practice dress and came into the studio to preen and practice."

Interestingly, *Afternoon of a Faun* makes no reference to popular dance steps, and is recognizably "American" only in the lightness of its touch. It is as if Robbins, having first made his mark with a frankly popular dance like *Fancy Free,* now felt the need to establish his legitimacy with a classical work set to the music of a European composer. This foreshadowed his mature style, in which the techniques and preoccupations seen in the ten-minute-long *Faun* were to be writ increasingly large.

By 1954, however, Robbins's commitment to ballet had also temporarily lessened. For the next decade, picking up from his success ten years earlier with *On the Town,* he devoted most of his creative energies to Broadway. Not that *On the Town* was the only musical in which he had been involved. But starting in 1954 with *Peter Pan,* his adaptation of James Barrie's play, Robbins radically enlarged his responsibility for the shows with which he was associated. His credit now read, "Entire Production Directed and Choreographed by Jerome Robbins." This was not just a matter of billing, but a statement of principle: more than anyone else active on Broadway in the Fifties and Sixties, Robbins sought to create something not unlike the Wagnerian ideal of the *Gesamtkunstwerk,* a totally unified theatrical experience. According to Sheldon Harnick, the lyricist for *Fiddler on the Roof:*

> When Robbins takes over a show, it's his vision in every department. He drives the set designer crazy, he drives the orchestrator crazy, he has a total vision of what he wants. He presses you and presses you on every point, no matter how trivial, until it isn't trivial any more.

Robbins was no less driven in his dealings with performers, and some of the tales of his backstage behavior during his years on Broadway are appalling. Yet the results of his bullying were memorable, especially in the three musicals for which he is best known: *West Side Story,* in which Shakespeare's *Romeo and Juliet* was recast as a clash between New York street gangs; *Gypsy* (1959), the story of the stripper Gypsy Rose Lee; and *Fiddler on the Roof* (1964), the musical-comedy adaptation of Sholem Aleichem's tales of ghetto life in czarist Russia. In these shows, the theatricality that in his ballets of the Fifties often seemed at odds with an uncertainly grasped classicism found its perfect expression. Even the tough-minded Arlene Croce has called *Gypsy* "a master-piece of poetic theater and radical design."

Why, then, did Robbins abandon the musical-comedy stage after *Fiddler*? Having previously had the opportunity to make ballets precisely to his satisfaction, he may have found it galling to have to deal with commercial-minded Broadway producers. More importantly, though, the ideal of the *Gesamtkunstwerk* was by definition evanescent. None of Robbins's Broadway shows has ever been revived successfully in anything approaching its original form; even where the dances survive, as in *West Side Story,* their surrounding theatrical context has been lost. Only in ballet would it be possible for him to create unified theatrical works that could have a lasting life in repertory.

IN 1969, AFTER A THIRTEEN-YEAR ABSENCE, ROBBINS RE-turned to New York City Ballet with *Dances at a Gathering,* a work for ten dancers set to eighteen piano pieces by Chopin. This work—the definitive realization of the artistic vision toward which he had been striving since he joined NYCB twenty years earlier—marked the beginning of his major phase as a ballet choreographer.

In this ballet, a group of young men and women meets under a blue sky and dances in ever-changing combinations for an hour. Some of the variations are lyrical, others comic. At one point, five dancers strike snapshot-like poses to the music of Chopin's C Major Mazurka, Op. 7, No. 5. In another dance—set to the F Minor Waltz, Op. 70, No. 2—a girl flutters flirtatiously around three boys who successively ignore her, after which she shrugs and runs offstage. Though the work is long, the scale of the individual variations is intimate and there are no full-ensemble dances. At the end, the dancers gather together—the only time they all appear at once—and gaze at a threatening cloud as it crosses the horizon. They then bow to one another and pair off, and the curtain falls.

"There are no stories to any of the dances in *Dances at a Gathering,*" Robbins has said. "There are no plots and no roles. The dancers are themselves dancing with each other to that music in that space." But *Dances,* while plotless, is not neoclassical: the dancers are strongly characterized, both individually and collectively (it is clear from the staging that they "know" each other), and the work as a whole embodies an overarching dramatic situation. Robbins described that situation to Edward Villella, a member of the original cast: "When you walk out onstage, you're actually beginning the ballet. You look around. It's as if it's the last time you'll ever dance in this theater, in this space. And this is your home, the place you know." *Dances at a Gathering,* then, is a dance about dancers — an approach first employed by Robbins in *Afternoon of a Faun* and recurrent in most of his later ballets.

Unsympathetic critics have applied the word "cute" to *Dances at a Gathering,* not only because it avoids direct classical statement but because Robbins makes effective use of certain obvious theatrical tricks. (Many of the variations, for example, end with an eye-catching lift as the dancers make their exit.) Others have been troubled by the ballet's length — at sixty-three minutes, it is twice as long as most one-act ballets — and by the final, solemn tableau, which in a bad performance can seem embarrassingly heavy-handed. Yet the actual dance content is for the most part very beautiful, and Robbins's knack for characterization is, as always, uncanny. As the great dance critic Edwin Denby has perceptively written:

> Robbins's genius in focusing on a decisive momentary movement — almost like a zoom lens — makes vivid the special quality of each dance. . . . You see each dancer dance marvelously and you also see each one as a fascinating individual — complex, alone, and with any of the others, individually most sensitive and generous in their relationships.

The result is a ballet that occupies an uneasy middle ground between neoclassicism and dance drama. Its virtues, as well as its problems, would be reflected in all of Robbins's subsequent work.

Between 1970 and 1990, when he retired from the company, Robbins produced ballets regularly for New York City Ballet. The most ambitious of these, *The Goldberg Variations,* uses a large cast to imaginative but uneven effect. More consistently successful are those which seek to please rather than impress, including *In the Night* (1970, music by Chopin), *Ma Mère l'Oye* (1975, music by Ravel), *Piano Pieces* (1981, music by Tchaikovsky), and *I'm Old Fashioned* (1983, music by Morton Gould). While these works differ greatly in tone, they have two things in common: none is a pure-dance ensemble piece in the manner of Balanchine, and all are in some sense "about" dancers (or a particular style of dance). *Ma Mère l'Oye*, for example, makes ingenious use of costumes and set pieces borrowed from other dances in the NYCB repertory, and *I'm Old Fashioned* is a tribute to Fred Astaire (a clip from one of Astaire's films is shown at the beginning and end).

Throughout the second half of the Eighties, Robbins's choreographic output dwindled, and most of his new dances were obviously minor efforts or *pièces d'occasion*. The chief exception was *Ives, Songs* (1988, music by Charles Ives), a reminiscence of childhood and adolescence set in World War I, around the time of Robbins's birth; its valedictory overtones, while affecting, are also uncomfortably blatant. He returned to Broadway the following year with *Jerome Robbins' Broadway*, a virtuoso retrospective consisting of scenes and dances from ten of his musical-comedy productions. The juxtaposition of these two events suggested to many that Robbins's long career had at last neared its end, and it came as no surprise when in 1990 he announced his retirement from NYCB. No new ballets came until 1994, when Mikhail Baryshnikov premiered *A Suite of Dances*, a solo work set to excerpts from Bach's unaccompanied cello suites. Later that same year, students of the School of American Ballet (founded by Balanchine and closely associated with NYCB) did *2 + 3 Part Inventions*, a piano-accompanied dance also set to the music of Bach. Rumors began to circulate that these works were studies for a major ballet, and the rumors proved true when NYCB premiered *Brandenburg*, a dance for two solo couples and a corps of sixteen set to Bach's Third Brandenburg Concerto and individual movements from three of the other Brandenburgs.

At first glance, *Brandenburg* appears to be the missing link in Robbins's output. A large-scale ensemble piece structured along classical lines, it contains no implied relationships, and the dancers are not individually characterized. But a closer look reveals that it is also merely the latest in Robbins's long series of dances about dancers — specifically, a corps of Robbins-style dancers performing a "neoclassical" ballet that incorporates all the choreographer's signature moves (down to the cartwheels first seen in *Fancy Free*). No more a direct dance statement than *Dances at a Gathering*, *Brandenburg* is a theatricalized portrayal of neoclassicism, and one that, for all the fetching grace and fluidity of its complex ensembles, is to George Balanchine's *Symphony in C* as *West Side Story* is to *Romeo and Juliet.*

THAT ROBBINS SHOULD SUFFER BY COMPARISON WITH HIS mentor is no shame: what choreographer would not? But comparisons between the two men, while inevitable, nevertheless obscure the fact that their sensibilities are vastly different. Balanchine was the ideal type of what the playwright Friedrich Schiller called the "naive" poet — the wholly natural genius unburdened by romantic self-consciousness. Robbins, by contrast, is a no less ideal example of Schiller's "sentimental" poet, beset by ideas, intensely aware of his alienation from the natural world, forever seeking redemption through his art.

The irony is that Robbins has long admired and aspired to Balanchine's "naïveté." Everything he has said about his art makes that clear, from his statement that the dancers in *Dances at a Gathering* "are themselves dancing with each other to that music in that space" to the revealing remark he made to the dance critic Deborah Jowitt in 1974:

> Essentially what I care about is working; that's what I feel my job is. I don't want to fall into profundities and artistry and surround everything with whipped cream. I work, only instead of being a plumber, I'm a choreographer. I like my job.

Not surprisingly, then, Robbins's most successful ballets are those in which he operates as a craftsman, shunning what Arlene Croce has called "the pursuit of cosmic bellyaches." Profundity is his weakest suit, angst a close second. It is in striving for "naïveté" that Robbins loosens the bonds of his sentimentality and most closely approaches the direct expressiveness of pure neoclassicism; his failure to free himself altogether from those bonds has prevented him from becoming an artist of the first rank.

But how many artists of the first rank have there been in twentieth-century dance? The list proves unexpectedly short: Balanchine, Paul Taylor, Mark Morris, and possibly Merce Cunningham and Frederick Ashton. And judged by any standard other than the most exalted, Jerome Robbins ranks very high indeed. Not only is he the sole American-born ballet choreographer to have created an oeuvre of demonstrably long-lasting interest, but his fusion of classical and vernacular movement set the tone for American dance — modern as well as ballet — from the Seventies on.

In this respect as in others, it is finally more appropriate to compare Robbins not to Balanchine but to his old friend and collaborator, Leonard Bernstein, with whom his name will always be linked. For the positions of the two men in the hierarchies of their respective domains have proved over the years to be strikingly similar: though never attaining the indisputable greatness after which they so passionately sought, both gave pleasure their whole lives long, left behind distinguished and memorable works of theater, and have earned permanent places of honor in the annals of American art.

Commentary 1997

How Good Was Leonard Bernstein?

YOUNGER READERS ACCUSTOMED TO HEARING THE NAME of the late Leonard Bernstein uttered only in reverential tones may find it hard to believe that America's best-known classical musician was for a long time treated as something perilously close to a figure of fun. Harold C. Schonberg, chief music critic of the *New York Times* throughout Bernstein's decade-long tenure as music director of the New York Philharmonic, regularly portrayed him as a flamboyant poseur: "Toward the end of the Liszt concerto, he rose vertically into the air, *à la* Nijinsky, and hovered there a good fifteen seconds by the clock." Virgil Thomson, perhaps the most influential American music critic of the twentieth century, was even more dismissive of Bernstein as a composer: "Bernstein . . . does not compose with either originality or much skill. His pieces lack contrapuntal coherence, melodic distinction, contrapuntal progress, harmonic logic, and concentration of thought." And Tom Wolfe's "Radical Chic: That Party at Lenny's," in which Bernstein was mercilessly caricatured as the ultimate limousine liberal, exploded whatever claims he still had to being taken seriously as an intellectual.

But the rise and fall of reputations is a futures market, and Leonard Bernstein is looking more and more like a blue-chip stock. More than fifty years after his debut as a conductor, and well after his death at the age of seventy-two, he remains the only American-born performer to have found a secure place in the first tier of such classical-music superstars as Toscanini, Horowitz, and Callas. Sales of his recordings reportedly doubled between 1990 and 1993, and although his concert works have yet to win widespread popularity, two of his musical comedies,

West Side Story and *Candide,* and one of his ballet scores, *Fancy Free,* are performed regularly around the world. Nevertheless, many of the old doubts about Bernstein persist. Norman Podhoretz once said of Saul Bellow that "there was a sense in which the validity of a whole phase of American experience was felt to hang on the question of whether or not he would turn out to be a great novelist." The musicians of my generation—born after World War II—felt that way about Leonard Bernstein. To us, he *was* American music, and we wanted him to be great. It was as if his success would somehow ratify our own strivings, and prove that we, too, could do great things.

I suspect that Bernstein was aware of the extent to which so many people had an emotional stake in his career, and that he found it intimidating. It was a cliché, even a joke, that he could never decide what to do with himself: compose, conduct, play the piano, write Broadway shows, do TV. But what Bernstein really wanted was to be a great composer. "I never had a career," he said in 1984. "Conducting is really just a thing." It was a theme to which he returned days before his death in 1990: "The obvious fear is that I'll be remembered—however vaguely—not as a composer but as a conductor." Thus far, that fear is being realized. But the story of Leonard Bernstein's impact is far from over. Indeed, those of us who grew up with "Lenny on our minds" (in Samuel Lipman's perfect phrase) are still left with the need to decide, at least tentatively, just how good he really was.

In making that effort, we have the help of two recent biographies. *Leonard Bernstein,* by far the longer of the two, is by Humphrey Burton, a British producer who directed the many televised concerts and documentaries Bernstein made during the last twenty years of his life. Though the book was written with the cooperation of Bernstein's family and with exclusive access to his huge personal archive, it is not, Burton says, "an 'authorized' biography. Nobody has told me what to say or prevented me from saying what I wanted." Be that as it may, Burton's biography has the tone of a brief for the defense, albeit one written by a lawyer with mixed feelings about his client; it is also, less obviously, a book by an Englishman about an American, and suffers at times from an inadequate feel for various aspects, some of them significant, of American culture. Rich but unselective in detail, *Leonard*

Bernstein contrives to be at once slightly pedestrian and thoroughly engrossing. Meryle Secrest's *Leonard Bernstein: A Life* is both considerably shorter and very different in tone, mainly because the author was not allowed to make use of the Bernstein archives and because Bernstein's family discouraged his closest friends from talking to her. (An exception was Shirley Bernstein, Leonard's sister, who spoke candidly to Secrest about his younger years.) As a result, Secrest was forced to rely more extensively on secondary sources than Burton, and her book, while mostly admiring, tends to take a drier, more jaundiced view of Bernstein the man.

Neither Burton nor Secrest has much of interest to say about Bernstein's compositions, or his place in the history of American music. (Joan Peyser's much-criticized 1987 biography, for all its blatant errors and reliance on unsourced scandalous gossip, gives a better idea of how Bernstein stood in relation to the musical crosscurrents of his time.) For this reason alone, neither of these books can be considered definitive. Taken as preliminary reports, however, and especially when read side by side, they are very useful, partly because they tend to correct each other: Burton's intimacy is balanced by Secrest's skepticism. Though there remain a few gaping holes — we still await, for example, an account of Bernstein's long relationship with Jerome Robbins — it is now possible for those wishing to take stock of his work to do so based on a detailed knowledge of his life.

THE TEMPTATION TO CONCENTRATE ON BERNSTEIN THE MAN at the expense of Bernstein the musician is easy to understand. From the beginning, Leonard Bernstein had an uncanny knack for self-dramatization. Even his angst felt stagey. ("I remember saying to him," the composer Lukas Foss told Burton, "that he had such an expansive luxurious way of being miserable that it didn't seem miserable to me, ever.") In addition, he exuded at all times the tangy odor of scandal. Though stories about Bernstein's private life were sanitized by friendly journalists well into the Seventies, tales of his elephantine ego, heavy drinking, and increasingly flagrant homosexuality were long the common coin of conversation wherever musicians gathered.

Perhaps one should call it bisexuality, since Bernstein married and had three children. But going strictly by the weight of documentary evidence, it would appear that Bernstein was mainly attracted to men. (A close woman friend believed that "he required men sexually and women emotionally.") And despite the oft-expressed wishes of some of his friends, his sex life cannot simply be dismissed as a purely private matter. For one thing, traces of Bernstein's sexual interests can be found in many of his compositions, among them the Serenade After Plato's *Symposium* and, less predictably, *West Side Story,* a parable of forbidden love as unabashedly homosexual in its subtext as any Tennessee Williams play. Even more to the point, Bernstein was part of the informal network of gay artists that played a key institutional role in American classical music and dance during the Thirties and Forties. Though the doings of this group have yet to be chronicled in any detail by historians of American music, its existence has always been common knowledge, and one of its great successes was to help boost the career of the young Leonard Bernstein. It is, to put it mildly, no coincidence that three of Bernstein's earliest patrons — the conductor Dimitri Mitropoulos and the composers Aaron Copland and Marc Blitzstein — were homosexual. Bernstein appears to have been sexually involved with all three men; Secrest even speculates that he "made the decision to abandon his heterosexual pursuits for the good of his career." But one need not go that far to recognize that the young Bernstein's homosexuality gave him entrée to artistic circles not normally open to a Harvard undergraduate.

Of special interest is Bernstein's relationship with Copland, which has never before been discussed honestly in print, least of all in Copland's own poker-faced memoirs. Copland was for all intents and purposes Bernstein's composition teacher; Bernstein returned the favor by championing, as a conductor, his mentor's music. Indeed, the eventual recognition of Copland as the outstanding American composer of the twentieth century owed much to Bernstein's advocacy. But the relationship, it turns out, went deeper than that. Burton's book contains hitherto unpublished excerpts from the Copland-Bernstein correspondence which show not only that the two men were lovers at one point (probably in 1940), but that Copland also went to great lengths to encourage Bernstein to become a conductor: "I keep being properly impressed by all the offers, interests, contacts, personalities that flit through your life. But don't forget *our* party line — you're heading for conducting in a big way — and everybody and everything that doesn't lead there is an excrescence on the body politic."

The irony is that homosexuality proved to be an agonizing dilemma for Leonard Bernstein, both because it left him wracked with seizures of guilt (as a young man, he spoke of having "a canker in my soul") and because it forced him to lead a life of hypocrisy in order to achieve his main professional goal, the musical directorship of a major American orchestra. Not until 1959 did Bernstein take charge of the New York Philharmonic, eight years after he married the Chilean actress Felicia Montealegre. Had he wished merely to be a composer, Bernstein's sexuality would not have stood in the way, any more than it did for Copland, Thomson, or Samuel Barber. It was his additional desire to be a public figure — a community leader, as it were — that made it impossible for Bernstein to be openly gay.

Being Jewish seemed to present another obstacle to winning the leadership of a major orchestra. Certainly Serge Koussevitzky, music director of the Boston Symphony and Bernstein's most important mentor as a conductor, thought it did. Koussevitzky, who himself had converted from Judaism to Christianity as a young man, knew well that the upper-class boards of trustees of America's leading orchestras were reluctant to hire Jewish conductors. He therefore advised his young protégé to change his name to "Leonard S. Burns." But Bernstein refused. Burning though he was with ambition, he seems never at any time to have considered concealing his Jewishness to further that ambition. On the contrary: unlike Koussevitzky, Bernstein probably sensed that Jewishness was becoming more of an advantage than a liability in postwar America.

In any case, having grown up in Boston, the son of mildly observant immigrant parents, Bernstein, both in his life and his work, always made a great point of his Jewishness (and was always passionately devoted to Israel). Burton even claims that Bernstein created "the most significant body of specifically Jewish work achieved by a Jewish composer working in the field of classical music." This may be excessive, but Burton's description of Bernstein's relation to Jewishness is fair enough:

[O]ne is struck by how deeply the interior life of this worldly man was influenced by his Jewish inheritance, by the Hebrew texts he learned as a child (at his father's behest), and by the synagogue music he heard sung in Temple Mishkan Tefila every Friday evening. His first major composition, the *Jeremiah* Symphony, was a setting of beautiful Hebrew words about desolation and despair, taken from the Book of Lamentations. His big choral works, the *Kaddish* Symphony (a Jewish requiem in all but name), the *Chichester Psalms,* and *Mass,* all include settings of Hebrew or Aramaic religious texts, while the *Dybbuk* ballet score is the most obvious demonstration of his concern for the mystic aspect of his Jewish blood and faith.

BURTON IS LESS ACCURATE IN DESCRIBING BERNSTEIN'S POLITICS. Like Secrest, he tends to take Bernstein's simple-minded leftism at face value, seeing it as an expression of idealism and humanism. A more discerning judgment comes from Hilton Kramer, writing in the *New York Post* after it was revealed that the FBI had kept tabs on Bernstein:

> There can hardly have been a single committee, publication, open letter, or organization promoting the interests of the Soviet Union, the Communist party, and their fellow-travelers during the years of Bernstein's ascent to international stardom to which the conductor-composer did not contribute his name and money.
>
> About all such causes, he proved to be a perfect fool, apparently believing to the end—and against mountains of evidence to the contrary—that they were "good" causes.

Moreover, both Burton and Secrest fail to convey the extent to which Bernstein became one of the emblematic figures of American culture. In Bernstein, the left-wing populism of the Thirties and the politics of liberation of the Sixties joined hands, driving him to embrace not only every front organization in sight but almost every other lunatic political tendency of his time. Whether or not this mattered in the larger scheme of things, it mattered greatly for him. For the fact is that in Bernstein's politics lay the seeds of his ultimate destruction: seeking liberation, he found chaos instead.

A monster of self-indulgence, Bernstein nonetheless managed to keep his appetites under control during the Sixties, mainly because the New York Philharmonic would have fired him had he become an object of scandal. In 1969, he retired from the Philharmonic and became an itinerant conductor beholden to no one; eight months later, he and his wife Felicia threw the fund-raising party for the Black Panthers immortalized in "Radical Chic." In the course of the following decade, he temporarily deserted Felicia for a young man, proclaimed his homosexuality to the world (thereby astonishing his children, to whom he had earlier denied it), surrounded himself with an entourage of handsome sycophants, wrecked his health with drugs and drink, composed a smallish portfolio of appallingly pretentious music, and became a public embarrassment whenever he opened his mouth. There can seldom have been a midlife crisis quite like it.

The death of Felicia Bernstein in 1978 accelerated her husband's disintegration. He continued to brag to awestruck reporters about his invulnerability:

> I was diagnosed as having emphysema in my mid-twenties, and I've been smoking for decades. I was told that if I didn't stop, I'd be dead by age twenty-five. Then they said I'd be dead by age forty-five. And fifty-five. Well, I beat the rap. I smoke, I drink, I stay up all night and screw around. I'm overcommitted on all fronts.

But his children knew better. His daughter Jamie (who once discovered to her horror that her father had encouraged her to have an affair with a man with whom he himself had previously had sexual relations) told Burton, "After my mother was gone, there was no one to check him except us and there were limits for us because we didn't live with him. So after that it was just Maestro City all the way."

Even the sympathetic Burton lets slip a certain amount of tight-lipped distaste at the pitiful carousing of Bernstein's final years, and Secrest and Joan Peyser, lacking the inhibitions of friendship, are a good deal more frank. But none of Leonard Bernstein's biographers sums up his last years as unsparingly as did his wife. In 1976, Bernstein informed Felicia, who had had a mastectomy two years before and was (though she did not yet know it) dying of cancer, that he was leaving her for a male lover. "You're going to die a bitter and lonely old man," she told him. And so he did.

THROUGHOUT LEONARD BERNSTEIN'S CAREER, MANY CRITICS tended automatically to assume that, for all his great gifts, there was necessarily something slick and second-rate about his use of them. This assumption was a function of his celebrity. Some, to be sure, were blinded by Bernstein's relentless charm. Others, knowing what they knew about the man, found it difficult to take the artist seriously. But Bernstein's fellow musicians saw through his grotesque antics. They recognized, among other things, the truth of a remark he made to the BBC's Huw Wheldon in 1959: "I'm extremely humble about whatever gifts I may have, but I am not modest about the work I do. I work extremely hard and all the time." While he may not have been above going to bed with men who could help push him up the ladder of success, he also studied with some of the toughest teachers in America—for example, piano with Isabelle Vengerova, whose other American pupils included Gary Graffman and Jacob Lateiner, and conducting with Fritz Reiner, one of the supreme baton technicians of the century. They were all impressed by his talent and application, and predicted great things for him.

He also succeeded in impressing the New York Philharmonic, the hardest-boiled gang of conductor-haters in the world, to which some witty musician long ago gave the nickname "Murder, Inc." In 1943, the twenty-five-year-old Bernstein, then assistant conductor of the Philharmonic, was called on at the last minute to substitute for the great Bruno Walter at a Sunday broadcast matinee. Not only had Bernstein not rehearsed the program, he had never before led the orchestra in public. What happened when he mounted the podium and gave the downbeat for Schumann's *Manfred* Overture, as described to Secrest by a violist who had recently joined the Philharmonic, could never have been brought off by a mere glamor boy:

> The idea was, he'd follow us, only it didn't work out that way. . . . Here were players in their fifties and sixties with long experience. And here

this little snot-nose comes in and creates a more exciting performance. We were supposed to have gone over it with Bruno Walter, we had rehearsed it with him and performed it with him, and this had nothing to do with Bruno Walter. The orchestra stood up and cheered. We were open-mouthed. That man was the most extraordinary musician I have met in my life.

It is worth remembering, too, that Bernstein distinguished himself as conductor, composer, pianist, *and* teacher, a fourfold achievement virtually unprecedented in the history of music. True, he hardly devoted himself with equal fervor to all these pursuits. Once past his student days, for instance, Bernstein never again played a solo piano recital, preferring occasional appearances with the Philharmonic and other orchestras as pianist-conductor. But the few recordings he made at the keyboard are all superbly vital and imaginative, suggesting that he could have had a major career as a soloist had he wanted it.

Bernstein's teaching, too, was basically a sideline, though it brought him well-deserved fame. The fifty-three Young People's Concerts he televised with the Philharmonic between 1958 and 1972 remain a singular achievement in the field of music appreciation. Especially when compared with the tinselly way classical music is hawked on public television today, these commercial broadcasts come across as admirably straightforward both in substance and style. As always, he made ample use of his charm, but he never let it get in the way of the music.

This was not necessarily the case when Bernstein conducted for adults. "Routine, with its loveless mediocrity, lies like hoar-frost on the surface of the world's greatest masterpieces," the conductor Wilhelm Furtwängler once said. Musicians who worked with Bernstein are unanimous in praising his ability to lift everyday music-making out of the swamp of routine, to turn each concert into a once-in-a-lifetime occasion. The trouble was that the occasions in question were all too often celebrations of the man on the podium rather than the masterpieces on the program. At his worst, Bernstein was the Barbra Streisand of conductors, an ego-filled blimp who used the classics as a backdrop for his dramatic posturing.

Given his monumental vanity, however, the remarkable thing was not that Bernstein sometimes conducted badly, but that he managed so often to conduct brilliantly. Once again, the recordings tell the story better than any biography. The problem is in sorting them out. Bernstein made literally hundreds of records in the course of his fifty years as a conductor. He recorded everything from Handel's *Messiah* to Wagner's *Tristan und Isolde* to Stravinsky's *Le Sacre du printemps* (three times). It is risky to generalize about so large and varied a body of work, but he tended to be at his best in his Philharmonic days, particularly in the music of Haydn, Mozart, and Beethoven, where his performances were brisk, volatile, essentially serious in temperament yet dramatic to an appropriate degree.

The nineteenth-century Romantics, on the other hand, inspired in Bernstein interpretations that could be wildly undisciplined, most of all in his old age, when he developed a taste for ultra-slow tempos. But in the twentieth-century repertoire (and Bernstein, following Koussevitzky's lead, programmed more modern music, much of it by American composers, than any other conductor of his generation), he was consistently satisfying. Even when he gave his ego full throttle — something that happened not infrequently in his later recordings of Mahler, who in his earlier days he had done more than anyone else to revive and popularize — the performances that resulted were often as exciting as they were overwrought.

BERNSTEIN'S WORK AS A COMPOSER WAS ANOTHER MATTER. After *West Side Story,* he made a deliberate decision to concentrate on conducting rather than composing. It was a choice with which, according to Burton, he was never fully at ease: "To the walling up of a fruitful stream, to the dominance of the extrovert side of his personality over introspection, can perhaps be attributed the increasing number of black depressions experienced by Bernstein from his forties onward, and the occasional impression that he was not completely in touch with reality."

Bernstein's despair must have been deepened by the knowledge that the quality as well as the quantity of his compositional output fell off sharply after *West Side Story.* "Lenny had a bad case of important-itis," Stephen Sondheim told Meryle Secrest. It was a canny diagnosis. From 1960 on, much of Bernstein's creative energy was poured into repeated attempts to write the Great American Opera. He tried out and discarded one ambitious libretto idea after another: Nabokov's *Lolita,* Brecht's *The Exception and the Rule,* Thornton Wilder's *The Skin of Our Teeth.* But trying to produce a masterpiece through sheer force of will can leave a composer impotent. Only four of Bernstein's post–*West Side Story* theatrical projects—*Mass* (1971), the ballet *Dybbuk* (1974), the musical comedy *1600 Pennsylvania Avenue* (1976), and the opera *A Quiet Place* (1983) — made it to the stage, and all were failures, both aesthetic and commercial.

Harold Schonberg, who had a talent for getting under Bernstein's skin, once said that he could have been the American Offenbach. This must have enraged a man whose greatest desire in later life was to write an opera about the Holocaust. "You know what's made me really distraught?" a drunken Bernstein asked at a party in Rome seven years before his death. "I am only going to be remembered as the man who wrote *West Side Story.*" Judging by this remark, it would seem that Bernstein had come to share the view of those critics who dismissed his earlier music as trivial. They were wrong, and so was he. Although Bernstein never succeeded in becoming a great composer, he did manage to write a number of pieces that seem likely to endure.

To Bernstein, as to George Gershwin before him, the distinction between "popular" and "serious" was one of complexity rather than style; also like Gershwin, he was a natural melodist, making it possible for him to shuttle between Broadway and Carnegie Hall with ease. As a young man, he took plenty of heat from snobbish critics (and from Koussevitzky, who loathed what he insisted on calling "jezz") over his ventures into musical comedy. But Aaron Copland, a composer-critic scarcely less shrewd than Virgil Thomson, declined to see them as a mistake. Writing in 1948, he went so far as to single out Bernstein as one of "the best we have to offer among the new generation" of American composers:

> The most striking feature of Bernstein's music is its immediacy of emotional appeal. Melodically and harmonically it has a spontaneity and warmth that speak directly to an audience. . . . At its worst, Bernstein's music is conductor's music — eclectic in style and facile in inspiration.

But at its best, it is music of vibrant rhythmic invention, of irresistible élan, often carrying with it a terrific dramatic punch. It is possible that some form of stage music will prove to be Bernstein's finest achievement.

This appraisal, made just five years after Bernstein's first major premiere, was right in every particular. He was, indeed, at his best writing for the theater — though not, I think, in *West Side Story*, a work whose manipulativeness is more apparent now that its music and libretto must stand on their own, divorced from the electric context of Jerome Robbins's staging. But *Fancy Free* (1944) is at least as good as any of Copland's own ballet scores, and *On the Town* (1944), *Wonderful Town* (1953), and *Candide* (1956) have long since established themselves as classics of American musical comedy. As for the concert works, the *Jeremiah* Symphony (1942), the *Age of Anxiety* Symphony (1949), the Serenade (1954), and *Chichester Psalms* (1965), all but the last written before Bernstein succumbed to "important-itis," combine open-hearted romanticism and polished craftsmanship to compelling effect.

This is by no means a universally accepted judgment. There are critics who still wince at the sound of Bernstein's name, not least because of his once-unfashionable commitment to tonality:

All [musical] forms we have ever known — plainchant, motet, fugue, or sonata — have always been conceived in *tonality*, that is, in the sense of a tonal magnetic center, with subsidiary tonal relationships. . . . And the moment a composer tries to "abstract" musical tones by denying them their tonal implications, he has left the world of communication.

In the Sixties and Seventies, such views were the musical equivalent of preferring Adam Smith to Karl Marx. But now that the pendulum of taste has swung back from the hermetic austerity of serialism toward the directness and simplicity of tonality, Bernstein's music may be about to come into its own.

It goes without saying that, in the end, Bernstein did not fulfill the extravagant expectations of his admirers, nor did those of us who looked to him for validation finally get what we were looking for. Yet anyone capable of composing *Fancy Free,* reviving the music of Mahler, and introducing millions of Americans to the joys of classical music deserves to be praised for what he did, not criticized for what he failed to do.

This does not mean that we should—or can—whitewash him. In this respect, Bernstein reminds me of Richard Wagner, a composer to whose music he was increasingly drawn in his later years. "Some of us grow up more successfully than others," Bernstein said in 1985. "I have the feeling that Wagner never grew up in this sense, that he retained all his life that infantile feeling of being the center of the universe." Every person I have ever met who knew Leonard Bernstein at all well similarly describes him as a child who never grew up. As long as Wagner is remembered, it will be as a man in whom genius and beastliness were inseparably commingled; as long as Bernstein is remembered, it will be as an artist whose every achievement bore the scars of a deeply flawed character. It remains to be seen whether Bernstein will be remembered as long as Wagner has been. But my guess is that he will not soon be forgotten.

Commentary 1994

Brand-Name Opera

ANDRÉ PREVIN'S OPERATIC VERSION OF *A STREETCAR Named Desire* received its premiere by the San Francisco Opera in one of the most widely noticed classical-music events of recent years. Critics from around the world covered the opening-night performance, and the production, which starred the much-admired American soprano Renée Fleming in the role of Blanche Du Bois, was recorded live by Deutsche Grammophon for release on CD and videotaped for later telecast by PBS.

It stands to reason that Previn's first opera should have received such attention, not merely on account of his celebrity — he is one of the few classical musicians whose name is known to the public at large — but also because opera in America has lately entered a period of unprecedented popularity. Attendance, stimulated by the general adoption of English-language supertitles and the mass-market success of singers like Luciano Pavarotti and Cecilia Bartoli, has risen 34 percent since 1980, and several American operas composed in the last decade, among them John Adams's *The Death of Klinghoffer,* John Corigliano's *The Ghosts of Versailles,* Anthony Davis's *Amistad,* Tobias Picker's *Emmeline,* Conrad Susa's *The Dangerous Liaisons,* and Stewart Wallace's *Harvey Milk,* have attracted media coverage not unlike that showered on *A Streetcar Named Desire.* All these operas were produced by major American houses; most were telecast by PBS; and several have been recorded commercially.

Yet despite the initial receptivity of audiences, none of these operas as yet show any sign of entering the standard repertory, whether in America or abroad. To judge by the mostly tepid reviews of its premiere, moreover, *Streetcar* is unlikely to break the pattern. American operagoers, it seems, are willing to give new works the benefit of the doubt, especially if the casts are stellar and the productions sufficiently expensive-looking, but a single viewing usually proves sufficient to slake their curiosity. Though every opera is a case unto itself, in important ways *A Streetcar Named Desire* exemplifies the underlying reasons why this should be so.

FIFTY-ONE YEARS AFTER IT OPENED ON BROADWAY, *A STREET-car Named Desire* remains one of the most frequently produced plays of the twentieth century — it is still well-known enough, for instance, to have been parodied on *The Simpsons* — and the 1951 film version, directed by Elia Kazan and starring Vivien Leigh and Marlon Brando, continues to be shown regularly on TV. As a result, most literate Americans know the story of Blanche Du Bois, the impoverished Southern belle who comes to New Orleans to live with her sister Stella, runs afoul of Stanley Kowalski, Stella's brutish husband, and ends up in an insane asylum, having proved incapable of reconciling her fantasies of gentility with the coarse realities of working-class life.

Because the play is so famous — and because the Tennessee Williams estate required him to do so — Philip Littell, the librettist, stuck closely both to its broad structural outlines and to its verbal essence. "The trick," Littell has said, "is to make [the audience] think, 'Why'd they hire a librettist?'" In this he has succeeded; despite extensive cuts and countless small textual changes, anyone who has seen the play will find Littell's libretto to be impressively true to its spirit. But to turn a famous piece of literature into an effective opera libretto entails far more than merely compressing the original text. Every great opera based on a familiar literary source involves an imaginative transformation of the original, one that typically goes far beyond the setting of old words to new music. In Verdi's *Otello* and *Falstaff,* Shakespeare's English words are freely translated into the Italian of Arrigo Boito; in Tchaikovsky's *Yevgeny Onegin,* Alexander Pushkin's verse novel is opened up into a series of "lyrical scenes"; in Benjamin Britten's *The Turn of the Screw,* Henry James's narrative voice is jettisoned in favor of dialogue, almost none of which appears in the original novella.

In the absence of such a transformation, one is almost inevitably left with an impression of mere tautology; and that is the case with *Streetcar*. Lotfi Mansouri, the general director of the San Francisco Opera, had long wanted to turn Williams's play into an opera, and approached several composers before settling on Previn. "I cornered Stephen Sondheim," he has recalled, "and he said, 'Oh, it's such a good play — it doesn't need music.' Well, you can say that about Shakespeare's *Othello* too." But Boito's *Otello* is a good libretto precisely because it is so *different* from Shakespeare's *Othello*. By contrast, Littell's *Streetcar* is so much like the original play that it is difficult at first glance to see why Previn felt the need to set it to music.

As it happens, Previn's own answer to this question bespeaks a similar misunderstanding of operatic dramaturgy: "I always thought [*Streetcar*] was an opera that was just missing the music, with all the excesses of lust and madness in the plot." In fact, many opera libretti are melodramatic to a fault, but this is not because "excesses of lust and madness" are somehow intrinsic to opera — a notion that would have surprised Mozart. Rather, it is the nature of lyric theater that the underlying dramatic premises of an opera must be immediately intelligible to an audience. It takes far longer to sing a sentence than to speak it. For this reason, opera libretti cannot rely on lengthy exposition but instead must go directly to the point; subtlety in opera is a function not of the words but of the music. Hence the need for boldly drawn yet believable characters, caught up in clear-cut dramatic situations that require prompt resolution. Yet as a play, *Streetcar*, far from being immediately intelligible, is full of decidedly peculiar people who fail to ring true. The only exception is the character of Blanche, whose very name has become a universally recognized symbol of feminine self-deception.

In the end, *Streetcar* is an "operatic" play only in the limited sense that its language is poetic to the point of overripeness. But in a libretto, language per se is the least important thing. Some libretti are elegantly wrought, others baldly functional, but no normal listener, even in the age of supertitles, attends more than casually to the *verbal* music of an opera. To say it again, great operas are not about words and music but about situations and music — and the music comes first.

Music is so central to the effect of opera that it can justify even the most contorted dramaturgy. Beethoven's *Fidelio*, Berlioz's *Les Troyens*,

Verdi's *Il Trovatore,* Wagner's *Gotterdämmerung,* Tchaikovsky's *Onegin,* Debussy's *Pelléas et Mélisande:* all these works pose theatrical problems of one kind or another, but all are readily acknowledged as operatic masterpieces because of the powerful individuality of their musical content. Unlike them, Previn's score for *A Streetcar Named Desire,* though polished and accessible, is eclectic to the point of facelessness; by turns frankly romantic, mildly dissonant, and explicitly jazzy, it moves so freely from style to style that no personal voice emerges.

No doubt this has much to do with the fact that Previn spent his younger years working as a staff composer for MGM, where he scored a wide variety of films, among them *Elmer Gantry* and *Bad Day at Black Rock,* and served as music director for popular musical comedies like *Gigi* and *My Fair Lady.* Composers of film music not infrequently acquire a chameleonlike ability to change styles at will, and though Previn's virtuosity and professionalism were justly admired by his Hollywood colleagues, he never developed the kind of recognizable signature style heard in the scores of such renowned film composers as Bernard Herrmann and Erich Wolfgang Korngold.

Previn later turned his back on the movie industry, writing with witty contempt of its lack of culture in his 1991 memoir, *No Minor Chords: My Days in Hollywood.* On many occasions he has complained about the initial reluctance of the classical-music establishment to take him seriously. "I would have been more readily forgiven for being the Boston Strangler," he has said, "than for having written a film score." All the more ironic, then, that *Streetcar* so clearly betrays his training. In much the same way that film composers "underscore" dialogue, Previn keeps the text well to the fore at all times; the overall impression one carries away is of overlong stretches of tonal but tuneless *arioso* supported by an orchestral commentary strangely devoid of independent musical life. Even the arias — nearly all of them for Blanche — are melodically unmemorable. No less ironically, the jazzy passages of *A Streetcar Named Desire* are bland and unidiomatic, giving no hint that they are the work of a highly gifted jazz pianist.

Most troubling of all is Previn's singular inability to come to grips, musically, with the character of Stanley Kowalski. Granted, it is by definition difficult to write music for an inarticulate man — still another reason why *Streetcar* is a dubious subject for operatic adaptation—but Previn's elegantly scored music fails altogether to suggest the character's crude sensuality. A case in point is the scene in which Stanley, angered by the fact that Blanche has mysteriously squandered her sister's inheritance, reminds Stella: "In the state of Louisiana, we have what is known as the Napoleonic Code. . . . What that *means* is what belongs to you belongs to me and vicey-versa." Spoken by Marlon Brando in the film of *Streetcar,* these words instantaneously convey Stanley's swaggering, semiliterate belligerence; as sung in Previn's setting by the baritone Rodney Gilfry, they evoke a prissy solicitor warning his stubborn client of the perils of defalcation.

That Previn's score has turned out to be a major disappointment, however, should have surprised no one. A fine orchestral conductor as well as an outstanding piano soloist and accompanist, he has spent little of his performing career in the opera house. As a composer, although he has written effective occasional pieces for such artists as the sopranos Kathleen Battle and Barbara Bonney, the cellist Yo-Yo Ma, and the pianist Vladimir Ashkenazy, this was his very first venture into opera. Previn is now sixty-nine, whereas virtually all repertory operas are the work of musicians who began writing for the stage at a comparatively early age—usually in their twenties—and who either specialized in opera (like Verdi and Wagner) or (like Mozart and Britten) devoted a substantial portion of their composing lives to it. The chances that a part-time composer would have succeeded in setting so problematic a libretto on his first try were therefore slim at best.

GIVEN ALL THIS, ONE INEVITABLY WONDERS WHAT POSSESSED the San Francisco Opera to commission an operatic version of *A Streetcar Named Desire* in the first place, or to ask André Previn to write the score. For as I have already indicated, the opera was not Previn's idea at all, but rather that of Lotfi Mansouri, the company's general director.

That *Streetcar* was conceived not by a composer but by an impresario is wholly characteristic of today's media-driven classical-music culture. Indeed, to nothing does the making of *Streetcar* bear so great a resemblance as to a modern-day film-studio deal. Mansouri, the producer, acquired the rights to a road-tested vehicle for a world-famous female star, hired Previn and Littell as the writers and Colin Graham as the director, then pitched the idea to Renée Fleming. No matter that the original property was clearly unsuitable for operatic adaptation, or that Previn was just as clearly the wrong choice as composer. The presence on the marquee of three highly marketable brand names — Renée Fleming in André Previn's *A Streetcar Named Desire*! — guaranteed a pre-sold audience whether or not the finished product was any good.

To be sure, Mansouri did not invent the brand-name approach to opera. Its imprint can be found on most of the new American operas that have attracted significant media attention in recent years. *The Death of Klinghoffer,* for example, dealt with a well-known news story of the recent past, while *Harvey Milk* and *Amistad* were politically correct historical passion plays. But Mansouri has done much to perfect the formula. Witness his first commission for the San Francisco Opera, *The Dangerous Liaisons.* An adaptation of Choderlos de Laclos's *Les Liaisons dangéreuses,* the celebrated eighteenth-century epistolary novel that had recently been made into a successful play and a popular movie, *The Dangerous Liaisons* starred Fleming, Frederica von Stade, and Thomas Hampson, three of the biggest names in opera. The only thing missing was an equally famous composer, a flaw Mansouri hastened to correct with *Streetcar.*

There can be little doubt that more such operas will be produced in the near future, both by the San Francisco Opera — it has already announced its next major commission, an adaptation by Jake Heggie and Terrence McNally of Sister Helen Prejean's best-selling book, *Dead Man Walking,* the film version of which starred Sean Penn and Susan Sarandon — and by other, similarly inclined companies. John Harbison is currently composing *The Great Gatsby* for the Metropolitan Opera in New York, and the possibilities are all but endless. "I'm a populist," Mansouri has said. "I want to prove opera is for everyone, and I pick subjects with that in mind." So why not *Gone With the Wind*? *The Silence of the Lambs*? *Titanic*?

It is, of course, dangerously easy to make fun of the desire to bring opera to a wider audience — dangerous precisely because there is nothing intrinsically "elitist" about the great repertory operas. Masterpieces like *Le Nozze di Figaro, Carmen,* and *Tosca* — all of them, incidentally, adapted from once-famous literary sources — were deliberately designed to speak to the widest possible audience, and continue to do so to this day. The fact that a growing number of contemporary composers (and even producers) now seek to do the same thing is not contemptible but admirable. "I didn't want twelve-tone," Mansouri has said of *Streetcar.* "I wanted a gorgeous piece of music theater, accessible but not tacky, written for an audience, not academia." Musically speaking, what could be more desirable?

Unfortuantely, brand-name opera is noteworthy above all for its lack of musical distinction. In this, it resembles such recent Broadway shows as *Phantom of the Opera, Miss Saigon,* and *The Lion King,* little more than grandiose visual spectacles accompanied by innocuous music. At the same time, it also recalls the lavishly produced five-act historical pageants put on by the Paris Opera in the nineteenth century, grand operas like Meyerbeer's *Les Huguenots* and Auber's *La Muette de Portici* that were once as popular as *Miss Saigon.* Now they are forgotten, not because their librettos are dated but because their scores are dull. And therein lies the fatal flaw in Lotfi Mansouri's recipe. Impresarios don't write opera — composers do. The San Francisco Opera made every effort to bring André Previn's score to life: Colin Graham's direction was admirably straightforward, Michael Yeargan's sets were wonderfully vivid, and the excellent cast, especially Fleming and Elizabeth Futral as Stella, performed with skill and conviction. But while a musical genius could perhaps have risen to so auspicious, amply funded, and deeply problematic an occasion, Mansouri perversely chose to entrust the central element of *A Streetcar Named Desire* to a weekend composer whose chief credential was his celebrity. It is hard to imagine a more telling metaphor for the condition of American high culture in the age of the media event.

Commentary 1998

The David Helfgott Show

DAVID HELFGOTT, A MIDDLE-AGED, MENTALLY-ILL PIA-
nist from Australia, was all but unknown outside his native
land a year ago. Today, he is one of the hottest tickets in
classical music. His recording of the Rachmaninoff Third Piano Concerto rose within weeks of its release to the number-one spot on the *Billboard* classical chart, and had sold 200,000 copies by the time of his New
York recital debut, which took place at Lincoln Center's Avery Fisher
Hall. This concert, part of a North American tour that attracted mass-
media coverage comparable to that received by Van Cliburn when he
won the Tchaikovsky Competition in 1958, sold out within days of its
announcement, as did two hastily scheduled repeat performances.

The immediate cause of Helfgott's near-overnight success was not his
musicianship but an Australian-made movie, *Shine.* Although movies
about classical music and classical musicians were a staple of Hollywood
studios in the Thirties and Forties, they ceased to be popular long ago.
But something about *Shine,* which purports to tell the story of Helfgott's life, appealed to the public; the film became a sleeper hit, in the
end receiving seven Academy Award nominations, making its subject a
celebrity, and preparing the way for the recording and recital events to
come.

Prior to the release of *Shine,* the known facts of David Helfgott's life
could have fit neatly into a paragraph. Born in Melbourne in 1947, he
went to London in 1966 to study at the Royal College of Music, winning the college's Dannreuther Award three years later for a performance of the Rachmaninoff Third. He then returned to Australia,
where he suffered what his publicity material euphemistically describes

as a "breakdown," subsequently spending "many years under treatment and out of a mainstream existence." In 1983, he met Gillian Murray, a professional astrologer; they were married the following year, and under her influence Helfgott began playing concerts again, eventually appearing throughout Australia and in Europe.

So much for the facts. *Shine,* directed by Scott Hicks, is a fictionalized account of Helfgott's life, and one whose essential accuracy has been disputed by members of his family. Yet the film remains the principal source of what can only be called the Helfgott myth, and on that ground must be considered seriously. In *Shine,* then, we learn that Helfgott is the child of poor Polish-Jewish immigrants to Australia, virtually all of whose relatives died in the Holocaust. His father, Peter, is presented as a smothering sadist who beats his son, a bespectacled, bookish prodigy, whenever he shows any signs of independence, musical or otherwise. The American violinist Isaac Stern, impressed by young David's playing, arranges for him to study in America; but Peter, unwilling to let his family be broken up, forces the boy to refuse the offer.*

A few years later, David is offered a scholarship to the Royal College of Music in London. This time he defies his father, who disowns him with a prophecy of doom. Peter's words come true when David suffers a psychotic break in the middle of his prize-winning performance of the Rachmaninoff Third. After undergoing electroshock therapy, he returns to Australia, where his father refuses to speak to him. David is then institutionalized. When we next see him, years later, it is apparent that he is suffering from a comparatively mild but incapacitating form of schizophrenia (though the precise nature of his illness is nowhere specified in the film). Helfgott's doctors refuse to let him play the piano, and it is only after he is finally deinstitutionalized that he starts once again to perform, not in a concert hall but at a wine bar, where his virtuoso rendition of Rimsky-Korsakov's "Flight of the Bumblebee" makes him a local star. He meets Gillian, they fall in love and are married, and in the film's climactic scene he succeeds in giving a formal concert for the first time since returning to Australia.

As portrayed by the actor Geoffrey Rush, Helfgott is an irresistibly

*Isaac Stern has said that he does not remember having met Helfgott.

engaging fellow whose tendency to smash up apartments and speak in jittery, high-speed "word salads" of alliterative free association (a well-known symptom of schizophrenia) is less frightening than charming. Even at his least intelligible, Rush/Helfgott is fairly easy to understand, and given to gnomic utterances about war and the soul that are meant to show that his illness has made him both likable and wise. This characterization is central to the message of the film: Helfgott, we are to understand, suffers not from a chronic disease of the brain, treatable by drugs, but from a character disorder, caused by his father's abuse and curable through love. Revealingly, it is after he sleeps with his wife for the first time that he is able at long last to play a concert; in the final scene, his verbal tics have diminished to something resembling a bad stammer.

HOWEVER DUBIOUS ITS MERITS AS A DISQUISITION ON THE nature of mental illness, *Shine* is certainly a slick and effective piece of commercial entertainment. As such, it was all but predestined for success in the United States, a fundamentally optimistic country whose moviegoers like nothing better than watching affable heroes overcome seemingly insurmountable obstacles, have great sex, and live happily ever after. But how much does the real-life David Helfgott have in common with the benign savant seen in *Shine*?

As it happens, Gillian Helfgott has published a memoir that, though no more specific than the film about the nature of her husband's illness, is considerably more candid about its continuing symptoms. In it, she acknowledges implicitly that he is not competent in the legal sense of the word, describing him at the time of their first meeting as "a three-year-old in a body of a thirty-six-year-old." Yet she firmly insists that Helfgott's inability to function as "a regular member of society" is not an affliction but a choice — though one, it emerges, which she appears to have made in his behalf. "One could," Gillian Helfgott acknowledges, "give [David] enough medication that shops and restaurants and crowded streets would not bother him." But, she goes on,

> then his time would be taken up with doing all the little tasks that regular members of society do, and he'd be robbed of his passion to play, each and every day of his life. It wouldn't be difficult to try and

"adapt" him to some arbitrary standard of normality, but then David would no longer be David and, by destroying the individual, one would risk destroying his magic.

I shall return to these extraordinarily presumptuous words later. But here I must pause to ask: just how "magical" *is* David Helfgott's artistry? His best-selling CD, *David Helfgott Plays Rachmaninoff,* reveals that while at one time he must clearly have been a pianist of considerable accomplishment, he is no longer capable of performing Rachmaninoff's technically demanding music to anything remotely like a respectable concert standard. Indeed, upon the release of the CD, most of the reviews were negative, some quite sharply so. This, however, did not prevent his managers from following up *David Helfgott Plays Rachmaninoff* with the announcement of "The *Shine* Tour," in which he would make his North American debut at Boston's Symphony Hall and next give performances in Montreal, Toronto, New York, Los Angeles, and other large cities.

It was this tour, coming as it did on the heels of the Academy Award nominations, that made Helfgott news. Its promoters sought to neutralize possible adverse criticism by wrapping the pianist in greeting-card sanctimony (his American concerts, for instance, were billed as "The Celebration of Life"), and the reaction of concertgoers to his sold-out debut in Boston was overwhelmingly enthusiastic. Once again, though, the reviews were just as overwhelmingly unfavorable, with Anthony Tommasini, the critic for the *New York Times,* stating flatly that Helfgott was "not a finished pianist in any sense."

To this, Helfgott's handlers responded by going on the offensive: "I think there are some critics who perhaps act as sort of self-appointed guardians of an elite culture," Scott Hicks told reporters. "Maybe there are barricades that need to be stormed. Maybe the public has a right to be heard." And indeed, it could be argued that Helfgott's concerts were attracting large numbers of people who had never before attended a piano recital, and the pianist they were paying to see was by all accounts delighted to be playing for them. What harm could come of that?

At his New York debut, this question was answered as soon as Helfgott came on stage. No one even slightly familiar with the symptoms of schizophrenia could have failed to see that Geoffrey Rush's brilliant performance in *Shine* was—to put it bluntly—a lie. The real David Helfgott, it turned out, still wore the mask of insanity: the tic-like mannerisms shown in softened, romanticized form in *Shine* were in fact dismayingly pronounced. Moreover, his playing was far more disorganized in person than on disc, and his technique, though to some extent still intact, was divorced from any meaningful musicality. It was as if his hands remembered how to play the piano, but were doing so without the guidance of his mind.

A handful of people in Avery Fisher Hall realized what was happening. Isaac Stern fled at intermission, and I spoke to a pair of professional pianists who were shocked by the spectacle unfolding before their eyes: a mentally incompetent man was being paraded before a paying audience for the financial gain of his managers. It was this latter fact, not the abysmal quality of Helfgott's playing, that I myself stressed when I reviewed the concert for the *New York Daily News:*

> [I]t seems to me that many people have been unwilling to grapple with the harsh truth about Helfgott, the subject of the movie *Shine:* he has been, and gives every indication of still being, profoundly mentally ill. He grunts, mutters, sings, and talks to himself—very loudly—as he plays. He seems not fully aware of where he is (a handler came on stage at concert's end, presumably to make sure Helfgott understood it was time to leave). And while he is undeniably capable of playing the music of Beethoven, Mendelssohn, Liszt, and Rachmaninoff, at least in the limited sense of pushing down the right keys in the right order, the results suggested a weird cross between a gifted but uninhibited child and a player piano that has been badly regulated. . . .
>
> Two centuries ago, nice people went to asylums on Sunday, and gawked at the inmates. But times have changed. Today, we let the inmates out of the asylums and encourage them to live "normal" lives. Some preach strange religions on street corners; others give concerts at Avery Fisher Hall, and nice people pay $50 a head to watch them, and call it progress.

My review went further in this regard than those of other critics who wrote about Helfgott's New York concert. But they, too, were unanimous in their judgment that he was mentally ill, and that his physical presence on the stage of a great concert hall was thus utterly inappropriate. This unanimity seemed to me noteworthy at the time, and in retrospect, and upon reflection, it seems more noteworthy still.

A few days after hearing David Helfgott play at Lincoln Center, I went to the Museum of Modern Art in New York to see *Willem de Kooning: The Late Paintings, the 1980s.* The canvases hung at MoMA were painted well after de Kooning had developed Alzheimer's, and it should have been apparent to anyone acquainted with the effects of the disease that the man responsible for these pale, meaningless squiggles was no longer the painter whose landmark work of the Forties and early Fifties had changed the face of American art. The signs of mental disintegration were impossible to ignore. Yet ignored they were, both by the curators of the exhibit and by most of the art critics who wrote about it and who, unlike the music critics writing about David Helfgott, proved incapable of observing the bright line that separates mere eccentricity from outright insanity. For them, the senile de Kooning was not merely the equal of his early self, but arguably superior, with one critic going so far as to claim that "what's there may approach perfection as closely as human performance can."

In so saying, of course, this critic was merely taking the last, postmodernist step on a path down which many intellectuals have tripped in our time. Starting in the Sixties, the intellectual historian Michel Foucault and the psychiatrists Thomas Szasz and R. D. Laing, among many others, argued that major mental illness was not a disease but an artificial construct, brought into being by our particular social arrangements — that, for instance, in Szasz's words, "the identity of an individual as a schizophrenic depends on the existence of the social system of psychiatry." This theme melded nicely with the closely related notion, inherited from Romanticism, that insanity is actually a higher state of awareness, and the two ideas have since infiltrated our culture to the point where the products of genuinely deranged artists can be exalted, given the name of "visionary art," and even displayed in museums built especially for this purpose. In popular culture, these same ideas have given us not only *Shine* but such hit movies as *Rain Man* (1988), in which Dustin Hoffman plays an autistic savant who breaks the bank at a

Las Vegas casino, and *Forrest Gump* (1994), featuring Tom Hanks as a retarded man who achieves wealth, fame, and sexual fulfillment through his own unaided efforts.

In calling attention to the very different way David Helfgott's performance was treated by music critics, I hardly mean to argue that the musical world is free in general of the corrosive effects of cultural relativism. Far from it. Many a critic, after all, has written approvingly of the gender theory that elevates the efforts of third-rate women composers to the status of masterpieces, while others just as surely have praised the anti-music of John Cage or the intensely politicized operas of John Adams. What, then, stopped them from praising David Helfgott's recital as a sterling example of visionary art? Perhaps it was merely a lingering bourgeois scruple, a nostalgic (if inconsistently applied) belief in the discredited notion of "quality" in art. Whatever it was, there is reason to be grateful for it.

DAVID HELFGOTT'S MOMENT IN THE SUN IS NOT QUITE UP. HE is still giving concerts, and his CD continues to sell. But the David Helfgott Show is over, and he himself, in his real person, seems to have been forgotten almost entirely.

For the moviegoing public, of course, David Helfgott never existed in the first place: he was and is Geoffrey Rush, likable and wise, living proof that madness is just as good as sanity. For those who saw him in the flesh, or at this year's Oscar ceremonies (during which he played "Flight of the Bumblebee"), he is simply another freak in the electronic freak show that is postmodern culture, his tormented soul carved into a consumable good. Whether he is being exploited by those who have a stake in his career — indeed, whether the mere act of exhibiting him publicly might in and of itself be a moral wrong — goes undiscussed. Yet it is for this reason above all that we should be haunted by the image of that pitiful man at the piano, whose wife has deliberately chosen to deprive him of the chance to live as others do. For it is an especially ghastly irony that events like "The *Shine* Tour" and *Willem de Kooning: The Late Paintings, the 1980s* should be taking place just at the moment when medical science has largely abandoned older psychodynamic theories of insanity in favor of objective "disease models." We know now that such psychiatric disorders as schizophrenia and manic depression can, in many cases, be treated effectively, allowing their victims to lead comparatively normal lives.

Whether David Helfgott's is such a case, we will probably never know. Even now, Gillian Helfgott can still write blandly in her memoir, "I will always fight for David's right to stay extraordinary, and do whatever is necessary to protect him from any pressures to conform." The more one ponders these self-righteous words, the clearer it becomes that to speak of the marketing of David Helfgott as an act of exploitation is to use too weak a word. It is, rather, a sin.

Commentary 1997

Classical Barbie

I FIRST HEARD OF THE EROICA TRIO, A GROUP OF JUILLIARD alumnae who have been playing together since 1986, at the time of their Weill Recital Hall debut. Weill is the small auditorium next door to Carnegie Hall that presents up-and-coming young classical performers who, while not quite ready for prime time, are nevertheless considered worthy of wider notice by Carnegie's management. I rarely cover such concerts, though, and the press release made a big deal out of the fact that the members of the trio were all women, implying that this alone was reason to come hear them; I don't play that game, so I stayed home.

I next heard of the Eroica Trio when I received in the mail a special promo copy of their debut CD for EMI. It was shipped well in advance of the album's official release date, a tip-off that the label had decided to give the group an extra promotional push. As recently as five years ago, I would have paid close attention to the signing by EMI of a chamber-music ensemble, but times have changed, and the label of Artur Schnabel, David Oistrakh, and Jacqueline du Pré is now best known for having dropped the Philadelphia Orchestra from its roster, preferring to put its money on such rising stars of the future as Roberto Alagna and Vanessa-Mae. So I placed the CD in my file-and-forget pile, and forgot about it.

A few weeks later, I received what in book publishing is known as a "finished copy" of *Eroica Trio*. Special promo copies are shipped without art — all you get is the CD itself, housed in a cardboard sleeve or a plain jewel box — so this was my first opportunity to find out what the members of the Eroica Trio looked like. In fact, the finished product offers three such opportunities, for color photographs of Adela Peña, Sara Sant'Ambrogio, and Erika Nickrenz appear on the front and back of the jewel box as well as inside the booklet, and it turns out that they are, in a word, babes: their eyes are bright, their hair tousled, their lipstick glossy, their smiles Barbie-blank. In all three photos, the girls (I use this loaded term for reasons that will soon become clear, if they haven't already) are wearing designer dresses, and Andrew Eccles has shot them in such a way as to leave no possible doubt that they also have nice figures. What is nowhere to seen on the front cover of *Eroica Trio* is any indication of what music the CD contains. To find out, I had to look on the back, where the contents are listed in tiny print superimposed on the bosoms of Peña, Sant'Ambrogio, and Nickrenz: Gershwin's Three Preludes, the Ravel A Minor Trio, Benjamin Godard's Berceuse from *Jocelyn*, and Paul Schoenfield's *Café Music*. The Gershwin is performed in a vulgar, overblown adaptation by one Raimundo Penaforte; the Godard, a nineteenth-century salon staple, is a "single" short enough to be suitable for broadcast on Classic Lite FM stations; the Schoenfield is a more-than-half-sincere spoof of the potted-palm music that used to be played by trios in fancy restaurants.

I hasten to point out that the Eroica Trio is by no means the high-culture counterpart of the Monkees: Peña, Sant'Ambrogio, and Nickrenz may not be Jacques Thibaud, Pablo Casals, and Alfred Cortot, but they definitely know how to play their instruments, and while their slowish performance of the Ravel Trio isn't going to end up in any time capsules, it's much better than adequate. As for the rest of the program, I wouldn't have paid to hear it in concert, but suffice it to say that I've heard far worse. The trouble I have with *Eroica Trio* is not so much the program, fluffy though it is, as the slightly sleazy manner in which it is presented. Consider, for instance, the first paragraph of the liner notes: "Whether they are playing the great standards of the piano trio repertoire or daring contemporary works, the three striking young women who make up this world-class chamber ensemble electrify the concert stage with their combination of virtuosity, vivid artistic interpretation and sheer exuberance in performance." *Three striking young women.* Get it? I read this paragraph to a Gen-X friend of mine, and her answer was devastating: "Oh, I see—Charlie's Angels play Ravel."

Reading on, I learned that the trio "first came to international attention in 1991 when they took First Prize in the Walter F. Naumburg Chamber Music Competition." Now the Naumburgs, as they're known in the business, are a deadly serious affair, and you can bet these ladies didn't win first prize by playing the Berceuse from *Jocelyn* in body stockings. But winning the Naumburgs, prestigious though they are, didn't make the Eroica Trio famous, not even slightly: I get around, and I hadn't heard of them prior to last January. Presumably at some point between 1991 and then, Peña, Sant'Ambrogio, and Nickrenz got tired of playing Mozart in the sticks (for which I can hardly blame them), looked in the mirror, decided it was time to try something completely different, hired a high-powered publicist and started pitching themselves as the Spice Girls of classical music. The rest is easy enough to figure out. Virtually every classical record executive in New York is obsessed to the point of mania with getting his artists on TV, especially Steven Murphy, president of Angel Records, the American division of EMI, for which the Eroica Trio records. Murphy may not know anything about classical music—I've certainly never heard a word to the contrary—but I'm sure he knows a babe when he sees one, not to mention a salesworthy gimmick, without which damned few major-label classical recording contracts are signed nowadays.

Which brings us back to the CD I hold in my hand, and I know what some of you are thinking: what's wrong with a little cheesecake? The members of the Eroica Trio are consenting adults, and if they want to sell records by displaying the pretty faces and hard bodies God gave them, that's their business. Besides, they have perfectly good reasons for doing so. ("The terrible thing about this world," observes a character in Jean Renoir's *The Rules of the Game*, "is that everybody has his reason.") After all, the audience for classical music is shrinking daily, and anything that helps to interest young people in Ravel can't be all bad, right? Just ask Sara Sant'Ambrogio. "To attract new generations to classical music," she says, "we have to realize that we don't exist in a vacuum. We are competing for audiences with everything from MTV to *Rent*."

But what Sant'Ambrogio seems to have forgotten is that classical music, like the other fine arts, isn't for everyone. It takes a little work, which is why Beavis and Butt-head prefer MTV to Ravel. Unfortunately, the American arts establishment has spent the greater part of the last half-century operating on the precisely contrary assumption that high culture should be made available to the masses by any means necessary, and that if they don't want it, the fault lies not with them but with high culture itself. This is what the National Endowment for the Arts had in mind when it released a report last fall claiming that our arts insitutions are too "elitist." Edward Rothstein, writing in the *New York Times,* replied by pointing out the once-obvious fact that art is "an essentially undemocratic achievement by extraordinarily gifted individuals" — that it is elitist, in other words, by definition. The only way for classical music to attract a mass audience is to dilute it to the point where it ceases to be recognizable as classical music.

Therein lies the hidden danger of the Eroica Trio's dress-for-success marketing strategy. No, it's not the worst thing in the world — far from it. But what if Sara Sant'Ambrogio and her colleagues do end up making a potful of money playing Gershwin in low-cut designer gowns? Couldn't they make still more money by renaming themselves the Erotica Trio and playing Paul McCartney in wet T-shirts? More to the point, what's to stop EMI from making fifty times as much money by stuffing four child prodigies in catsuits and calling them the Obsession String Quartet? I'll bet they'd sell out Carnegie Hall in ten minutes flat, and I can just hear some oily corporate flack explaining how great *that* would be for classical music. As for those unlucky artists whom God absentmindedly neglected to equip with pretty faces and hard bodies, I somehow doubt there'll be much room for them on EMI's roster, no matter how beautifully they play, should the Eroica Trio hit the jackpot. (You want us to record Itzhak Perlman? Lose the crutches, baby.)

It was only a year ago that I sat in Avery Fisher Hall and watched with horror as an undermedicated schizophrenic played piano for a packed house that lapped it up and yelled for more. The exploitation of David Helfgott was the most morally repugnant spectacle I have witnessed in a quarter-century of concertgoing, yet there was no shortage of earnest people willing to go on TV and talk earnestly about how this, too, was somehow good for classical music. I wonder if it has occurred to the well-meaning members of the Eroica Trio that what they are doing to classical music by marketing themselves as "three striking young women" is not entirely dissimilar to what Helfgott's handlers did by marketing him, for all intents and purposes, as "that crazy pianist who plays Rachmaninoff." I wonder, too, if they have ever heard the haunting words of W. B. Yeats: "Evil comes to us men of imagination wearing as its mask all the virtues."

Fi 1998

Angelic Disorders

THE CULTURAL SEISMOGRAPHS OF HOLLYWOOD HAVE FI-
nally registered the Next Great Awakening: *City of Angels,* a
tearjerker about a soulful-looking angel who falls in love with a
perky heart surgeon, blew *Titanic* out of the top box-office slot. No
doubt this is the film industry's idea of divine intervention—James
Cameron, the writer-director-producer of *Titanic,* was showing signs
of hubris in the wake of his near-clean sweep of the Oscars—but
moviegoers who attend church more than once a year are unlikely to be
fooled by *City of Angels,* which is to religion what a Big Mac is to steak.

Religion isn't the only thing that gets ground up in *City of Angels,* an
adaptation of *Wings of Desire,* Wim Wenders's much-admired 1987
movie about an angel who longs to know what it's like to be human.
Remakes of good foreign films are almost always vapid, and this one is
no exception. "I love *Wings of Desire,*" says Dana Stevens, who wrote
the screenplay for *City of Angels,* "and I felt I could capture its essence."
Translated from the original Hollywoodese, that sentence reads: *We
kept the basic idea but dumbed everything else down.* In the process of
rendering Wenders's quirky, poignant fantasy safe for consumption by
American teenagers, Stevens and Brad Silberling, the director of *City of
Angels,* jettisoned everything that made *Wings of Desire* memorable in
the first place. Comparing the two films is thus a meaningless exercise
in pedantry: *City of Angels* should be judged on its own treacly terms.

The film's opening line ("I don't really pray, but if you could just help
me out here . . ."—a nice touch, but don't get your hopes up) is spoken by a terrified mother unaware that her dying child is being watched
over by a fashionably black-clad angel named Seth (Nicolas Cage). It

subsequently emerges that Seth is one of a host of guardian angels whose duties range from comforting the sick to persuading small-time crooks not to shoot convenience-store clerks. When not on duty, they hang out atop tall buildings and chat about the day's work, gathering on the beach at sunrise and sunset to listen to the music of the spheres. It sounds like a wonderful life, but there's trouble in paradise: Seth has developed a morbid fascination with the pleasures of the flesh, and no sooner does he meet Maggie (Meg Ryan), who is in despair because one of her patients has died on the operating table, than he realizes that he loves her. Nothing that happens from this moment on is even slightly unexpected, least of all the ending, in which Seth, having voluntarily surrendered his place in the angelic order so as to become Maggie's earthly lover, is left alone to face his mortality when she is killed in a car accident.

The one surprising thing about City of Angels is its dogged earnestness. Not only does the script hedge no bets as regards the question of God's existence, but it goes so far as to implicitly criticize the spiritual emptiness of its mortal characters. Maggie, for instance, is an agnostic, but though she listens to Jimi Hendrix in the operating room and makes flippant remarks about religion, the brightly skeptical facade with which she faces the world cannot conceal her growing sense of anguish at the apparent meaninglessness of her life. Her boyfriend, sensing that she is starting to have doubts about doubt, testily warns her not to become "one of those doctors who prays in the O.R." (Talk about telegraphing your punches.)

Hollywood has been seeking in recent years to capitalize on the angst with which the baby boomers are confronting middle age, but City of Angels is the first movie to place their anxieties in an explicitly religious context, and for that reason alone it is more interesting than, say, Lawrence Kasdan's unbearably fatuous Grand Canyon. Alas, City of Angels is forever bumping up against its own shallowness. Much is made of Seth's unfulfilled longing to experience the goodness of God's bounty — to taste a pear, or feel the wind on his face — but in the end, the film's real message is that having sex with a movie star in a really expensive house on Lake Tahoe is worth giving up heaven for. Sex, in fact, is the whole point of City of Angels (and also the source of its fundamental conceptual flaw: if sex is *that* good, why are there any angels left at all?). That's what makes the religious angle so smarmy. Right from the start, you know there's no way Maggie and Seth aren't going to end up in bed together, with Gabriel Yared's violin-enriched New Age score pumping up the sugar count in the background.

To the limited extent that *City of Angels* works, it's because of its cast, and particularly because of Meg Ryan. The star of *When Harry Met Sally . . .* and *Sleepless in Seattle* once seemed doomed to become the Doris Day of the Nineties, but her spunkiness is firmly under control here, and she actually contrives to suggest the sort of woman whom a moderately depressed man might not necessarily want to strangle. Nicolas Cage is good, too, though his own tendency toward self-caricature is starting to get out of hand—he looks more like a cocker spaniel than ever. Dennis Franz, who showed us his bare buttocks in the first episode of *NYPD Blue,* does so again as a surf-loving fallen angel who urges Seth to exercise his free will and take the plunge. Fortunately, Franz is a fine actor, as is André Braugher, another TV cop trying to make it in the movies (he's from *Homicide*), who gets much more out of the ungrateful role of Seth's angelic partner than the makers of *City of Angels* put into it.

But good acting can never do more than provide a veneer of plausibility for a bad script, though the failings of *City of Angels* are less repellent than sad. More Americans are talking and thinking about religion now than at any previous time in the past quarter-century, and they appear to be doing so in direct response to the widespread feeling that something has gone terribly wrong with our culture. Yet few seem prepared to change their lives in response to the call of faith, much less to boldly assert the universal validity of the commandments in which they claim to believe. (Nothing says more about the children of the baby boomers than their oft-repeated motto, "Whatever.") Small wonder such uncertain folk are flocking to see a movie that simultaneously asserts the existence of life after death *and* the superiority of flesh over spirit. Do we contradict ourselves? Very well, then, we contradict ourselves! What could be more American? Or more consoling?

It is surely no accident that for all its ostensible antimaterialism, everything about *City of Angels* looks fabulously expensive, especially

John Seale's swoopy, self-consciously beautiful cinematography. Every third shot seems to have been made from a helicopter, including the one in which we see an angel perched on the famous HOLLYWOOD sign. This scene sums up *City of Angels,* in which Hollywood's version of religion is expounded with the force of epiphany: you can't take it with you, so why not enjoy it now, then produce big-budget movies about how it didn't make you happy?

Crisis 1998

The Land of No Context

A S ANYONE FAMILIAR WITH THE COLLECTED WORKS OF
Frank Sinatra can tell you, the very best time to reflect on love
gone wrong is at a quarter to three, when there's no one in the
place except for you and Joe the bartender. But should you be doing
your drinking at two A.M. on a Thursday night in New York City, in a
joint with a television at the end of the bar, you might consider asking
Joe to tune in *Cheaters,* a nightmare version of *Candid Camera* in which
private detectives armed with video gear burst in on unsuspecting men
and women who are cheating on their significant others. *Cheaters* is
shown in some 190 American markets, and Bobby Goldstein, the
show's creator and executive producer, claims to receive roughly four
thousand inquiries each month from cheatees who are willing to swap
their privacy for the prospect of exposing their errant lovers on syndi-
cated TV. (They must also agree to pay for the investigation if they
later decide to back out.) Most get in touch by phone or through
www.cheaters.com, which also sells *Cheaters* videos, T-shirts, sweat-
shirts, and underwear, though some write directly to the show's offices
at — really — 4516 Lovers Lane, Dallas, Texas.

Unlikely as it may sound, *Cheaters* appears to be, as each episode
proudly proclaims, "real reality television." According to Goldstein, a
Texas lawyer turned independent producer, the show never stoops to
using actors or re-enactments, and the cheaters typically prove as coop-
erative as their victims. "They may not be so willing in the beginning,"
he explains, "but in order for them to be able to give us a follow-up
interview, which we do as often as possible, they have to give us a
release so that they can tell *their* side of the story." *Cheaters* doesn't

go beyond a preliminary investigation unless it seems likely that the cheaters in question are in fact cheating. Segments are broadcast only if all parties sign release forms. (In addition, some cheaters are paid small sums after the fact as a further inducement to cooperate.) "We don't start going down the path unless we've got a pretty good case going in," Goldstein says. "A few of them just don't pan out, but I'd say that 85 to 90 percent of the cases we investigate get on the air."

Adultery is usually a complicated business, but *Cheaters* presents it in in a starkly simple way. We start by meeting the Complainant, who sketches the situation in a few terse unrevealing sentences, after which hidden cameras stalk the Cheater. It may take weeks, but sooner or later the Cheater is caught in a compromising situation, and the resulting video is shown to the Complainant, who writhes and moans as an unseen narrator describes the on-screen action in unctuous tones reminiscent of Rip Torn at his smarmiest ("Their behavior is improper and shameless, made even more repugnant by Cari's open deceit of Robert on the phone that same night!"). Next comes the Confrontation, in which the Complainant, escorted by a phalanx of private eyes and cameramen, crashes in on the Cheater, catching him or her *in flagrante delicto*. After the obligatory commercial, a *Dragnet*-like epilogue tells us how it all ended, and it's off to the next case.

Watching an episode of *Cheaters* is not unlike watching the first ten minutes of *Chinatown*, in which Jake Gittes shows a client pictures of his wife having sex with another man. The trouble is that you never get to see the rest of the movie—you just watch the first reel over and over again. Who are these utterly ordinary people? What strange passions drive them into strange beds? In the Land of No Context that is reality TV, nobody cares about such irrelevancies, least of all the participants themselves. They offer up their pitiful intimacies as fodder for unseen voyeurs, then slip quickly off the stage, having proved themselves real by virtue of appearing on TV at two in the morning.

As for the voyeurs, it's tempting to turn to La Rochefoucauld for an explanation of their prurient interest: "In the adversity even of our best friends we always find something not wholly displeasing." Still, *triple-sec* French cynicism isn't necessarily a trustworthy guide to the American national character. If it were, then Bobby Goldstein Productions might well consider branching out with, say, a companion show in which hidden cameras grind away as doctors tell patients that they have six months to live. Yet somehow I doubt *Terminal!* would go over quite as big as *Cheaters*.

No doubt it says something significant about *Cheaters* and its viewers that Goldstein feels obliged to gild his show's essential salaciousness with a thick coat of sanctimony. Each episode begins with the following announcement: "*Cheaters* presents to you inspirational chronicles of humankind. The heroic men and women of these stories overcome the challenge of relationships and restore health and happiness to their lives by taking charge and holding accountable the unfaithful." Inspirational? *Heroic?* Now that self-esteem, earned or not, has become an absolute value, even an entitlement, I suppose one could use those two adjectives to describe a show in which cuckolds contrive for their faithless partners to be unmasked on TV. You might even call it "empowering," if you're the sort of person who uses that sort of word.

Me, I prefer straighter talk, though perhaps not quite so straight as that of La Rochefoucauld. As for *Cheaters,* I don't plan to make it part of my weekly TV diet, though I'm not sorry to have seen it. If nothing else, it reminded me of the wisdom of the anonymous seventeenth-century "Bachelor's Prayer" that H. L. Mencken, another deep-dyed cynic, made a point of including in his *New Dictionary of Quotations:* "I pray thee, O Lord, that I may not be married; but if I am to be married, that I may not be a cuckold; but if I am to be a cuckold, that I may not know it, but if I am to know, that I may not mind." That might not make for red-hot reality TV, but as advice goes, I'd say it beats anything the folks at 4516 Lovers Lane have to offer.

New York Times 2002

The Myth of "Classic" TV

AS FRANK SINATRA MIGHT HAVE SAID, IT WAS A VERY
good year for *The Sopranos,* which wrapped up its third season
recently on HBO. Snobs who claim not to watch any other
show (yeah, right) will be tuning in to see who gets whacked and who
lives to whack again. Policy wonks who salt their op-eds with pop-
culture references in order to simulate youth now have a new catch
phrase, "disrespecting the Bing," to kick around. (For those benighted
folk who don't keep up with *The Sopranos,* the reference is not to Bing
Crosby but to Bada Bing, the mob-owned strip joint that figures prominently in the series.) James Gandolfini even managed to walk away
from the smoldering wreckage of *The Mexican* smelling like a cannoli.

Meanwhile, critics continue to fumble for fresh superlatives with
which to praise the continuing adventures of Tony Soprano and his
trigger-happy extended family. Stephen Holden of the *New York Times*
set the bar high when he wrote that *The Sopranos* "just might be the
greatest work of American popular culture of the last quarter-century,"
but many of his colleagues have since jumped even higher. "While the
sheer entertainment and suspense of the plot twists are reminiscent of
Dickens and his early serials," Ellen Willis wrote in *The Nation,* "the
underlying themes evoke George Eliot: the world of Tony Soprano is a
kind of postmodern *Middlemarch.*" Tom Shales, writing in a similar
vein in the *Washington Post,* went so far as to claim that *The Sopranos*
"has gone beyond the status of mere TV series and is rife with reverber-
ation — 'social significance,' trite as that term may be."

These comments, and others like them, set me to thinking. Yes, *The
Sopranos* is an exciting and innovative series, and perhaps it will still be

reverberating five years from now. But before *The Sopranos* there were *Twin Peaks* and *Northern Exposure,* before them *Wiseguy* and *Moonlighting,* and before them *Miami Vice, St. Elsewhere,* and *Hill Street Blues,* all exciting and innovative series that were praised to the skies by critic after critic . . . and when did you last happen to watch an episode of any of them? I come not to bury *The Sopranos,* which I love, but to point out that there seems to be something in the nature of even the best TV dramas that renders them ephemeral.

The term "classic" is commonly used to describe fondly remembered TV shows of the past. (I searched for the phrase "classic TV" on Google the other day, and came up with 86,300 hits.) To call a work of art "classic," however, implies that it is something to which we return time and again, making new discoveries with each successive encounter. I can't tell you how many times I have looked at George Balanchine's *The Four Temperaments,* but though I suppose the day may come when it no longer has anything new to say to me, I still find it a source of apparently inexhaustible interest, and try to see it at least once a year. Every art form has produced innumerable masterpieces that, like *The Four Temperaments,* demand to be experienced repeatedly — every art form, that is, except for series television.

Granted, *TV Guide* is forever publishing lists of the 100 Wackiest Sitcoms of All Time, but how many times have you seen "Chuckles Bites the Dust"? If you failed to recognize the title of the most famous episode of *The Mary Tyler Moore Show,* you've proved my point: though viewers may happen to see an episode of a TV series more than once, it is rare that they seek out particular ones to watch again. What is true of sitcoms is trebly true of hour-long dramas, especially those whose individual episodes are not free-standing but assembled out of tightly interwoven story lines (what TV writers call "arcs") that may run for a season or more. Such series are even harder to watch piecemeal, since each new episode carries the narrative baggage of all the ones that have gone before. I watched the first *Sopranos* of the current season with a friend who had not previously seen the show, and spent much of the evening explaining to her who the characters were and why they behaved the way they did.

This cumulative quality is part of the charm of serial art. As Philip

Larkin observed, much of the pleasure of reading *A Dance to the Music of Time,* Anthony Powell's twelve-volume serial novel, "resides in the small reminiscential effects Mr. Powell's grip on his by now enormous cast enables him to bring off." But even the longest novels are portable and can be picked up and put down at will, thus making it far easier to invest the necessarily large amounts of time needed to read them. Not so TV shows: you can't watch them in the subway, and though the VCR makes it possible to view an episode at your leisure, it isn't very rewarding to do so in ten-minute chunks. To appreciate an hour-long drama, you have to consume it in a single sitting.

As it happens, only thirteen episodes of *The Sopranos* are aired each season, and the series is expected to have a fairly limited run. More typical is *St. Elsewhere,* which ran for 137 consecutive episodes, each of which grew organically out of its predecessors. Such long-running series can only be experienced serially, which for all practical purposes means during their original runs; once they cease to air each week in regular time slots, they cease to be readily available as total artistic experiences, and thus can no longer acquire new viewers, or be re-experienced by old ones. This is why there is no such thing as a "classic" TV series: we never see *any* series enough times to know whether its overall quality justifies the multiple viewings that are the hallmark of classic status. (Needless to say, I'm not talking about those fanatical cultists who have seen each episode of *Star Trek* a hundred times and can recite the dialogue from memory. To them, my heartfelt advice is: get a life.)

Some think *The Sopranos* will break this iron rule of ephemerality. I understand that a great many videocassettes of the first thirteen episodes have been sold, presumably to latecomers who weren't subscribing to HBO in 1999 and wanted to find out what they'd missed. But if you aren't already watching *The Sopranos,* you're probably not going to start now, unless you're prepared to sit through reruns of twenty-six additional episodes between now and next March, when the fourth season begins. Nor are even rabid fans likely to watch *The Sopranos* from beginning to end more than once. Who has the time? More likely, Tony and Carm and the late, lamented Big Pussy Bompensiero will eventually go the way of Frank Furillo, Joyce Davenport, and all the wonderful characters with whom I spent a happy hour each Thursday night back in the Eighties. *Hill Street Blues* was the first TV drama I ever went out of my way to see, and were there world enough and time, I might even consider watching the first few dozen episodes again. But while I still remember how much I liked *Hill Street Blues,* I can't recall much else about it—only a few isolated moments from two or three episodes — whereas I could easily rattle off fairly complete synopses of, say, *Citizen Kane* or *A Midsummer Night's Dream,* or whistle the exposition to the first movement of Mozart's G Minor Symphony. To qualify as a classic, a work of art must first of all be good enough to make you want to get to know it at least that well. Will any TV series ever be good enough to fill that exalted bill? With all due respect to the beloved Bing, I'm not betting on it.

New York Times 2001

Battle of the Brows

ITEM ONE: NEW YORK CITY HAS NOW HOSTED ITS FIRST large-scale, single-site, multidisciplinary arts festival. Sixty-four performances were staged in the three-week-long Lincoln Center Festival '96, under the slogan, "Classic, Contemporary, and Beyond." In an unusual move for Lincoln Center, which tends to keep to the middle of the cultural road, many of them had the unmistakable flavor of the avant-garde—or at least of yesterday's avant-garde.

Thus, the single playwright featured at the festival was Samuel Beckett, all nineteen of whose plays, including *Waiting for Godot* (1952) and *Krapp's Last Tape,* were performed by the Gate Theater of Dublin; the featured composer was the late Morton Feldman, an American precursor of minimalism who, though unknown to the public at large, continues to be treated as a cult figure by a tiny band of admirers. The Lyons Opera Ballet presented a postmodern, tarted-up restaging by Maguy Marin of the nineteenth-century ballet *Coppélia;* the Houston Grand Opera presented a production of the Virgil Thomson–Gertrude Stein nonsense opera *Four Saints in Three Acts,* which premiered in 1934 and which has been beloved ever since of music critics. But while the press was predictably delighted by Lincoln Center Festival '96, the public, though not indifferent, was predictably skeptical: in all, out of a possible 110,000 tickets, only 83,500 tickets were sold, or 76 percent of capacity.

Item two: only two days before Lincoln Center Festival '96 opened, Luciano Pavarotti, Placido Domingo, and José Carreras—the "Three Tenors"—gave a concert at Giants Stadium outside New York, accompanied by James Levine and the Metropolitan Opera Orchestra. The program consisted of standard operatic arias and pop tunes, the latter ranging from Neapolitan songs to "New York, New York." To attend the single performance, a capacity crowd of 56,000 fans paid up to $1,000 apiece.

In a sense, Lincoln Center Festival '96 and the Three Tenors concert were both aimed at the same potential audience, New Yorkers interested in the performing arts. So far as I know, no one in the press thought to discuss these two events in tandem, and few people seem to have attended both. But more significantly, just as the reviews of Lincoln Center Festival '96 were for the most part enthusiastic, so were those of the Three Tenors generally dismissive: an extravaganza, the critics said, worthy only of amused condescension.

In fact, both sets of reviews were wide of the mark.

IN THEORY, LINCOLN CENTER FESTIVAL '96 WAS THE BRAIN-child of one man, John Rockwell, who assumed the post of artistic director in 1994. During an earlier, two-decade-long tenure as a music critic for the *New York Times,* Rockwell had been noted for his propensity to deny the existence of meaningful distinctions between high and popular culture. His near-endless list of critical enthusiasms ranged from the minimalist composer Philip Glass to the rock balladeer Linda Ronstadt. And this year's festival, he told a reporter shortly before opening night, would represent "my interests and desires."

In practice, however, the festival also embodied a long list of artistic compromises, which finally rendered it miscellaneous to the point of incoherence. Its origins were strictly utilitarian: Lincoln Center's existing classical-music summer festival, Mostly Mozart, had been in decline for several seasons. The New York Philharmonic, which heretofore had no summer concert series, was looking for an opportunity to extend its performing schedule. The Philharmonic thus was already an integral part of the plan for the festival before Rockwell took over.

Certain other events in Festival '96 were presumably scheduled for reasons of political expediency. A case in point was *Sweet Release,* a shockingly bad dance choreographed by Judith Jamison to an original score by Wynton Marsalis and performed by the Alvin Ailey American Dance Company and the Lincoln Center Jazz Orchestra. The Ailey company already dances every winter in New York; Jamison, the company's current artistic director, is not generally regarded as a choreographer of importance; and Lincoln Center annually commissions a new work from Marsalis. It is hard to escape the conclusion that this work—incredibly, the only new dance premiered at the festival—was programmed not for artistic reasons but solely to increase the number of women and minority artists.

To the extent that the programming did seem genuinely to reflect Rockwell's eclectic tastes, it was—well, eclectic, though the "contemporary" aspect promised in the festival's slogan was almost nowhere to be seen. In fact, the most striking thing about Lincoln Center Festival '96 was its air of a trendiness decidedly faded. *Four Saints in Three Acts,* for example, was staged by Robert Wilson, still best known to American operagoers for *Einstein on the Beach,* his 1976 collaboration with Philip Glass; the choreographer Merce Cunningham, who made his first dance well over fifty years ago, presented *Ocean,* a full-evening dance in the round inspired by the works of James Joyce and John Cage; John Eliot Gardiner and the period-instrument Orchestre Revolutionnaire et Romantique gave a high-speed reading of Beethoven's Ninth Symphony, notable less for its "revolutionary" character (heavily touted in advance) than for its boorish insensitivity; and the brilliant Russian conductor Valery Gergiev offered three programs of music by Igor Stravinsky, Dmitri Shostakovich, and Sergei Prokofiev, including Prokofiev's agitprop *Cantata for the Twentieth Anniversary of the October Revolution,* set to texts by Marx, Lenin, and Stalin.

This is not to say that the festival was entirely devoid of merit. Wilson's staging of *Four Saints* was one of the most vivid operatic productions to be seen in New York in recent seasons; Cunningham's *Ocean,* while overlong and fitfully inspired, was nonetheless a major effort by an important choreographer deserving the serious attention of dancegoers. But Lincoln Center Festival '96 also served as a reminder that the very idea of the avant-garde has lately become a contradiction in terms. Not only is modernism dead and minimalism passé, but the "cutting-edge" status of avant-garde artists has long been blunted by their eagerness to seek institutional certification (and public funding). In any case, the appeal of their work, whether dating from the Twenties and Thirties or from the Sixties and Seventies, now has relatively little to do with its widely varying merits: for aging cultural radicals like Rockwell, it is all as much the stuff of nostalgia as, say, the music of the Grateful Dead, and it is essentially as nostalgia that Lincoln Center marketed it.

As for the continuing artistic vitality of Rockwell's avant-garde, it may be found in the following *New York Times* report of a festival nonevent:

> The Kronos Quartet has canceled its performance of Morton Feldman's String Quartet No. 2, saying that its players are no longer up to the physical demands of the uninterrupted six-hour work. The performance . . . was to have been the centerpiece of a Feldman retrospective at the Lincoln Center Festival '96. In a statement released yesterday, David Harrington, the group's first violinist and artistic director, said that "in our rehearsals we discovered that we are now unable to perform the work for purely physical reasons."

Taken together with the attendance figures for Lincoln Center Festival '96, this makes as pithy an epitaph for the American musical avant-garde as one could hope for.

THE THREE TENORS, BY CONTRAST, NEED NO EPITAPH: SIX years after Pavarotti, Domingo, and Carreras first sang together in Rome, they remain the most successful road show in the history of classical music. Their infrequent live performances sell out immediately; their TV broadcasts are repeated endlessly on PBS. In the same week they sang at Giants Stadium, their two CDs — recorded in 1990 and 1994 — were, respectively, the third and fourth classical best-sellers in the U.S.

Needless to say, artistic success cannot be measured by the golden yardstick of profit. But the experience of watching 56,000 people listening in rapt and respectful silence to three deservedly famous operatic tenors singing arias by Verdi and Puccini, accompanied by a distinguished conductor and orchestra, is not easily forgotten. Yes, there were those glossy pop medleys thrown in for good measure; but the applause that greeted them was no more thunderous than the applause for the arias. Indeed, the first encore, *La donna è mobile,* was cheered just as if it were a hit single, which was more or less what Giuseppe Verdi had in mind when he composed it 145 years ago.

To have been present at Giants Stadium was to be forcibly reminded that there used to be a cultural category — today, alas, no longer readily available — of which the Three Tenors furnish a faint but distinguishable echo and the legitimacy of which Lincoln Center Festival '96 implicitly denies. The word *middlebrow* has for so long been used by cultural radicals and intellectuals as a term of abuse that it is difficult to see through to the forgotten reality. As Dwight Macdonald defined it, middlebrow culture, made up of the intellectual and artistic products of capitalist society, was "an instrument of domination" by which the bourgeoisie was anesthetized and thus made passively accepting of its fate. But some critics of far greater discernment realized early on, however grudgingly, that middlebrow culture was a more complex and nuanced phenomenon. Here, for example, is Clement Greenberg:

> Middlebrow culture has to do in one way or another with self-improvement, and is born almost always out of the desire and effort of newly ascended social classes to rise culturally as well. . . . And while the middlebrow's respect for culture may be too pious and undifferentiated, it has worked to save the traditional facilities of culture — the printed word, the concert, lecture, museum, etc. — from that complete debauching which the movies, radio, and television have suffered under lowbrow and advertising culture. And it would be hard to deny that some sort of enlightenment does seem to be spread on the broader levels of the industrial city by middlebrow culture, and certain avenues of taste opened.

It is no exaggeration to say that many children of the baby boom were raised on just this sort of middlebrow culture at its best, and that some of them even used it as a path to higher things. For the underlying strength of middlebrow culture lay precisely in its "pious" acknowledgment of an ascending hierarchy of values, a ladder whose rungs could be climbed by anyone willing to make the effort.

The older generation of intellectuals attacked middlebrow taste from the perspective of high culture and (especially) the avant-garde. These were the precincts they wanted above all to defend, not only from the leveling influence of the middlebrow but especially from the depredations of the low and the popular to which middlebrow culture might provide a bridge. But a later generation of critics—including John Rockwell—reshuffled the categories. To them, genuine culture existed at the two extremes, the high (also known as the avant-garde) and the low (in music, rock and roll). Both were equally serious, and both equally meritorious, in large part because both were equally "subversive" of the bourgeois middle.

Today we live among the ruins of these various theories and the consequences they have brought upon us. Among those consequences is that high culture of virtually any kind has disappeared from commercial TV and the weekly newsmagazines. The earnest, self-improving middlebrow consumer is likewise increasingly a thing of the past, wandering helplessly between the mindlessly outré products of the so-called high culture and the wasteland of an electronic-era mass culture that is "debauched" (to use Greenberg's word) to a degree unimaginable in the 1950s.

In a way, the Three Tenors are the closest thing we have to the lost middlebrow culture. Far coarser in their approach than, say, Arthur Fiedler and the Boston Pops (that quintessential middlebrow institution), they are still capable of lifting aspiring music lovers from a more debased level of culture to a less debased one. For their pains, they are richly and rightly rewarded by those music lovers, and roundly and wrongly derided by the critics. But what they cannot do—what no performer, however charismatic, can do—is create a new mass audience for classical music, and certainly not one that will be receptive to the failed avant-garde experiments of the Sixties and Seventies. If the last middlebrows who continue to fill our concert halls and theaters are simply not interested in the likes of Morton Feldman, their offspring tend to view both Feldman and Stravinsky—not to mention Mozart and Verdi—with equal and utter indifference.

Such is the pass to which we have been brought, in no small part with the help of the middlebrow-hating radicals of the Sixties. Nevertheless, they continue to press their utopian cultural schemes, albeit with less and less self-assurance. In a post-festival press conference,

John Rockwell and his colleagues put the best possible face on Lincoln Center Festival '96: "Officials," reported the ever-upbeat *New York Times,* "said that the density and the variety in the first-year festival seemed about right, but that other adjustments would be made." Other adjustments? "Popular music may get a bigger slice of the pie next year."

In short, next year's festival will be more like the Three Tenors at Giants Stadium—only much more pretentious, arguably much less elevating, and, one suspects, nowhere near so entertaining.

Commentary 1996

Good Night, David

I DON'T WATCH MUCH TV NEWS ANYMORE, BUT WHEN I heard David Brinkley was retiring, I made a point of tuning in to ABC's *This Week* to see him say goodbye. It was business as usual for the first forty-five minutes or so: one of Marv Albert's lawyers did a star turn, and Roy Romer played his why-we-need-campaign-finance-reform soundbite two or three times—I lost count—before Sam Donaldson finally gave him the hook. Then there was a reel of goodnight-Chet-goodnight-David clips, after which Brinkley, looking all of his seventy-seven years but sounding far younger, took his last, elegant bow. Then it was all over, and I felt empty and disoriented, the way most baby boomers feel when another relic of their lost youth passes from the scene. Red Skelton had died the previous week, and Charles Kuralt went on the road for good a couple of months before that; Skelton got a half-page obit in the *New York Times,* not bad for a comedian whose name is completely unknown to anyone under the age of, oh, thirty-five. I wonder how many people read it.

I know a half-dozen Gen-Xers better than casually, and when I'm with them, I do most of the listening, pretending to keep up with what postmodernism has wrought. But I know I'm just going through the motions. Besides, you can't keep up with the culture by talking to a half-dozen Gen-Xers. They can't even keep up with it, because it doesn't exist anymore, not the way it did when I was a boy. Back then, my family watched *The CBS Evening News with Walter Cronkite,* and so did every other family I knew, except for the ones that preferred NBC's *Huntley-Brinkley Report.* Not that it mattered much, since there were only three TV networks to choose from, movie theaters showed only one film at a time, and *Billboard* had only one chart that mattered, the Hot 100, at the top of which you could find both the Beatles and, occasionally, Dave Brubeck, the same way you could see them both on *The Ed Sullivan Show*. If you want to know what America was like in 1962, there's your answer: it was a place where everybody watched Ed Sullivan and knew who David Brinkley was.

Conservative intellectuals who decry the death of the common culture in America usually have in mind the King James Bible, Shakespeare, and the Gettysburg Address, but more than that has died in the quarter-century since I graduated from high school: we have also lost the shared reference points of our popular culture. *Billboard* now publishes a dozen different charts, including Top Singles, Top Albums, Country, Adult Contemporary, R&B, Modern Rock, Latin, Hot Dance Music/Maxi-Singles, Jazz, and Classical. I get seventy-six channels on my cable TV, including three different all-news networks; more often than not, the six-screen theater on the corner of my Upper West Side block is showing at least four movies whose names I don't know, most of them intended for a niche market that in the polite parlance of the day could be described as Male Adolescents of Color. If I want to see a movie better suited to the interests of a Colorless, Middle-aged Male, I have to go somewhere else.

Needless to say, it's decidedly unfashionable to complain about this state of affairs. Not only is diversity the cultural trump card of the Nineties, but a surprising number of conservatives seem perfectly happy to be living in a land of niche markets. For them, diversity equals individualism, and the Internet is the ultimate symbol of individualism, a place where all can have their simultaneous say, be they lacto-vegetarians or neo-Nazis. As a result, I find it virtually impossible to convey to my younger friends any sense of what it was like when everybody watched the same TV shows and read the same magazines. They can't make the imaginative leap, and most don't particularly want to.

America was a different country then, and never more so than when you went someplace else. When Norman Podhoretz went to Cambridge in the early Fifties, he found that the young Americans he met there had more in common than "good teeth and smooth complexions."

> In those days before pop became fashionable we shared in a thousand guilty secret loves: the Shadow and the Green Hornet, Batman and Superman, James Cagney and Pat O'Brien, Harry James and Glenn Miller, "Did You Ever See a Dream Walking?" and "I Left My Heart at the Stage Door Canteen." *You too?* we would say delightedly to one another, after listening to initially sheepish confessions about the incorrigibility of our low American tastes, *you too?* And then, purifying ourselves in orgies of authenticity after days, weeks, months of genuflection in cathedrals and galleries and museums and chateaux, we would vie with one another in expertise in the culture that was really in our bones, dredging up the lyrics of long-forgotten popular songs, advertising slogans, and movie plots. . . . *Isn't it funny?* we would say to one another on a chance encounter in Paris or Athens or Rome, *isn't it funny? I never thought of myself as an American before.*

To be sure, pop culture didn't start with Harry James and *The Green Hornet.* It dates back to the invention in the mid-nineteenth century of the modern printing presses that first made possible the production of cheap, large-circulation daily newspapers aimed not at the well-to-do but the newly literate working classes. But it was the movies, the phonograph, and radio that created a full-scale opening for mass-produced middlebrow "art" intended for an audience whose members were literate to widely varying degrees, and these media soon became, for better or worse, the most powerful integrating forces in American life since the rise of the common school. Woody Allen's *Radio Days,* which shows how network radio helped weave second-generation immigrant families of the Forties into the fabric of middle-class America, reminds us that TV served only to accelerate a process that was already moving at a brisk clip by the time Podhoretz went off to Cambridge to study with F. R. Leavis.

It's foolish to romanticize middlebrow culture, but no less foolish to claim it was nothing more than an opiate of the masses. *Time* published Whittaker Chambers on Reinhold Niebuhr and Rebecca West; Arturo

Toscanini conducted on NBC for seventeen years. Even Clement Green-berg, that unrivaled scourge of middlebrowism, wrote about abstract art for the *Saturday Evening Post*'s "Adventures of the Mind" series. (I don't know what the cover of that issue was, but I like to think Norman Rockwell painted it.) Sir John Reith, the first director-general of the BBC, once said his policy was to give the public "something rather better than it thinks it wants"; similarly, the gatekeepers of middlebrow culture in America felt a genuine responsibility occasionally to give the public something rather better than *Gilligan's Island*. For all our latter-day worship of "inclusiveness," I'm struck by just how inclusive mid-dlebrow culture really was, as well as how much it demanded of its consumers. God knows TV news in the Fifties and Sixties had its prob-lems, but at least it tried to be serious, so much so that stylish, thoughtful writers like David Brinkley and Charles Kuralt could actually become on-camera stars.

Still, I know better than to pretend that once upon a time, TV was nothing but *Peter Pan, Playhouse 90,* and *The Bell Telephone Hour.* The point of network television in its heyday wasn't that it served up master-pieces around the clock; rather, it was that anybody could partake at will of the wide-ranging fare it *did* serve up. It was because CBS broad-cast both *Gilligan's Island* and Leonard Bernstein's Young People's Concerts that some people discovered the latter, and profited thereby. Watching Ed Sullivan on Sunday nights, you saw a little bit of every-thing, and so did your neighbors. Such shows were an important part of the cultural glue that helped hold this country together.

Now they are gone, and I miss them, the same way I miss the slow-moving America of my small-town youth, back when the word "every-body" was more than an abstraction. Red Skelton and Carol Burnett, Jack Paar and Johnny Carson, *What's My Line?* and *I've Got a Secret:* all are gone and few remembered, and none has been replaced. TV has become yet another instrument of social fragmentation, an anteroom to the World Wide Web in which we sit in separate cubicles, sovereign monads reigning over gated communities of the mind. Intelligent peo-ple who call themselves conservatives tell me this is progress, and I might believe them if I believed in progress. Instead, I surf the Web in search of tiny firms that sell flickering kinescopes of old game shows, and note with sadness the passing of the long-forgotten giants of the small screen. I wonder, too, what future encounters with their multicultural pasts will cause my brightly ironic Gen-X friends to suddenly start thinking of themselves as Americans. Will they remember *Seinfeld* the way I remember David Brinkley? Somehow I doubt it.

Weekly Standard 1997

PART THREE ~ DOWN TO THE CROSSROADS

Inner Chambers

L EAFING THROUGH THE INTRODUCTION TO THE COL-
lected correspondence of Felix Frankfurter and Oliver Wendell
Holmes, Jr., I found a passing reference to "the alleged Communist spy Alger Hiss." Time was when such lawyerly weaseling left me
speechless with anger. Now I just shrug. As Dostoyevsky, Whittaker
Chambers's favorite author, once put it, "Man gets used to everything,
the beast!" Alger Hiss was convicted of perjury in a court of law, and
everyone who knows anything about the Hiss case knows perfectly well
that he did what Chambers said he did. Allen Weinstein put the next-
to-last nail in the coffin in 1978 with the publication of *Perjury,* and the
coup de grâce came with the release by the National Security Agency of
intercepted Soviet cable traffic from the Forties revealing that Hiss flew
straight from Yalta to Moscow, where Andrei Vyshinsky personally
thanked him for his long years of service to the Soviet Union. But when
Hiss died, virtually no obituary writer was willing to say flat out that
He Did It, and Peter Jennings and Tom Brokaw both went so far as to
suggest that he was framed. Such was the nature of Alger Hiss's posthumous victory: by lying steadfastly for half a century, he succeeded in
hiding the truth behind the shadow of a doubt.

Today, long after the final collapse of the Soviet Union, we now
know that Chambers will be remembered not for having slandered a
prominent New Dealer, but for having told the truth about Communism at a time when few wanted to hear it. But Hiss's guilt was long
seen by many liberals as at best an open question, and throughout the
last decade and a half of his life, Chambers wandered in the wilder-
ness of public disrepute. His decision to testify before the House

Un-American Activities Committee had brought to an end his distinguished career as a magazine journalist; Henry Luce asked for his resignation from *Time,* for which he had written since 1939, and even after a jury convicted Hiss, no reputable magazine would consider hiring his accuser as a writer or editor. It was not merely that as an admitted ex-Communist, Chambers was by definition "controversial." He had also committed what many liberals, uneasily aware of the extent to which their own movement was tainted by Stalinism, saw as the ultimate act of heresy: he revealed that the administration of Franklin Roosevelt, the patron saint of American liberalism, had been infiltrated by Communists whose first loyalty was to the Soviet Union. For this, he could not be forgiven, since no ideology whose legitimacy is rooted in the myth of its own absolute rectitude can afford to admit having partaken of original sin.

Chambers then compounded his own offense by writing *Witness,* the 1952 memoir in which he expounded at length his belief that "the crisis of the Western world exists to the degree in which it is indifferent to God." Though he was not the first American to interpret the Cold War — and, by implication, modernity itself — as a struggle between faith in God and faith in man, it was his searing account of the struggle that reached the largest audience. *Witness* was serialized in the *Saturday Evening Post* and chosen as a main selection of the Book-of-the-Month Club; the trade edition was one of the ten best-selling books of 1952. That such a book should have found so vast a readership was even more disturbing to the thoroughly secularized liberal establishment, already shaken by the revelation that Hiss, who seemed the very personification of the fervent left-liberal idealism of the Thirties, had been a Soviet agent. Therein lay Chambers's immediate significance: for the first time since Roosevelt entered the White House in 1933, secular liberalism had a thoughtful, articulate opponent whom ordinary Americans took seriously.

It was for this reason that some liberals (though by no means all) chose to "respond" to *Witness* by smearing its author. "It can't be treated simply as a book," Mary McCarthy wrote to Hannah Arendt in 1952. "The great effort of this new Right is to get itself accepted as *normal,* and its publications as a *normal* part of publishing . . . and this, it seems to me, must be scotched, if it's not already too late." Arendt's response was to publish a savage review of *Witness* in the liberal Catholic magazine *Commonweal,* in which she declared that Chambers belonged "in a police state where people have been organized and split into two ever-changing categories: those who have the privilege to be informers and those who are dominated by the fear of being informed upon." In such a fashion did too many liberals turn their backs on anti-Communism, as the inconvenient truth about Alger Hiss and his fellow Communists slowly vanished beneath a sea of qualifications, evasions, and outright lies.

What also vanished was the truth about Whittaker Chambers. To be sure, his memory was kept bright by those who had known him in his post-trial days, not least those who had worked with him at *National Review* in the Fifties and the countless young Americans who had been converted to conservatism by reading *Witness.* But until the appearance of *Perjury,* Chambers was visible only through the glare of partisanship. To his enemies, he was the spiritual leader of the dark legion of reaction; to his admirers, he was a symbol of the great moral cause of the postwar era. More than a few conservatives were thus understandably unnerved when Allen Weinstein revealed that Chambers was, like all human beings, all too human: one suspects they preferred the symbol to the flawed, confused man himself.

I doubt that Sam Tanenhaus's long-awaited biography of Whittaker Chambers will change anyone's mind about whether Hiss or Chambers was telling the truth. Nor is it intended to do so (though Tanenhaus includes a devastatingly efficient six-page appendix summarizing the additional evidence against Hiss that has emerged in the five decades since his conviction). For *Whittaker Chambers: A Biography* is not a rehash of *United States of America v. Alger Hiss.* It is, rather, the richly detailed story of a representative modern man, one who embodied in his tortured person all the tensions and complexities of the Thirties, and I know of no book that does a better job of explaining that odious decade.

Modernity, as Tanenhaus reminds us, was Whittaker Chambers's birthright: he was taught from earliest childhood that there is no truth, and spent the rest of his life searching for it. His father was a bisexual magazine illustrator, his mother an arty, shabby-genteel agnostic. At Columbia University, he dazzled such teachers as Mark Van Doren (and such students as Lionel Trilling) with his literary gifts, but soon discovered that words alone could not fill the empty places in his soul. Tormented by inchoate homosexual longings, painfully aware of the squalor and misery in which the "other half" of America lived, Chambers sought deliverance in the secular religion that was Marxism, abandoning a promising career as a poet and translator to become a Communist journalist and, later, a spy. Idealism drove him into the arms of mass murderers, and idealism forced him in time to confront the enormity of what he and his Communist brethren had done: by choosing to testify against Alger Hiss, Chambers, in Arthur Koestler's striking phrase, "knowingly committed moral suicide to atone for the guilt of our generation."

All this is well known, at least in outline, to readers of *Witness* and *Perjury*. But Tanenhaus has put new factual flesh on the received view of Chambers, giving us, among many other invaluable things, the first fully convincing account of his college days — I came away from this book understanding at last why his fellow students admired him so extravagantly — and, no less important, the first adequate discussion of his famously stormy tenure at *Time:*

> Chambers was not reporting. He was explaining, reading political developments through the lens of Leninism. That lens collected its light from a narrow range of the spectrum, but the beam it threw on events was stunning in its clarity. Chambers overstated his case, often seeing dangers where they were not present. He was also not above crimping the evidence to suit his thesis. Still, he grasped, better than anyone else around him — and as well as any other American of the day — that the postwar world would be formed in the crucible of "power politics."

The drama, as is so often the case with biography, is in the details, which Tanenhaus supplies in abundance. What could be more potently symbolic than the fact (published here for the first time) that Chambers gave up the opportunity to translate the last volume of *A la re-*

cherche du temps perdu in order to go to work for *The New Masses*? And even when Tanenhaus revisits oft-tilled ground, as in his description of the Hiss perjury trials, he manages to make the familiar fresh. What could be more illustrative of Chambers's character than the fact that, as he waited for the first trial to get under way, he passed the time reading Dostoyevsky's *The Possessed* and W. H. Auden's *The Age of Anxiety*?

No small part of the strength of *Whittaker Chambers: A Biography* comes from its scrupulous avoidance of cheerleading. Indeed, I came away suspecting that Tanenhaus rather disliked Chambers, or at the very least found his Dostoyevskyan temperament unsympathetic. Yet there is no question in Tanenhaus's mind about Chambers's honesty, and he is just as certain that in spying for the Soviets, Chambers served an unambiguously evil end. The resulting detachment with which he considers Chambers's life and thought, while likely to unsettle conservative readers accustomed to thinking of the author of *Witness* as a latter-day saint, adds immeasurably to the book's vividness. Chambers's bisexuality is discussed frankly (though not salaciously), and his tendencies toward self-pity and self-dramatization are acknowledged straightforwardly.

TANENHAUS'S DETACHMENT ALSO SERVES HIM WELL IN ASSESS-ing Chambers's problematic stature as writer and thinker. He correctly points out that Chambers's interest in "the convergence of religion and politics . . . is what makes *Witness,* for all its morbid imagery and Slavic passions, a uniquely American book, for only in America do religious and political ideals become interchangeable, even indistinguishable." He acutely compares Chambers to Aleksandr Solzhenitsyn, noting that "Solzhenitsyn too would be misunderstood, his asperities interpreted as militant fanaticism." And his explanation of why Chambers proved incapable of finishing *The Losing Side,* his planned large-scale theoretical work on conservatism and Communism, seems to me exactly right:

> He wanted to create a myth of the universe, as Marx, Spengler, and Toynbee had done. Like them, Chambers had an authentic feel for history as poetic drama. But he lacked the intellectual requirements of a system builder. For all his immense reading and his considerable mental

strength, Chambers was neither a scholar nor a systematic thinker. . . .
His intellectual style was a hybrid of the autodidact's and the educated
publicist's. He was a forager of texts, who read widely and collected
memorable tag lines he employed as a form of illustrative shorthand,
filling out his intuitions and adding them to the accumulated wisdom of
his own experience. Much as Chambers deplored "attempts to explain
the Communist experience primarily in personal, psychological terms,"
it was the one thing he really knew how to do. And he had already done
it, in *Witness*.

It is, of course, impossible to consider Chambers solely as a writer or
a thinker. That is his tragedy. Like so many other men of the Thirties,
his life was cloven by history, and by his own fateful choice of action
over contemplation. Chambers the promising poet, Chambers the
gifted literary critic, Chambers the journalist of near-genius: all were
sacrificed on the altar of commitment. But the author of *Witness,* as
André Malraux truly said, did not return from hell with empty hands. If
anything justified Whittaker Chambers's acts of treason, it was his decision to tell the truth about them to the House Un-American Activities
Committee, whatever the personal cost; if anything justifies his youthful betrayal of his talent in the name of politics, it is the enduring
significance of *Witness,* which will be remembered not only as a classic
of American autobiography but as one of the founding documents of
postwar American conservatism.

Chambers's own place in the history of modern conservative thought
is easily defined: more than anyone else, he persuaded American conservatives that religious belief was central to the tradition they proposed to defend. "Political freedom, as the Western world has known it,
is only a political reading of the Bible," he wrote in *Witness.* "Religion
and freedom are indivisible. . . . Economics is not the central problem
of this century. It is a relative problem which can be solved in relative
ways. Faith is the central problem of this age." These words were anathema to laissez-faire individualists, who were far more concerned with
the rise of centralized government in America than the overall spiritual
condition of the West (and who for the same reason were in turn
anathema to Chambers, as his letters make surpassingly clear). But

while classical economic analysis would remain central to conservative dogmatics, it was in large part because of Chambers that the movement that crystallized around William F. Buckley, Jr., was from the outset committed to the proposition that, in Chambers's words, "God alone is the inciter and guarantor of freedom."

Whether or not conservatives of the twenty-first century will continue to share this certainty remains to be seen. One doubts, though, that Chambers would have been greatly surprised to learn that the movement at whose creation he was present had begun at century's end to doubt the central meaning of his witness. "I know that I am leaving the winning side for the losing side," he had famously declared in 1948, "but it is better to die on the losing side than to live under Communism." This pessimism, which disturbed many of his contemporaries, has come to seem all but inexplicable to those conservatives who fail to realize that when Chambers called the West "the losing side," he was speaking as much of the enemy within as the enemy without. His great fear was that his witness would prove vain, that America would be overwhelmed by the secular materialism it had uncomprehendingly embraced almost as completely as had the Soviet Union. One day late in 1952, as he lay in a hospital bed recovering from a heart attack, he was visited by a Passionist monk. "Father," he asked, "what am I to answer those people who keep writing me that I was wrong to write in *Witness* that I had left the winning side for the losing side? They say that by calling the West the losing side, I have implied that evil can ultimately overcome good." The monk replied, "Who says that the West deserves to be saved?"

As for the case of *United States of America v. Alger Hiss,* it was finally closed by the death of the ninety-two-year-old defendant, who presumably kept on lying to his last breath. Now he belongs to the ages, and one somehow doubts they will view his treachery as sympathetically as did his contemporaries. It is one of the not-so-minor consolations of history that Alger Hiss lived long enough to witness the protracted suicide of the evil empire he served so faithfully, and to see its archives thrown open to the searching scrutiny of Western scholars. Bit by bit, the record is being set straight on Communism, and the publication of

Whittaker Chambers: A Biography marks an essential step toward that goal. The journalists of today may casually subscribe to the notion that Whittaker Chambers was a man of dishonor, but the historians of tomorrow — guided by this indispensable book — will know better.

National Review 1997

The Great American Composer

WHEN BILL CLINTON AND AL GORE GAVE THEIR VIC-
tory speeches in Little Rock, the music used to introduce
them was Aaron Copland's *Appalachian Spring,* a piece,
one TV anchorman said, embodying "the spirit of the Midwest." Indeed, the composer of such "all-American" works as *Billy the Kid, Rodeo,*
and *Appalachian Spring* has become, by now, as iconic a figure in the
history of our culture as F. Scott Fitzgerald, Edward Hopper, or Louis
Armstrong. His music is played by symphony orchestras, marching
bands, and rock groups, danced to by ballet companies, used in TV
commercials, and performed on state occasions. If this country had an
official composer, it would be Copland.

There are numerous ironies in this circumstance, one of which is that
the "all-American" Copland was born in Brooklyn of Russian-Jewish
émigré parents, studied composition in Paris with an acolyte of Igor
Stravinsky, and was a homosexual and, during the Thirties, a fellow-
traveler of the American Communist party. More telling is the fact that,
despite his continuing popularity—or because of it—many critics today remain reluctant to treat Copland as a major composer. This is
mainly due to Copland's decision in the mid-Thirties to abandon the
high modernism of his youthful work in favor of a musical style of (in
his words) "imposed simplicity." The shift, which made him the most
successful classical composer in America, also brought into question his
artistic seriousness, and that question still echoes among those who
remain committed to the ideals of the musical avant-garde.

Surprisingly little of value has been written about any aspect of
Copland's life or work. No full-length biography has been published.

Copland: 1900 Through 1942 (1984) and *Copland: Since 1943* (1989), a two-volume "memoir" assembled by Vivian Perlis from oral-history transcripts and previously published writings, is guarded in its treatment of his politics and all but silent on his homosexuality. And Copland's correspondence, which (to judge by the handful of letters published in Humphrey Burton's 1994 biography of Leonard Bernstein) was both candid and illuminating, remains uncollected. The paradoxical result is that Copland is at once America's best-known composer and a mysterious figure. Until a full account appears of his eventful life, the history of American music in the twentieth century will have something of a blank spot at its center. Still, on the basis of what we do know, it is possible to speculate about what drove Copland, and to arrive at an estimate not only of his significance and influence but of his musical stature.

THE COMPOSER OF *FANFARE FOR THE COMMON MAN* GREW UP in what he would later describe as "a thoroughly bourgeois environment." His father, Harris Copland, emigrated from Lithuania in 1877 and settled in Brooklyn, where he opened a department store and married Sarah Mittenthal in 1885. The Coplands lived over the store with their five children, of whom Aaron, born in 1900, was the youngest. Aaron wrote his first songs as a child, determined to become a professional musician at fifteen, and began studying composition two years later; Rubin Goldmark, his first teacher, had been a student of Antonin Dvořák and gave his own students (another of whom was George Gershwin) a solidly conservative grounding in harmony, counterpoint, and sonata form.

Copland's memoirs say nothing about whether his "thoroughly bourgeois" parents disapproved of his decision to go into music, but they seem to have made no serious objection when he won a scholarship to Fontainebleau, a French summer school for American musicians. So Copland went to Paris in 1921, where he studied with Nadia Boulanger, the twentieth century's most influential teacher of composition. Though Boulanger was a master of traditional technique, she was also passionately committed to the cause of contemporary music, especially the neoclassical scores of Igor Stravinsky, and was firmly post-

Wagnerian in her stylistic orientation; her taste and methods accorded with Copland's anti-Romantic inclinations, and he quickly became her star pupil.

Copland's progress under Boulanger was so swift that his graduation piece, the Symphony for Organ and Orchestra, was premiered in 1925 by Walter Damrosch and the New York Symphony, and performed again shortly thereafter by Serge Koussevitzky and the Boston Symphony — a heady accomplishment for a twenty-four-year-old who had never before heard any of his music played by an orchestra. Though it now comes across as a thoroughly accessible example of mid-Twenties modernism, the Organ Symphony shocked its first listeners with its tart harmonies and jazz-derived rhythms. "Ladies and gentlemen," Damrosch told his horrified concert-hall audience, "I am sure that if a gifted young man can write a symphony like this at twenty-three, within five years he will be ready to commit murder."

If Damrosch's widely reported *mot* brought Copland his first national publicity, the work itself had a galvanizing effect on his contemporaries. "The piece that opened the whole door to me," reminisced Virgil Thomson many decades later, "was that Organ Symphony of Aaron's. I thought that it was the voice of America in our generation." Thomson was responding both to the musical merits of the Organ Symphony and to the fact that it was among the first large-scale works by an American composer to owe nothing to the German Romantic tradition that had dominated American musical life throughout the nineteenth century. Copland was not, of course, the first to turn his back on this tradition. Charles Ives began composing in a proto-modernist style shortly after the turn of the century, and Charles Griffes incorporated Debussyan techniques into his music starting in 1911. But Ives remained isolated throughout his composing life, and Griffes died too young fully to realize his potential. Copland, by contrast, came along at a time when young American composers were looking both for a new style and for a leader, and in the wake of the Organ Symphony's premiere he emerged not only as a composer of promise but also as a musical entrepreneur: he organized concerts, wrote criticism, taught composition and music appreciation, encouraged young talents to study with Nadia Boulanger, and recommended their scores to conductors like Koussevitzky, who performed Copland's own music regularly from 1925 on.

All this activity served a larger goal: advancing Copland's vision of a music that would be international in appeal yet unmistakably reflective of the American national character. "Our concern," he wrote later,

> was not with the quotable hymn or spiritual: we wanted to find a music that would speak of universal things in a vernacular of American speech rhythms. We wanted to write music on a level that left popular music far behind — music with a largeness of utterance wholly representative of the country that Whitman had envisaged.

For elements of this American style, Copland searched both at home and abroad. In his Piano Concerto (1926) and Symphonic Ode (1927–29), he sought to combine the harmonic clarity and rhythmic vitality of Stravinsky's neoclassical scores with the "largeness of utterance" found in the symphonies of Gustav Mahler (another composer to whom he had been introduced by Boulanger), coloring the whole with the syncopations and blues-inflected melodies of jazz. By the early Thirties, the jazz was mostly gone, and the Mahleresque grandiosity had been replaced by the laconic approach of such tightly organized works as the Piano Variations (1930) and Short Symphony (1933). Yet all these pieces were strikingly individual and recognizably American in tone, and they established Copland as the most important American composer of his generation.

THUS FAR, THE OUTLINES OF COPLAND'S STORY ARE FAMILIAR to anyone with more than a casual awareness of the history of American music. But starting in the Thirties, the received version of Copland's life — one the composer himself recounted on numerous occasions — diverges from the facts.

According to Copland's own account, he came in time to feel dissatisfied with the failure of ordinary American concertgoers to respond to his music, and resolved to change his style accordingly:

> The old "special" public of the modern music concerts [of the Twenties] had fallen away, and the conventional concert public continued

apathetic or indifferent to anything but the established classics. . . . I felt that it was worth the effort to see if I couldn't say what I had to say in the simplest possible terms.

The result was *El salón México* (1933–36), a musical portrait of a visit to a "popular-type" dance hall in Mexico City. Based on folk melodies, *El salón México* contains all the fingerprints of the composer's "modernist" style—the angular rhythms and shifting time signatures, the bright, brassy orchestral palette, the piquant bitonal harmonies—presented in a simplified, more readily appealing form. *El salón México* was an immediate success: within a year of its publication, it had been performed by sixteen American orchestras (including two radio orchestras) and five foreign orchestras, and it remains to this day one of the most popular orchestral pieces ever written by an American composer.

Copland subsequently wrote many other "American-style" works aimed at a popular audience, including the ballets *Billy the Kid* (1938, choreographed by Eugene Loring) and *Rodeo* (1942, choreographed by Agnes de Mille); the scores for the Hollywood films *Of Mice and Men* (1939), *Our Town* (1940), *The Red Pony* (1948), and *The Heiress* (1948); and several shorter pieces for orchestra, among them *Prairie Journal* (1937), *An Outdoor Overture* (1938), *John Henry* (1940), *Lincoln Portrait* (1942), the ubiquitous *Fanfare for the Common Man* (1942), and *Letter from Home* (1943). Though some of these pieces are of greater musical interest than others, all are beautifully crafted, and, taken together, they constitute, in Virgil Thomson's words, "a high-level contribution to light music that may well be [Copland's] most valued legacy." But Copland's decision to simplify his musical language arose from more than just an understandable desire to reach out to a larger (and more remunerative) audience. At least in part and at least at first, it also constituted a specifically political statement, one that ran parallel to the cultural policies of the American Communist party in the mid-Thirties.

Copland had been interested in left-wing politics since 1919, when he played piano at dances held at Brooklyn's Finnish Socialist Hall and learned about the philosophy of Eugene V. Debs from the clarinet player in the house band. In 1930 he helped to organize the Group Theater, where he met the playwright Clifford Odets, the director Elia Kazan, and various other young radicals. Starting in 1934, Copland became involved with numerous Communist-controlled groups, including the Composers Collective of New York (whose members included the Stalinist composer Marc Blitzstein), and began writing for the *New Masses*, the Communist-party periodical. In its pages he reviewed the *Workers' Song Book No. 1* of the Composers' Collective (to which he had contributed) and published a "mass song" called *Into the Streets May First*.

The key date in Copland's political life, however, was 1935, the year that the Moscow-directed Communist International (Comintern) proclaimed the establishment of the Popular Front. This was the "antifascist" alliance through which the Soviet Union sought to coopt liberals in America and elsewhere by, among other things, encouraging the development of a Stalinist-shaped middlebrow culture, comparable in its stultifying high-mindedness and philistine utilitarianism to the "socialist realism" imposed on Soviet artists by the Kremlin. To speak of American culture in the Thirties is in large part to speak of the fruits of the Popular Front and its adherents, both conscious and unconscious: the plays of Odets and Lillian Hellman, the novels of Steinbeck, the poetry of Archibald MacLeish — and, inevitably, the music of Aaron Copland.

Though Copland had begun work on *El salón México* prior to 1935, the shift of party policy in that year must surely have struck him as opportune. His own public statements on the virtues of proletarian art had been ambiguous at best; he was, it seems, understandably uncomfortable with the idea of using his music as a weapon in the fight against capitalism. Now the advent of the Popular Front, according to which the bourgeois artist was no longer to be considered a class enemy of the revolutionary cause, simultaneously solved Copland's political problem and gave him a new sense of artistic direction. In Vivian Perlis's revealing words:

> Never again would Copland attempt to reach a more popular audience with a "workers' song" or for political reasons. When the Popular Front came along in 1935, bringing a wider recognition and apprecia-

tion of American folk music, the way was opened for Copland to adopt a simpler, more direct music style using quotation or simulation of folk tunes in productions outside the concert hall—ballet, theater, radio, and film.

While Copland claimed never to have joined the Communist party, he remained close to its members throughout the Thirties and Forties, composing the score for the 1943 pro-Soviet Hollywood movie *North Star* (written by Lillian Hellman), lending his name to numerous Communist-front organizations (in some cases apparently at the behest of Serge Koussevitzky), and playing a prominent part in the Soviet-controlled Waldorf Peace Conference of 1949.

It was thus predictable that Copland would later be tarred with the same critical brush as the Steinbecks and Blitzsteins, and that his reputation as a serious artist would suffer as a result. But there was a crucial difference between the composer of *El salón México* and the author of *The Grapes of Wrath:* Copland knew he was writing light music, while Steinbeck believed himself to be writing a great novel. And whatever his initial reasons for simplifying his style, Copland did not intend his light pieces to be musically unserious, merely accessible. "I like to think," he told a friend in 1943, "that I have touched off for myself and others a kind of musical naturalness that we have badly needed."

In any case, the acid test of Copland's seriousness is not to be found in his lighter pieces, but in the "abstract" compositions that he also produced during the middle years of his career, ranging from such large-scale utterances as the Piano Sonata (1939–41) and Third Symphony (1944–46) to the more intimate Violin Sonata (1942–43) and *Twelve Poems of Emily Dickinson* (1944–50). These works are self-evidently the work of the "all-American" composer of *Billy the Kid.* But they are sparer in texture and more concentrated in expression. Here, the open-prairie plainness of the light music has been transposed into a minor key, and there can be little doubt that the composer's psychic "subject matter" is the loneliness and alienation of urban life: in a piece like the masterly *Quiet City* (1941), the grandly proclamatory gestures of the early works have been transformed into a controlled yet intensely melancholy lyricism. And here, too, Copland's Jewishness came to the fore: the long arches of melody heard in the middle-period music are like modern songs of lamentation, rooted in the cantillations of a much older culture. "I thought he was a prophet calling out to Israel," Virgil Thomson told Vivian Perlis, "the Jewish preacher telling people right and wrong."

Interestingly, Copland sought to fuse his popular and "serious" manners in several of his middle-period works, most notably the Third Symphony, the scores for *Our Town* and *The Heiress,* the Clarinet Concert composed for Benny Goodman (1947–48), and the opera *The Tender Land* (1952–54). But it is in his score for Martha Graham's *Appalachian Spring* (1943–44) that Copland's two musical sides achieve their fullest synthesis: in this piece, his light-music style is elevated to greatness by an extreme refinement of means and intent. Scored with uncanny transparency for an ensemble of thirteen instruments, *Appalachian Spring* is Copland's masterpiece, a work comparable in quality to the ballet scores of Stravinsky and Tchaikovsky.

To praise the music of Copland's middle period is not to dismiss as unimportant his earlier works, some of which, the Piano Variations and Short Symphony in particular, are no less masterly than *Appalachian Spring* or *Quiet City.* But the overall superiority of the middle-period music lies in its increased economy and directness — qualities that were brought out in Copland by his decision to adopt a populist style. Whether he made that decision for personal or for political reasons (more likely, for some mixture of the two), the fact is that in turning away from the high modernism of his youth, Copland found his true voice as a composer.

IT WAS NOT UNTIL AFTER THE WALDORF CONFERENCE IN 1949, at which he was reportedly shocked by the conduct of the Soviet composer Dmitri Shostakovich (who announced under painfully obvious duress that "Stravinsky is not a good composer — he does not compose for the masses"), that Copland ceased to involve himself in leftist causes. By this time, however, his political activities had come to the attention of anti-Communist investigators. He was listed in *Red Channels,* a booklet containing the names of suspected Communists in the broadcast media, and his *Lincoln Portrait* was subsequently dropped from the program of Dwight Eisenhower's inaugural concert in 1952; the following year, he was interrogated by Senator Joseph R. McCarthy. Thereafter, he had nothing to say about politics, save to his closest friends.* Even at the height of the McCarthy era, however, Copland remained a genuinely popular composer. Ironically, his greatest difficulties in the postwar period lay not with the public, which seemed ready enough to forgive him his politics, but with his colleagues, who may or may not have disapproved of his politics but who could not forgive him his popularity. As far back as *El salón México,* many of Copland's contemporaries had begun to view him as a traitor to the modernist cause. By 1970, Leonard Bernstein, his beloved friend and loyal interpreter, wrote ruefully that young musicians, among whom the "Schoenberg syndrome" had taken hold, had "gradually stopped flocking to Aaron."

Like Stravinsky, Copland did seek in later life to master the international language of postwar modernism, producing a series of works that make highly personal use of the twelve-tone method of composition associated with the name of Arnold Schoenberg. But none of these pieces found favor with concertgoers, and it is possible that the seeming resurgence of creativity inspired by his flirtation with serialism actually served to mask a loss of inspiration. Starting in the Fifties, Copland launched a second career as a guest conductor of symphony orchestras; he devoted less time and energy to composing, and after the early Seventies he produced nothing but fragments. The reason for Copland's decline as a composer may also have been organic. From the Seventies on, his lapses of memory were the subject of concerned talk in the musical community, and they eventually forced him to stop conducting in 1982; though he subsequently published his memoirs, it became known that he was suffering from Alzheimer's disease. He died in 1990, not long after Leonard Bernstein.

*The sections of Copland's memoirs dealing with political matters were written not by him but by Vivian Perlis, and were not published until after the onset of Alzheimer's disease had forced him to stop making all but the most perfunctory public appearances.

AROUND THE TIME AARON COPLAND STOPPED COMPOSING, THE critic Samuel Lipman wrote: "We have come to the end of a chapter in American music, as we have come to the end of a chapter in our national life. In music, if nowhere else, internationalism has triumphed, and we are all homogenized. Whatever the future shape of American music, it will not follow in the directions toward which Aaron Copland's music once seemed to lead."

But the ensuing years have given grounds to qualify Lipman's prediction. The future of American music, in fact, now seems to be leading back to Copland. Young American composers, themselves increasingly disenchanted with the "triumph" of internationalism, are once again quick to cite him as an influence, and his music is played more widely than ever before. Of course it may be that in our present age of identity politics, Copland serves a number of extramusical agendas. If so, however, he serves them illegitimately, for Copland was his own melting pot. No "queer theory" can account for his musical achievement; no cultural politician can explain how he drew from the stifling banality of the Popular Front the inspiration for his deservedly most memorable works. The only explanation is genius.

Whatever the future brings, its historians will record that Aaron Copland's music served as the model for the modern American style of classical composition. In developing that style, he proved yet again the truth of Ralph Vaughan Williams's dictum that "if the roots of your art are firmly planted in your own soil and that soil has anything individual to give you, you may still gain the whole world and not lose your own soul." By expressing the American national character in music, Copland gave full expression to his own genius, and so created masterpieces of universal appeal that continue to speak to listeners around the world. He is, in every sense, the great American composer.

Commentary 1997

The Man Who Watched Bogart

AMONG MY PRIZED POSSESSIONS IS A BATTERED COPY OF Robert Warshow's *The Immediate Experience: Movies, Comics, Theatre, and Other Aspects of Popular Culture,* an obscure collection of critical essays published in 1962 to no special acclaim. I doubt it sold more than a couple of hundred copies, and I know it didn't go over big in Kansas City, because mine is a discarded library copy, and the faded date-due stamps on the first page indicate that between 1962 and 1979, the year in which I acquired it, *The Immediate Experience* was checked out just fifteen times, the last in 1972.

That *The Immediate Experience* was published at all is the unlikeliest of stories, for Warshow, though greatly admired by his colleagues, was anything but famous. A bred-in-the-bone New York Jew and second-generation socialist, he made his living as an editor for *Commentary* and a writer for *Commentary, The Nation,* and *Partisan Review,* mostly about film. His essays did not go entirely unnoticed beyond the tiny circle of influential readers of those legendary little magazines, and in 1955, he was invited to write for the *New Yorker.* He died the next day of a heart attack, aged thirty-seven. Seven years later, Warshow's desolated friends assembled nineteen of his essays, virtually the whole of his slender output, and Doubleday published the resulting book with an introduction by Lionel Trilling. Five years after that, Norman Podhoretz wrote vividly about Warshow in *Making It,* his memoir of life among the New York literariat. But lasting critical reputations are rarely based on a single volume of essays, however brilliant, and Warshow's star soon faced to near-black. For a long time, the only people likely to know his name were aging neoconservatives and abnormally well-read film buffs.

Not that such folk are mutually exclusive, but they are rarely seen at the same cocktail parties, and it is a decided oddity that the man whom Podhoretz called "one of the best essayists in the English language" also figures prominently in the pages of *Roger Ebert's Book of Film,* an anthology whose other contributors include Rex Reed, Mario Puzo, and John Waters.

Ebert's collection was until recently the only volume in print containing any of Warshow's essays, and while that one, "The Gangster as Tragic Hero," ranked among his best, it conveyed only a limited sense of what he was about. So it was with real surprise that I learned of the appearance of an expanded edition of *The Immediate Experience* containing the complete text of the original book, eight previously uncollected pieces by Warshow, and a newly commissioned pair of accompanying essays by David Denby, the film critic of the *New Yorker,* and Stanley Cavell, a philosopher who also writes about film. I can think of no essay collection of the past half-century more richly deserving of republication—and none more likely to be misunderstood.

TO THE EXTENT THAT WARSHOW IS REMEMBERED TODAY, IT IS for what he wrote about the movies. Two of his pieces, "The Gangster as Tragic Hero" (1948) and "The Westerner" (1954), continue to be cited in the scholarly literature on film, with good reason.* Warshow was one of the first American intellectuals to pay sustained attention to those over-familiar genres, and what he had to say about them has not yet lost its ability to command our attention:

> The gangster is lonely and melancholy, and can give the impression of a profound worldly wisdom. He appeals most to adolescents with their impatience and their feeling of being outsiders, but more generally he appeals to that side of all of us which refuses to believe in the "normal" possibilities of happiness and achievement; the gangster is the "no" to that great American "yes" which is stamped so big over our official culture and yet has so little to do with the way we really feel about our

---

* "The Westerner," for instance, is cited in *The Oxford History of World Cinema,* though the passage in question is both misquoted and wrongly attributed to "The Gangster as Tragic Hero." (In addition, Warshow's name is misspelled.)

lives. . . . The Western hero, by contrast, is a figure of repose. He resembles the gangster in being lonely and to some degree melancholy. But his melancholy comes from the "simple" recognition that life is unavoidably serious, not from the disproportions of his own temperament. And his loneliness is organic, not imposed on him by his situation but belonging to him intimately and testifying to his completeness.

The power of "The Westerner" arises from the way Warshow uses his experience as a moviegoer to illuminate a two-sided aspect of the American national character—the untragic optimism to which we are so deeply committed as a people, even when experience causes us to question it as individuals. Simply written yet full of implication, "The Westerner" is a masterly example of the critic's art, as fresh today as it was a half-century ago. But what the modern reader may not realize is just how unusual it was a half-century ago. Nowadays, we take it for granted that the oaters of John Wayne and Randolph Scott have something interesting, even important, to tell us about ourselves and our country; indeed, to dissent from that orthodoxy is to court excommunication from certain circles of academe. In 1954, though, few American critics were prepared to take lowbrow movies seriously, and fewer still wrote about them with Warshow's rigorous, laconic clarity.

Eleven of the nineteen essays included in the original edition of *The Immediate Experience,* and one of the newly collected pieces, are about film, and it seems fairly clear from the choice of Denby and Cavell to introduce it that Harvard University Press regards the book primarily as a contribution to the literature of film studies. But as the subtitle of his book indicates, Warshow was interested in a wider range of topics, though most of them, from the "sick" humor of *Mad* magazine to the middlebrow dramaturgy of Arthur Miller, fit into the pigeonhole of what we now unapologetically refer to as "pop culture." David Denby describes Warshow as "one of the inventors" of the genre of pop-culture criticism. In fact, it was more or less singlehandedly invented by George Orwell, the writer to whom he can most usefully be compared (as Lionel Trilling did in his introduction to *The Immediate Experience*). Orwell's pithy essays about such plebeian topics as boys'-school stories and pornographic postcards taught Warshow's generation of critics how popular culture could be used as a prism through which to view and interpret modern life. From Orwell, too, they learned to write straightforwardly and personally, and with a scrupulous, even self-conscious honesty made necessary by their increasingly problematic relationship to an intellectual class enthralled by Communism, a political movement built on lies.

Warshow, like Orwell, was a left-wing anti-Communist, an affiliation that is (if possible) even less fashionable today than in the Thirties and early Forties, though for a different reason. Back then, a great many American artists and intellectuals were unabashedly in love with Joseph Stalin, and happily blacklisted those who dared to disagree. Today, one is hard pressed to find a leftist prepared to so much as acknowledge Stalin's existence, much less hint at the damning fact that his ardent admirers once played a hugely influential role in the shaping of American popular culture. Certainly the anonymous author of the flap copy for the new edition of *The Immediate Experience* is unwilling to admit any such thing, saying only that, according to Warshow, "a 'disastrous vulgarization of intellectual life' [had] corrupted American liberalism from the 1930s to the 1950s." Conspicuously missing from this careful filleting of Warshow's thought is the word "Stalinism," an omission that would have enraged the man who wrote bluntly and fearlessly of the corrosive effects of "the mass culture of Stalinist liberalism" on American intellectual life: "In the '30s radicalism entered upon an age of organized mass disingenuousness, when every act and every idea had behind it some 'larger consideration' which destroyed its honesty and its meaning. Everyone became a *professional* politician, acting within a framework of 'realism' that tended to make political activity an end in itself. The half-truth was elevated to the position of a principle, and in the end the half-truth, in itself, became more desirable than the whole truth."

Merely to praise Warshow as a great film critic is to ignore the extent to which all his criticism was concerned with the long-term effects on American culture of the loose coalition of liberals, Stalinist fellow travelers, and full-fledged Communists known as the Popular Front. Among the many undertakings of this unholy alliance was the manufacture of watered-down pop-culture artifacts intended to teach educated Americans the necessity of Soviet-style "anti-Fascism," which sympathetic critics duly praised as high art. The insidious and inevitable result of such activity, Warshow argued, was to corrupt art, as well as liberalism itself: "The whole level of thought and discussion, the level of culture itself, had been lowered. . . . *The Grapes of Wrath* was a great novel. Eventually, *Confessions of a Nazi Spy* was a serious movie and 'Ballad for Americans' was an inspired song. The mass culture of the educated classes — the culture of the 'middle-brow,' as it has sometimes been called — had come into existence."

It was out of this insight that Warshow drew his finest essay, "The 'Idealism' of Julius and Ethel Rosenberg," originally published in *Commentary* in 1953, in which he turned his unsparing gaze on the letters exchanged in prison by the martyrs of the postwar left as they awaited execution for having passed atomic secrets to the Soviet Union. For Warshow, the Rosenbergs were the ultimate embodiment of the Popular Front, a robot couple incapable of harboring any unpolitical opinions whatsoever, even about baseball: "It's that indomitable spirit that has endeared [the Brooklyn Dodgers] to so many. But it is chiefly in their outstanding contribution to the eradication of racial prejudice that they have covered themselves with glory." In such crude fatuities, Warshow heard the death knell of American liberalism:

> Whether he cheers the Yankees or the Dodgers, whether he damns Franklin Roosevelt as a warmonger or adores him as the champion of human rights, the Communist is always celebrating the same thing: the great empty Idea which has taken on the outlines of his personality. Communists are still "idealists" — perhaps all the more so because their "idealism" is by now almost entirely without content — and the surprising degree of sympathy and even respect that they can command among liberals is partly to be explained by the liberal belief that "idealism" in itself is a virtue.

Small wonder it took so long for *The Immediate Experience* to be reprinted. Fifty years later, the cold-eyed honesty of "The 'Idealism' of Julius and Ethel Rosenberg" is still capable of making liberals squirm. Judith Shulevitz, writing in the *New York Times Book Review,* called it "amazingly nasty." But David Denby, for all his obvious discomfort with Warshow's directness, is at least prepared to openly acknowledge that at a time when many liberals "remained sympathetic to the Communist 'experiment' and were infuriatingly slow to comprehend that they were supporting the cause of murder," Warshow was dead right about the pernicious effects of Stalinism on American culture: "The horror of American Stalinism, he says again and again, is that it prevents its adherents from having any kind of direct and honest relationship to experience. . . . The culture that resulted from this effort—a spreading rot of liberal middle-brow kitsch—was also prevented by will and by habit from knowing that it was lying."

STANLEY CAVELL'S EPILOGUE TO *THE IMMEDIATE EXPERIENCE*, as befits a professional philosopher, is more than a little bit turgid, but it starts off with a sentence with which I could not agree more: "Robert Warshow's *The Immediate Experience* is one of those books whose discovery, early or late, can create so specific a feeling of personal gratitude for its existence that it is almost a surprise to learn that others know how good it is." I know just what he means. Back when I was still trying to decide what kind of writer I wanted to be, looking for mentors and trying on styles for size, his plain speaking hit me right between the eyes.

Warshow was fascinated by popular culture, but he wrote about it with a sense of proportion, something lacking in most of the other critics whose work I was reading in the Seventies. He showed how it was possible to appreciate, say, the movies of Howard Hawks—even to love them—without jumping to the conclusion that the director of *The Big Sleep* and *To Have and Have Not* was just as good as Shakespeare:

> I have had enough serious interest in the products of the "higher" arts to be very sharply aware that the impulse which leads me to a Humphrey Bogart movie has little in common with the impulse which leads me to the novels of Henry James or the poetry of T. S. Eliot. That there is a connection between the two impulses I do not doubt, but the connection is not adequately summed up in the statement that the Bogart movie and the Eliot poem are both forms of art. To define that

connection seems to me one of the tasks of film criticism, and the definition must be first of all a personal one. A man watches a movie, and the critic must acknowledge that he is that man.

His unfaked faithfulness to the immediate experience of the unpretentious genre films he loved stands in stark contrast to the deep-dyed falseness of the Popular Front liberals who, like the Rosenbergs, approved only of art, good or bad, that served their political ends—an attitude that has since metamorphosed into what we now call political correctness. In addition to teaching me how to write about pop culture, his essays demonstrated how the Stalinist habit of mind not only survived its evil inventor but became part of the very essence of postmodern thought. To have read *The Immediate Experience* as a young man was to know ever after, in the fullest possible sense, what it means to say—and to believe—that the personal is political. I have made plenty of mistakes in my life, but not that one: Robert Warshow inoculated me against it, forever.

Weekly Standard 2002

Scoundrel Time

ERE THEY COME AGAIN: DASHIELL HAMMETT AND Lillian Hellman, the Nick and Nora of the limousine left, the ultimate fun couple of a decade when martinis before breakfast were de rigueur and mass murder was politically correct so long as the KGB was picking the victims. Even under the best of circumstances, the prospect of wading once more into the moral muck of the Hammett-Hellman ménage turns the stomach, and the subtitle of Joan Mellen's dual biography, the first book to be based on Hellman's private papers, isn't exactly encouraging: surely it's a bit late in the day to be paying homage to "the legendary passion of Lillian Hellman and Dashiell Hammett," which in point of fact appears to have been worthy of Krafft-Ebing at his most picturesque.

In fact, Mellen does seem at times to be half in love with Hammett and Hellman, especially the latter. "Often in the perilous crossings between men and women," she writes in her preface, "I found myself wondering: what would Lily do? And it always comes back to me. She would act; she would throw her hat into the ring, take a stand, present herself, draw on her strengths: wit, great intelligence, perseverance, and the inspiration and courage she had learned from Hammett, who had taught her to trust no authority, to do her damnedest to outsmart a cynical and corrupt society." But the sticky heroine-worship of this passage is not borne out by the bulk of *Hellman and Hammett,* whose cumulative effect is devastating.

One wonders if Mellen's shifting tone is to some extent a reflection of her own disillusionment. Time was, after all, when a great many people saw Hellman and Hammett as heroic figures. Feminists in particular, as

Mellen points out, have been much enamored of their affair, at least the version of it enshrined in Hellman's four volumes of famously unreliable reminiscence. "Feminists thought: here was a woman who had not married the great love of her life, had not bought into the motherhood myth, who was too shrewd not to know a woman can't have it all, and who had produced meaningful work." But Mellen, having sifted through Hellman's diaries and correspondence, has come to a very different conclusion. In the memoirs, she argues, Hellman spun out of whole cloth "what she had been denied: a lifelong emotional attachment with a man, not the actual one she had with Hammett, but one more romantic."

According to Mellen, Hellman was a hopelessly premodern woman whose whole life was shaped by the belief that she was unattractive. Once she realized that the alcoholic, wildly promiscuous Hammett (who comes across here as the next worst thing to a sociopath) would never commit himself fully to her, she decided that "if she could not have Hammett, she would become him. She would behave exactly as he did, even as she would teach herself to write in his style. Only thus could she avoid the danger of becoming merely the wallflower, the homely woman ever grateful, waiting for him to beckon her to his temporarily unoccupied bed."

This overly deterministic thesis has the unconvincing effect of explaining away the sort of bad behavior whose true explanation is to be found in bad character. Even so, it does not tempt Mellen to whitewash the thuggish conduct of her subjects, whether in affairs of the heart or in politics. Many younger readers are doubtless unaware that the authors of *The Children's Hour* and *The Maltese Falcon* were unregenerate Stalinists, and they may well find it instructive to learn that Hellman and Hammett publicly endorsed the verdicts in the Moscow purge trials, signed a petition (written by Hammett and dated nine days before the Hitler-Stalin pact) stating that only "fascists" and "reactionaries" could have been responsible for the "fantastic falsehood that the U.S.S.R. and the totalitarian states are basically alike," and at no time in their later lives recanted their oft-stated belief that the Soviet Union under Stalin was, in Hellman's words, "the ideal democratic state."

Here again, Mellen's efforts to show how two presumably intelligent people could have gobbled such hogwash are too pat: she contends that Hammett, having given up writing after the publication in 1934 of *The Thin Man,* took up Stalinism as a way of lending meaning to "a life devoid of purpose," and that Hellman went along mainly as "a means of sharing life with him, ingratiating herself as she could not as a wife." But to her credit, Mellen does not pretend that the American Communist party was anything other than "a crude transmission belt for Stalin's dictates, a carbon copy of his authoritarian rule," or that the willingness of Hammett and Hellman to do its bidding, whatever their inner motivations, was anything other than contemptible.

AS A CASE STUDY IN PSYCHOPATHOLOGY, *HELLMAN AND Hammett* is engrossing, if repetitious; as a portrait of applied Stalinism, it is frank and forthright. What it fails to do is make a persuasive case that Lillian Hellman still matters. Hammett's place in American literature is secure, though minor: he and Raymond Chandler will always be remembered as the Washington and Lincoln of detective fiction. Not so Hellman. Her once-popular memoirs can no longer be taken seriously (least of all as records of fact), while her plays hardly rise above the level of political cartoons — one can almost see the captions printed in big block letters across the chests of the characters. What life they have, ironically enough, derives from their shrewd use of the forms of bourgeois melodrama. (It was not for nothing that George S. Kaufman, a man who knew a thing or two about commercial theater, responded to *The Little Foxes* by sending Hellman a three-word telegram: "That's telling them.")

In the end, Hellman was no more loyal to her art than she was to anything or anyone else, except for Stalin, whom she revered to the bitter end. Much the same thing could just as easily be said of Dashiell Hammett, of course; once he stopped writing, he became a spiritual corpse responsive only to the call of Johnnie Walker Red, prostitutes, and Communism. Perhaps that is the best explanation of why these two coldhearted creatures cleaved to each other through thick and (mostly) thin: they had their love of power politics to keep them warm.

New York Times Book Review 1996

Cradle of Lies

S IX DECADES AFTER ITS OPENING NIGHT, MARC BLITZ-
stein's *The Cradle Will Rock* remains one of the most celebrated
events in the annals of Broadway. Orson Welles, the director,
and John Houseman, the producer, had originally intended to present
Blitzstein's pro-union musical under the auspices of Project #891,
the classical-theater wing of the New Deal's Federal Theatre Project
(FTP). But when the Works Progress Administration (WPA) — the
New Deal relief agency of which the FTP was a part — canceled the
premiere, the cast marched twenty-one blocks to another theater. There
an improvised performance, accompanied by the composer on a rented
piano, was given before a crowd of passionate supporters.

The story of *Cradle*'s premiere has been told many times, most memorably in *Run-through,* the first volume of Houseman's memoirs. Now
it has been filmed by the leftist actor-director Tim Robbins with a cast
whose members include such Hollywood luminaries as John Cusack,
Bill Murray, Vanessa Redgrave, and Susan Sarandon. Though the reviews of *Cradle Will Rock* (as the film is titled) were mixed, many
prestigious critics, ranging from Janet Maslin of the *New York Times* and
Anthony Lane of the *New Yorker* to John Simon of *National Review,*
praised it enthusiastically.

The credits describe *Cradle Will Rock* as "a (mostly) true story."
Though Robbins has made no secret of his having fictionalized real
events, most commentators took it for granted that his script was essentially faithful to what happened in 1937 and that (in Simon's words)
"despite some oversimplification, the film works." Whether *Cradle Will
Rock* "works" is a matter of opinion, but the word "oversimplification"

is a gross understatement. Except for the names of some of the participants and the use of excerpts from Blitzstein's score, virtually every
aspect of Robbins's script varies significantly, often drastically, and always tendentiously from the historical record. The real story of how
The Cradle Will Rock came to Broadway is both more nuanced and far
less heroic than the version that has passed into American theatrical
folklore and that Robbins has used as the basis for his film.

The Works Progress Administration, founded in 1935, was charged
by Congress with creating federally funded jobs programs for healthy,
non-handicapped Americans who were unable to find work during the
Great Depression. Harry Hopkins, the confidant of Franklin Roosevelt
who administered the WPA, created a white-collar division intended to
provide employment for writers, musicians, artists, and actors; under
its rubric, Hallie Flanagan, who ran an experimental theater program at
Vassar, was invited to organize the Federal Theatre Project, which hired
out-of-work actors and other professionals to present plays throughout
the country for free or nominal admission.

Flanagan was deeply committed to the ideal of a socially relevant
theater. In 1926, she had used a Guggenheim fellowship to study theatrical techniques in the Soviet Union; six years later, she co-authored a
stage version of *Can You Make Out Their Voices?* a proletarian short
story by Whittaker Chambers, then an open member of the Communist party. The story had been originally published in the *New Masses,*
the party-controlled magazine that Chambers briefly edited before em-
barking on his underground career as a Soviet spy.

Not surprisingly, the FTP reflected Flanagan's own "socially conscious" priorities. Though she claimed, then and later, that no more
than 10 percent of its productions were politically oriented (a con-
venient assertion whose basis in fact has never been established), it
was the newly commissioned political plays, most notably such pro-
Roosevelt productions as *Triple-A Plowed Under, One-Third of a Nation,*
and *Power,* theatrical documentaries known as Living Newspapers, that
attracted the greatest attention. Of *Power,* Harry Hopkins said: "People
will say it's propaganda. Well, I say what of it? It's propaganda to
educate the consumer who's paying for power. It's about time someone
had some propaganda for him. . . . I want this play and plays like it

done from one end of the country to the other." These frankly partisan productions soon brought the FTP to the attention of Republicans in Congress, who already suspected (correctly) that Flanagan was seeking to create a permanent, federally funded national theater under the guise of a temporary relief project. Ironically, the situation was brought to a head by Project #891, one of the few FTP units specifically charged with presenting *non*-political plays.

Project #891 was launched by Orson Welles and John Houseman in the wake of the success of their all-black version of *Macbeth,* produced in Harlem in 1936 by the FTP's Negro Theatre Unit. Flanagan then allowed the two men to start their own FTP troupe, based on Broadway at Maxine Elliott's Theater and devoted to classical revivals. They responded with a brilliantly innovative version of Christopher Marlowe's *Doctor Faustus* and *Horse Eats Hat,* a zany adaptation by the dance critic Edwin Denby of Eugène Labiche's *The Italian Straw Hat.*

It was at this point that Welles and Houseman, taking a sharp left turn, decided to stage *The Cradle Will Rock.* Marc Blitzstein, still an obscure composer-critic in 1937, had embraced Communism only three years before. *Cradle,* written not long after his political conversion, was a musical parable about the rivalry between Mister Mister, the boss of Steeltown, U.S.A., and Larry Foreman, a labor organizer who works for a union modeled after John L. Lewis's Congress of Industrial Organizations (CIO), which at that time was heavily infiltrated by Communists. Strongly influenced by the Bertolt Brecht–Kurt Weill *Three-Penny Opera* of 1928, *Cradle* is a piece of broad-brush agitprop set to a sophisticated but accessible score in which Blitzstein manipulates a variety of popular-music styles to pungent effect.

Given the ongoing recovery of the American economy, Congress's growing hostility to large-scale federal relief programs, and the controversy caused by such overtly political productions as the Living Newspapers, the decision of Welles and Houseman to mount a pro-union musical by a composer known for his close ties to the Communist party inevitably put the entire FTP at risk. As Houseman would recall in his memoirs, events quickly conspired to make *Cradle* more controversial still:

The day *The Cradle Will Rock* went into rehearsal there were riots in Akron and Pontiac and strikes halted work at the Chrysler and Hudson auto plants. . . . During the first week of June, as we were starting our technical rehearsals, 5,000 CIO sympathizers invaded the business section of Lansing, Michigan, forced the closing of factories and stores and blocked all traffic in protest against the arrest of pickets.

Four days before the first public dress rehearsal, the WPA ordered the FTP to cut its payroll by 30 percent and postpone any new play, concert, or art exhibit set to open prior to July 1, a move generally regarded as a bill of attainder aimed at *Cradle*. On June 15, the day before the first official preview performance, a dozen uniformed WPA guards sealed Maxine Elliott's Theater; the next day, Actors' Equity refused to allow the cast of *Cradle* to take part in any other production of the play. Welles and Houseman then decided to undertake a "wildcat" performance on their own, heedless of its likely effect on the rest of the FTP. "There is nothing to prevent you from entering whatever theater we find," Welles told the cast, "then getting up from your seats, as U.S. citizens, and speaking or singing your piece when your cue comes." The show opened that night at the Venice Theater in precisely that manner: Blitzstein sat on stage, narrating and vigorously pounding out the score on an upright piano, while the members of the cast, stationed throughout the house, performed from their seats and in the aisles.

The next morning, the premiere made the front pages. Capitalizing on the publicity, the members of Project #891 took a two-week leave from their relief jobs that made it possible for them to present a brief run of *Cradle* at the Venice Theater. The FTP then officially canceled its own production and destroyed the sets, and Welles and Houseman left to start the Mercury Theater. A year later, the House Un-American Activities Committee investigated the FTP, finding that "a rather large number of [its] employees . . . are either members of the Communist party or sympathizers with the Communist party." In 1939, Congress voted to shut down the FTP for good.

IN TRANSFERRING THIS TALE TO THE SCREEN, ROBBINS HAS stripped away its myriad subtleties. The participants are rendered as black-and-white caricatures—Flanagan (Cherry Jones) is a noble earth mother in suits, Welles (Angus MacFayden) a blowhard with a Scots-Irish accent, Houseman (Cary Elwes) a flamboyant crypto-homosexual—and the underlying issues are reduced to leaden bumper-sticker orations. (Here, for instance, is Flanagan's initial response to Blitzstein's *Cradle:* "Marc, you've written something groundbreaking here. Never before, to my knowledge, has an American musical dealt with content, social issues, dramatic themes.") At the same time, the FTP's tendency to mount high-profile productions of propagandistic plays is subtly downplayed, while the presence of hardline Communists in its ranks, though freely acknowledged later by Houseman and others, is treated as a joke.

Robbins has rewritten history in other ways, some obvious, some less so. To take one egregious example, Blitzstein (Hank Azaria) is asked by Welles in the film if he is "a Red." His answer: "Officially, no. I am a homosexual and that excludes me from membership in the party. I am faithful to the ideals of the party." Indeed, Blitzstein was a homosexual. But in his 1958 appearance before HUAC he also readily acknowledged having joined the Communist party in 1938. Eric A. Gordon, his highly sympathetic biographer, adds that Blitzstein's "activities of the preceding three years suggest earlier membership. . . . Blitzstein had accepted Communist party leadership on the Left, had worked closely with it, publicly supported its line, and wrote for its press." By all accounts an ardent Stalinist—among many other things, he played a conspicuous role in the Waldorf Peace Conference—he did not leave the party until 1949, around the same time the *Daily Worker* published an unfavorable review of *Regina,* his musical version of Lillian Hellman's *The Little Foxes.*

Another example: in the film, numerous musicians join Blitzstein and the cast in the opening-night performance. In fact, however, only one instrumentalist, an accordion player, took part in the premiere, since the American Federation of Musicians, affiliated with the American Federation of Labor, was uninterested in supporting a performance of a work regarded by its leaders, in Houseman's candid recollection, as "straight CIO propaganda or worse." The subsequent run of *Cradle* at the Venice Theater and the Mercury Theater's 1938 revival were also accompanied by Blitzstein alone (though the Mercury was required to pay for a union conductor-contractor and a twelve-piece orchestra whose members played cards backstage while the show was performed).

In the film, Flanagan casually dismisses a colleague's warning that the production might put the entire FTP in jeopardy. "It's pro-union, yes, but so is our audience," she says, going on to deny that the play is an attack on capitalism: "Not at all. It's an attack on greed." Aside from misrepresenting the show's actual content, this scene entirely obliterates the well-known fact that Flanagan, though she admired *Cradle*, was horrified that Welles and Houseman would choose to imperil the FTP at so sensitive a juncture. As she later wrote to Blitzstein:

> Important as the issue raised by *The Cradle Will Rock* was, it was not the only issue facing us. The thing that people on the New York project never cared about, never understood, and never took the trouble to find out, is that this is a big country. Federal Theatre was bigger than any single project in it. It included not only *The Cradle Will Rock* but the theater for the children of coal miners in Gary, Indiana, the enterprise for vaudevillians in Portland, Oregon, the Negro theater in Chicago, the research being done in Oklahoma — and other projects employing several thousand people in other states.

Robbins never so much as hints that, from their own point of view, it might have been grossly irresponsible for Welles and Houseman to proceed with *Cradle* in light of these awkward political realities.

A final example: in the film, Flanagan testifies before HUAC immediately prior to opening night (the hearings actually took place more than a year later). Her cross-examination focuses on Communist infiltration of the FTP, leaving the impression that the project was closed down for that reason alone. In fact, however, HUAC's final report on "un-American propaganda activities" in the U.S. devoted only a single paragraph to the FTP. Congress's decision to terminate the project, though driven in part by the content of the plays, derived primarily from other considerations. As John O'Connor and Lorraine Brown write in their history of the FTP:

> According to the chairman of the House Committee on Appropriations, Clifton Woodrum, the Project had forgotten its purpose — "to furnish relief assistance to unemployed theatrical people" — in its desire

to "enter the field of amusement and entertainment," in competition with private enterprise.

Nor, it may be assumed, were Republicans interested in continuing to spend tax dollars on a federal agency that from its outset had produced explicitly partisan plays described by Harry Hopkins himself as "propaganda." But such matters, too, go unmentioned in Robbins's script.

The obvious purpose of these distortions is to present a sanitized account of the making of *The Cradle Will Rock* in which each and every leftist, union member, and supporter of a federally funded national theater is shown to be a paragon of political virtue. But Robbins's most fantastic departures from reality are to be found in the film's two subplots. The first concerns the commissioning by Nelson Rockefeller (John Cusack) of a fresco for Rockefeller Center by the Marxist painter Diego Rivera (Ruben Blades) and his later decision to have the painting razed upon discovering that it contains a portrait of Lenin and other anticapitalist symbols. The actual events took place several years prior to *Cradle,* but in the film, Rivera's fresco is destroyed on the day the show opens.

In the second, more convoluted subplot, Gray Mathers (Philip Baker Hall), a fictional anti-Communist steel magnate and art collector, brokers a deal between William Randolph Hearst (John Carpenter) and Mussolini's government in Italy by whose terms Hearst will funnel money to the fascist regime and Mathers will "put frames on Italian trucks" in return for Old Master paintings. In his afterword to the published script, Robbins implies that these paintings were confiscated from European Jews: "We may never know the complete truth about where confiscated art wound up after World War II, but we do know from recent lawsuits that many of these pieces are now in private collections."

This flight of Oliver Stone–like paranoia has nothing to do with the prosaic reality of ongoing legal disputes over the provenance of several paintings stolen during the war by the Germans (not the Italians) and subsequently shown in blockbuster exhibitions in Europe and America. Robbins spun it out of whole cloth in order to make possible the most absurd scene in *Cradle Will Rock*. In this scene, Hearst, Rockefeller, and Mathers discuss Rivera's pro-Soviet fresco:

HEARST: We control the future of art because we will pay for the future of art. Appoint people to your museum boards that detest the Riveras of the world. Celebrate the Matisses. Create the next wave of art. . . .

MATHERS: Nonpolitical.

ROCKEFELLER: Yes, abstract. Colors, form, not politics.

HEARST: My papers will hail it as the next new thing. We will canonize the artists, make them rich. Before long all artists will be doing the next new thing.

MATHERS: Do you think? There's something about artists that always gets socially concerned.

HEARST: Sure. But they won't be paid for it. They'll have no influence. They won't be seen. And rather than starve, they'll adapt.

As anyone conversant with Marxist art criticism will recognize, this scene is very loosely based on the harebrained but nonetheless widely accepted theory that the postwar success of such abstract expressionist painters as Jackson Pollock and Willem de Kooning can be attributed in large part to the nefarious manipulations of the CIA and corporate America, aided and abetted by staunchly anti-Communist art critics like Clement Greenberg. These combined forces allegedly promoted abstraction over representational art because it was "nonpolitical," and thus less likely to incite the masses.

Preposterous as this theory is—the inclusion of Hearst here is an especially surrealistic touch, since he had no use for Henri Matisse or any other modern artist, and would certainly never have "canonized" them in his newspapers—it is central to *Cradle Will Rock*. The movie ends with a montage cutting back and forth between the opening night of *Cradle* and lingering shots of Rivera's portrait of Lenin. The last thing we see is a long shot of Times Square circa 1999, dominated not by Broadway marquees but by brightly lit corporate billboards. Robbins's message is clear: had the Federal Theatre Project been allowed to continue disseminating state-subsidized left-wing propaganda, the soul of America might have been saved. Instead, art as a weapon was replaced by art as a tranquilizer, and corporate fascism won the battle for American hearts and minds. In place of *The Cradle Will Rock,* we now have *Beauty and the Beast;* in place of Rivera, Matisse.

"I'M INSPIRED BY DANGEROUS ART," ROBBINS WRITES IN HIS introduction to *Cradle Will Rock: The Movie and the Moment,* the published version of the script. But it is hard to see what dangers he courted in making a politically correct movie that caters slavishly to the preening limousine liberalism that has long dominated the American entertainment industry. And what of *Cradle* itself? How did it endanger the men and women who produced and performed it at the Venice Theater in 1937? Welles and Houseman went on to long and illustrious theatrical careers. Some of the cast members, to be sure, later found themselves on the anti-Communist blacklist of the Fifties, but that short-lived, famously porous ban applied only to film, radio, and TV. It was never honored on Broadway, where Howard da Silva, who had played Larry Foreman in the original *Cradle,* worked regularly for the rest of his life.

Even Marc Blitzstein found his Communist ties to be no obstacle to a successful career. During World War II he served in the army air force, working as an official military composer and turning out such earnest pieces of propaganda as the *Airborne Symphony* (1946). His English-language adaptation of *The Three-Penny Opera,* which opened off Broadway in 1954, ran for 2,611 performances. *Cradle* was revived on several occasions during his lifetime, the last time in 1960 by the New York City Opera. That same year, the Ford Foundation commissioned him to write an operatic treatment of the lives of Sacco and Vanzetti, the Italian anarchists who were patron saints of the Communist Party. The Metropolitan Opera would have produced this work had he not left it unfinished at his death in 1964.

In the end, the only "dangerous" thing about Blitzstein's radicalism was the devastating effect it had on his art. *Cradle* remains his best-known piece, but it is now rarely revived, not because the music is uninteresting but because of the irredeemable banality of his libretto, in which men of flesh and blood are turned into crude, lifeless symbols. The rest of his output is also largely forgotten, mostly for similar

reasons. As for the cause to which he devoted much of his adult life —
Stalinism — outside Hollywood and the academy one would have to
search far and wide to locate defenders of a political system whose sole
achievement was the butchering of several million innocent human
beings.

Not that any of this matters to Tim Robbins. He continues to see
"something deeply inspiring in the idealism and courage of artists from
the Thirties" who refused to "prostitute themselves" by selling their
services to the highest bidder. Evidently, in Robbins's moral calculus,
prostituting one's art in the name of the foremost mass murderer of
modern times does not in the least derogate from one's idealism and
courage, any more than utter ignorance of the crosscurrents of cultural
politics in the Thirties disqualifies one from making a relentlessly
preachy movie about that decade's complex history. Clearly, what is
"dangerous" in Robbins's case is a little learning — very little.

Commentary 2000

Willa Cather: No Way to Treat a Lady

IN 1920, H. L. MENCKEN CALLED WILLA CATHER "A WOMAN who, after a long apprenticeship, has got herself into the front rank of American novelists." As usual, the Great Mentioner of American letters was right on the money. But her cool chronicles of prairie life and its discontents contained no Joycean word-juggling, no torrid sex scenes, no class consciousness—none of the ingredients, in short, that literary intellectuals of the Thirties deemed indispensable. So a new generation of tastemakers dropped Cather down the memory hole, leaving her to middle-aged, middlebrow critics and the common readers who never swerved in their loyalty to the author of *My Ántonia* and *Death Comes for the Archbishop*. It said everything about her that she won the Pulitzer Prize and made the cover of *Time:* one moist kiss of death for each cheek.

The mills of trendiness grind ceaselessly, and in the age of feminist criticism, Willa Cather became a potentially hot property once again. But getting her back into the classroom wasn't quite as simple as it looked. For in addition to being a woman, she was also a New Deal–hating Republican, a fellow traveler of Roman Catholicism, a firm believer in the gospel of art for art's sake, and a testy anti-feminist who dismissed most lady poets as wet-eyed halfwits and most lady novelists as simply incompetent: "Has any woman ever really had the art instinct, the art necessity? Is it not with them a substitute, a transferred enthusiasm, an escape valve for what has sought or is seeking another channel?"

How, then, to detoxify her politically incorrect life and work and render them fit for consumption by delicate undergraduates? The answer turned out to be breathtakingly simple. In 1984, Sharon O'Brien published an essay in an obscure journal announcing that Cather was a "self-identified" lesbian, and that her homosexuality was the "emotional source of her fiction." Presto, change-o: today, virtually all Cather criticism takes these assertions for granted. The woman whom Granville Hicks had dismissed in proper Marxist fashion as being unequal to "the harshness of our world" is now a major novelist — or, to be exact, a major *lesbian* novelist, every bit as good as Virginia Woolf and Alice Walker, and maybe even Radclyffe Hall. There was only one catch: O'Brien made it all up.

One of the most unlikely things about the tale of how Willa Cather became a lesbian is that it was first told in the *New Yorker* (yes, the *New Yorker*!) by a dance critic. Joan Acocella is also a literary scholar by avocation, and by means unknown and unimaginable to me, she not only persuaded Tina Brown to print her exposé in 1995, but has now contrived to have an expanded version published by a reputable academic house. This devastatingly concise book isn't going to win its fearless author any prizes — she marches through the ranks of Cather scholars the way Sherman marched through Georgia — but anyone who has had it up to here with PC should buy a copy of *Willa Cather and the Politics of Criticism* and get ready to cheer, long and loudly.

According to Acocella, Cather probably was romantically attracted to women. But there is no documentary evidence that she ever did anything about it, and scarcely more proof to be culled from her novels. Indeed, that was the very point of her work: she sought to be the kind of novelist who writes not about "who marries whom, or at least who goes to bed with whom," but about the full panoply of human interests, of which love is but a single aspect. (Acocella herself has a special interest in artists who seek to break through what she calls "the boundary of the sex plot," a theme she also explores in her fine 1993 biography of the choreographer Mark Morris.) Human, mind you, not female: Cather felt equally competent to write about men, and did so no less memorably. But O'Brien, by her own admission, was determined to turn her idol into a single-issue cultural politician, thereby "rewriting one of the silencing stories of my own life, my domination by women who tried to erase me without ever seeing who I was." (How very Eighties: biography as therapy.) So, Acocella says, she cooked the books, falsely paraphrasing an unpublished Cather letter in such a way as to suggest that its author was confessing to "unnatural" feelings for a female friend. O'Brien made this "evidence" the centerpiece of the scholarly article that she later parlayed into a book-length "psychosexual study," which established her as the queen of Cather studies.

Since then, Willa Cather's lesbianism, such as it was or wasn't, has become the grain of sand around which a thousand costume pearls of critical theory have accreted: "In a 1986 essay Judith Fetterley accused Jane Rule of antihomosexual bias for describing *My Ántonia* as a serene book — in other words, for refusing to acknowledge its latent lesbian agony. 'Homophobia can go no further,' Fetterley declared." But Acocella, though she has assembled quite a nifty little chamber of critical horrors, is not your ordinary outrage-collecting cultural conservative. In fact, she is not a conservative at all, but an old-fashioned, determinedly non-radical feminist who insists that the proper goal of art is to describe life in all its proliferating, ideology-transcending complexity: "Will it be useful if we argue that while men and heterosexuals can write about anything they want, women can only write about gender, homosexuals only about sexuality? 'Why would Willa Cather celebrate male bonding?' asks O'Brien. And why would Leo Tolstoy celebrate a girl's experience at her first ball? Because they wanted to write about life."

To which I would add that an unintended effect of the criticism Acocella decries is to make its subjects seem too narrow to bother with. The irony, of course, is that far from being a purveyor of proto-identity politics, Cather was in fact an artist of extraordinary breadth, and the more I read her, the surer I am that she is not merely a woman novelist, or a regional novelist, or even an American novelist: she is a *great* novelist, clear-eyed and strong-hearted, who describes the harshness of the world in words of calm and consoling beauty. Among other things, she is close to unique in her ability to convey the feel of small-town life without any of the sentiment or self-pity that have poisoned the work of so many other American writers. "Out of her father's children," she writes of Alexandra Bergson, the heroine of *O Pioneers!* "there was one who was fit to cope with the world, who had not been tied to the plow, and who had a personality apart from the soil. And that, she reflected, was what she had worked for. She felt well satisfied with her life."

Yet there is still more to Cather than her matchlessly sympathetic chronicles of hardscrabble prairie lives. *Death Comes for the Archbishop,* her greatest novel, embodies a vision of life that might be described, however paradoxically, as Christian stoicism. Certainly this chronicle of two French priests consecrated to the mission of bringing the gospel to the American southwest is unambiguously spiritual in its implications. But its author is no less deeply imbued with the tragic sense of life— hence her elegiac tone—and far too tough-minded to stoop to the overfragrant piety that turns religious art to religious kitsch:

> During those last weeks of the Bishop's life he thought very little about death; it was the Past he was leaving. The future would take care of itself. But he had an intellectual curiosity about dying; about the changes that took place in a man's beliefs and scale of values. More and more life seemed to him an experience of the Ego, in no sense the Ego itself. This conviction, he believed, was something apart from his religious life; it was an enlightenment that came to him as a man, a human creature. And he noticed that he judged conduct differently now; his own and that of others. The mistakes of his life seemed unimportant; accidents that had occurred en route. . . .

It is an act of cultural vandalism in the first degree to sum up with a single trendy adjective the woman who wrote those lines, and Joan Acocella swells with righteous anger at those theory-mad pigeonholers who would dare to try it: "She broke out of jail, and now they are putting her—and all other women writers—back in." Out of that anger, she has made this eloquent, wholly admirable book.

National Review 2001

Another Sun Person Heard From

T HE ANTICS OF LEONARD JEFFRIES, CHAIRMAN OF THE black-studies department at City College of New York, noted Afrocentrist, and originator of the terms "sun people" (i.e., blacks) and "ice people" (i.e., whites), were widely reported in the press in the spring of 1993. Nominally removed from his chairmanship in 1992 for incompetence, Jeffries was in fact dismissed for engaging in gross, flagrant, and — most important — public anti-Semitism. His formal evaluations by college officials had been satisfactory right up to (and, incredibly, after) the day he gave a taxpayer-supported speech at the Empire State Black Arts and Cultural Festival in which he explained, among other things, how Jews financed the African slave trade, a revelation he had previously vouchsafed to his students. Jeffries promptly sued the City University of New York, of which CCNY is a part, claiming he had been given the boot not for being a bad chairman but for having lawfully exercised his constitutionally protected right to free speech. A federal jury agreed with Jeffries, ordering CUNY to fork over four hundred thousand dollars in recompense, and Judge Kenneth Conboy subsequently ordered him restored to his chairmanship.

One of the interesting things about Jeffries is the fact that he has so few respectable defenders. Most of what has been written about him in the mass media since he lurched into the spotlight (Jeffries helped draft "A Curriculum of Inclusion," the now-infamous report on multicultural education commissioned by New York State Education Commissioner Thomas Sobol) has been contemptuous in the extreme. Even the *New Yorker* took time out from sucking up to Bill and Hillary Clinton to devote eleven pages to a brutally frank profile of Jeffries. The piece, written by James Traub, was full of quotes from prominent black academics who hastened to distance themselves from Jeffries's ravings. Michele Wallace, a professor in CCNY's English department, went so far as to suggest that his conduct threatened to undermine the legitimacy of black studies itself:

> Leonard Jeffries is not rational. It's not possible to absorb sun people and ice people into a rational view. My view of Leonard Jeffries is that he's a maniac — and you can't assimilate a maniac. Jeffries should be marginalized. . . . A lot of students are confused. They don't understand the difference between Edmund Gordon [Jeffries's temporary replacement as chairman] and Leonard Jeffries. And I think a number of us need to take on this task if black studies is ever going to be a serious area.

A few days after James Traub's profile of Leonard Jeffries was published, I read Houston A. Baker, Jr.'s *Black Studies, Rap, and the Academy*. Viewed from one angle, Houston Baker is everything that Leonard Jeffries is not. So far as is known to the fact checkers of the *New Yorker,* Jeffries has published nothing; Baker is the author of numerous books. Save among his Afrocentric buddies, Jeffries is disreputable; Baker is not only reputable but fashionable, or so one gathers from the dust jacket of *Black Studies, Rap, and the Academy,* on which can be found snippets of praise from such publications as the *New York Times Book Review, Washington Post Book World,* and the *Village Voice Literary Supplement* ("If one person could embody the trajectory of black literature and literary theory in the post-apartheid era of American higher education, Houston Baker is that person"). He is even a past president of the Modern Language Association. But Jeffries and Baker have two relevant things in common: both are black, and both are in charge of black-studies departments. Baker directs the Center for the Study of Black Literature and Culture at the University of Pennsylvania, where he is professor of English and Albert M. Greenfield Professor of Human Relations.

Looking at Houston Baker's résumé, one naturally supposes him to be the sort of person Michele Wallace has in mind when she speaks of black studies as a "serious area." His books, for example, are published by the University of Chicago Press, which is also, a glance at my bookshelves reminds me, the publisher of Leslie Marchand's *Byron: A Portrait*, Richard Posner's *The Essential Holmes*, Leo Strauss's *Natural Right and History*, Anthony Powell's *Miscellaneous Verdicts*, and Clement Greenberg's *Collected Essays and Criticism*, to pick five titles at random. That is fast company, but the University of Chicago Press is plainly unafraid of the implicit comparison. Indeed, *Black Studies, Rap, and the Academy* is the first volume in the series "Black Literature and Culture," edited by none other than Houston A. Baker, Jr. To top it all off, the book is, according to the preface, "the result of a short-term visiting fellowship at Princeton University. Professor Arnold Rampersad of American Studies and Professor Victor Brombert of the Council of the Humanities graciously invited me to present lectures as a Whitney J. Oates Fellow during the spring of 1992." Morris Zapp couldn't have put it better.

I didn't know much about Houston Baker prior to reading his latest book, though I had run across his name more than once. Nor do I know much about black studies as an academic discipline, other than what I read in the magazines; it was still getting off the ground when I was going to school. I do, however, know something about rap, partly because I live in Manhattan, where it is ubiquitous, and partly because I mugged up the subject a couple of years ago at the request of an editor, producing in due course an article from which Baker quotes (without comment) on page 49 of his book. More to the point, I know serious scholarship when I see it, having consumed a carload of it in my time. The arrival of *Black Studies, Rap, and the Academy* thus seemed to me in the highest degree opportune — a chance to find out at first hand about one of the "serious" practitioners of black studies whose reputation Leonard Jeffries is allegedly damaging.

The argument of *Black Studies, Rap, and the Academy* can be summed up briefly: (1) Black studies is an indispensable part of American higher education. (2) Rap is a creative and authentic expression of the urban black experience and should thus be taken seriously by academics, particularly those working in the field of black studies. (3) Anyone who disagrees with (1) or (2) is a racist. Mind you, Baker doesn't actually call critics of black studies (or rap) "racists"—he's too smart for that. There are subtler ways to sling the mud:

> The late Allan Bloom's influential *The Closing of the American Mind* commences with a sullen and dyspeptic account of the arrival of Black Studies [the term is always capitalized in *Black Studies, Rap, and the Academy*] at Cornell. This arrival is described by Bloom in darkly Miltonic terms as Paradise Lost, an expulsion from the academic garden of White Male Philosophical Privilege.
>
> From a Black Studies perspective, the past twenty-five years have been a journey from bare seasons of migration to the flowering of scholarly innovation. From a conservative white male perspective, these same years must have seemed an enduring crisis, each new day and work of Black Studies bringing fresh anxieties of territorial loss.

Forgive me for not wheeling out the big guns, but life is too short to waste time wrangling over this kind of prattle, or the ideology that drives it. Neither is it worth summarizing Baker's views on rap, since they are, controlling for polysyllables, mostly indistinguishable from those of the average thirteen-year-old, and are in any case asserted rather than demonstrated. Instead, I want to concentrate on certain stylistic aspects of *Black Studies, Rap, and the Academy,* which reveal far more about Houston Baker than any respectful parsing of his ideas ever could.

BAKER SHIFTS INTO HIGH RHETORICAL GEAR ON THE VERY first page, informing us that black studies is "a narrative of Hagar's children redeemed from exile by the grace of affirmative action and the intentionality of Black Power. It is a vernacular tale, resonant with rhythm and blues." Having read the remaining 109 pages of *Black Studies, Rap, and the Academy* with some care, I can assure you that this one is wholly representative. Indeed, the book is a veritable omnium-gatherum of latter-day academic clichés. Here are a few of the more noteworthy varieties:

Loud, flatulent praise of the Sixties. "In the midsixties, the quiet of the American university—whether garden or factory—was shattered forever by the thundering 'NO' to all prior arrangements of higher education in America issued by the Free Speech Movement (FSM)."

Even louder and more flatulent denunciation of the Eighties. "Most of the population of the United States is financially hard-pressed, crippled by the absence of justice in everyday life, and distressingly aware that an unseemly white-male profittaking during the 1980s has brought the United States to the precipice of human disaster."

Pseudo-heterodoxy. According to the dust jacket, "the book's most controversial moment" comes when Baker supports the banning by Florida's Broward County of 2 Live Crew's album *As Nasty as They Wanna Be,* which Henry Louis Gates, Jr., praised on the op-ed page of the *New York Times* for its "exuberant use of hyperbole." (One wonders how Gates would react were one of his white students to stand up in class and deliver himself of an exuberantly hyperbolic speech in praise of rape consisting mainly of the words *bitch* and *motherfucker.*) Says Baker, striding fearlessly into single combat with the grand panjandrum of black studies:

> I believe 2 Live Crew's album was understandably banned. And I believe [wait for it] that if women and minorities were empowered to assume genuine agency in American society, other such albums would probably be banned, along with Andrew Dice Clay, *Hustler, Penthouse,* and peep shows. Though social scientists and policy analysts are fearful of declaring a correlation between the volume of violent, obscene, antiwoman drivel available in the Unites States and the incidence of violence against women, common sense alone suggests such a correlation. . . . I am certainly *not* suggesting that the criminal prosecution of popular artists should become a United States norm. Nor am I advocating the institution of a kind of State PC (in this instance, "popular culture") police force to roam the land instituting "standard" words and works in lieu of popular idioms. . . . I believe Tipper Gore *is* a puritanical busybody who should not be listened to by anyone under the age of 135.

Now *that's* controversial.

Preening. "I recently (February 1990) had the experience of crossing the Atlantic by night, followed by a metropolitan ride from Heathrow

Airport to North Westminster Community School in order to teach Shakespeare's *Henry V* to a class of GCSE (General Certificate of Secondary Education) students. . . . To make an exciting pedagogical story brief, we took off—as a group. I showed them how Henry V was a rapper—a cold dissing, def con man, tougher-than-leather and smoother-than-ice, an artisan of words. . . . eight or nine of the students surrounded me after class seeking, as they put it, 'scholarships' to go back with me to America—'now, Sir!'"

Incessant use of tin-eared jargon. "*Black Studies* became a sign of conjuncture that not only foregrounded the university as a space of territorial contest, but also metaphorized the contest itself in a way that allowed the sign to serve as a simulacrum."

Embarrassing use of teenage slang. "It seems high time, then, for those of us who are inside to get seriously busy about the business of Black Studies for the nineties—to bust a move and rigorously bring the scholarly noise for a new generation." (Get down, Grandpa.)

Simple ignorance. Among the names Baker misspells: S. I. Hayakawa, Carol Iannone, Catharine MacKinnon, Salman Rushdie.

Plain old bad writing. "Then perhaps we would not only see the horror of that black woman who was forced to a Brooklyn rooftop, raped, and murdered in the same time frame as the Central Park jogger assault, a rape and murder that were very much unreported [if so, how did Baker hear about them?]; we might also find in our new public concern both exacting and effective ways to channel the transnational capital of everyday rap into a spirited refiguration of black urban territories—a refiguration that would foreclose even the possibility of such horrendous black woman victimization as that in Brooklyn, and a refiguration that certainly would prevent the veritable silencing of such obscenity."

Here we arrive at the heart of the matter. Put aside Baker's politics for a moment and concentrate on the *aesthetics* of that last sentence, and the hundreds of others like it with which *Black Studies, Rap, and the Academy* is stuffed to the eyeballs. Can there really be any doubt that a man capable of publishing such prose is demonstrably unworthy of being entrusted with the education of English majors, whatever their race, creed, color, or sexual orientation?

As I said earlier, I know very little about black studies as a formal discipline, though I'm not especially sympathetic to it in the abstract. I don't see that it makes a great deal of sense to study "black history" or "black art" in ghettoized isolation. This approach, taken to the lunatic extremes to which academics take everything nowadays, is at once condescending and destructive. If Richard Wright is worth taking seriously as an artist, surely it is because he was, to borrow Bruce Bawer's formulation, a gifted writer who happened to be black, not a Black Writer who happened to be gifted. Least of all does he profit from being yoked with the woozy likes of, say, Alice Walker. Who gains from *that* comparison?

At the same time, I recognize that black studies is, at least in theory, a coherent concept. It is not at all difficult to imagine what an intellectually responsible black-studies department might choose to teach, and how it might go about doing so. And while my own feeling is that such cultural separatism is a mistake—I would much rather see the artistic achievements of, say, Count Basie or Alvin Ailey presented as integral parts of Western culture—I'm not reflexively hostile to a program of study that simultaneously considers such artists as representatives of a specifically black culture.

The problem is that black studies in practice is too often the product not of responsible intellectual inquiry but of far baser motives. Consider the case of the black-studies department at City College of New York, which was founded two decades ago in response to—what else?—student protests. (*Though we know we should defeat you, we have not the time to meet you. / We will therefore pay you cash to go away.*) Leonard Jeffries was hired straight out of graduate school to head the department and immediately granted tenure, presumably as a condition of his hiring, after which he was left almost entirely to his own devices. "It was never much of a department," a lawyer for City University of New York claimed at Jeffries's trial. "In the last fifteen years or so, you could count the published scholarly works of City College's black-studies department on the fingers of two hands." Yet no one at CCNY was willing to challenge Jeffries on the merits—to openly assert that he and his colleagues (virtually all of whom he hired) were incompetent hacks—until he forced the issue by dragging his employers to court. Not that CCNY officials subsequently leapt to the defense of academic standards. Indeed, it was precisely because their testimony was so half-hearted, and because Jeffries's formal evaluations had all been satisfactory, that Joseph Fleming, Jeffries's lawyer, was able to persuade a jury in essence that his client was fired not because he was incompetent but because he was anti-Semitic.

Arguing in court against Jeffries's reinstatement as chairman, New York Assistant State Attorney General Kathie Ann Whipple played what she doubtless assumed to be the ultimate trump card by claiming that Jeffries "does not grasp the sensitivities and sensibilities essential for working in an ethnically diverse environment." This statement is worth a closer look. In CCNY's eyes, Leonard Jeffries's besetting sin was *insensitivity*. (That is a pretty flossy word for the man who once called Diane Ravitch "the ultimate, supreme, sophisticated debonair racist . . . a sophisticated Texas Jew," but never mind.) His scholarship, or lack of it, was viewed as a purely secondary consideration. And so it was, at least to the cynical administrators who built the bully pulpit from which Jeffries continues to cram the gospel of Afrocentrism down the throats of ignorant undergraduates who know no better.

One would like to think this sordid tale an exception to the rule. But, as James Traub explains in his *New Yorker* profile, it is in fact characteristic of many, perhaps most, black-studies departments:

> Black students at campuses all over the country began demanding separate programs and living facilities; above all, they demanded the establishment of programs of black studies — in effect, a department of their own. For many scholars, black and white, such ultimatums represented an assault on the intellectual integrity of the university. But college officials found that a black-studies department was a relatively cheap way to buy campus peace. The Marxist historian Eugene Genovese accused these administrators of practicing "a benevolent paternalism that is neither more or less than racist." The subsequent neglect of conventional academic standards in many black-studies departments suggests that Genovese was right.

So, I hasten to add, does the fact that the University of Chicago Press chose to publish *Black Studies, Rap, and the Academy*, a vulgar, stupid, and totally unscholarly book that is "literate" in precisely the same sense that a man who tarts up his prose with two-dollar words gleaned from *Roget's* is literate. If I were an editor at a publishing house, and this book had been submitted to me by an unknown author, I would have rejected it without a second thought. But, of course, it is not the work of an unknown author. It is the work of a specialist in black studies who has been deemed worthy of an endowed chair, a book series of his own, and — I would venture to bet — a six-figure contract that doesn't require him to teach very much.

TO BE SURE, HOUSTON BAKER, JR., IS NO WORSE THAN THE rest of his fellow literary-theory racketeers. He commits no literary offenses that cannot be found in a hundred other equally stupid books published by a hundred other professors of other colors. More important, he is no Leonard Jeffries. But these things are beside the point. Everybody admits that Jeffries is the living embodiment of black studies at its worst. If the author of *Black Studies, Rap, and the Academy* is truly representative of the *best* black studies has to offer, then it necessarily follows that black studies is a joke, a pitiful and preposterous burlesque of scholarship foisted on the academy in the holy name of diversity.

Which brings us back to the anguished words of Michele Wallace: "A lot of students are confused. They don't understand the difference between Edmund Gordon and Leonard Jeffries. And I think a number of us need to take on this task if black studies is ever going to be a serious area." Well, Ms. Wallace, I have news for you: the marginalization of Leonard Jeffries is not the only task you need to take on if black studies is ever going to be a serious area. There is something else you and your colleagues need to be saying, loudly and clearly: *What* we *do is not what Houston Baker and his ilk do. If we are scholars, they are something else.* The day I see those words published in the *New York Times Book Review* under the byline of a tenured professor of black studies is the day I read another book by a tenured professor of black studies. Until then, I'll take my Richard Wright, Louis Armstrong, Romare Bearden, E. Franklin Frazier, and B. B. King neat, thank you very much.

New Criterion 1993

The Color of Jazz

GRP RECORDS, WHICH OWNS THE CATALOGUE OF
Decca, a prominent record label of the Thirties and Forties,
recently released a two-CD set of jazz performances originally recorded by the older company. The set contains classic recordings by Louis Armstrong, Count Basie, Duke Ellington, Jelly Roll
Morton, Sidney Bechet, Coleman Hawkins, Fletcher Henderson, Billie
Holiday, and other artists. More significant than the album's contents,
however, is its title: *Black Legends of Jazz*.

As recently as a decade ago, it would have been inconceivable for a
major label to release such an album. Not only would the title have been
considered offensive, it would have been seen as untrue to the spirit of
jazz. To be sure, black and white musicians did not perform together on
stage until the mid-Thirties, and even now, racially mixed bands, like
racially mixed couples, are uncommon enough to catch the eye. But
the cultural ethos of jazz was for the most part firmly free of race-
consciousness. Louis Armstrong, the most important figure in jazz,
spoke for most musicians when he said, "It's no crime for cats of any
color to get together and blow." But American culture has changed
greatly since Armstrong died in 1971, and jazz has changed with it.
Race-consciousness — on the part of individuals and institutions alike —
is now a powerful force in the world of jazz, one whose effects have only
just begun to come clear.

In October 1994, Representative John Conyers, Jr. (D-Mich.),
learned that the Smithsonian Jazz Masterworks Orchestra, an ensemble
organized by the Smithsonian Institution to play the music of the big-
band era, normally engages a half-dozen black musicians out of its total

of sixteen members. In a letter sent to the Smithsonian and later published in the *Washington Times,* Conyers said he found this proportion "extremely disturbing," adding that

> I want people who experience the Orchestra in performance to hear and see jazz for what it has been and is—a product of the African-American cultural experience. While jazz has certainly inspired the participation and creativity of all Americans, as well as other people around the world, the lack of real racial, ethnic, and gender diversity among the Orchestra's members presents an unrealistic image of who plays this music which I urge you to expeditiously correct.

As it happens, Conyers's letter was not only crudely threatening but historically ill-informed. So far as can be determined, jazz was "invented" around the turn of the twentieth century by New Orleans blacks of widely varying musical education and ethnic background (many were Creoles, the mixed-blood descendants of French slaveholders and their female slaves). But whites were playing jazz within a decade of its initial appearance, and began making important contributions to its stylistic development shortly thereafter. Until fairly recently, most musicians and scholars agreed that jazz long ago ceased to be a uniquely black idiom and became "multicultural" in the truest, least politicized sense of the word. As the white guitarist Jim Hall said, "I've always felt that the music started out as black but that it's as much mine now as anyone else's."

But Conyers is hardly alone today in dissenting from this consensus. (As for the Smithsonian, it responded to his threat, predictably, by ordering the orchestra's musical directors to ensure that its "makeup . . . reflect racial balance"—that is, have more blacks and fewer whites.) Perhaps the first to do so was the black novelist and literary scholar Albert Murray in his 1976 book, *Stomping the Blues.* Murray is not a musician, and his book is an idiosyncratic interpretation of American popular music in which jazz is treated not as an independent musical form but as part of the blues, an older idiom that originated among Southern blacks at some point in the late nineteenth or the early twentieth century.

For Murray, the ability to play the blues is the defining trait of "authentic" jazz musicians. Those who do not play the blues are not authentic—and white musicians, Murray implies, cannot play the blues. In the caption to the only photo in *Stomping the Blues* in which white musicians are shown, Murray succinctly describes these whites—including Pee Wee Russell and Gerry Mulligan, two of the most admired players in jazz—as members of the "third line," carefully explaining that in a New Orleans street parade, the "first line" consists of the musicians, while the "second line" is made up of "dancing-and-prancing fans and proteges . . . [who] are permitted to carry the instruments of their favorite musicians for several blocks while the band takes a breather before striking up again." The "third line" is left undefined, but its meaning is clear.

Now, just as there have always been black and white players, there have always been "black" and "white" styles in jazz. But there has also been substantial racial overlap in every important jazz style since the Twenties, and it is impossible consistently to distinguish white players from black simply by listening. When the black trumpeter Roy Eldridge claimed to be able to do so, the jazz critic Leonard Feather gave him a "blindfold test" (subsequently described in the jazz magazine *Down Beat*), which Eldridge failed.

Feather also popularized the term "Crow Jim" to refer to the reverse-racist belief that white jazz musicians are by definition derivative and second-rate. Indeed, some were—and are. But three of the most influential players in the history of jazz, the cornetist Bix Beiderbecke, the clarinetist Benny Goodman, and the pianist Bill Evans, were white, and the list of white jazz instrumentalists universally acknowledged by their peers as artists of the first rank also includes Jack Teagarden, Bunny Berigan (whom Louis Armstrong cited as his own favorite trumpeter), Artie Shaw, Bobby Hackett, Dave Tough, Red Norvo, Buddy Rich, Jimmy Rowles, Art Pepper, Stan Getz, Paul Desmond, Jim Hall, and countless others. Moreover, as the songwriter and jazz journalist Gene Lees has amply documented in his book, *Cats of Any Color: Jazz, Black and White*, many noted black jazz musicians have readily acknowledged the influence of white players.

Murray deals with these awkward facts by ignoring them—just as, on the other side, he ignores the fact that such indisputably major jazz figures as Earl Hines, Coleman Hawkins, Fats Waller, Teddy Wilson, and Art Tatum, all of them black, were not blues players. With the sole exception of the drummer Gene Krupa, who is described as a "white drummer of the so-called Swing Era," no white musician is mentioned in the main text of *Stomping the Blues,* favorably or otherwise. Murray does not say explicitly that whites cannot play jazz, but that is what he means. Whites who try to play the blues are by definition derivative, and thus of no interest; whites who do not play the blues are by definition not playing jazz, and thus also of no interest.

Only Whitney Balliett of the *New Yorker* drew attention to the racist implications of Murray's thesis when *Stomping the Blues* was published. The failure of other critics to do so, though inexcusable, is easily understood. By 1976, the audience for jazz was predominantly white, a fact of which black jazz musicians were intensely aware. Books like *Stomping the Blues* were seen by most jazz writers as part of the larger project of fostering "black pride," and their ideological underpinnings were accordingly downplayed or ignored.

ONE CRITIC WHO READ *STOMPING THE BLUES* CLOSELY WAS Stanley Crouch, who called it "the most eloquent book ever written about African-American music" and, even more interestingly, "the first real aesthetic theory of jazz."

Crouch, an erstwhile drummer with little musical training, is best known for his provocative essays on American culture, many of which were collected in his 1990 book, *Notes of a Hanging Judge*. These essays have earned him a reputation as one of the few prominent black writers willing to challenge the prevailing left-liberal orthodoxy on racial matters. Thus, Crouch has called the black filmmaker Spike Lee a "fascist"; described the black novelist Toni Morrison as a "literary conjure woman" who is "as American as P. T. Barnum"; and suggested that "the sob squad of white liberals . . . spend some time talking to the victims of the third-world criminals they sympathize with so much."

Given Crouch's consistent, even courageous opposition to the conventional wisdom on race in America, it is all the more dismaying to find that in his jazz criticism he paradoxically adopts a Crow Jim line very nearly as rigid and ahistorical as that of Albert Murray. Unlike

Murray, Crouch has on occasion expressed admiration for certain white players. But in his critical lexicon, "the Afro-American approach to sound and rhythm" is the only true way to play jazz, and even celebrated black players like Miles Davis are diminished in value to the degree that they succumb to "the academic temptation of Western music." (Crouch here presumably means "classical" music, since jazz is self-evidently a form of Western music.)

In "The Duke, the King, and the City of Jazz," a 1989 review of Gunther Schuller's *The Swing Era,* Crouch comments on only one white musician, Benny Goodman, whose big band he calls "inferior" in quality to its black counterparts (an opinion that, while politically correct, is musically questionable). Given the fact that some 150 pages of *The Swing Era* are devoted to white bands and soloists of the Thirties and Forties, one must conclude that, like Murray, Crouch considers their work to be of no interest.

When Crouch does deign to notice white musicians, his remarks are often scathing. He has publicly called Bill Evans, perhaps the most admired jazz pianist of the Sixties and Seventies, a "punk." In a 1990 essay on Miles Davis, Crouch describes that trumpeter's recorded collaborations with the white composer-arranger Gil Evans, one of the two or three most important arrangers in the history of jazz, in terms no less contemptuous of the white contribution to jazz:

> [T]hose albums . . . reveal that Davis could be taken by pastel versions of European colors (they are given what value they have in these sessions by the Afro-American dimensions that were never far from Davis's embouchure, breath, fingering); if Davis's trumpet voice is removed, in fact, a good number of Evans's arrangements sound like high-level television music.

Whether or not these remarks are "racist" is a matter of opinion. But that they are *racialist* — manifestations, that is, of an ideology in which race is a primary factor in the making of aesthetic judgments — is unquestionable. Moreover, through his connection with the black trumpeter Wynton Marsalis, Stanley Crouch is in a position to act on his convictions.

Crouch met Marsalis in the early Eighties, introduced him to Albert

Murray, and, by his own account, undertook to teach him the history of jazz. Today, Crouch supplies obsequious liner notes for Marsalis's recordings ("Marsalis brings his own heroic individuality to the expression of tenderness magnified and recalled by a stretch of trumpet tones and ensemble colors that are themselves contrasted by the celebratory swing of eroticism ascended to the diamond point of romantic precision") and, more important, under the title of artistic adviser, plays a key role in the programming of Jazz at Lincoln Center, the New York concert series led by Marsalis.

Under Marsalis and Crouch, Jazz at Lincoln Center presents mostly programs about black musicians. Whites are allowed to play with the Lincoln Center Jazz Orchestra, but the historic contributions of earlier white players, composers, and arrangers are systematically ignored, and contemporary white composers are rarely commissioned to write original pieces for the full orchestra. This policy is so egregiously race-conscious that it has even been attacked by admirers of Wynton Marsalis, including Peter Watrous, jazz critic for the *New York Times*. As Watrous has been quoted, bluntly, in the magazine *Jazz Times:* "They say . . . they have to put on all the important figures before they get to the lesser-knowns, and that there happen to be more important figures who are black. That's complete bullshit."

Marsalis is unapologetic about such matters, and apparently he can afford to be. At thirty-three, in addition to having performed and recorded much of the classical trumpet literature, he is the most famous jazz musician in America. He has appeared on the covers of *Time* and the *New York Times Magazine;* he has been under exclusive contract to Sony, one of the biggest record labels in the world, since 1981; and he has composed ballet scores for New York City Ballet and American Ballet Theater, and extended concert works presented by Jazz at Lincoln Center. Young musicians who have worked in his band subsequently find it easy to get lucrative recording contracts of their own. If there is a jazz counterpart to Leonard Bernstein, it is Wynton Marsalis.

Interestingly, not all of these achievements hold up equally well under scrutiny. Technically speaking, Marsalis is a virtuoso by any conceivable standard, and even so formidable a music critic as B. H. Haggin considered him a first-rate classical trumpeter. But his jazz playing is felt by many to be cold and, ironically enough, derivative. In a sense, it is derivative by design: Marsalis was one of a number of stylistically conservative players of the late Seventies and early Eighties who rejected the avant-garde techniques of the Sixties in favor of a "neoclassical" approach in which older jazz styles, rather than being rejected out of hand as outmoded, were revived and updated. He has deliberately sought to incorporate in his playing a wide variety of stylistic elements from great jazz trumpeters of the past. But the results, especially when he uses Louis Armstrong–derived techniques, have a generic quality that suggests an incomplete assimilation of his sources.

As an educator and a presenter of Bernstein-style "young people's concerts" intended to introduce children to jazz, Marsalis is widely recognized as having done admirable work. Indeed, I would venture to say that in the long run, he will be best remembered as a middlebrow popularizer — one who in particular has done more than any other figure of his generation to revive interest in jazz among young black listeners. About his large-scale compositional efforts there is also little disagreement, at least among musicians not connected with his various enterprises, though here the verdict is unfavorable: they are unfinished, sometimes even frankly amateurish, and betray a lack of technique startling in an artist so generously equipped in other areas. The fact that he has been the frequent recipient of commissions from Jazz at Lincoln Center is thus little short of scandalous.

Marsalis takes seriously his job as unappointed spokesman for Albert Murray's and Stanley Crouch's version of the jazz tradition. Ever since he began giving interviews in the early Eighties, he has been quick to criticize other musicians, notably Miles Davis and Sonny Rollins, for "selling out" to commercial music. He is just as quick to attack his critics, especially those who accuse him of reverse racism. And he is adamant in defending his conduct as artistic director of Jazz at Lincoln Center. "I get no flak from the general public and I get no flak from musicians," he told a reporter for *Jazz Times*.

The latter is untrue. Indeed, whether or not Wynton Marsalis is a racist is a common topic of conversation among New York musicians. Although he uses white players both in the Lincoln Center Jazz Orchestra and in his own groups, it is widely believed that he harbors a general disdain for white musicians, and the belief seems to be borne out by facts. As the jazz journalist W. Royal Stokes pointed out earlier this year, "the ratio on concert dates in [Jazz at Lincoln Center] . . . has consistently been in the neighborhood of ten black musicians to one white."

In one strikingly unguarded moment on the black-oriented TV talk show *Tony Brown's Journal,* Marsalis went even farther, complaining that the music business is controlled by "people who read the Torah and stuff. . . . Every idiom of black music, be it jazz, rhythm-and-blues, or whatever, has declined in its negroidery and purpose. It became more whitified. It's not the white people's fault. The white people, they do what they do to support the misconceptions that they started when they brought the brothers and sisters over here as slaves. We are, in effect, in a state of war." Anyone seeking to understand the "aesthetic theory" behind Marsalis's artistic leadership of Jazz at Lincoln Center should examine these remarks closely, side by side with the following passage in Stanley Crouch's liner notes for the Marsalis album *The Majesty of the Blues:* "But we must understand that the money-lenders of the marketplace have never EVER known the difference between an office or an auction block and a temple, they have never known that there was an identity to anything other than that of a hustle, a shuck, a scam, a game."

THE COMMERCIAL SUCCESS OF WYNTON MARSALIS HAS LED several major labels to start recording jazz again. Precisely because their interest is not artistic but commercial, however, they approach jazz in the same way Hollywood seeks to replicate successful movies: by looking for Marsalis clones. The Marsalis family itself has provided several candidates, starting with Branford Marsalis, an accomplished tenor-saxophone player who started out as a sideman with his younger brother's group and eventually became Doc Severinsen's successor as bandleader on the *Tonight Show.*

An entire "school" of young jazz neoclassicists, many of whom have worked with Wynton Marsalis, has lately emerged, collectively known in the jazz press as the "Young Lions" and referred to by more skeptical colleagues as "young black men in suits." (Many of them emulate

Marsalis's taste in clothing.) Most of these players are still too young and inexperienced to have developed individual styles, though a few, including the tenor saxophonist Joshua Redman and the bassist Christian McBride, have considerable talent.* But virtually all have one thing in common: their race. It is, by contrast, comparatively rare for a major record label to sign a young white player, and all but unheard-of for a middle-aged white player to be signed.

In the long run, market forces will restore some kind of balance to the present situation in recorded jazz. (It has not escaped the attention of music-business insiders that sales of Wynton Marsalis's records have been declining for the last few years.) But jazz is also affected by non-commercial institutions funded in whole or part by public money, and thus subject not only to market forces but also to political pressures. The intimidation of the Smithsonian Jazz Masterworks Orchestra by Representative Conyers is an example of such pressure at work. Another, cited by Gene Lees, is the American Jazz Masters Fellowship awards. Between 1982 and 1994, thirty-nine of these awards, worth $20,000 each, were made by the National Endowment for the Arts. Only two went to white musicians.

One can easily multiply such examples to show how reverse racism has become, if not universal, then powerfully legitimate in jazz, and indeed how it has insinuated itself throughout the jazz community. When an important historical study like Ted Gioia's *West Coast Jazz* fails to be reviewed in major publications, is it because the book is thought unworthy of serious attention by book-review editors — or because West Coast jazz, dominated as it was by whites, is itself presumed unworthy of attention? When a white jazz critic like Tom Piazza complains that Bill Evans "doesn't swing enough" and "can't play the blues," is he making a genuine critical judgment — or merely aping the Crouch-

---

* In a "blindfold test" published in the August 1995 issue of *Down Beat,* the black drummer Marvin "Smitty" Smith made the following penetrating comments about a recording by some of the most prominent of the Young Lions: "Here, there's a high level of proficiency, but the spirit of really forging forward, striving to create a new direction of sound, I don't get. . . . I don't get a strong individual personality out of any of them."

Murray white-boys-can't-play-jazz party line? In a cultural environment where race has become an admissible criterion for aesthetic judgments, there is no way to answer these questions: the mere fact that they have to be asked is evidence of the corrosion wrought by racialist thinking.

THE NEW REVERSE RACISM IN JAZZ IS NOT, OF COURSE, AN isolated phenomenon. It has arisen at a time when such government policies as quota-based affirmative action have made race-consciousness a pervasive feature of American society. In the absence of those policies — and the underlying political beliefs that drive them — it is unlikely that public institutions like Lincoln Center and the Smithsonian Institution would lend the prestige of their names to artistic enterprises run on racialist lines, or submit meekly to the demands of cynical politicians playing the "race card."

But that is just what makes the current epidemic in the world of jazz so disturbing, and its implications so far-reaching. Throughout much of its century-long history, jazz has been a relatively safe haven from the storms of ideology, a meritocracy of comrades in which, as musicians say, "every tub sits on its own bottom." No such society-within-a-society is perfect, and jazz is no exception, as anyone at all familiar with its history must inevitably be aware. Older black musicians remember all too well the personal and professional roadblocks placed in their paths by a country that long refused to treat them as first-class citizens. Yet those who have lived and worked in the world of jazz know how close it has come to the ideal of a culture in which artists are judged not by the color of their skin but by the content of their choruses.

Albert Murray, Stanley Crouch, and Wynton Marsalis all claim as their musical heroes Louis Armstrong and Duke Ellington, both of whom knew the sting of racism their whole lives long. Yet Armstrong, a man of extraordinary generosity of spirit, never yielded to the temptation to treat white musicians as he had been treated by the white world. Instead, he accepted them as colleagues. "I'm a spade, and you're an ofay," he said to the trombonist Jack Teagarden, one of his closest musical associates. "We got the same soul — so let's blow." As for Duke Ellington, the man who composed *Black, Brown, and Beige* also told an interviewer in 1945:

Twenty years ago when jazz was finding an audience, it may have had more of a Negro character. The Negro element is still important. But jazz has become a part of America. There are as many white musicians playing it as Negro. . . . We are all working along more or less the same lines. We learn from each other. Jazz is American now. *American* is the big word.

Five decades later, this spirit is being undermined by cultural politicians for whom the word "American" has validity only when it lies on the far side of a hyphen. That jazz, the ultimate cultural melting pot and arguably America's most important contribution to the fine arts, should have fallen victim to such divisive thinking is an especially telling index of the unhappy state of our culture at the end of the twentieth century.

Commentary 1995

(Over)praising Duke Ellington

WRITING SHORTLY AFTER DUKE ELLINGTON'S DEATH in 1974, the jazz scholar Gunther Schuller placed the composer of "It Don't Mean a Thing (If It Ain't Got That Swing)" in "the pantheon of musical greats—the Beethovens, the Monteverdis, the Schoenbergs, the prime movers, the inspired innovators." Though few other critics have gone so far, it is certainly true that Ellington is widely considered to be the most important composer, and one of the most important bandleaders, in the history of jazz. Many of his songs, including "Mood Indigo," "Sophisticated Lady," "Solitude," "In a Sentimental Mood," and "Prelude to a Kiss," remain popular to this day, and the more ambitious instrumental pieces he wrote for his orchestra starting in the late Twenties won him lasting worldwide acclaim.

Paradoxically, the strength of Ellington's reputation rests in part on the fact that even his most enthusiastic admirers, including Gunther Schuller, have not praised his music indiscriminately. In particular, there has long been a consensus that Ellington's postwar output was far less successful than the music of his early and middle years. As Schuller explains in *The New Grove Dictionary of Jazz:*

> [I]t is generally agreed that [Ellington] attained the zenith of his creativity in the late 1930s and early 1940s, and that he worked best in the miniature forms dictated by the three-minute ten-inch [78 rpm] disc. Ellington's creativity declined substantially after the mid-1940s, many of the late-period extended compositions suffering from a diminished originality and hasty work, often occasioned by incessant touring.

But this measured appraisal has come under withering assault in recent years, especially in the race-conscious interpretation of jazz history formulated by Albert Murray, elaborated by Stanley Crouch, and popularized by Wynton Marsalis. According to Murray, for example, Ellington is not merely the most important jazz composer but "the most representative American composer." Indeed, Murray implies that Ellington was the greatest of *all* American composers, in or out of jazz:

> Not unlike Emerson, Melville, Whitman, Twain, Hemingway, and Faulkner in literature, [Ellington] quite obviously has converted more of the actual texture and vitality of American life into first-rate, universally appealing music than anybody else. . . . By comparison the sonorities, not to mention the devices of Charles Ives, Walter Piston, Virgil Thomson, Aaron Copland, Roger Sessions, John Cage, and Elliott Carter, for example, seem if not downright European, at least as European as American.

Although Murray has had little to say about Ellington's experiments in extended musical form, Crouch, for his part, asserts that Ellington was at his peak not in the "four-year streak of three-minute masterpieces he and his orchestra produced between 1939 and 1942," but rather in the Fifties and Sixties, when he was chiefly occupied with the multi-movement suites regarded by Schuller and most other critics as inferior in quality to his earlier work. But Murray and Crouch are united in the belief that Ellington was altogether a talent so great as to belong to a realm beyond criticism. In the recent "Black in America" issue of the *New Yorker,* Crouch called Ellington "the most protean of American geniuses":

> In his music he assayed a multitude of forms and voices as successfully as Herman Melville, satirized the skin off pomposity as gleefully as Mark Twain, matched Buster Keaton for surreal slapstick, equaled the declarative lyricism Ernest Hemingway brought to lonely moments of tragic resolution, rivaled William Faulkner in the dense intricacy of his tonal colors, conjured up a combination of Bill (Bojangles) Robinson and Fred Astaire in the way his percussive accents danced through suave billows of harmony, was a twin to John Ford in the deployment

of his phenomenal repertory team of players, mixed satire and gloom with as much innovation as his good friend Orson Welles.

As can easily be deduced from such deep-purple passages, Murray and Crouch are not musicians. But their amateur appraisals have nonetheless been influential, to some extent because Ellington scholarship remains rudimentary. There is at present no scholarly biography of Ellington — the only fully serious book-length study by a musicologist, Mark Tucker's *Ellington: The Early Years* (1991), stops at the end of 1927 — and surprisingly little criticism of his work has been produced by trained musicians. In the absence of a more thoughtful critique of Ellington's oeuvre, the Murray-Crouch line is fast acquiring the status of an orthodoxy. Yet it is false, or distorted, in nearly every particular. In order properly to understand and appreciate his achievements, it is necessary to distinguish the real Duke Ellington from the mythical figure who exists only in the heated prose of his uncritical advocates.

BORN IN WASHINGTON, D.C., IN 1899, EDWARD KENNEDY ELlington (he acquired the nickname "Duke" as a teenager) began to study piano at the age of seven. But he was not a prodigy, and his lessons lasted no more than a few months; thereafter, he never again studied music formally, and seems not to have taken any special interest in classical music until long after he had become famous.

The full extent of Ellington's talent became dramatically evident within a few years of his emergence as a bandleader. By 1930, he had composed and recorded numerous scores that, though technically not as sophisticated as those played by the big bands of Fletcher Henderson, Jean Goldkette, and Paul Whiteman, were easily comparable in originality to the music of the much-admired New Orleans pianist-composer Jelly Roll Morton. Such early efforts as "Black and Tan Fantasy" (1927) and "The Mooche" (1928) were exceptional in their combination of exotic orchestral colors and innovative harmonies, and quickly attracted the attention of other musicians.

Ellington composed directly "on" his band, an unrivaled collection of musical eccentrics whom he chose for their idiosyncratic styles. He taught himself how to orchestrate by using the band as a laboratory, gradually mastering the art of blending individual timbres into a collective sound of unique richness and complexity. By the mid-Thirties, the Ellington band was consistently producing some of the finest music in jazz, and from 1940 to 1942 Ellington turned out a steady stream of compositions, among them "Ko-Ko," "Concerto for Cootie," "Harlem Air-Shaft," and "Warm Valley" (all from 1940), that were justly hailed as masterpieces.

But by this time, Ellington's fertile musical imagination had in certain ways outstripped his homemade technique. If his earliest orchestrations were worked out in collaboration with members of the band, as his scores grew more elaborate he began to make use of assistants who "extracted" instrumental parts from his rough sketches. This practice continued in varying degrees throughout Ellington's life (he used orchestrators, for example, in all the works he composed for symphony orchestra), as did his reliance on collaborators, both acknowledged and anonymous. Many of Ellington's early hits were based on themes supplied by his soloists: the clarinetist Barney Bigard had to sue him to receive credit (and royalties) for "Mood Indigo," and the trombonist Lawrence Brown, who claimed to have written part of "Sophisticated Lady," famously said to his employer, "I don't consider you a composer. You are a compiler."

From 1939 on, Ellington worked closely with Billy Strayhorn, the exact nature of whose contribution to the Ellington oeuvre may be the single most important unresolved issue in jazz scholarship. Initially billed as "staff arranger," Strayhorn — who, unlike Ellington, had extensive formal training in music — received full composing credit for several of the Ellington band's best-known recordings, among them "Take the 'A' Train" and "Chelsea Bridge" (both 1941), and collaborated on many other works, a fact Ellington himself admitted far more readily than did many of his admirers. (In his *New Yorker* essay, Stanley Crouch gives Ellington sole credit for several compositions for which the two men actually shared equal billing.)

But Strayhorn, because he was homosexual, deliberately kept a low profile. Little was written about him until after his death, and it was not until recently that the first biography, David Hajdu's *Lush Life: A Biog-*

raphy of Billy Strayhorn, was published. In the course of his research, Hajdu examined Strayhorn's private papers, on the basis of which he states unequivocally — though often without documentation — that in addition to their acknowledged collaborations, Strayhorn wrote parts of several of Ellington's most important works, including *The Tattooed Bride* (1948) and *A Tone Parallel to Harlem* (1950), both of which have been cited by Crouch in support of his claim that Ellington's later compositions are superior to his earlier ones.

On the question of Ellington's professional relationship with Strayhorn, Hajdu's book is of value mainly as a road map for future scholars. And even on the assumption that his claims prove true, it is important not to overstate their significance: there can be no doubt that Ellington was primarily responsible for the bulk of the music performed and recorded under his name. Still, the awkward fact remains that some of Ellington's work poses major problems of attribution.

PART OF WHAT LED ELLINGTON TO EMPLOY BETTER-TRAINED musical collaborators was his own lack of technical assurance — the same thing that led him, in general, to shun longer forms. In 1935, Ellington told a reporter he would never write an opera or a symphony. "I have to make a living and so I have to have an audience," he explained. But at the same time, he was working on his second extended composition, a twelve-minute single-movement work called *Reminiscing in Tempo,* and eight years later, in 1943, he would unveil a fifty-minute-long "tone parallel to the history of the American Negro" called *Black, Brown, and Beige.* It received its first performance at Carnegie Hall, the quintessential American symbol of musical legitimacy.

It is hardly surprising that Ellington should have sought to move beyond the narrow compass of the miniatures in which he specialized. Starting in the Thirties, he was praised by classical musicians who found in his work a sense of compositional unity unprecedented in jazz. In 1934, the English composer-critic Constant Lambert called him "a real composer, the first jazz composer of distinction," while in 1938, Aaron Copland, writing in the magazine *Modern Music* about big bands and their leaders, observed:

[T]he master of them all is still Duke Ellington. The others, by comparison, are hardly more than composer-arrangers. Ellington is a composer, by which I mean, he comes nearer to knowing how to make a piece hang together than the others.

Yet it was not until 1931 that Ellington first recorded an original composition, *Creole Rhapsody*, greater in length than a three-minute 78 side, and the experiment was not repeated until 1935 and *Reminiscing in Tempo*. Thereafter, Ellington attempted only rarely to compose in longer forms, most notably in *Diminuendo and Crescendo in Blue* (1937), *Black, Brown, and Beige, The Tattooed Bride,* and *A Tone Parallel to Harlem*. The vast majority of his "extended" works are actually suites whose purported structural unity is more a matter of clever titling (*The Perfume Suite, A Drum Is a Woman*) than anything else, and which are extremely uneven in musical quality.

The reason Ellington avoided longer forms is clear from his occasional attempts at working in them: he had only a superficial grasp of the techniques necessary to create organically larger musical structures. While all his extended pieces contain passages of great beauty and originality, none — with the possible exceptions of *Reminiscing in Tempo* and *The Tattooed Bride* — can be said to "work" structurally. The difficulty facing Ellington was not lack of talent, but lack of training. As Gunther Schuller explains:

> There are some talents involved in the art of composition which can be inborn, intuitive, or acquired subconsciously by absorption of a given musical environment. . . . But other compositional skills have to be learned, usually by some form of systematic study. From this requirement even the genius is not exempt, although obviously he does not need to acquire these in academic or formal settings. . . . Ellington's lack of technique and formal skills hindered him. He was content [in his longer works] to repeat thematic material, mostly with only the scantest of variations (or indeed none), too frequently relying on endless pedal points, on rambling piano interludes filled in by himself. . . . At best, themes and ideas simply succeeded each other; rarely did one have that sense of inevitability which marks great art.

Creole Rhapsody, Ellington's first sustained attempt at breaking the bounds of repeating-chorus song form, was in all likelihood inspired by the example of George Gershwin, and a comparison between the two men is illuminating. Like Ellington, Gershwin was a master miniaturist; and *Rhapsody in Blue,* his first attempt at large-scale composition, was also structurally incoherent. But unlike Ellington, Gershwin realized early on that he would never master the larger forms on his own. Not only did he study composition, he also familiarized himself with a wide range of classical music, up to and including the works of such modernists as Arnold Schoenberg and Alban Berg. This course of study made it possible for Gershwin to produce a series of "classical" compositions of increasing structural complexity, culminating in *Porgy and Bess.* None of these works are completely successful from a formal standpoint (though *An American in Paris* comes close), but it is nonetheless plain that Gershwin understood what he was trying to do, was intimately familiar with his models, and, had he lived, would almost certainly have solved the problems with which he was still grappling at the time of his death in 1937.

Ellington, by contrast, gave no indication of even recognizing that his limitations were limitations. At no time did he seek formal training, and to the end of his life his musical culture remained severely restricted. ("Instead of studying larger forms," the composer Alec Wilder once remarked, "Duke simply hired Billy Strayhorn.") His rare "symphonic" pieces appear to have been inspired by the mere desire to produce such works, not by any genuine comprehension of their structural imperatives. And in time he found an easier way to win the exalted reputation of a "classical" composer: the much-publicized suites of his later years allowed Ellington and his admirers to claim that he had done what in fact he had not done, and could not do.

IT IS NOT NECESSARY TO MISREPRESENT DUKE ELLINGTON'S gifts in order to assure him of a secure place in the history of American music. Whatever his shortcomings, he did create music of extraordinary individuality, and there seems little doubt that his best work — most of which is from the Thirties and Forties — will last.

Why, then, do Albert Murray and Stanley Crouch make claims for Ellington that cannot be justified by an objective appraisal of his work? Partly, I think, out of simple musical ignorance. But it should also be noted that the Ellington of their writings may be to some extent the product of a racial myth, and as such not accessible to rational discussion. How else are we to explain, for example, Murray's insistence that Ellington was more authentically "American" than Ives or Copland, or his implication that this alleged authenticity somehow made Ellington a better composer? Or Crouch's insistence that Ellington was equally at home in short and long musical forms? The oddly defensive belligerence of such extravagant comparisons tells us nothing useful about Ellington, but much about the degree to which even the most confident black intellectuals may be afflicted by self-doubt.

Such comparisons, however, also do a grave disservice to Ellington himself. If he was a great musician — as I believe he was — then his greatness will hardly be diminished by the searching scrutiny of qualified critics and scholars. By contrast, his reputation is clearly diminished by insupportable claims that he produced (in Crouch's words) "masterpieces, long or short, in every decade," or that his music is in any meaningful sense superior to that of such "European" composers as Ives or Copland. Ellington himself would have been appalled by such claims. "To attempt to elevate the status of the jazz musician by forcing the level of his best work into comparisons with classical music," he wrote in 1944, "is to deny him his rightful share of originality." This statement is as true today as it was a half-century ago. There is nothing to be learned by directly comparing a three-minute blues like Ellington's "Ko-Ko" with a forty-five-minute symphony by Copland. The composer of the former was incapable of composing the latter (and vice versa), yet both were masters of American music, each in his own way. The inability of the Ellington mythmakers to accept this fact separates them from those who revere the achievements — while acknowledging the limitations — of the real Duke Ellington.

Commentary 1996

Sins of the Fathers

IT IS A COMMONPLACE AMONG CONSERVATIVE ROMAN Catholics that anti-Catholicism is the last politically correct form of bigotry. Such folk will find plenty of red meat on which to feed in *The Priest,* Thomas M. Disch's new novel. The Rev. Patrick Bryce, the title character, is a hard-drinking hypocrite who likes to perform oral sex on pubescent boys when not otherwise occupied supplying anti-abortion sound bites to local television stations. His clerical colleagues include two ex-lovers whose dialogue could have been written by Terrence McNally ("You were so droll at dinner—and such a flirt") and a right-wing dunderhead who has sired a pair of illegitimate twins (one of whom turns out to be Father Pat). Every other practicing Catholic in *The Priest* is guilty of one or more of a gaudy panoply of sins ranging from anti-Semitism to multiple murder. The Inquisition and the Shroud of Turin also figure prominently in the action, the latter in a manner for which the word "blasphemous" is something of an understatement.

What we have here, in short, is an omnium-gatherum of Anti-Catholicism's Greatest Hits, not a few of which are getting a trifle long in the tooth. But the interesting thing about Disch, a spectacularly prolific author whose thirty previous books, plays, and librettos range from *The Brave Little Toaster* to *The Cardinal Detoxes,* is that he has recycled these chestnuts not in a crudely printed no-popery tract but in a novel of considerable originality and some brilliance, published by a reputable house whose other recent titles include Pope John Paul II's *Crossing the Threshold of Hope.* It is worth noting that the word "controversial" is nowhere to be found in the flap copy for a book likely to impact on orthodox Catholics with roughly the same muzzle velocity *The Satanic*

Verses had for Islamic fundamentalists. Presumably the publicity depart-ment of Alfred A. Knopf saw nothing controversial about *The Priest,* a judgment that says more about the current reputation of Catholicism among American intellectuals than it does about the content of Disch's novel. It also says something about the extent to which genre novels are taken seriously by their publishers. *The Priest* is the sort of book known to the trade as a "horror" novel, though Disch's subtitle, "A Gothic Romance," speaks more directly to his central conceit: supernatural forces cause Father Patrick Bryce to swap bodies in mid-novel with Silvanus de Roquefort, Bishop of Rodez and Montpellier-le-Vieux, en-thusiastic fornicator and apparatchik of the Inquisition, whose profes-sional activities include delivering fire-and-brimstone homilies and performing amateur mastectomies on female heretics. Short of actual bloodsucking, you can't get much more Gothic than that.

The Gothic novel has a long history of lip-smacking anti-Catholicism, going all the way back to *The Monk,* Matthew G. Lewis's 1796 shocker about a Capuchin abbot whose sexual misconduct sends him tumbling into hell. But there is an important difference between *The Monk* and *The Priest.* Most anti-Catholicism in the eighteenth and nineteenth cen-turies, Monk Lewis's included, was the fruit of ignorance and class prejudice; the ideas that drive *The Priest,* by contrast, derive not from simple bigotry but ideology. Disch puts sermons on the evils of the Catholic Church into the mouths of several of his characters, all of which boil down to the familiar complaint that the church's positions on sexual matters are life-denying and hypocritical. "We're all hypocrites nowa-days," one priest says. "The Vatican has made it a condition of employ-ment, so to speak. If we're not hypocrites about being gay, then we're hypocrites about birth control or abortion. We preach one thing in public, but in the confessional it's another story."

It is the specificity of this complaint that has kept Disch from making the most of a novel about which there are a great many good things. I was particularly impressed by his willingness to enlist Gothic tech-niques in the service of serious artistic aims. Even in an age of rational-ism run rampant, Gothicism remains a useful arrow in the novelist's quiver—one need only cite such disparate writers as Thomas Mann, Isaac Bashevis Singer, and Flannery O'Connor to make the point—and

Disch's animating conceit is an extraordinarily clever and fertile one, which he deploys with great panache. The trouble with *The Priest,* artistically speaking, is that Disch lets his outrage get in the way of his imagination. The fact that not one practicing Catholic character is allowed to show a glimmer of decency (except for the campy priest who resigns his post to become a chef at novel's end) is a problem, as is the denouement, which is curiously adolescent in its can-you-top-thisness. Least convincing of all is the way in which the plot pivots on the desire for revenge of one of the many altar boys Father Pat molested, who grows up to become a transvestite *and* a member of Act Up *and* a loyal member of the Catholic Church: "I don't want to destroy the church. . . . I *love* the church. I need the church." That, as the British say, is coming it a bit high.

But, of course, it is impossible to judge Disch's book solely as a novel. It is also a political statement, and a timely one. I read *The Priest* two days after Pope John Paul II released *Evangelium Vitae,* his latest encyclical, and the coincidence struck me as opportune. *Evangelium Vitae* does not deal with homosexuality, but the points it makes, particularly its straightforward attack on moral relativism, are quite relevant in this connection. "In a way," one of Disch's gay priests says of the Catholic Church, "that may be its problem — that it's in the nature of the church that it *can't* change. What's changed is the world around us." This is the heart of the homosexual case against Catholicism: the church is unwilling to update its dogma to suit the desires of contemporary worshipers. Yet the whole point of the Catholic Church is its unequivocal rejection of moral relativism in favor of natural law, which is by definition timeless and universal. Were the church to start inching away from this stance, it would cease to be the church.

Disch understands this. Rather than reforming the church, he would clearly prefer to sow salt on its ashes, a point of view more widely shared among American liberals than is commonly realized — or admitted. Nor is it simply to be dismissed as mere "Catholic bashing" (a term that in any case sounds uncomfortably whiny coming from conservatives who are quick to criticize other Americans seeking to exploit their "victim status"). The Vatican is arguably the last conservative institution in the West that takes its own ideas seriously enough to seek to apply them with absolute consistency; it makes perfect sense that those who oppose those ideas, Disch included, should do so with quasi-religious fervor.

"If intolerable alternatives are to be avoided," Sir Isaiah Berlin once said, "life must achieve various types of often uneasy equilibrium. I believe this deeply: but it is not a doctrine which inspires the young. They seek absolutes; and that usually, sooner or later, ends in blood." The American political system was designed to achieve uneasy equilibrium among a wide variety of competing forces; it is utterly ill suited to resolving the irreconcilable differences that separate Thomas Disch from John Paul II. Yet it is now being asked to resolve those differences, by fiat if necessary: that is what the present-day "culture wars" are all about. Though one may rightly bemoan the fact that yet another novelist of talent has chosen to join these bloody wars, Thomas Disch surely deserves full credit for having gone straight to the root of the matter. Compared with the Vicar of Christ, Rush Limbaugh and Newt Gingrich are strictly small potatoes.

New York Times Book Review 1995

The Anti-Victim: Arlene Croce

TWO KINDS OF CRITICS PROVOKE ANGER: BAD ONES AND great ones. Arlene Croce is widely acknowledged as the preeminent dance critic of her generation, Edwin Denby's only peer. Yet long after she stopped contributing regularly to the *New Yorker,* the mere mention of her name is still capable of making certain people hopping mad. Just the other day, I mentioned to a dance buff that Croce was about to publish a one-volume collection of her reviews, and received a reply altogether unsuitable for quotation in a family newspaper. Now that book is out, a chunky, clunkily titled anthology containing eighty-seven pieces culled by Robert Cornfield from Croce's three previous collections of dance criticism, plus nineteen later, uncollected essays. Though a few important things have slipped through his net, Cornfield has done his work well, and I have no doubt that a hundred years from today, *Writing in the Dark, Dancing in the New Yorker* will be ranked among the half-dozen indispensable books about dance to have been written in the twentieth century.

Croce's foremost gift as a critic is her ability to write vividly and indelibly about what dances and dancers look like. Though she confesses to being a "dance illiterate" who has "never formally studied dance, never taken a music lesson, never performed on any stage," she has given us such little miracles of poetic observation as this snapshot of the "Melancholic" variation of George Balanchine's *Four Temperaments:* "We have an expansive field of vision, but the solo dancer does not seem to know how much room he has. . . . The corps is a few small girls, a small menace. But they are enough to block and frustrate his every attempt to leap free. He leaps and crumples to earth. We recognize this man: his personal weather is always ceiling zero." We should all be so illiterate.

In addition to a first-class eye, Croce has a first-class mind. Most American intellectuals are hopelessly provincial when it comes to dance. Were it not so, Balanchine would be fully as legendary as Stravinsky, and Paul Taylor as much of a cultural icon as Robert Rauschenberg. But thanks to her (and to William Shawn, who not only hired her in 1973 but had the good sense to give her sufficient space with which to make an impression), the *New Yorker* was paying deeply informed attention to dance at a time when most so-called highbrow magazines were otherwise occupied. When I came to New York City, I had yet to see a single dance by Balanchine or Taylor or Merce Cunningham, but I had been *reading* about them in the *New Yorker,* and the pieces I was reading were set within a wide frame of cultural reference. Any art form that can inspire criticism like this, I thought, is worth knowing about. And so it was.

Reading Arlene Croce in bulk is a different experience from consuming her in weekly doses, one that put me in mind of the experience of reading the collected essays of Clement Greenberg, another critic who still makes people angry (and whom Croce cites to brilliantly apposite effect in an essay on the crisis of the proscenium stage). Unlike Greenberg, she has no overarching theory of dance, but her taste, if atheoretical, is nonetheless consistent: she is a classicist who believes that great art is not about ideas, but beauty. The whole of her anti-ideology can be found in a deceptively casual remark she slipped into a 1975 review (inexplicably omitted from this collection) of New York City Ballet's Ravel festival: "The audience for the Ravel festival probably included a lot of people who prefer acting to dancing — who like ballets that make you think. I never saw a good ballet that made me think." This lethal two-liner was self-evidently intended to enrage those painfully earnest modern-dance buffs who believe that art is valuable only to the extent that it makes the world a cleaner, better-lighted place. For those who thought otherwise — who believed, like Greenberg and Croce, in art for pleasure's sake — it was both electrifying and liberating to see such cheeky words in print.

What changed on Croce's watch was the prevailing political climate of art in America. By the late Eighties, the notion that the personal is political — or, to put it another way, that opposition to ideology-driven art is itself a form of ideology — had become central to "progressive" artistic thought. "I can recall even then," Croce writes dryly, "having to defend in many a seminar or panel discussion the right of the critic to be 'judgmental' in a democracy." At the same time, the creative energies that fueled the postwar dance boom were starting to dissipate. For Croce, 1989 was "the last year of ballet, the end of the wondrously creative and progressive ballet I'd known all my life," a terminus signaled by the retirement of Suzanne Farrell and Lincoln Kirstein from New York City Ballet and the departure of Mikhail Baryshnikov from American Ballet Theater. Within a matter of years, the philistines had seized the field. Paul Taylor and Merce Cunningham were still doing major work, but of the younger generation of choreographers, only Mark Morris, whose deliberately outrageous bad-boy antics concealed a profoundly subversive commitment to the supremacy of art over ideas, was turning out consistently compelling dances. Everyone else, it seemed, was busy creating bad ballets that made you think, usually about racism, sexism, and AIDS, the unholy trinity of postmodern art.

As the present volume reminds us, it was Croce who brought Morris to the attention of the public at large — perhaps her most historically significant achievement as a critic. But Morris was a modern-dance choreographer, unwilling to submit to the natural law of classicism as redefined by Balanchine. Where was the Mark Morris of classical ballet? Unable to find him and unwilling to settle for anything less, Croce began to lose interest in the dance scene, increasingly content to hurl occasional thunderbolts at Peter Martins for his dubious stewardship of the Balanchine repertory at New York City Ballet. (One of these later pieces, "Dimming the Lights," actually led to the departure of Robert Gottlieb, Shawn's successor at the *New Yorker,* from the City Ballet board. Greater loyalty hath no editor.) It was at this juncture that Croce wrote "Discussing the Undiscussable," the now notorious 1994 essay in which she announced that she was boycotting Bill T. Jones's *Still/Here,* a piece of performance art about real people suffering from terminal illnesses, in the belief that the advent of "victim art" would eventually prove disastrous for art in general and dance in particular: "I can live with the flabby, the feeble, the scoliotic. But with the righteous I cannot function at all. . . . Instead of compassion, these performers induce, and even invite, a cozy kind of complicity." By then, she had become vulnerable to attack from those who in earlier years might have been reluctant to speak out against so formidable a critic, and now that she has apparently quit the scene altogether, her reputation may be entering a Greenberg-like period of eclipse, the inevitable fate of strong-minded critics who make the mistake of being right at the wrong time.

To be sure, Croce was far from infallible (her fulsome early praise of Twyla Tharp, for example, now sounds less like prophecy than a school-girl crush), and merely because she has stopped writing about dance in America does not mean there is nothing left to write about. No, New York City Ballet isn't what it used to be, but the Balanchine Celebration held at the Kennedy Center in Washington served as a galvanizing re-minder that Balanchine's legacy is alive and thriving outside the erst-while capital of the dance world. And with the opening of the Mark Morris Dance Center in Brooklyn, the greatest choreographer of the baby-boom generation will finally have an institutional base from which to promulgate *his* gospel of modern dance for art's sake.

I wish Arlene Croce were interested in chronicling these develop-ments, but the bounty she gave us in her twenty-five years at the *New Yorker* was surely generous enough. *Writing in the Dark, Dancing in the New Yorker* demonstrates that you don't have to produce a magnum opus in order to write yourself into the history of an art form: you can also do it on the installment plan.

New York Times Book Review 2000

PART FOUR ∼ POST-POSTMODERN

Life with Camille

CAMILLE PAGLIA, WHO CLEARLY BELIEVES THAT BIG books should start with a big bang, makes the following pronouncements on the first page of *Sexual Personae: Art and Decadence From Nefertiti to Emily Dickinson*: "*Sexual Personae* seeks to demonstrate the unity and continuity of western culture." "The book accepts the canonical western tradition and rejects the modernist idea that culture has collapsed into meaningless fragments." "My stress on the truth in sexual stereotypes and on the biologic basis of sex differences is sure to cause controversy." "My method is a form of sensationalism." That's quite a laundry list, even for a seven-hundred-page book. Still, Paglia manages to keep most of her promises. Ostensibly a critical study of the representation of human sexuality in Western art, *Sexual Personae* is also a scorched-earth attack on the underlying philosophical assumptions of liberalism and feminism. Such attacks are not taken lightly in the academy these days, and Paglia is doubtless being picketed at this very moment by a gang of irate undergraduates. But she is no conservative, either, and any canon-loving traditionalist who takes the trouble to read her book from cover to cover is more than likely to join the picket lines.

The argument of *Sexual Personae* runs roughly as follows: Nature is barbarous and violent, though people choose to pretend that it is benevolent rather than succumb to utter despair. Art can be either Apollonian, camouflaging the "dehumanizing brutality" of nature, or Dionysian, accepting and celebrating it. The Apollonian striving for order is central to the Judeo-Christian tradition, which is responsible for "western personality and western achievement." Western culture nonetheless contains a Dionysian dimension (Paglia prefers the term "chthonic") that liberal humanists prefer not to acknowledge. In art, the chthonic realities of nature are typically represented by sexual symbolism, which is usually violent and compulsive. "The amorality, aggression, sadism, voyeurism, and pornography in great art," Paglia argues, "have been ignored or glossed over by most academic critics." To this end, *Sexual Personae* serves as an illustrated catalogue of the pagan sexual symbolism that Paglia believes to be omnipresent in Western art; a sequel devoted to popular culture is in the works.

All of this may sound rather conventional, if not actually stodgy, but Paglia heats things up considerably by drawing a flashy assortment of extreme conclusions from her basic premises. Not only does she praise "the spectacular glory of male civilization," she flatly rejects Rousseau's vision of "benign Romantic nature" and its offspring, "the progressivist strain in nineteenth-century culture, for which social reform was the means to achieve paradise on earth." Feminism, she claims, is "heir to Rousseau" in that it "sees every hierarchy as repressive, a social fiction; every negative about woman is a male lie designed to keep her in her place. Feminism has exceeded its proper mission of seeking political equality for women and has ended by rejecting contingency, that is, human limitation by nature or fate. . . . If civilization had been left in female hands, we would still be living in grass huts."

Paglia's aggressive antiliberalism is deceptive, however. While she pays lip service to traditional Western values ("The banning of pornography, rightly sought by Judeo-Christianity, would be a victory over the west's stubborn paganism"), her incessant assaults on liberalism and feminism are in fact profoundly anticonservative. Far from merely arguing for the significance of the chthonian dimension of Western art, Paglia positively wallows in it. A self-styled "advocate of aestheticism and Decadence," she seems to believe that decadent art is great precisely because it is decadent—that is, because it offers a truer vision of "the amorality of the instinctual life" and thus provides Apollonian civilization with a necessary catharsis for its chthonic fears and fantasies. "We may have to accept an ethical cleavage between imagination and reality," she says happily, "tolerating horrors, rapes, and mutilations in art that we would not tolerate in society."

The ability to infuriate both antagonists in an ideological struggle is often a sign of a first-rate book. *Sexual Personae* will undoubtedly antagonize the vast majority of its readers, and it contains patches of real brilliance, but Paglia is constantly tripping over her own pretentiousness. "My largest ambition," she says at the outset, "is to fuse Frazer with Freud." The pages of *Sexual Personae* are littered with equally prideful little packages of self-regard ("Chaucer's comic persona resembles that of Charlie Chaplin's Little Tramp, whom I seem to be alone in loathing." "Unlike older scholars, some of us find *King Lear* boring and obvious, and we dread having to teach it to resentful students.")

Paglia's aesthetic judgment is as erratic as her self-esteem is healthy. Her standard gimmick, endlessly repeated, is the high-low cultural comparison: Lord Byron and the Beach Boys, Coleridge and Rod Serling, Sir Frederick Ashton's ballets and *The Avengers*. Some of these yokings are so ludicrous as to seem almost campy: "Patrick Dennis' *Auntie Mame* (1955) is the American *Alice in Wonderland* and in my view more interesting and important than any 'serious' novel after World War II." But there is nothing intentionally funny about *Sexual Personae,* which is all too clearly the work of a lapel-grabbing fanatic with a universal theory to hawk. Paglia's elaborate schema of sexual symbolism, impressive though it may sound in the telling, has led her to construct a bizarre anticanon of decadence in which earnest dullards like Charles Dickens and Henry James are shoved aside in favor of that old fraud, the Marquis de Sade.

Sade, to be sure, is not without his significance. Mario Praz and Edmund Wilson, to name only two critics of distinction, recognized and acknowledged his noxious influence on various key figures in the Romantic movement. But Paglia is not merely interested in Sade — she *admires* him. She is, in fact, the latest of the Sade cultists who have been haunting the fringes of serious literary criticism for decades. Like the rest of her fellow Sadeans, she complains that her idol is underrated and ignored, "the most unread major writer in western literature. . . . No education in the western tradition is complete without Sade." Comparison with Sade, not surprisingly, is the ultimate superlative in her critical vocabulary: "William Blake is the British Sade, as Emily Dickinson is the American Sade."

After reading *Sexual Personae,* one rather expects Camille Paglia to turn up, whip in hand, as a character in David Lodge's next novel, locking horns with Morris Zapp at a Modern Language Association convention. Paglia is quite real, though, and she is also a conspicuously gifted writer. She is an exciting (if purple) stylist and an admirably close reader with a hard core of common sense. For all its flaws, her first book is every bit as intellectually stimulating as it is exasperating. But *Sexual Personae* is tainted with the kind of symbol-mongering reductionism that sees one thing in everything, and despite its considerable virtues, it left me thinking of Earl Long's pithy appraisal of Henry Luce and his notoriously single-minded magazines: "Mr. Luce is like a man that owns a shoe store and buys all the shoes to fit himself. Then he expects other people to buy them."

New York Times Book Review 1990

Tolstoy's Contraption

IN 1987, *THE BONFIRE OF THE VANITIES*, TOM WOLFE'S much-discussed novel about life in New York, spent fifty-six weeks on the *New York Times*'s bestseller list — but *A Man in Full,* published last year to still louder fanfare, dropped off the list after just nine weeks. Could it be that Wolfe's second novel was simply not good enough (or too good) to hold the attention of the reading public? Or was its comparative failure a sign of far-reaching changes in the once-privileged place of the novel in American culture?

It's no secret that the power of novels to shape the national conversation has declined precipitously since the days when J. D. Salinger and Norman Mailer were household names, and further still in the past decade alone. According to one recent study, 55 percent of Americans spend less than thirty minutes a day reading anything at all. Today, a book need only sell fifty thousand copies to crack the bestseller lists; even the biggest-selling pop novelists, Tom Clancy and Stephen King, top out at around a million copies per book. (The final episode of NBC's *Cheers,* by contrast, was seen by forty-two million people.) But who now wields this agenda-setting power? Certainly not the three major TV networks, whose viewership has also been declining, in part because of the rise of cable TV and the fast-growing popularity of the Internet as a source of news and entertainment. Yet cable TV and the Internet exist to serve niche markets; they do not yet wield broad-based cultural influence and may never do so. In our atomized culture, going to the movies is the one thing "everybody" does — perhaps the last cultural experience to be shared by very large numbers of Americans.

Nor are the movies solely a mass-culture phenomenon. For Americans under the age of thirty, film has largely replaced the novel as the dominant mode of artistic expression, just as the compact disc has become the "successor technology" to the phonograph record. No novel by any Gen-X author has achieved a fraction of the cultural currency of, say, Quentin Tarantino's *Pulp Fiction*. Movies like this are to today's twenty- and thirtysomethings what *The Catcher in the Rye* and *On the Road* were to the baby boomers.

What happened to the novel? Public schools ceased to emphasize the development of reading skills starting in the Sixties, around the same time that TV became ubiquitous. For this reason, most Americans born after 1970 are image-oriented: they spend more time looking at pictures than the printed word. This is a development of fearful significance, since a culture based solely on images is condemned to shallowness. (If you doubt this, consider the effect of TV on politics.) But it does not follow that the decline of the novel is therefore a wholly catastrophic event. It might even be that movies have superseded novels not because Americans have grown dumber but because the novel is an obsolete artistic technology.

We are not accustomed to thinking of art forms as technologies, but that is what they are — which means they can be rendered moribund by new technological developments, in the way that silent films gave way to talkies and radio to TV. Well into the eighteenth century, for example, most of the West's great storytellers wrote plays, not novels. But the development of modern printing techniques made it feasible for books to be sold at lower prices, allowing storytellers to reach large numbers of readers individually; they then turned to writing novels, and by the twentieth century the theatrical play had come to be widely regarded as a cultural backwater. To be sure, important plays continue to be written and produced, but few watch them (unless they are made into movies).

Until recently, two things stood in the way of the possible emergence of the sound film as a successor technology to the novel. One was the prohibitively high cost of filmmaking. The other was the fact that movies, like plays, could only be viewed by congregations of people. Accordingly, Hollywood made films in factory-like settings and marketed them as commodities (in the Thirties and Forties, one went not to "a movie" but "the movies"). But it is now possible to shoot a theatrical-quality film for $100,000 or less, while the invention of the videocassette means that anyone can watch *The Rules of the Game* or *Citizen Kane* alone and at his convenience.

As a result, Americans under thirty are habituated to the characteristic narrative style of film — it is far more familiar to them than that of prose fiction — and many talented young American storytellers who once might have chosen to write novels are instead making small-scale movies of considerable artistic merit. Such films as Brad Anderson's *Next Stop Wonderland,* Darren Aronofsky's *Pi,* Tom DiCillo's *Living in Oblivion,* Doug Liman's *Swingers,* Greg Mottola's *The Daytrippers,* Alexander Payne's *Election,* Kevin Smith's *Chasing Amy,* and Whit Stillman's *The Last Days of Disco* may not be able to compete with the high-school sex farces that clog the gigaplexes. But the astonishing box-office success of *The Blair Witch Project,* a starless horror film shot for $35,000, suggests that young audiences are open to more adventurous styles of filmmaking. In any case, it is only a matter of time before similar films are routinely released directly to videocassette and marketed like books (or made available in downloadable form over the Internet), thus circumventing the current blockbuster-driven system of film distribution. Once that happens, my guess is that the independent movie will replace the novel as the principal vehicle for serious storytelling in the twenty-first century.

Those who reflexively reject all cultural change will of course be disappointed by the decline of the novel, and they will be right — up to a point. No film director can provide more than a pale simulacrum of the verbal richness and fully articulated psychological and intellectual complexity of a novel like Henry James's *The Portrait of a Lady,* as Jane Campion proved in her maladroit film version. But it is also true that no novelist can illustrate his words with pictures shot by Gregg Toland and music composed by Bernard Herrmann, as Orson Welles did in *Citizen Kane.* Film has its own unique expressive resources, and it is wrong to assume that they are necessarily inferior to those of the novelist.

As it happens, Leo Tolstoy predicted not long before his death in

1910 that "this little clinking contraption with the revolving handle will make a revolution in our life — in the life of writers. It is a direct attack on the old methods of literary art. . . . This swift change of scene, this blending of emotion and experience — it is much better than the heavy, long-drawn-out kind of writing to which we are accustomed. It is closer to life." Though it took a century, Tolstoy's audacious prophecy will soon come to pass — and the results may not be so terrible as you think.

Wall Street Journal 1999

Is That All There Is?

Tight shot of a door opening to reveal a pleasant-looking MAN *in a business suit, briefcase in hand. (Soundtrack: birds chirping.)*

PULL BACK *to show the neatly painted house, well-kept lawn, and brand-new station wagon. It's a sunny morning in suburbia. As the man glances at his watch and starts down the walk to the waiting car, neatly stepping around a tricycle, his pretty* WIFE, *twelve-year-old* DAUGHTER, *and eight-year-old* SON *appear in the doorway, smiling and waving....*

Time out for a pop quiz. This man is:

(a) sleeping with his secretary
(b) beating his wife
(c) molesting his daughter
(d) molesting his son
(e) a caring, considerate breadwinner who goes to church every Sunday and loves his family more than life itself.

If you answered (e), you don't get out much. In Hollywood, suburbia is hell, a clean, well-lit place where benighted souls afflicted by the false consciousness of the middle classes are sentenced to lead empty lives of not-so-quiet desperation, from which they take time out only to get high, abuse a child, or go shopping. The sole exceptions to this iron rule are teenagers, provided they dress down, affect surly expressions, treat their parents with casual contempt, have sex early and often (or at least try to), and promise to vote Democratic once they turn eighteen. Small wonder, then, that Sam Mendes's *American Beauty* is being advertised, accurately enough, as "the best-reviewed movie of the year," since at first glance — not to mention second and third — it appears to embody nearly every cliché on the above list.

Lester Burnham (Kevin Spacey), the protagonist of *American Beauty*, is a supercilious cynic whose meaningless job (he's a low-level reporter for a media magazine) is about to be downsized out of existence. He hasn't made love to his wife Carolyn (Annette Bening) for so long that his principal sexual outlet now consists of masturbating in the shower. Jane (Thora Birch), Lester's teenage daughter, regards him with scorn and pity, while he in turn lusts after Angela (Mena Suvari), her Lolita-like best friend. Meanwhile, Carolyn, a tightly wound real-estate agent who plays Bobby Darin records at dinnertime and cares more for her roses than her family, is having a torrid affair with her chief competitor. As if this weren't enough, the Burnhams have just acquired an exceedingly creepy set of next-door neighbors. Colonel Fitts (Chris Cooper) is a retired marine who collects Nazi memorabilia, subjects his son Ricky (Wes Bentley) to monthly drug tests, and beats him up from time to time just to keep him on his toes. Ricky, who affects a mask of quiet submission in his father's presence, is in fact a black-clad aesthete and amateur filmmaker who runs a thriving little dope-dealing business on the side. Having dealt these well-thumbed cards, Mendes and script-writer Alan Ball proceed to play them in ways that are occasionally smart and funny but more often embarrassingly predictable. Lester blackmails his employers into giving him a huge severance package, goes to work at a fast-food joint, and starts pumping iron and smoking marijuana to impress Angela. Jane falls in love with Ricky, whose father, a raving homophobe, falls madly in love with the new, pumped-up Lester.

American Beauty is just that smug, just that obvious, just that contemptuous of ordinary middle-class family life — except when it isn't. For somewhere beneath the thick veneer of cheap laughs and easy answers, Mendes and Ball seem to have been trying to make quite a different sort of film, one that comes honestly to grips with materialism and its discontents. To see that film, though, you have to ignore much of the one on screen (including absolutely everything having to do with Ricky's father, who is approximately as believable as Bill Clinton). Therein lies the paradox of *American Beauty:* the liberal intolerance of its makers systematically undercuts the very points they are trying to make.

"I'm forty-two years old," Lester announces at the outset in a voice-over shamelessly pinched from *Sunset Boulevard.* "In less than a year, I'll be dead. Of course, I don't know that yet. In a way, I'm dead already." What Lester means, of course, is that he is *spiritually* dead, the proof of which is that even when he is finally jolted back into consciousness by the loss of his job, his automatic response is to cleave even more frantically to the visible world, turning his back on his real life — his wife and child — to pursue the nubile Angela. Lester's increasingly obsessive attempts to get into shape are a metaphor for his deluded materialism: at film's end, he looks fabulous but is empty inside.

In the last ten minutes of *American Beauty,* much of the nonsense of the preceding hour and a half abruptly peels away as Angela offers herself at long last to Lester, who realizes in a terrible moment of epiphany that he has been pursuing a mirage (for it turns out that she is in fact a frightened virgin). All at once the scales fall from his eyes, and instead of having sex with Angela, he comforts her like the father he has forgotten how to be. In that moment, we can see his shriveled soul coming back to life, and here, too, we see for the first time just how good Spacey is. Throughout most of the film, he takes the script's elephantine ironies at face value, turning in a performance notable mainly for its snideness. But as soon as Lester gets real, so does Spacey, and in the final scene, a parade of complex emotions — delusion, dawning comprehension, self-loathing, repentance — marches across his face with the galvanizing clarity only a great actor can summon.

Alas, at this point, things take an irreversibly wrong turn (the final plot twist will make you groan out loud), and as a result, you are likely to go home fixated on all that is banal about *American Beauty,* of which there is no shortage. My cliché meter nearly broke, for example, once it became clear that Ricky was being offered up as the film's moral touchstone, the only character in tune with his soul. Similarly, the way Lester's wife is presented as a robot of ambition is so gratuitously cruel, so devoid of true sympathy, as to border on the hateful (an impression that Bening's wonderfully precise performance inadvertently serves to reinforce).

Such coarseness makes it difficult to give full credit to Mendes and Ball for what appears to have been a genuinely serious attempt on their parts to make a quasi-religious movie. To be sure, most critics have been notably reluctant to impute religious significance to *American Beauty,* no doubt in many cases out of ignorance, but to me the point is self-evident. When Ricky explains to Jane that he films the seemingly meaningless occurrences of everyday life in the hope of catching glimpses of what he calls "an entire life behind things," surely he is speaking of the supernatural world, just as Lester's final monologue (which poaches as shamelessly from *Our Town* as the opening did from *Sunset Boulevard*) plainly implies that the spiritual life can and must be pursued everywhere — yea, even unto the suburbs!

Too bad that so powerful a message had to be obscured by the reflexive youth-worship and bourgeois-baiting that prevent *American Beauty* from adding up to more than the sum of its not infrequently compelling parts. Being bourgeois, after all, is not the same thing as being good, and a film whose clever makers had dared to question their own moral superiority (no preacher should ever be smug) might have been vastly more effective in persuading its comfortable viewers that hard bodies do not always harbor beautiful souls.

Crisis 1999

Beasts and Superbeasts

HUMAN BEINGS LOVE TO FLIRT WITH FEAR, WHICH can be made even more attractive by placing it under lock and key, visible but inaccessible. We caress the iron bars that keep the caged lions from slashing our faces; we queue up to ride mechanical contraptions designed to make us vomit. Yet nothing thrills us more than stories implying that there are dark forces in the world too powerful to be tamed by human hands. Such tales, be they Gothic novels or the latest slasher movie, speak to us with a directness that slices through our painstakingly acquired veneers of sophistication: a bloodstained man materializes without warning in a doorway and we scream, half afraid and half ecstatic. But there is a difference between the stories that scared our great-grandparents and the ones that scare us. Nineteenth-century horror stories operated on the assumption, shared by reader and writer alike, that while ghosts and vampires might or might not exist in real life, there could be no doubting the existence of *some* sort of supernatural realm, meaning that devils might well walk among us. Not for nothing were such novels as *Dracula* shot through with specifically Christian iconography and symbolism. Indeed, they could never have been written in the absence of Christianity, or something very much like it.

With the ebbing of the sea of faith, ambiguity crept into the ghost story, sometimes to striking effect ("The Turn of the Screw" is all the more frightening precisely because we do not know for sure whether the ghost of Peter Quint is real). Once the tide was out for good, though, horror fiction, like modernity itself, was reduced to living on spiritual credit. Agnostic authors cynically spun new tales of the supernatural, drawing on a millennium's worth of accumulated faith in order to make their readers' flesh creep. Of late, the account has been running low, and cinematic horror has entered a decadent phase in which vampires have mostly given way to serial killers whose murderous frenzies are coolly explained away by psychiatrist-sleuths, while semi-satirical movies like *Scream* openly spoof the all-too-familiar conventions of their genre, like a shipwrecked explorer who eats his own flesh in order to survive.

Far more interesting, if ultimately no less decadent, is *The Blair Witch Project,* a no-budget film shot for $35,000 that is well on its way to becoming the most profitable independent movie ever made. It is a near perfect exercise in postmodernism, a horror film whose subject is film itself. The improvised script is as thin as a summer suit: three student filmmakers (Heather Donahue, Michael Williams, and Joshua Leonard) set out to shoot a documentary about a Maryland forest that is said to be haunted. They lose their way and are forced to camp in the woods, growing colder, hungrier, and steadily more terrified as they come to realize that an unknown assailant is stalking them. In the end, they vanish without trace, leaving behind the undeveloped film that directors Daniel Myrick and Eduardo Sanchez have edited into a movie called — what else? — *The Blair Witch Project*.

Blair Witch was shrewdly designed to appeal to media-savvy teenagers lured by an Internet-based publicity campaign, which left the false impression that Donahue, Williams, and Leonard were not actors playing parts but actual students who actually disappeared in the Blair woods. (All three actors are referred to by their own names in the film.) This impression is reinforced by the deliberately amateurish cinematography — the actors shot the film themselves — while the alleged "horrors" are suggested rather than shown, a time-honored technique beloved of cash-strapped producers, though none the less effective for its familiarity. Alas, *Blair Witch,* though hugely entertaining, is not especially scary, no doubt because it was all too clearly made by people who do not believe in the demons whose presence they have so cunningly implied. To be sure, there are moments when the movie breaks free of its ingenious conceit and becomes something more than merely artful; near the end, Donahue turns the camera on herself and records a final message to her family that is unexpectedly moving, and the climactic scene, in which the students meet their invisible tormentor, leaves a sharp aftertaste of genuine fear. Elsewhere, though, one rarely feels that the very clever people who made *The Blair Witch Project* thought they were doing anything more than making a very clever film.

Not so M. Night Shyamalan, the twenty-eight-year-old writer-director of *The Sixth Sense,* whose labyrinthine plot centers on Dr. Malcolm Crowe (Bruce Willis), a Philadelphia psychiatrist charged with the care of Cole Sear (Haley Joel Osment), a nine-year-old boy obsessed with violence whose arms are covered with mysterious scars. At length, Cole makes a confession to Dr. Crowe — "I see dead people" — and the doctor, not unreasonably, concludes that his young patient is a paranoid schizophrenic. But Cole's problem turns out to be not nearly so simple, and the more time Dr. Crowe spends with the boy, the more he comes to doubt his diagnosis.

For once, the convention of not giving away the surprise ending of a popular film will be honored here. If you're not floored by the last couple of twists in *The Sixth Sense,* you ought to consider taking up script-writing yourself. But Shyamalan is no ordinary horrormonger, and *The Sixth Sense,* while it contains more than a few moments scary enough to make you grab a stranger's arm, is no ordinary horror movie but the work of a greatly gifted director who has the power to make reality itself seem hallucinatory. Though the dialogue is nicely turned, *The Sixth Sense,* like *Vertigo* or *North by Northwest,* is meant to be seen as much as heard, and in Shyamalan's knowing hands, everyday sights — autumn leaves whisking down a South Philadelphia street, a helium balloon floating to the top of an empty stairwell — all but quiver with numinous implication.

Yet the film's impact arises in even larger part from the fact that unlike *Blair Witch,* not to mention every other horror movie made in the past quarter-century, it takes its own subject matter seriously. Not coincidentally, Cole is a Catholic — when he recites the "De Profundis," Dr. Crowe is forced to dig out his college Latin dictionary and translate it word by word — and at no time is it suggested that his faith is in any way foolish, perverse, or otherwise inferior to the secular religion of psychiatry. (In fact, it is the only thing keeping the boy from going mad.) Just as important, Cole's credibility as a character hinges on the audience's willingness to believe that he really *does* see dead people, for his appalling visions are not explicable as mere metaphors, or wishful thinking: they are real or they are nothing.

The Sixth Sense is not overtly religious — otherwise, it wouldn't have become a hit — but its spiritual underpinnings are not extraneous to the film's phenomenal success, which seems to have taken its producers by surprise and is by all accounts the result not of paid publicity but the kind of word-of-mouth enthusiasm no money can buy. My guess is that a good percentage of its viewers, whether they know it or not, are reveling in the rare opportunity to see a movie that accords with their own convictions. Most Americans, after all, believe in God, heaven, and hell, and while I have no information as to Shyamalan's own religious opinions, I have a sneaking suspicion that they are not dissimilar. This may explain why *The Sixth Sense* has replaced *The Blair Witch Project* at the top of the box-office charts: all other things being equal, a film about something is more interesting than a film about nothing.

Crisis 1999

Whit Stillman, Class Clown

ONCE UPON A TIME, I WAS RUNNING A MONTHLY COCK-tail party-salon headquartered in a townhouse on the Upper East Side of Manhattan that had once belonged to Alan Jay Lerner. One evening, I showed up to unlock the bar and saw to my amazement that the room in which we gathered each month was full of strange-looking equipment, and the furniture draped with white sheets. Upon further inquiry, I learned that our digs would be temporarily doubling after hours as an interior for a movie, written and directed by a casual acquaintance of mine. People one knew didn't make movies back in 1989, nor did the acquaintance in question seem even slightly plausible in the role of *auteur*, but we all made a point of not spilling any booze that night, little knowing that our meeting place would someday come to be revered by independent-movie buffs as the home of the Sally Fowler Rat Pack, the anxiously earnest young debs and escorts of Whit Stillman's *Metropolitan*.

The rest is cinematic history. Stillman shot *Metropolitan* on a shoe-string, followed by two more utterly personal movies, *Barcelona* and *The Last Days of Disco*, completing a trilogy that has long since established him as one of the wittiest filmmakers of his generation, or any other. My guess is that a quarter-century from now, he'll be talked about the way today's critics talk about, oh, Billy Wilder. And now he is the subject of a book of essays, a few of which are high-minded enough to make a doctoral candidate blush. *Doomed Bourgeois in Love* — the perfect title is the advertising slogan for *Metropolitan*, cleverly shorn of its internal punctuation — contains an introduction and nine new essays about Stillman's three films and one novel, followed by an appendix consisting of four previously published but uncollected reviews. The contributors range from such impeccably usual suspects as Luc Sante and Donald Lyons to a number of smart people whose names I didn't know. All agree that Stillman is the real deal, though certain of them, as Lauren Weiner admits in her very fine consideration of his use of irony, "run the risk of investigating away all the charm" of his films. One essay (not hers) starts out like this: "'Amerika, du hast es besser!' Goethe exclaimed." Yikes!

In between these occasional miscalculations, the authors of *Doomed Bourgeois in Love* have a great many shrewd and illuminating things to say about Stillman and his art, and if they sometimes lapse into over-seriousness, it is the vice of a virtue, which is that they take him very seriously indeed. For Whit Stillman is a comedian of the best kind, one with a highly developed moral imagination: his films are rooted in a clear-eyed understanding of just how hard it has become for nice young men and women to figure out the right thing to do in a culture without rules. Fresh out of school, his well-heeled, angst-ridden twentysome-things find themselves swept up in a complicated, unforgiving world for which their sheltered lives have left them unprepared. Certainly it is hard to believe that *The Last Days of Disco,* which deals with the messy love lives of a group of young New Yorkers who frequent a club not unlike Studio 54, was intended to be nothing more than a charming story of romance in the early Eighties. No sermons are preached: we merely see what happens to the characters as they make their hapless way in a world that has renounced religion as a guide to life. Yet their collective misadventures add up to a withering critique of contempo-rary American culture, one that is all the more effective for having been played for laughs.

The elaborate plot centers on Alice Kinnon (Chloe Sevigny) and Charlotte Pingress (Kate Beckinsale), two publishing-house flunkies — a coveted entry-level job for bright young things with brand-new Ivy League degrees and allowances from home — who spend their nights partying at the most fashionable club in New York, where they become acquainted with a group of similarly situated men. More than anything else, they long to be thought worldly ("I live dangerously — on the edge"), but neither girl knows all that much about sex, and their male friends, it soon emerges, are scarcely more knowledgeable. In downtown New York, such ignorance is unforgivable, so Alice and Charlotte move into a railroad flat together and plunge into the high waters of sexual experience. For the agonizingly shy Alice, the club appears at first glance to be a haven where she can shed her unwanted inhibitions to the pounding beat of dance music, but it is in fact a sinister place where money is laundered and cocaine snorted, and an air of decadence and doom hangs over its drab facade and glittering interior. "I have a very bad feeling about the club," one character says. "It's like a meteorite is headed straight for it. It's going to destroy everything." Nor is his apocalyptic prediction far wrong: at film's end, the club has been shuttered by the police, and the young men and women who once danced there have lost their virginity, their jobs, and their innocence.

Bleak though this description may sound, *The Last Days of Disco* is on the surface a soufflé-light romantic comedy in the manner of *Metropolitan* and *Barcelona*. But just as their witty dialogue concealed a hard core of moral seriousness, so does *The Last Days of Disco* speak pointedly of the myriad ways in which the sexual revolution has laid waste to countless lives. "Thank God, this is a whole new era," Charlotte blithely informs Alice as they look down at the dance floor. "We're in complete control. There are a lot of choices out there. . . . I just think it's so important to be in control of your own destiny." Little do they realize that the ideas they have picked up so casually from their older siblings carry with them dire consequences, and that their freely made "choices" will soon bring them pain and grief — and, in Alice's case, sickness.

One of the most thought-provoking aspects of *The Last Days of Disco* is the unobtrusive manner in which it shows how organized religion has largely ceased to be a part of upper-middle-class American life, though it is omnipresent in the script, slightly out of focus but nonetheless unmistakable for those with eyes to see. Churches are forever popping up in the background, but no one ever speaks of them, much less goes into one to worship; one character admits to believing in God, but his confession is explained away (or is it?) as a symptom of manic depression. In the last scene, Stillman's chastened children march off to adulthood as church bells toll softly in the background: the meteorite has struck at last, destroying the last redoubt of their youth and leaving them to figure out what to do with the rest of their lives.

MARK C. HENRIE, THE EDITOR OF *DOOMED BOURGEOIS IN Love,* is well aware of what Whit Stillman is up to. "The perplexity that animates each of Stillman's films," he explains in his introduction, "is how to find our way, how to live well, when the cake of custom has been broken. . . . Perhaps in an age such as ours, it is not tragedy but comedy which is the mature response." Accordingly, much of the book is devoted to this theme, and variations on it. Joseph Alulis, for instance, reads *Metropolitan* as a "defense of virtue," while Peter Augustine Lawler, in "Nature, Grace, and *The Last Days of Disco,*" contends that Stillman's films are "rather Socratic, Christian, and at least ambiguously conservative." But several essays range further afield, among them George Sim Johnston's "Whit Stillman, Novelist," a review of Stillman's novelization of *The Last Days of Disco,* a book that failed to receive the close attention it deserved. Unlike most critics, Johnston saw that *The Last Days of Disco, With Cocktails at Petrossian Afterwards,* far from being a casual knockoff of the original screenplay, was in fact a fully imagined reconception of the film, worthy of consideration in its own right as a free-standing work of literary art:

> [T]he metamorphosis of *The Last Days of Disco* (the movie) into *The Last Days of Disco* (the book) is as miraculous and unexpected as anything in Ovid. It is as though the author had a burden of social knowledge that he could not fully discharge in one medium and so turned into a novelist to get the job fully done. If Stillman's movies remind you of a European art film that is actually fun, this novel puts one in mind of the good old days of elegant social fiction — of Wharton and Fitzgerald, Marquand and Cheever.

At the same time, Johnston's typically acute review points to a weakness of *Doomed Bourgeois in Love,* which is that many of the contributors are not especially responsive to the specifically *cinematic* aspect of Stillman's work. With a few notable exceptions, they seem to think of his films as more or less equivalent to their scripts, an admiring but equally misguided inversion of one of the two criticisms leveled most frequently at Stillman, which is that his characters are too talky, a "defect" about which he is rightly unapologetic. As it happens, the screenplays to *Metropolitan* and *Barcelona* have been published, and to read them is to see at once that he really does think in theatrical terms, if not necessarily visual ones (though he is marvelously good at using décor to evoke a strong sense of time and place). No more than Jean Renoir or John Sayles is he interested in "pure" cinema: like them, he understands that there is more than one way to make a movie. "Some visual purists still think film is pictures at an exhibition," he once said to me in an interview. "They seem to forget that we've been making sound films ever since the Twenties. Talk is incredibly important. . . . Of course you have to be very careful with it, and I understand why all the screenwriting gurus warn against too much dialogue, but I think they're making a mistake. Even action films often have very good dialogue, though there isn't necessarily a lot of it. What's the charm of a buddy comedy? Just to see two guys shooting bullets? It's what the two guys *say* to each other that matters."

The other criticism, of course, is that he makes movies about young people with money, which is both a silly oversimplification and — to coin an epithet — classist. In any case, as James Bowman points out in "Whit Stillman: Poet of the Broken Branches," he uses the besieged values of the Urban Haute Bourgeoisie as a symbol of "a much less subjective and more accessible kind of goodness and innocence." That's what makes his tough-minded but sweet-tempered tales of uncertain youth as much a part of the indie-flick subculture as, say, Kevin Smith's *Clerks,* an edgy, sexually blunt comedy set in a convenience store somewhere in deepest New Jersey. Stillman's real interest is not in old money but young love, and how it has fared in the wake of the sexual revolution; his droll, oddly formal-sounding preppies and yuppies, just like Smith's grubby, potty-mouthed Gen-X slackers, are lost in postmodern America, looking for an exit sign. He is the poet of their touching plight, and *Doomed Bourgeois in Love* pays due tribute to the singular subtlety with which he has given them voice.

National Review 2001

Pictures of Words: John Sayles

ON PAPER, JOHN SAYLES WOULD SEEM TO BE THE QUIN-tessence of a critics' darling. He writes, directs, and edits serious-minded independent films shot on skin-tight budgets. What's more, these films are politically conscious (to use his own olive-drab phrase), and the politics are both explicitly presented and impeccably liberal-populist, with a pinch of curdled Sixties radicalism stirred in for extra sourness. Is it any wonder that he's among the handful of filmmakers to have won a "genius grant" from the MacArthur Foundation? He might have been genetically engineered to be suitable for so politically correct an honor. Yet Sayles is by no means the Woody Allen of the Big Chill generation. Indeed, the grudgingly respectful reviews of *Sunshine State,* his latest movie, left me wondering whether there are all that many critics who really *like* his work — which I, unlikely as it may sound, happen to love.

Why this lack of enthusiasm? What is it about Sayles that inspires a normally sharp-eyed moviegoer like David Denby to declare that the creator of such wonderfully varied works of cinematic art as *Baby, It's You, Eight Men Out, Passion Fish,* and *Lone Star* is not "a natural film-maker, or much of a dramatist"? Part of the problem is that most people who write about film are either modernists or postmodernists. Modernists hold, with Clement Greenberg, that artists should "eliminate from the specific effects of each art any and every effect that might conceivably be borrowed from or by the medium of any other art." For this reason, they like films about film — that is, movies whose primary impetus is visual, not verbal. Alfred Hitchcock and Buster Keaton are their gods, and they're always ready to go into rhapsodies over any film that contains a scene without dialogue. (Don't get a modernist critic started on the first reel of *Rio Bravo*—he'll talk about it all the way through dessert.) The worst thing they can say about a movie is that it's "talky." Postmodernists, on the other hand, like films about *films,* and so they favor directors, like François Truffaut, Joel Coen, or Steven Soderbergh, whose subject matter is other movies. As kids, they preferred going to the movies to playing outside; as grownups, they'd rather watch a remake of *Citizen Kane* than the real thing.

John Sayles doesn't fit into either of these pigeonholes. His films aren't devoid of action, or of visual interest, but they do consist mainly of actors and actresses talking—pictures of words, so to speak. And while he does sometimes make genre-like movies (*Lone Star,* for example, is a noirish whodunit), you never get the feeling that he's particularly interested in commenting on the history of the medium. His subject matter is not film, or other films, but people, usually unglamorously ordinary people trying to make the best of the moderately bad situations with which life presents them, portrayed with sympathetic but clear-eyed realism. Off the top of my head, I can't think of a Sayles movie in which anything explodes, or whose principal character is a head-turning beauty.

Sayles's method can be seen at its purest in *Sunshine State,* the unabashedly rambling story of what happens when a group of unscrupulous real-estate developers tries to take over Delrona Beach, a shabby Florida town famous for nothing, and bulldoze it into a gorgeously landscaped beachfront community full of rich golfers. (Among the bad guys is Alan King, a superannuated stand-up comedian whom old age has miraculously transformed into one of the craftiest character actors around.) While their shady machinations are central to the complicated plot, *Sunshine State* is not a *Chinatown*-like study of moral corruption, and it doesn't even matter all that much that the bad guys lose— sort of—in the end. Sayles's real interest is in the citizens, past and present, of Delrona Beach, in particular Marly Temple (Edie Falco), a sun-dried motel manager who hates her unadventurous life but lacks the nerve to change it, and Desirée Stokes (Angela Bassett), who left town at fifteen, black, pregnant and unmarried, and has now come back home as an adult to try to make peace with her genteel, censorious mother (Mary Alice).

If you're thinking that all this sounds like a cross between a soap opera and an eat-your-spinach editorial in *Mother Jones,* I can see why. Many of Sayles's films sound painfully stilted — on paper. It's only when you see them, or hear him talk about them, that you realize how essentially unideological he is. This has nothing to do with politics, at least as that term used to be construed. I'm sure he's never voted for a Republican in his life, but as a filmmaker, he doesn't go in for political caricature, or any other kind of caricature. (Significantly, he is one of the very few filmmakers whose middle-class black characters invariably act like real people, not secular saints.)

Asked by a fawning interviewer why so few American directors make politically conscious movies, Sayles gave this typical reply:

> It's easier not to, and sometimes it's really not the point of a movie. Sometimes it would really get in the way. I think more than being political or not political, it's often the problem of being complex: The characters aren't heroic. Sometimes they do things you don't like, even if you may like them, and it's hard to know exactly who the good guys and bad guys are, because everybody is a little bit compromised. And if you put that into your average adventure movie, it makes it complicated in ways that slow the movie down and really aren't appropriate for that particular movie.

That's John Sayles in a nutshell, political but never doctrinaire, not even about the nature of filmmaking. You get the feeling that unlike most critics, he believes there are any number of ways to make a movie, including but by no means limited to his own.

The only American writer-director I can think of whose work is at all like Sayles's is Whit Stillman, and the comparison says a lot about both men, since their films don't seem at first glance to have much in common. It's a long way from the Sea-Vue Motel of Delrona Beach, Florida, to the Upper East Side of New York City, just as it is hard to imagine Edie Falco (whose deceptively unflashy performance in *Sunshine State* is the work of a first-class actress) having anything to say to

Chris Eigeman, the archer-than-arch super-WASP who is Stillman's on-camera alter ego. But Sayles, like Stillman, is unafraid to plant his camera firmly in one spot, point it at his characters, and let them talk. He knows that two people talking can be every bit as dramatic — and as visually rich — as two people trying to kill each other with digitally enhanced light sabers.

Back in the days when Barbara Pym couldn't get her novels published, Philip Larkin wrote to an editor he knew to try to persuade him of her virtues. "I like," he said, "to read about people who have done nothing spectacular, who aren't beautiful or lucky, who try to behave well in the limited field of activity they command, but who can see, in little autumnal moments of vision, that the so called 'big' experiences of life are going to miss them; and I like to read about such things presented not with self pity or despair or romanticism, but with realistic firmness & even humour, that is in fact what the critics wd call the moral tone of the book." That's just what most Hollywood movies don't do — and what makes *Sunshine State* one of the finest American films of the past decade.

Crisis 2002

The Tilt-a-World of David Ives

EVERY WORK OF ART IS A WORLD UNTO ITSELF, GOV-erned by its own rigorous laws. Usually these laws are familiar ones (gravity) or simulations of familiar ones (perspective). When they're wholly unfamiliar, you get atonal music or *Finnegans Wake*. But what happens when all the laws are familiar, save one? Then you've wandered into the parallel universe of surrealism. If you're watching television, it's *The Twilight Zone;* if you're looking at a painting, it's a quiet suburb whose sky is dense with a hundred gentlemen in bowler hats, floating serenely away to some mysterious paradise. And if you should be sitting in a New York theater laughing hysterically, chances are that it's a play written by David Ives, whose latest show is a mixed bill of six one-act comedies called *Mere Mortals and Others*.

This is the sort of thing that happens in Ives's plays:

- A man comes into a café, tries a pickup line on a woman reading at a table and gets brushed off. A bell rings offstage. The man tries a different line and gets brushed off again. Then the bell rings again, and the man tries again. And again. And again. (She: "Girlfriend?" He: "No, I don't have a girlfriend. Not if you mean the castrating bitch I dumped last night." Bell.)

- A nervous young woman with a stutter enters a classroom, where she's heartily greeted by a fellow in a lab coat who says, "Velcro! Bell jar, Froyling! Harvard*yu?*" She's come for her first lesson in a "universal language" called Unamunda, advertised as "the language that will unite all humankind." (In Unamunda, the word for *English* is *Johncleese.*)

- A foul-mouthed big-city milk distributor goes home to his wife each night, puts on a red dress, black lace panties, and stiletto pumps, and promptly sheds his cares.
- The lights go up on Leon Trotsky's Mexico retreat. Trotsky is seated at his desk, scribbling furiously and talking to himself. "The proletariat is right," he mutters. "The proletariat must always be right." Then you see an ax handle sticking out of the back of his head.

You were expecting maybe Neil Simon? Nice, neat three-act plays crackling with cookie-cutter one-liners? Not a chance. Ives is a very amusing man, and his plays — some of which take up as little as two printed pages — are full of good lines, but they have as much in common with your standard rolling-in-the-aisles Broadway show as *Sunday in the Park with George* has with *The Sound of Music*. His singular achievement is that he brings to the high-speed world of sketch comedy an oddly tilted vision for which "surrealistic" is the only possible adjective. Yet Ives's plays are never, ever pretentious. Sometimes they're drop-dead funny; sometimes they're shot through with startlingly intense ruefulness. Often they are structured more like a piece of music — a fugue, a rondo, a theme and variations — than a conventional theater piece: the chiming of a bell, or the repetition of a catch phrase, divides up a scene with the crispness of a cadence. And always, they are as individual as the voice of an old friend, albeit one with a penchant for playing slightly sadistic practical jokes.

Fourteen of David Ives's plays, ranging from *Sure Thing* (that's the one about the man, the woman, and the bell) to *Philip Glass Buys a Loaf of Bread* (which defies description, except to say that once you've seen it performed, you'll never again hear Glass's minimalist music without giggling), have been published in a Vintage paperback called *All in the Timing*. The book (named after Ives's breakthrough 1993 production) includes a preface in which the author answers various questions about his life and work — without bothering to say what the questions were. Here are some of the answers:

8. My aunt Jo.

12. By moistening the tip and saying, "Wankel Rotary Engine," of course.

25. Yes I said yes I will Yes.

27. Mrs. Peacock, in the library, with the lead pipe.

38. Two reams of paper, several bottles of Jim Beam, and a seemingly indestructible copy of Bizet's "The Pearl Fishers."

A few plausible-sounding facts about Ives can be picked up in the interstices of such answers as *18. Panty hose.* Born and raised on the south side of Chicago, he determined to write for the theater at the age of sixteen, when he saw Hume Cronyn and Jessica Tandy in Edward Albee's *A Delicate Balance.* He went to Yale Drama School, had his first professional production, at twenty-one, in 1972 ("It catapulted me into immediate and total obscurity"), and has been turning out plays more or less ever since. To learn more about him, you have to go to the source, though reading the preface to *All in the Timing* may leave you a bit anxious at the prospect of sitting down with its author for a little chat. Talking to Ives on the phone is also unnerving, though in a different way: he ejects punch lines like a squid releasing a cloud of ink in order to swim away unseen.

After all this, the polite, soft-spoken man who opens the door of his apartment on Manhattan's Upper West Side comes as something of an anticlimax. He is tall, thin, not obviously demented and perfectly capable of conducting an ordinary conversation in Johncleese, though one involving considerably more laughter than is the norm. In between the laughs, he is refreshingly matter-of-fact about his craft. "I don't really write jokes — setup, payoff, setup, payoff," he explains. "People tell me my plays are funny, but it's hard to look at them and extract a joke. With Neil Simon, you can sort of walk out of the theater and hum the jokes, like humming the tunes from a musical. What I do is try to set up situations that are funny. Usually, I know a good thing when I see one, though sometimes it takes me years to get around to working it out. The idea for *Sure Thing* — a conversation that corrects itself — is something I wrote down in a notebook years and years ago. Originally, it was a man walking up to a woman at a bus stop and saying, 'Does this bus go to X?' I was fascinated by the problem of how many possible conversations could come out of that, and which one eventually leads to the young man and woman getting married."

Ives's plays grow from unlikely seeds. The inspiration for *Variations on the Death of Trotsky,* for example, was an article in the *New York Times* that described the assassination of the Russian revolutionary in 1940. "It mentioned that he'd had a mountain-climber's ax bashed into his skull," Ives recalls, "and that he lived for thirty-six hours. I was on the phone with a friend of mine, and I said, 'This is the funniest thing I've ever read. What does one *do* with a mountain-climber's ax in one's head for thirty-six hours? At what point do you notice it? What movies do you rent?' We just laughed and laughed. This friend had just directed a play of mine, and his birthday was coming up, so as a birthday present I wrote him this play, which I never really intended to be produced—it was just a joke gift. But he read it and said, 'This is kind of good.'"

Not surprisingly, the author of *Philip Glass Buys a Loaf of Bread* and *Foreplay, or The Art of the Fugue* is a passionate music lover, and readily admits that this influences his writing. "The hard thing about plays," he says, "is giving them a form. There's something so terribly satisfying about musical form—even the thirty-two-bar Broadway song or the two-and-a-half-minute Louis Armstrong 78. And the feeling that you've gone through a lot in that tiny period of time, and come out different, is something I really like. Part of what makes me write the way I do is sheer impatience. There is no worse feeling than sitting down in a theater and, five minutes into a play, thinking, 'My God, I've got two more hours of this stuff.' I think Wagner's operas were created by the same people who invented baseball."

Some of Ives's plays, including *Ancient History* and *The Red Address,* seem at first glance to take a dim view of the possibility of human communication—especially between men and women. But the newly married playwright begs to differ: "I think one of the reasons why *All in the Timing* was so popular with audiences is that the people in the plays get over these incredible obstacles in the end, and actually somehow get to the other side. Two people in a café who have nothing in common actually find their way to going out to the movies together. Philip Glass actually does get his loaf of bread. A man who speaks a made-up language actually gets through to a woman who stutters. I mean, if these two people don't fall in love, who cares about the play? Sure, the way there may be a little rocky, but the plays do seem to say that one can succeed in getting through." Which also seems to sum up David Ives quite nicely. You might, in fact, call him a hopeful surrealist — a dark comedian firmly committed to the belief that there is a way out of the twilight zone.

Civilization 1997

The New New Music

A CHAPTER IN THE HISTORY OF AMERICAN CLASSICAL music is quietly drawing to a close, and — though unknown to most music lovers — another has already opened.

For the past fifteen years, a group of American composers, collectively known as the minimalists, has dominated the new-music scene. Their works, immediately recognizable by the use of endlessly repeated melodic fragments and slow-moving harmonic sequences, have been performed by first-tier orchestras, opera companies, and chamber ensembles, recorded by major labels, fought over by critics, and imitated by students. They are the first classical composers since the Forties to have achieved broad-based popularity, and as such, they have set the tone for contemporary classical music in America, and more recently in Europe as well.

But while these composers — the best-known of whom are Philip Glass, Steve Reich, and John Adams — remain active, they are no longer the sole source of creative vitality in American musical life. The past years have seen the emergence of a clutch of younger composers, all born since 1945, who have turned their backs on minimalism. Their music, too, is being performed, and in many cases recorded, by the symphony orchestras of Atlanta, Baltimore, Denver, Houston, Phoenix, Pittsburgh, San Francisco, Seattle, and other cities here and abroad; it is receiving increasingly respectful critical attention; and it is drawing audiences in steadily growing numbers.

Who are these composers? How good is the music they write? What does their arrival portend? In order to answer these questions, it is necessary to take a quick look backward at the musical course of our century.

History is written by the victors. Until recently, the received version of the modern movement in classical music has reflected the prejudices of those modernist composers who controlled the musical establishment from the late Fifties until the advent of minimalism two decades later. Their ideology — an ideology of revolt against tradition — continues to distort our understanding of how modern music actually developed, and why it finally reached a dead end.

Contrary to the received wisdom, musical modernism at its inception represented a revolt not against tradition in general but against German Romanticism in particular. By the end of the nineteenth century, Richard Wagner, the quintessential German Romantic composer, had become the dominant, style-setting figure of the age, a fixed star by which all progressive musicians navigated. But Wagner's example proved to be not liberating but stifling. To many ambitious young composers at the turn of the century, his operas were too long, too loud, too lavishly orchestrated, too self-absorbed, and above all — at least for the non-Germans among them — too German.

It was a Frenchman, Claude Debussy, who led the revolt against Wagnerism. Starting with *Prélude à l'après-midi d'un faune,* Debussy moved away from Wagner's oppressively hyperchromatic harmonic language, creating a more open and flexible form of tonal organization that served as a model for succeeding generations who wished to work within the classical tradition without slavishly aping German models.

It was largely because of Debussy, who happened to be an intense French nationalist, that no "international style" emerged during the first decades of musical modernism. Instead, composers adopted widely varied styles that, though recognizably modern in their use of the expanded language of post-Debussyan tonality, were also rooted in the melodic and rhythmic inflections of specific cultures. Virtually without exception, the key figures of the modern movement, from Hungary's Béla Bartók to America's Aaron Copland, wrote music that vividly reflected their diverse origins; even Igor Stravinsky, who spent much time and energy denying his heritage and claiming to be a musical cosmopolitan, was Russian to the core.

By the Thirties, the new harmonic worlds discovered by Debussy had been explored to their uttermost limits. Indeed, it seemed possible that all subsequent stylistic developments in classical music would take place within the framework of tonal modernism. Perhaps the most eloquent statement of this belief was by the German modernist Paul Hindemith:

> Music has now entered the phase of its life that corresponds with the natural permanent state of poetry. . . . Everybody who understands the national language of a writer knows his poetic material of construction thoroughly. Yet poetry has not come to an end, and never will, so long as there are spoken and intelligible languages. Why, then, should music have reached the final epochs of its existence after all the material of harmonic construction is equally well known?

That the essentially conservative modernism of Hindemith, Stravinsky, and their contemporaries was, in fact, an outgrowth of the classical tradition is proved by the fact that so many of the numerous works they composed between 1930 and 1945 have long since entered the standard repertoire. Stravinsky's *Symphony of Psalms,* Ralph Vaughan Williams's Fourth Symphony, Sergei Prokofiev's *Romeo and Juliet,* Bartók's Music for Strings, Percussion, and Celesta, Dmitri Shostakovich's Fifth Symphony, Francis Poulenc's Organ Concerto, Samuel Barber's Violin Concerto, Hindemith's *The Four Temperaments,* Copland's *Appalachian Spring,* Benjamin Britten's *Peter Grimes* — all these masterpieces date from a time when it seemed that modernism was here to stay.

BUT IN CLASSICAL MUSIC, AS IN THE OTHER ARTS, THERE WERE really two modernisms — one conservative, the other profoundly radical — and the chief architect of the second modernism made it his life's work to subvert the first.

Arnold Schoenberg was a German Romantic turned modernist who, unlike his contemporaries, refused to accept that German and Austrian composers would no longer chart the course of classical music. Initially, the young Schoenberg sought to restore German musical hegemony by extending Wagner's hyperchromatic harmonic vocabulary. But the unexpected result of this experiment was that traditional tonality, already stretched to the breaking point in Schoenberg's *Verklärte Nacht, Gurrelieder,* and *Pelleas und Melisande,* dissolved altogether in the finale of the Second String Quartet and the song cycle *Das Buch der hängenden Gärten.* These are the first pieces of modern classical music that can properly be called nontonal—or, to use the generally accepted term, atonal.

Schoenberg spent the next decade working out the implications of his discovery in such influential compositions as *Pierrot lunaire.* But he eventually found atonality too unstable to serve as a basis for formally coherent musical works. What was needed was a more systematic approach to composition, one that would integrate atonal harmony with the precisely articulated formal structures of the Austro-German classical tradition. To that end, he invented in 1920 the method now known as serialism, in which the twelve tones of the chromatic scale are arranged in "rows" whose various permutations provide the material for large-scale, nontonal compositions.

For Schoenberg, serialism was not merely a source of creative renewal but also a means of reversing the trend that had toppled Central European composers from their position of absolute stylistic dominance. In serialism, he boasted, "I have discovered something that will ensure the supremacy of German music for the next hundred years." But he attracted only two disciples of importance, Alban Berg and Anton Webern, and both men, like their teacher, were Viennese. Elsewhere, serialism was dismissed as a solution to a problem that did not exist. The vast majority of concertgoers throughout Europe and America detested serial music, finding it sterile and nonsensical, and the rest of the modern movement continued to embrace tonality.

All this changed, however, after 1945. The chaos into which the West had been plunged by World War II created an opening for cultural ideologues with comprehensive, world-ordering systems, and serialism filled the bill to perfection. Young composers, most notably Pierre Boulez in France and Milton Babbitt in the United States, took up Schoenberg's methods and applied them in an even more systematic manner than did the master. Soon it was being said that the triumph of serialism was historically inevitable, with Boulez going so far as to declare that "every musician who has not felt . . . the necessity of the serial language is USELESS."

The Marxian echoes of such rhetoric exercised a strong appeal to intellectuals, and similarly attractive, at least to academic scholars of music, was the mathematical rigor of serial technique. Thanks to Boulez and Babbitt, what had once been a style soon became a discipline, and one that could be taught to students much more easily than tonal modernism with its emphasis on stylistic diversity. By the Sixties, serialist composers had become ensconced on the faculties of America's most prestigious schools of music. In Europe, state-subsidized radio orchestras and new-music ensembles (especially England's BBC Symphony) adopted aggressively pro-serialist programming, to the point where younger tonal composers often found it all but impossible to get a hearing.

To revisit the postwar literature of serialism is to be struck by the smugness with which it proclaimed that the lineage of classical music descended not through the tonal modernists but through Schoenberg and his successors. Charles Wuorinen, for instance, wrote in 1979 that the tonal system "is no longer employed by serious composers of the mainstream," while the pianist and critic Charles Rosen claimed that those who continued to use tonality were "retreating from the ideal of original invention that has been imposed on art since the Renaissance." These claims, as it happens, were no more valid two decades ago than they are today. Britten and Shostakovich continued to produce "original" tonal masterpieces well into the Seventies, and many younger American composers of note, including Leonard Bernstein, John Corigliano, David Diamond, and Ned Rorem, also saw no reason to abandon tonality. At the same time, only one piece of serial music, Alban Berg's Violin Concerto (in which the tone row is manipulated in such a way as to permit pseudo-tonal effects), became part of the international concert repertoire. To this day, no other fully serial composition has been programmed regularly by star performers or embraced by more than a handful of listeners.

Nevertheless, the general perception in musical circles was that serialism had triumphed. Even Stravinsky and Copland finally converted in old age. As more and more composers submitted to the method's lockstep discipline, the public, too, came to agree with this judgment — and it responded by, in effect, giving up on new music altogether.

PERHAPS FITTINGLY, IT WAS A PUPIL OF ARNOLD SCHOENBERG, the American composer John Cage, who did more than anyone else to undermine the serialist orthodoxy.

Unlike the serialists, who continued to believe in the validity of their own version of musical tradition, Cage believed in nothing. He was the first composer to transplant the anarchic credo of Marcel Duchamp into the rigidly ordered environment of late-modern classical music. Just as Duchamp had taken snow shovels and bicycle wheels and displayed them as "ready-made" sculptures, so did Cage tune twelve radios to different stations and call the resulting cacophony music. In 1952, he "composed" *4'33''*, a piece for any instrument or combination of instruments that consists solely of four minutes and thirty-three seconds' worth of silence. Though Cage and his fellow avant-gardists were no more successful than the serialists in appealing to the public, their ideas foreshadowed the emergence of a new strain of musical thinking. Starting in the late Sixties, a number of American composers became convinced that modernism, at least as it had come to be defined by the serialists, was at a dead end. Comparable conclusions were being drawn in the fields of writing and the visual arts. By the mid-Seventies, the term *postmodern* was being widely invoked to describe a new style in which the high moral seriousness and technical complexity of modernism were supplanted by a playful nihilism.

In music, the chief manifestation of this development was minimalism, developed more or less simultaneously by Steve Reich and Philip Glass. Reich and Glass constructed their pieces out of simple melodic, harmonic, and rhythmic cells, repeated ad infinitum in gradually shifting patterns. The effect of their music was "tonal" in the limited sense that it was not atonal, but it did not constitute a genuine return to functional tonality. For the minimalists had no more use for the classical tradition than they did for modernism. Rather, they wrenched familiar devices from their traditional contexts, transplanting them into new settings for ironic effect.

The irony, however, rebounded. Hungry for new music that made sense, concertgoers took minimalism at face value, hearing in the compositions of Reich, Glass, and their younger follower John Adams not a distanced commentary on Western musical tradition but a comparatively straightforward use of tonal materials. Other young composers, having caught a glimpse of the once-forbidden delights of sold-out performances and respectable record sales, abandoned serialism for minimalism in droves.

As things inevitably turned out, minimalism, for all its surface flair, was musically too insubstantial to appeal for very long either to listeners or to most composers. Once the novelty wore off, the underlying shallowness of content became all too apparent. What did not wear off, though, was the now-widespread conviction that serialism, far from having been historically necessary, had in fact represented a drastically wrong turn. For this reason, once minimalism ran its course, there would be no revival of that particular branch of modernism. Instead, starting in the mid-Eighties, a new generation of American composers began producing scores influenced neither by serialism nor by minimalism but by the music of the long-unfashionable tonal modernists. Operating largely out of sight of the media, these "new tonalists" embarked on the task of going back to the future—of reattaching classical composition to the mainstream of musical tradition.

Among the leading exponents of the new tonalism are ten young Americans: Daniel Asia, Richard Danielpour, Michael Daugherty, Elliott Goldenthal, Aaron Jay Kernis, Libby Larsen, Lowell Liebermann, Paul Moravec, Christopher Rouse, and George Tsontakis. Though their music varies widely in style, all of them speak the language of tonality, and do so without irony or self-consciousness. This is what sets them apart from the postmodern movement: they are neither embarrassed nor paralyzed by tradition. Rather, they accept it as a given.

The new tonalists are similarly united in their rejection of the hermeticism of late modernism. Rather, they seek to compose serious music intelligible to the common listener, and they therefore tend to work in conventional forms, writing symphonies, operas, chamber music, and ballet and film scores (Elliott Goldenthal, for instance, scored *Batman Forever* and *Interview with the Vampire*). Some also make use of more contemporary stylistic developments; in *Jackie O* (1997), an opera based loosely on the life of Jacqueline Kennedy Onassis, Michael Daugherty incorporates rock rhythms and instrumental techniques drawn from film and TV music.

Many of the characteristic features of the new tonalism can be heard in Paul Moravec's masterly Violin Sonata (1992). This twenty-two-minute work, cast in standard three-movement sonata form (fast-slow-fast), opens with a striking high-register passage for violin, backed by a nervously fluttering piano figure that outlines the key of D in the dissonance-tinged manner of the tonal modernists. Yet Moravec uses post-Debussyan tonality not to comment retrospectively on an older style but to make a direct statement of his own. The writing for both violin and piano is resourceful but idiomatic — there are no avant-garde "special effects" — and the thematic material, especially in the contemplative slow movement, is richly melodic.

In evaluating the work of Moravec and his contemporaries, it is important to keep in mind that the new tonalism has existed as an identifiable idiom for just over a decade. Many of its practitioners have yet to develop fully original styles of their own, and some are distinctive only to the extent that they are consistent in their borrowings. Richard Danielpour, Elliott Goldenthal, and Libby Larsen, for example, have produced numerous pieces that, though attractive and well-made, often fail to transcend their easily identifiable sources (Danielpour, whose music often bears an uncanny resemblance to that of Leonard Bernstein, is especially problematic in this regard). Others — Christopher Rouse and Aaron Jay Kernis being cases in point — are so concerned with making "big statements" that their music, striving for high seriousness, occasionally stumbles instead into portentous excess.

But several of the new tonalists have turned out scores that bode well for the long term. Despite their shared penchant for overstatement, Rouse and Kernis are composers of undeniable accomplishment. In addition, Moravec's Violin Sonata, George Tsontakis's Fourth String Quartet (1988), Daniel Asia's Third Symphony (1991), and Lowell Liebermann's Second Piano Concerto (1992) are all major musical statements, fully worthy of comparison (as is much of their recent work) with the music of Copland or Barber. No less interesting in his own witty, unassuming way is Michael Daugherty, whose *Jackie O,* though it suffers from Wayne Koestenbaum's pretentious libretto, is surely the work of a born theater composer.

PAUL HINDEMITH, IT TURNS OUT, WAS RIGHT: CLASSICAL MU-sic has not yet reached its final epoch. Now that the wreckage of serialism and the nihilist avant-garde have been cleared away, it can be seen that late modernism, together with its postmodernist coda, constituted nothing more than a hiatus in the continuity of a classical tradition that had run uninterrupted from the seventeenth century to the end of World War II.

The new tonalists are making it possible once again for American composers to walk in the paths blazed by the geniuses of that tradition. To be sure, we cannot yet say whether any of them is writing music that will permanently endure. But we can already say that because of their efforts, American classical music has recaptured the potential for greatness, and the masters of the future will stand on their shoulders.

Commentary 1997

Death of the Concert

IN 1965, THE PIANIST GLENN GOULD MADE A CASUAL RE-mark that attracted worldwide attention. As he later recalled: "In an unguarded moment . . . I predicted that the public concert as we know it today would no longer exist a century hence, that its functions would have been entirely taken over by electronic media. It had not occurred to me that this statement represented a particularly radical pronouncement. . . . But never has a statement of mine been so widely quoted — or so hotly disputed."

At the time, Gould's prediction was generally dismissed as the special pleading of a brilliant neurotic. A near-incapacitating case of stage fright had forced him to stop giving concerts in 1964, and thereafter he played only in the recording studio and on radio and TV. To anyone who cared to listen, he stated with assurance that his personal inhibitions were, in effect, the wave of the future.

As it happens, in the three decades since Gould announced the coming death of the concert, no other classical performer has followed his hermitlike example. Pianists, violinists, and singers continue to crisscross the country, donning evening dress and performing for enthusiastic audiences in concert halls, gymnasiums, and multipurpose arts centers; since 1980, more than 110 new orchestras have been founded in the United States. "Forget the Stereotype: America Is Becoming a Nation of Culture," read the headline in a front-page story published in the *Wall Street Journal*. Yet in private — and sometimes even in public — promoters and managers are far less sanguine. The loyal concert subscribers of the Sixties and Seventies are fast approaching retirement age, and younger listeners are so far failing to replace them in sufficiently large numbers. Though opera attendance is up, ticket sales for traditional concert programs are declining: the Phoenix Symphony, for example, claims that it sells about 90 percent of the tickets for its pop concerts, but only 55 percent for its classical programs. (Significantly, opera singers have become the only classical musicians whose activities are routinely covered by the mass media.) At the same time, new recordings of the classics have stopped selling, and many of the major labels are concentrating on pop-flavored "crossover" music.

Why are Americans losing their taste for classical concertgoing? The stock explanation is that secondary schools are devoting less time and money to music education, thus reducing the likelihood that children will be exposed to the classics. This is true enough. But other, more complex historical factors are also at work, and if they continue unchecked, Glenn Gould's seemingly outrageous prophecy may well come to pass.

MORE OFTEN THAN NOT, A CLASSICAL CONCERT IS A TWO-hour-long event in which three or four large-scale works by well-known composers of the eighteenth and nineteenth centuries are performed by a celebrity soloist (or a celebrity conductor and orchestra). "Modern" music — by which is usually meant music composed between 1910 and 1945 — is occasionally heard, but popular soloists rarely program pieces written in the last fifty years.

This is not the way things used to be. In the nineteenth century, opera companies and symphony orchestras programmed new music as a matter of course. In addition, most of the major composers of this new music, including Hector Berlioz, Felix Mendelssohn, Franz Liszt, Frédéric Chopin, Richard Wagner, Richard Strauss, and Gustav Mahler, also had active careers as performers, in the course of which they frequently played or conducted their own works.

Surprising as this may sound, the music that dominates today's concert programs — the works of the past that, taken together, comprise what is known as the "standard repertoire" — was largely unfamiliar to nineteenth-century concertgoers, as indeed it was to many performers.

Baroque music, for example, was heard only in romanticized transcriptions. Of the large-scale instrumental works of Haydn, Mozart, and Beethoven, only a few were performed with any regularity, and Schubert's instrumental music was all but unknown.

The change occurred as nineteenth-century music grew technically more complex. In time, it became increasingly common for conductors and instrumentalists to leave the job of composition to specialists, while they themselves came to specialize in the art of performance. These new, noncomposing virtuosos were naturally more inclined to explore the output of older composers, and their programs came to be increasingly devoted to the music of the past. By World War I, the age of the composer-performer was drawing to a close (Sergei Rachmaninoff was the last important composer who also toured extensively as a celebrity virtuoso), and soloists and orchestras were programming old and new music in roughly equal proportions.

The decline of the composer-performer coincided with the rise of the modern movement in music. The listening public initially resisted modernism, but no more so than it had resisted such "advanced" composers as Liszt, Wagner, and Brahms. For a while, therefore, it seemed reasonable to believe that the music of the tonal modernists — Béla Bartók, Aaron Copland, Paul Hindemith, Francis Poulenc, Sergei Prokofiev, Igor Stravinsky, Ralph Vaughan Williams, and their many followers in Europe and America — would eventually find favor among concertgoers.

Instead, history intervened. The Russian Revolution and the subsequent Nazi takeover of Germany led to the installation of reactionary cultural commissars who sought to extirpate modernism from the European musical scene, if necessary by brute force. At the same time, dozens of famous soloists and conductors emigrated to the United States, among them the pianists Vladimir Horowitz, Artur Schnabel, and Rudolf Serkin; the violinists Jascha Heifetz and Fritz Kreisler; the conductors Serge Koussevitzsky, George Szell, Arturo Toscanini, and Bruno Walter; and the members of the Budapest and Busch String Quartets. Not surprisingly, these extraordinarily talented artists quickly found favor with American listeners (particularly in light of the fact that there were as yet no native-born conductors or instrumentalists of

comparable distinction). But few of them played any but the most conservative of new music. The only famous émigré to take a serious and
sustained interest in American music was Koussevitzky, under whose
leadership the Boston Symphony became the sole first-tier American
orchestra consistently to premiere new scores by young American composers. Much the same thing was true of the Central European émigrés
who would thereafter make up a significanat portion of the American
audience for classical music. For them, the canon of nineteenth-century
classics was a source of emotional reassurance — a way of reconstituting
the lost world of prewar Europe. And many, one suspects, came sub-
consciously to associate musical modernism with the political chaos
they had gratefully left behind.

By war's end, a seemingly unbridgeable chasm had opened between
younger modernist composers and conservative audiences. Many such
composers retreated into the academy, there to write willfully abstruse
music that was in turn ignored by most listeners. Thus it was that the
postwar classical-music business came to be based almost entirely on
performances by celebrity artists of the standard repertoire.

The introduction in 1948 of the long-playing record served to con-
solidate the hold exerted by the music of the past on the classical-music
industry. Between 1948 and 1970, the major labels released hundreds of
top-selling recordings of the standard repertoire by a new generation of
musical celebrities, including the sopranos Maria Callas and Elisabeth
Schwarzkopf; the baritone Dietrich Fischer-Dieskau; the pianists Van
Cliburn, Glenn Gould, and Dinu Lipatti; and the conductors Leonard
Bernstein, Herbert von Karajan, and Georg Solti. To be sure, these
artists were also powerful presences on the concert stage. But it was
recordings, not concerts, that made them stars. And although Gould
was the only one who ultimately decided to specialize in recording,
there is no question that the others took it every bit as seriously as live
performance — if not more so. "I do not want to give any more concerts," Lipatti told Walter Legge, his producer, not long before his
untimely death in 1950, "except perhaps as rehearsals for recording. Let
us give our lives to making records together."

But the success of the LP also created the conditions that eventually
brought about the current crisis of the concert. With the advent of the

digital compact disc, it became possible to reissue the classic recordings of the Fifties and Sixties in a durable, modern-sounding format; the major labels, having long ago amortized their investment in these recordings, thereupon proceeded to market them at lower prices than new versions by younger artists. The result was the near-total paralysis of the classical-recording industry. For why would the average record buyer, having purchased a digitally remastered CD of Beethoven's Ninth Symphony by Karajan and the Berlin Philharmonic, want to acquire a more expensive, less interesting new recording by a younger conductor? Nor did the unintended consequences of recording stop there. By the mid-Sixties, it was possible to purchase high-quality renditions of virtually every important piece of classical music composed prior to 1910. Similarly, good-sounding hi-fi systems had become cheap enough for anyone to own. An entire generation of music lovers thus became accustomed to experiencing classical music not in the concert hall but at home. As the Horowitzes and Bernsteins died off, these listeners began to question the need to attend *any* public performances of the classics, whether by callow young artists or by middle-aged celebrity performers who had already committed their repertoires to disc one or more times.

To understand the implications of this change in attitude, one need only look at the programs of the famous soloists who are performing at Carnegie Hall this season, most of them playing works they have previously recorded. Thus, among pianists, Daniel Barenboim is doing the Liszt B Minor Sonata; Alfred Brendel is offering a series of recitals devoted to solo piano music, chamber music, and song cycles by Haydn, Schubert, and Mozart; Maurizio Pollini is playing the Schumann C Major Fantasy and the Chopin B Flat Minor Sonata; and András Schiff is performing Bartók's three piano concertos. No doubt all of these concerts will be worth hearing, and some may well be exceptional. But to what extent is it reasonable to expect that Alfred Brendel has something so dramatically new to say about the Schubert A Major Sonata, D. 959, that it is worth paying $60 to hear him play it in person? For the veteran concertgoer, the answer is obvious: recordings are at best a pale substitute for the immediate experience of live performance. But for the younger person who can sit in his living room and listen to the same sonata being performed by Pollini, Schiff, Vladimir Ashkenazy, Richard Goode, Murray Perahia, or Artur Schnabel — not to mention Brendel himself — this argument is unlikely to withstand close scrutiny.

Truly charismatic performers, of course, will presumably always be able to draw enthusiastic crowds. But charisma is in remarkably short supply among the present generation of instrumentalists. This season, for example, Carnegie Hall is presenting in recital only one instrumental soloist under the age of fifty, the pianist Evgeny Kissin, who can genuinely be said to have something of the same galvanizing appeal as the great virtuosos of the past.

GIVEN ALL THIS, HOW CAN THE PUBLIC CONCERT CONTINUE to compete with the concert-hall-of-the-mind that has been made possible by the introduction of the compact disc? Is there a musically serious alternative to the lowest-common-denominator pops programs that are becoming increasingly prevalent outside America's major cities? Consider two recent orchestral concerts, one in New York and the other in San Francisco.

In September, the New York Philharmonic, America's oldest orchestra, opened its season with a two-week-long Beethoven festival conducted by its music director, Kurt Masur. Not only is Masur a superlative interpreter of Beethoven, but this was the first time the Philharmonic had performed the nine symphonies in chronological order since Toscanini led a similar cycle in 1942. Yet critical responses ranged from measured praise to open hostility, and it was hard to escape the feeling that by launching the season in so conventional a manner, Masur and the Philharmonic had demonstrated yet again the extent to which they are out of touch with the changing realities of contemporary concertgoing.

In the same week as the first installment of Masur's Beethoven cycle, Michael Tilson Thomas and the San Francisco Symphony presented a program that typified a radically different approach: Charles Ives's *From the Steeples and the Mountains,* Henry Cowell's *Music 1957,* Samuel Barber's *Knoxville: Summer of 1915,* and the Mahler First Symphony. It was obvious on entering the hall that the audience was far younger than that which turned out to hear Masur and the Philharmonic. No less surprising was the way the concert began: Thomas came on stage and spoke lucidly and engagingly about the complexities of the Ives piece. As a result, the audience, which might otherwise have found the composition impossibly difficult, responded to it with unfeigned enthusiasm.

I should stress that there was no significant difference in the musical quality of the two concerts. The New York Philharmonic is a better orchestra than the San Francisco Symphony, but not by much, and Thomas and Masur are both greatly gifted conductors. The difference, rather, was in the program — and the attitude behind it. The German-born Masur remains deeply attached to the traditional concept of the public concert as an occasion for music-lovers to hear live performances by well-known musicians of the accepted canon of eighteenth- and nineteenth-century classics. Thomas, who was born and trained in America (and who is seventeen years younger than Masur), believes just as deeply that in order to attract younger listeners, it is necessary to offer them a different kind of musical experience, one that goes beyond merely duplicating what is readily available on record.

The electrifying effect that Thomas has had on San Francisco audiences suggests one possible solution to the problem of the concert: change its focus from old music to new. Especially now that atonality and serialism have run their course, there is no good reason why American soloists and orchestras, as often as they perform the music of Beethoven, Brahms, or Tchaikovsky, should not also be playing the masterpieces of the earlier tonal modernists, including the Americans among them like Ives and Barber — as well as the accessible yet challenging music of such "new tonalists" as Daniel Asia, Aaron Jay Kernis, Paul Moravec, Lowell Liebermann, and George Tsontakis.

Why do we need new music? Because without it, our musical culture will sicken and die — as it came perilously close to doing in the Sixties and Seventies when "new music" more often than not meant ugly music, and concertgoers learned from hard experience to reject in advance any piece composed after 1945. Throughout this period, concertgoers were forced to look exclusively to performers, not creative artists, as sources of novelty and vitality. The resulting concentration on celebrity performances of the standard repertoire, though understandable, was nonetheless unhealthy: even the greatest masterpieces can temporarily lose their savor from overexposure. This is exactly what has happened to much of the standard repertoire, and it is why the institution of the classical concert is in trouble.

To be sure, Kurt Masur and the New York Philharmonic are not having trouble selling tickets — yet. Beethoven cycles and Tchaikovsky nights continue to draw crowds, and the celebrity system is still the backbone of the classical-music business. But the point of diminishing returns, especially outside the largest urban areas, has clearly been reached, and the recent experience of the classical-recording industry suggests that it is no less essential for soloists and orchestras to rethink the way they do business.

If they do not, the concert hall will someday become a place where old men and women gather forlornly to listen to the same symphonies and concertos they first heard a half-century ago, while their children, if they are interested in classical music at all, will stay home and listen to compact discs or whatever newer marvel is destined to replace them.

Commentary 1998

Life Without Records

I N THE YEAR 2001, FOR THE FIRST TIME, BLANK COMPACT discs outsold prerecorded ones. This statistic has been widely reported in the news media, usually in connection with the fact that prerecorded CD sales in the United States dropped by 10 percent in the same year. Most observers of the music business took it to be further proof that the recording industry is in a state of acute crisis. But nowhere was it suggested that the CD-R (to use the trade name by which "blank" recordable CDs are known) might be anything more than a superior replacement for the now-obsolete audio cassette, much less that its burgeoning popularity is only the latest sign of a radical and irreversible change in the way we experience music.

Just as significant, and even less well known, is the fact that thirty-one million Americans to date have used their personal computers to share music files — that is, to send recordings to one another over the Internet. It is no secret that record companies see file-sharing as a threat to their existence, for which reason they are making futile attempts to impede its use, mostly through aggressive litigation and the introduction of new software that would make it harder to copy a CD. Again, however, the wider implications of this development have gone mostly unexplored. Anyone reading a typical newspaper story about file-sharing would be likely to conclude that the process, for all its unprecedented technical sophistication, does not differ in any essential way from making a cassette copy of a favorite album and giving it to a friend.

Of course, when it comes to the effects of technology on culture, skeptics are in good company. The prophets of the twentieth century, utopian and dystopian alike, had no doubt that middle-class Americans would by now be routinely conversing on picture phones and traveling to work in personal aircraft, à la George and Jane Jetson. And even as they were wrong about that, none of them foresaw the rise of the Internet, or the speed with which a relatively simple application such as e-mail would become part of the everyday routine of tens of millions of people around the world.

I do not claim the gift of prophecy, but I have been using computers in my daily work for twenty-five years, longer than most Americans, and in that time I have acquired a healthy respect for their culture-changing power. At the same time, I have become aware of a paradox: just as it is very difficult to grasp the potential of a new technology if one does not actually use it, so can using it make it seem so routine as to be unremarkable. Since comparatively few people over the age of thirty have downloaded music files from the Web and "burned" them onto CD-Rs, they may find it hard to imagine how these technologies work, or to understand the dramatic impact they are having. By contrast, people *under* thirty, having spent their whole lives using personal computers, tend to take CD-burning and file-sharing for granted, and are less prone to speculate about their cultural implications.

Let me, then, offer some thoughts on what it feels like to use the new computer-based listening technologies, and on how they are changing our larger musical culture and its existing institutional structures.

FOR THREE-QUARTERS OF A CENTURY, RECORDS WERE MADE BY a process now known as analog recording. In its earliest form, a musician sang or played into the large end of a megaphone-like horn, which funneled the resulting sound waves to a recording needle. These waves made the needle vibrate, and the vibrating needle in turn incised a correspondingly wavy groove into a rotating wax plate or cylinder. When the process was reversed, the needle was moved by the groove in such a way as to generate new vibrations that resembled the original sound waves and could be used to reproduce them.

This process was replaced by digital recording, invented in 1976, in which a computer is used to convert sound waves not into an analogous physical object—a wavy groove in a wax plate or an electronically recorded array of magnetized particles on a strip of plastic tape—but a sequence of descriptive binary digits. When *this* process is reversed, these digits are first decoded and only then used to generate a fluctuating electrical signal analogous to the original sound waves. This signal is sent to a loudspeaker, which converts it into new waves closely resembling the original ones.

The initial advantage of digital recording was that it offered a more accurate way to reproduce sound. With the introduction in 1983 of the laser-scanned compact disc, in which sounds are stored in actual digital form rather than being etched into the needle-cut grooves of a vinyl disc (as was the case with the first digital recordings to be commercially marketed), it was widely thought that the digital revolution was complete. The larger significance of the break with analog recording had yet to penetrate. It was, simply, this: instead of manufacturing physical objects from which sounds could be reconstituted, engineers were now converting those same sounds into strings of numbers. As a result, it was no longer necessary to own the physical object in order to reproduce the music. All one needed was the numbers.

This was the true digital revolution. When recorded sound is converted to numbers, it exits the realm of objects and enters the realm of ideas. To put it another way, it becomes pure information, transmissible from person to person by an infinite variety of means. In theory, I could call you up on the phone and read aloud a string of numbers representing a recorded performance of Beethoven's Fifth Symphony, and you in turn could write those numbers down, type them into a computer, and eventually translate them back into sound. The only catch is that such a "conversation" would last for weeks, or however long it would take to read out the millions of binary numbers comprising a digitized version of a piece of music. Hence the importance of the Internet, which allows computer users around the world to electronically transmit digitized data — including audio files — to one another over commercial telephone lines.

At first, it was impractical to do this. The sheer volume of information packed into a single CD was too great, meaning that it took hours to transmit even a fairly short piece of music. But two recent developments have changed this situation dramatically. The first is the rapidly spreading availability of broadband cable modems that give high-speed

Internet access to ordinary computer users. The second is the invention of mp3, the popular "data-reduction" software that compresses sound recordings into data files small enough to be stored on the hard drive of a personal computer, sent via e-mail, or downloaded from Web sites. Such files can also be downloaded from "peer-to-peer" file-sharing sites, the best known of which is the now-defunct Napster. These sites are Web-based clearinghouses that allow their users to make mp3 files available, free, to all other users. In addition, many record labels have launched or are launching online delivery systems from which their recordings can be downloaded for a fee.

How easy is it to do these things? I own an iBook, a laptop computer made by Apple. Bundled into its software is a program called iTunes. Whether I am downloading music directly from the Web or uploading from CDs I already own, the process is the same. So far, I have loaded about 190 hours of music onto my iTunes player, ranging from sonatas and symphonies to bluegrass and rock-and-roll. The exercise is so simple that I started using the player without bothering to look at an instruction manual. I insert one of my pre-recorded compact discs into the computer and click a few keys. The computer then takes the contents of the disc—all of it or any combination of tracks, just as I choose—and converts them into mp3 files that are stored on my hard drive. It takes about thirty seconds to "rip" a three-minute song from a CD. (Downloading works the same way, and just as fast.) To play any of the 2,300 selections that are now on my iTunes player, I go to the "library" screen, find the title, and click on it twice. The music begins playing instantly. I like to listen through headphones, but if I wanted, I could also connect a set of external speakers to my computer, or use it as a component in my stereo system, just like a CD player. Since mp3 files are compressed, the resulting sound is not of the highest possible quality, but my forty-six-year-old ears are rarely capable of telling the difference between an mp3 file and the original CD from which it has been ripped.

My iTunes player also burns CD-Rs. In a matter of seconds, I can instruct it to burn up to seventy-five minutes' worth of mp3 files from my computerized library, arranged in any order I want. Within a few minutes, I have a custom-made compact disc that I can play on my stereo, give to a friend, or drop in a mailbox and send to my mother. Should I find that process laborious, I can e-mail the same files to anyone equipped to receive them.

If, after hearing all this, you still doubt the power of the new computer-based technologies, consider: what I have done is to pack the equivalent of seven shelves' worth of CDs into a plastic box not much larger than a stack of eight magazines. This box also contains the personal computer on which I do my writing and from which I send my e-mail. I can use it whenever and wherever I want—at my desk, in a hotel room, on a plane. Were I to find this box insufficiently portable, I could also purchase an iPod, Apple's version of a Walkman, into which the contents of my iTunes player can be dumped in about twenty minutes. An iPod is roughly the size of a cellular phone, and at present costs about three hundred dollars.

None of these devices is a science-fiction fantasy. They are on sale now, and I use them every day.

AS PEOPLE START USING PERSONAL COMPUTERS IN THE WAYS I have just described, their relationship to the experience of listening to recorded music will change accordingly.

The nature of this experience has yet to be adequately described by theorists of art, most of whom make flawed assumptions about the nature of what the Marxist critic Walter Benjamin, in his 1935 essay of the same name, called "the work of art in the age of mechanical reproduction." Benjamin, for example, feared the loss of authenticity that he thought to be an inevitable consequence of the mass production of replicas of art works, a process that (in his words) substitutes "a plurality of copies for a unique existence." Conversely, André Malraux, writing in *Le Musée imaginaire* (1947), praised the prospect of a democratic "museum without walls" made possible by the availability of such replicas. But in fact, traditional museums, rather than falling into desuetude, now attract larger audiences than ever, precisely because they offer viewers the opportunity to see handmade art objects whose existence *is* unique. Even the most unsophisticated museumgoer quickly comes to realize that no reproduction of a painting by Rembrandt or

Cézanne can possibly convey more than the smallest part of the impact of the original.

But music is different. Unlike a painting, the printed score of a Schubert song is not an art object in and of itself. It is a set of instructions that, if followed faithfully, will cause the object to be made manifest — once. But if music exists only through the act of performance, a recording of a Schubert song, being also a performance, does not bear the same relationship to a live performance that a reproduction of a painting does to the original. It is not a mere "replica," but an independent and fully valid way of experiencing the song. Indeed, a record album can be, and usually is, an art object in its own right. I own several thousand CDs, each of which consists of a series of musical selections arranged in a specific order and (normally) intended to be listened to in that order. Some were recorded in concert, but most were created in the recording studio, often with the help of such studio-specific techniques as tape splicing and overdubbing. Such famous albums as Glenn Gould's 1955 recording of the Bach *Goldberg Variations,* Frank Sinatra's *Only the Lonely,* Miles Davis's *Kind of Blue,* or the Beatles' *Sgt. Pepper's Lonely Hearts Club Band* are not attempts to simulate live performances. They are, rather, unique experiences existing *only* on record, and the record itself, not the music or the performance, is the art object.

Since 1950 or so, objects such as these have been the most significant forms of musical experience in the West — far more significant than live performances, and arguably even more so than specific musical compositions. Nor have they been rendered irrelevant by digital technology, any more than *Citizen Kane* made *War and Peace* irrelevant. But now something else is happening: when I load any one of these "objects" onto my iTunes player, I am opening myself up to the possibility of experiencing it in a completely new way. All at once, the concrete object — the original album, with its cover art, liner notes, and carefully arranged sequence of tracks — ceases to exist. In its place is a string of abstract digits that I can manipulate at will. If I want, I can listen to the twelve songs that make up *Only the Lonely* in the order that they appear on the album. But I can also listen to them separately, in a different order, as part of a Frank Sinatra "greatest hits" sequence of my own devising, or in any other way that suits my fancy. Instead of permitting an artist or a record company to tell me how to listen, I am making my own choices.

This enhanced capacity for choice is central to the appeal of computer-based listening systems. Should I care for only one track on a CD, I can buy that CD, load it onto iTunes, and throw away the original disc. Or I can go to a Web site and download only that one song—which is what young, computer-literate music lovers are increasingly doing. Instead of buying pop albums containing two or three good songs, they acquire the songs they like and listen to them in contexts of their own choosing. If record companies will not give them the power to make those choices themselves, they will take the power into their own hands by swapping mp3 files with friends, or downloading them from file-sharing sites.

The spread of computer-based listening has already started to alter the way records are made and marketed. A young jazz pianist who recently signed with a major label told me that to get people to buy his CDs, he now has to give them "something they can't get by going to hear me at a club, or downloading a couple of tracks off the Web." Instead, he has to make albums that are strong from start to finish—a unified experience, not just "a studio jam session or a bunch of unrelated selections." And, he added, "it's not just the music, either. The packaging has to contribute to the total effect, too. Interesting liner notes, interesting art—all that really matters now." Indeed it does, and more so than ever before. But such efforts, however ambitious and thoughtfully conceived, are still doomed to failure. In the not-so-long run, the introduction of online delivery systems and the spread of file-sharing will certainly undermine and very likely destroy the fundamental economic basis for the recording industry, at least as we know it today. Nor can there be much doubt that within a few years, the record album will lose its once-privileged place at the heart of Western musical culture.

IN ORDER TO GRASP THE POTENTIAL IMPACT OF THE DIGITAL revolution, it may be helpful to consider the effects that an earlier technological breakthrough of comparable significance—the invention of sound recording—has had on the culture of classical music.

A hundred years ago, the performance of classical music was for the most part a local, even provincial phenomenon. A modest number of major soloists toured internationally (that is, in Europe), but one could only hear them "live," by going to a concert hall or opera house, while larger resident ensembles such as symphony orchestras did not travel at all, save to nearby cities. This relative geographic isolation led to the evolution of distinctive regional styles and techniques. Russian violinists held their bows differently from Hungarians; Italian tenors sang with a cutting edge unknown in England. Moreover, symphony orchestras were typically composed of locally trained players whose "accents" coalesced into group styles as identifiable as the bouquet of a wine made from local grapes.

The invention in 1893 of the mass-produced phonograph record changed these circumstances dramatically. To begin with, it created the conditions that made possible the emergence of the international classical "superstar." For the first time in history, it was possible for an artist to be heard—and to make money—other than by performing before live audiences, one concert at a time. Enrico Caruso, who began recording in 1902, was the first classical musician to win a worldwide following through the sale of his records; thereafter, the major classical labels played a key role in conferring superstar status on the performers they chose to record. As the American mezzo-soprano Susan Graham has explained the system, "Until I started making records nobody outside the places where I regularly appeared knew who I was. . . . And the only way journalists become interested enough even to write about you is if you start to make records."

Recording also broached the walls of geographic separation behind which regional styles had flourished. Now it was possible for anyone with access to a phonograph to hear the Philadelphia Orchestra under Leopold Stokowski without traveling to Philadelphia—and to compare it to, say, the Berlin Philharmonic under Wilhelm Furtwängler. At first, this seemed an unimaginable boon, and for the connoisseur of old records it remains so. Thanks to the phonograph, it is possible for us to *know* how the great artists of yesterday played and sang, rather than having to rely on the impressionistic verbal descriptions of their contemporaries. Caruso, Fritz Kreisler, Nellie Melba, Ignace Jan Paderewski—

these "immortal" names of the now-distant past remain alive to us today chiefly because of the recordings they made a century ago.

In countless cases, the phonograph also had an immediate and salutary effect on the way artists made music. Never before had musicians been able to study their own playing and singing at leisure, and many of them profited from what they heard: between 1900 and 1940, classical performers collectively became more rhythmically exact and less tolerant of wrong notes and flawed intonation. In time, some performers began to use recordings not merely as a tool for the refinement of already established styles, but as a means of developing as yet unformed ones. The record producer Walter Legge left an unusually revealing account of how he played golden-age recordings for his wife, the German soprano Elisabeth Schwarzkopf, in order to "widen" her "imaginative concept of the possibilities of vocal sound":

> Rosa Ponselle's vintage port and thick cream timbre and noble line; the Slavic brilliance of Nina Koshetz; a few phrases from [Geraldine] Farrar's Carmen . . . all these were nectar and ambrosia for Schwarzkopf's musical appetite. Instrumentalists too: Fritz Kreisler for the dark beauty of tone, his nobility and cavalier nonchalance; [Artur] Schnabel for concentrated thinking over long musical periods, firmly rhythmical, seemingly oblivious to bar lines. From the analysis of what we found most admirable in these diverse models we made our own synthesis.

The problem with using recordings of the past in this analytic manner is that it can lead to the development of an eclectic style as lacking in genuine individuality as a cafeteria dinner. Fortunately, Schwarzkopf did not begin to work with Legge until after she had been performing in public for nearly a decade, and her artistic personality was strong enough by that time to allow her to profit from the experience. Nevertheless, the trap had been set, and artists with weaker personalities soon began to fall into it, with dire results. By the Fifties, the regional styles of yesteryear were fast becoming extinct, killed off by the deprovincializing effects of recordings, air travel, and the mass emigrations (and mass murders) of World War II. In only a few places, most notably Vienna and the Soviet Union, did identifiably regional schools of interpretation continue to flourish.

Yet the Fifties were also great years for classical recording, for they were dominated by performers who had grown up under the influence of prewar regionalism while simultaneously profiting from the enhanced self-awareness made possible by the phonograph. The German baritone Dietrich Fischer-Dieskau, the Greek-American soprano Maria Callas, the Hungarian conductors Fritz Reiner and George Szell, the Austrian pianist Rudolf Serkin, the Russian violinists Jascha Heifetz and Nathan Milstein: all combined idiosyncrasy with exactitude in a way that characterized classical music-making in the Fifties and early Sixties. These artists, and others like them, were at the center of the superstar system created by the major labels. Though they did not know it at the time, their recordings of the standard repertoire would in many cases come to be regarded as "definitive," and since their careers coincided with the invention of high-fidelity stereo, these recordings — unlike those made by older artists — were so technically advanced that they continued to sound as good as new long after the musicians who made them had died or retired.

But the economic exigencies of the industry demanded that the major labels continue to regularly release brand-new "product," so, starting in the mid-Sixties, they began to sign a new generation of very young virtuosos, among them the pianist Daniel Barenboim (born in 1942) and the violinist Itzhak Perlman (born in 1945). These musicians were born too late to acquire the regional "accents" of the prewar era; instead, they grew up listening to the records of the superstars of the Fifties. Not surprisingly, their playing was technically accomplished but eclectically "international" in style, lacking the inimitable regional tang of a Heifetz or a Serkin.

By the end of the Eighties, the Heifetzes and Serkins were all gone — but their recordings survived them. The invention of the digital compact disc made it possible for the major labels to reissue yet again the classic standard-repertoire recordings of the Fifties, only this time in durable, low-priced editions whose remastered early-stereo sound was directly competitive in quality with brand-new recordings. The

Barenboims and Perlmans were thus forced to compete head to head with the old masters from whom they had learned their craft, and were found wanting. Increasingly, collectors started to purchase digitally remastered CD reissues of old records in preference to more expensive new releases by younger artists. The major labels responded by ceasing to make new recordings of the standard repertoire, a decision that in turn undermined the superstar system, based as it had been on the ability of those labels to create an international market for emerging young artists. As a result, few classical musicians under the age of forty will receive the opportunity to record their Beethoven symphonies, Chopin sonatas, and Verdi heroines. If they do, it will be for small independent labels that cannot afford to spend the money on promotion necessary to turn promising young artists into established superstars.

The major classical labels have been severely shaken by these developments, but not destroyed — yet. What will finally put them out of business is the Internet. Several symphony orchestras and a few individual musicians, frustrated by the narrow commercialism of the major labels, are already using the Web to distribute self-made CDs. In addition to recording for DGG with the Emerson Quartet, the cellist David Finckel makes solo recordings in collaboration with his wife, the pianist Wu Han, and markets them exclusively through a Web site, www.AristLed .com. But in addition to recording their own performances, Finckel and Wu Han must also pay to have them pressed onto CDs, then mail them to individual buyers. These latter steps, and the costly overhead they generate, will be eliminated once it becomes possible to download AristLed's recordings directly from the Web.

What remains to be seen is whether existing classical labels can operate profitably on the Web, especially given the fact that sound recordings go out of copyright in Europe fifty years after their initial release. This means that by the year 2015, the classic early-stereo recordings of the standard classical repertoire currently being reissued by the major labels will have entered the public domain, meaning that perfect digital copies can be legally distributed by anybody who cares to make them available for downloading. Callas's *Tosca,* Heifetz's Beethoven and Brahms, Herbert von Karajan's Strauss and Sibelius — all will be up for grabs. Once that happens, it is hard to see how any of the major labels will be able to survive in anything like their present form.

WHAT WILL REPLACE THEM? I, FOR ONE, THINK IT HIGHLY likely that more and more artists, classical and popular alike, will start to make their own recordings and market them directly to the public via the Web. To be sure, few artists will have the patience or where-withal to do such a thing entirely on their own, and new managerial institutions will presumably emerge to assist them. But these institutions will act as middlemen, purveyors of a service, as opposed to record labels, which use artists to serve *their* interests. And while even the most ambitious artists will doubtless also employ technical assistants of various kinds, such as freelance recording engineers, the ultimate responsibility for their work will belong — for the first time ever — to the artists themselves.

What form that work will take is another question entirely. Prior to the invention of the LP, musicians usually recorded not albums but specific songs or pieces of music that were released on single 78s and meant to be experienced individually. Perhaps, then, there will be no more *Only the Lonely*s or *Kind of Blue*s, but only "One for My Baby"s and "All Blues." Or possibly new modes of presentation will evolve, in the same way that Internet "magazines" are developing Web-specific features like "The Corner," the chatty group-discussion page that is the most widely read department of *National Review Online*.

In addition, the collapse of the major classical labels and the rise of the Internet as a locus for decentralized recording activity will almost certainly prevent the re-emergence of anything remotely resembling the superstar system. What would classical music look like without superstars? A possible answer can be found by looking at classical ballet. Few ballet companies tour regularly, and some of the most important, like New York City Ballet, are rarely seen outside their home towns; videocassettes are a notoriously inadequate substitute for live performances, and thus sell poorly. For these reasons, the major media devote little space to ballet, meaning that there are never more than one or two international superstars at any given moment. Most balletgoers spend the bulk of their time attending performances by the resident companies of the cities in which they live, and the dances, not the dancers, are the draw. (It is *The Nutcracker* that fills seats, not the Sugar Plum Fairy.)

In the United States, regional opera works in much the same way. Only a half-dozen major American companies can afford to import superstars; everyone else hires solid second-tier singers with little or no name recognition, often using local artists to fill out their casts. Audiences are attracted not by the stars, but by the show—that is, by dramatically compelling productions of musically interesting operas. If the larger culture of classical music were to be reorganized along similar lines, then concert presenters, instead of presenting a small roster of international celebrity virtuosos, might be forced to engage a wider range of lower-priced soloists, possibly including local artists and ensembles with a carefully cultivated base of loyal fans. Similarly, regional symphony orchestras would have to adopt more imaginative programming strategies to attract listeners who now buy tickets mainly to hear superstar soloists play popular concertos in person. It is possible, too, that with the breakup of the single worldwide market created by the superstar system, we might see a similar disintegration of the blandly eclectic "international" style of performance that came to dominate classical music in the Seventies. Performers who play for the moment, rather than for the microphones of an international record company primarily interested in its bottom line, are less likely to play it safe—and more likely to play interesting music.

In the midst of these seemingly endless uncertainties, one aspect of life without records is not only possible but probable: henceforth, nobody in his right mind will look to classical music as a means of making very large sums of money. Of all the ways in which the invention of the phonograph changed the culture of classical music, perhaps the most fateful was that it turned a local craft into an international trade, thereby attracting the attention of entrepreneurs who were more interested in money than in art. Needless to say, there can be no art without money, but the recording industry, by creating a mass market for music, sucked unprecedentedly large amounts of money into the classical-music culture, thereby insidiously and inexorably altering its artistic priorities.

In 1978, Brown Meggs published a novel called *Aria* in which he candidly described the internal workings of a major classical label owned by a multinational corporation. (He had previously run Angel Records, then the American division of EMI.) The most revealing passage is a drunken confession that the protagonist, a middle-aged record producer named Harry Chapin, makes to his seatmate on a trans-Atlantic flight:

> Originally, records were a library function. We would capture for posterity the world's greatest scores as interpreted by fine old gentlemen who had spent lifetimes in determining inner truths. . . . Today we have this enormous, insatiable commercial pipeline to fill. With what? With *product*. Not art—*product*. . . . I am part of the problem. I encourage these long-haired Donnys and Barrys and Dannys and Zubies, who find themselves stepping straight from the conservatory, with their student scores marked up the way their professors told them, directly into the concert hall and recording studio, there to spout back the lessons learned by rote. . . . And I help perpetuate this hoax. I help tell the consuming public, such as it is, that these new records by these new artists—*artists?*—are worthy of permanent encapsulation in vinyl. I help put these unformed fetuses into our museums.

Now, after a quarter-century of Donnys and Barrys and Dannys and Zubies—of crossover and the Three Tenors and a hundred different recorded versions of Beethoven's Ninth Symphony, each one duller than the last—the classical recording industry appears to be on its last legs. Nor will it die alone. Hard though it may be to imagine life without records and record stores, it is only a matter of time, and not much of it, before they disappear—and notwithstanding the myriad pleasures that the major labels have given us in the course of their century-long existence, it is at least possible that the twenty-first century will be better off without them.

To be sure, this prospect is understandably disturbing to many older musicians and music lovers, given the fact that the record album has played so pivotal a role in the culture of postwar music. Nor do I claim that life without records will necessarily be better—or worse. It will merely be *different,* just as the lives of actors were irrevocably changed by the invention of the motion-picture camera in ways that no one could possibly have foreseen in 1900. But one thing is already clear: unlike art museums and opera houses, records serve a purpose that technology has rendered obsolete. The triumph of the digit, and the demise of the record album as culture-shaping art object, is at hand.

Commentary 2002

Three Roads to American Opera

IF YOU TALK TO ANY AMERICAN COMPOSER UNDER THE AGE of fifty, chances are that he will either have just written an opera or be planning to write one soon. This has as much to do with economics as with aesthetics. Professional composers follow the musical market no less closely than the Supreme Court is said to follow the election returns, and the ongoing explosion of interest in American opera shows no signs of abating. For the first time since the Fifties, it has become possible for an American composer seriously to contemplate the prospect of writing an opera that will receive multiple productions.

Take, for instance, John Harbison's *The Great Gatsby,* premiered by New York's Metropolitan Opera in December 1999, and William Bolcom's *A View from the Bridge,* premiered by the Lyric Opera of Chicago two months earlier. These works have much in common. Both are large-scale stage pieces by distinguished American composers of the late-modernist generation (Harbison and Bolcom were both born in 1938). Both are musical adaptations of preexisting works by famous American authors. And both are composed in straightforwardly tonal idioms that incorporate elements of American popular music. Most interesting of all is that Lyric Opera will be presenting the Met's production of *Gatsby* next season, and the Met will borrow *View* in 2002. Although the sharing of productions is now common in the opera business, it is nevertheless remarkable that the country's two biggest companies should be mounting two untested works by American composers in such a fashion. Clearly, American opera, long viewed by the directors of major houses as an ugly stepchild of the standard repertoire, has at last begun to come into its own.

But for all their similarities, *Gatsby* and *View* are also very different operas, and they take sharply dissimilar approaches — one promising, the other not — to the continuing problem of forging a viable American style. Nor do they represent anything like the full range of possibilities currently being explored by American composers and companies.

JOHN HARBISON'S VERSION OF F. SCOTT FITZGERALD'S 1925 novel was commissioned by the Met to honor the twenty-fifth anniversary of the debut of James Levine, the company's music director and this country's most successful opera conductor. Levine is not known for his commitment to American composers; insofar as his taste in modern music can be divined from the works he chooses to conduct at the Met and elsewhere, it runs to such prewar European serialists as Arnold Schoenberg and Alban Berg. Nor does the Met often produce new operas. In that light, it was no great surprise that, in honoring Levine, the company should have commissioned an essentially conservative work from a composer who in recent years has emerged as a pillar of the domestic new-music establishment.

Harbison's résumé says everything about his music. A graduate of Harvard and Princeton, and a longtime professor at the Massachusetts Institute of Technology, he is the academic composer par excellence. He has received a Pulitzer prize and a MacArthur fellowship, and has served as composer-in-residence with the Los Angeles Philharmonic, the Pittsburgh Symphony, and the Aspen, Marlboro, and Tanglewood music festivals. Yet none of his pieces have entered the working repertoire of any world-class performer or ensemble. Neither of his two previous operas, *A Winter's Tale* and *A Full Moon in March,* is particularly well-known.

Harbison can hardly be accused of opportunism in choosing to turn *The Great Gatsby* into an opera; his interest in the novel goes back many years. But the same cannot be said of the Met, whose desire to commission a stage version of so familiar a book smacks itself of an increasingly familiar phenomenon: the practice by which major companies put together readily marketable packages whose parts have been carefully assembled with an eye to high name recognition. As it happens, *Gatsby* is both a great work of art and, when it comes to name recognition, a literary property of blue-chip quality. The story of how James Gatz, a poor but earnest boy from the Midwest, turned himself into Jay Gatsby, the gorgeous, gold-hatted bootlegger who rented a mansion on Long Island and there sought with dire results to reclaim the Southern belle he had loved and lost, continues to resound in our collective imagination; rarely has the American dream of self-actualization without limit been so vividly embodied, or its discontents so unsparingly probed. The weak link in brand-name operas tends to be the music, and *Gatsby* is no exception. Harbison's slow-paced score is main-line modernist yard goods — mildly dissonant and determinedly tuneless save for the clever Twenties pop-song pastiches that brighten the party scenes. It is tonal in the limited sense of not being atonal, but at no point does Harbison show any grasp of how the great opera composers of the past used functional tonality to create, sustain, and release dramatic tension over extended periods of time. Instead, his harmonically static music continually reaches for grand gestures without ever grasping them.

No less troublesome is the composer's own libretto, a fillet of Fitzgerald in which all of the novel's action and most of its famous lines ("Her voice is full of money") are collapsed into a two-act plot. Moreover, where Fitzgerald's *Gatsby* is retrospectively narrated by Nick Carraway, through whose consciousness the unfolding action is filtered, in Harbison's adaptation Nick (sung by Dwayne Croft) is a secondary character and the mysterious Jay Gatsby (Jerry Hadley) is placed at center stage throughout. This was an inevitable decision, since the closeness of first-person narration is incompatible with the large musical gestures of major-house opera (in which the orchestra functions as the "narrator"). But it also deprives the opera of much of what made its source so distinctive.

Fitzgerald's *Gatsby,* after all, is a relatively intimate, even undramatic conversation piece whose effectiveness arises in large part from the contrast between the confiding tone of Nick's elegiac voice and the inscrutability of Gatsby, who proves in the end to be all surface and self-delusion. This critical contrast is completely missing from Harbison's libretto. Indeed, he has gone so far as to give Gatsby a pair of clumsily confessional arias, in the process betraying his incomprehension of Fitzgerald's intentions: Gatsby, the great mystery man of American fiction, would never have revealed himself in that way, not even *to* himself.

Another mistake was to make Gatsby a *lirico-spinto* tenor, the quintessentially "heroic" voice type of nineteenth-century Italian opera, rather than a baritone (as had been widely expected). Such singers can play flawed heroes, but their voices are too bright and affirmative for the role of ambiguous anti-heroes. Jerry Hadley is, to boot, middle-aged, stocky, and unglamorous—hardly the "elegant young rough-neck" of Fitzgerald's imagination—and his beefy tenor voice is badly frayed. The remainder of the cast was excellent, with Lorraine Hunt Lieberson, the celebrated baroque-opera mezzo-soprano, making a memorable company debut in the small but showy role of Myrtle. The production was sensitively directed by Mark Lamos and designed in high art-deco style by Michael Yeargan. But even the seemingly infinite resources of the Metropolitan Opera House were insufficient to conceal the fact that Harbison has turned Fitzgerald's quicksilver masterpiece into an overlong opera that is stolidly competent and hopelessly undramatic.

LIKE *GATSBY*, THE OPERATIC VERSION OF *A VIEW FROM THE Bridge* is aesthetically conservative. In a way it is even more so, since William Bolcom has deliberately taken as his model the naturalistic style of opera known as *verismo* that was popularized by such turn-of-the-century Italian romantics as Leoncavallo, Mascagni, and Puccini. But Bolcom has also carefully thought through the problem of how to write a tradition-based opera that is dramatically alive, and with impressive results.

To begin with, he chose to set not a novel but a play, and one whose own "operatic" qualities have frequently been remarked upon. Arthur Miller's 1955 drama, which Miller adapted in collaboration with Arnold Weinstein, tells the story of Eddie Carbone (Kim Josephson), a middle-aged Italian-American longshoreman from Brooklyn who is sexually attracted to his young niece Catherine (Juliana Rambaldi).

Unable to sleep with his wife Beatrice (Catherine Malfitano) and tortured by his illicit longing for Catherine, Eddie finds himself ostracized by his fellow immigrants. The events that flow from this forbidden passion are the stuff of which verismo opera is made—there is even a climactic knife fight. Furthermore, Miller's naturalistic dialogue is plain-spoken enough to profit from the heightened emotionality that is made possible by the singing voice. Having picked a subject that demands full-blooded musical gestures, Bolcom proved eminently capable of rising to the occasion. It is significant that, although of the same generation as John Harbison, he is not an "establishment" modernist. A key figure in the ragtime revival of the Sixties, Bolcom has long been involved in the study and performance of American popular music— among other things, he is widely known for the popular-song recitals that he gives with his wife, the mezzo-soprano Joan Morris—and his classical compositions are couched in a polystylistic idiom that incorporates an exceptionally wide variety of musical dialects.

Not surprisingly, then, the score to *View* is flecked with such pop-flavored devices as a "doo-wop" vocal quartet and a witty version of the popular song "Paper Doll" sung in the style of a Puccini aria. But Bolcom has succeeded in bending these idioms to his own purposes, and the results do not sound like a Broadway show with added dissonance but a brusquely laconic modernist score in which the popular music of the Fifties is refracted to powerful effect. For this reason and others, *View* will surely be taken up by other companies here and abroad, and in time might even become a permanent part of the international operatic repertoire.

For all its virtues, however, no one would call *A View from the Bridge* theatrically innovative. Miller's dramaturgy is conventional—*View* is as much a "well-made" opera as *Tosca* or *Pagliacci*—and, though Bolcom has succeeded in creating a recognizably American equivalent of verismo, he breaks no new musical ground. Rather, *View* represents a continuation of the naturalistic American-opera tradition originated in the Forties and Fifties by such composers as Gian Carlo Menotti and Carlisle Floyd. These composers, all of whom were committed to the language of functional tonality, produced text-driven operas with "well-made" libretti intended for performance in small- and medium-sized houses; the orchestras they required were modest in size, the scenic requirements comfortably naturalistic. Though some of their taut, concise melodramas were more musically memorable than others — some, indeed, are less like operas than stage plays with atmospheric background music — most have proved to be highly effective theater pieces.

Nevertheless, I suspect that in the century to come, a truly indigenous American-opera style will emerge not from the Menotti-Floyd tradition but from elsewhere. One of the most promising of the various possibilities currently on display is to be seen in the work of younger composers seeking self-consciously to re-create the idiom of musical comedy in the sophisticated image of Stephen Sondheim, the only Broadway songwriter to have consistently produced important new musicals throughout the past quarter-century. Such composers include Michael John LaChiusa, whose *Marie Christine* was produced by Lincoln Center Theater even as *Gatsby* was opening at the Met, and Adam Guettel, whose *Floyd Collins,* first seen off Broadway in 1996, has since been produced by regional theater companies across the United States.

Though billed as "a new musical," *Marie Christine,* which featured the phenomenally gifted Audra McDonald in the title role, has much in common with such *opéra-comique* works as Bizet's *Carmen* or a *Singspiel* like Mozart's *The Magic Flute,* both of which include spoken dialogue and song-like arias. Roughly two-thirds of the show is sung, and much of the dialogue is orchestrally accompanied; of the three dozen musical numbers, only one is a free-standing song that ends with a break for applause. The harmonic language is often quite dissonant, at least by the comparatively bland standards of contemporary popular music, and LaChiusa's own libretto, in which the Greek myth of Medea is transplanted to turn-of-the-century New Orleans and Chicago, is frankly tragic, with an ending far starker than anything previously attempted in a Broadway musical.

Interestingly, LaChiusa has insisted in print that *Marie Christine* is not an opera — an opinion echoed by several critics. (The most thoughtful of them, Anthony Tommasini of the *New York Times,* dismissed it as "neither an opera nor a musical" but "a clunky hybrid.")

And there are indeed good reasons for calling it a musical. For one thing, the cast and orchestra are electronically amplified; for another, the score's rhythmic language is almost entirely pop-based. But if *Marie Christine* is a musical, it is one that aspires, in my opinion successfully, to the expressive weight of opera — albeit a vernacular American opera employing singers who eschew the "legitimate" vocal techniques necessary in order to be heard over a full orchestra in a large house without benefit of amplification.

This last is an important qualification. Few American operas have achieved the double aim of being sufficiently grand in scale to "work" in a large house and sufficiently accessible in musical style to please mass audiences. Such works as Philip Glass's *Akhnaten* and John Adams's *Nixon in China,* both of which emphasized broad-brush pageantry over detailed drama, were quickly taken up by companies around the world, but their minimalist language has proved too limited to stand up to repeated viewings. Considerably more promising is Lowell Liebermann's *The Picture of Dorian Gray,* an opera that, though compact in scale and modern in the tradition-based manner of Liebermann's fellow "new tonalist" composers, has far more in common with the grandly rhetorical style of nineteenth-century European opera than the more intimate approach of Menotti and his followers. In this respect, *Dorian Gray* constitutes a break with recent American operatic practice — but one that, unlike minimalist opera, may prove in the long run to be better suited to the specialized needs of major houses.

Viewed from this perspective, it is by no means clear that the vernacular-opera style of LaChiusa, or of Adam Guettel in *Floyd Collins,* will feed into the mainstream of American opera. But it is worth noting that at least one serious company, Houston Grand Opera, is currently planning to revive *Floyd Collins* — and that another, Chicago's Lyric Opera, recently announced that it would produce Stephen Sondheim's *Sweeney Todd,* with the great Welsh bass-baritone Bryn Terfel in the title role. As more classical singers like Terfel, McDonald, Anne Sofie von Otter, Frederica von Stade, and Dawn Upshaw begin to devote substantial parts of their careers to the performance of American popular music, it will become increasingly feasible for opera companies to consider adding such works to their repertoires.

ULTIMATELY, THOUGH, IT IS COMPOSERS — NOT SINGERS, OR conductors, or even general managers — who will set the course of American opera in the twenty-first century. And it may well be that the best of those composers have yet to be heard from. Prior to World War II, it was widely felt that British opera was dead beyond hope of revival. The last work by an English-born composer to enter the standard repertoire had been Purcell's *Dido and Aeneas,* composed in 1689. But then, in 1945, Benjamin Britten, the greatest English composer of the twentieth century, decided to devote the bulk of his energies to opera. His *Peter Grimes* was an immediate worldwide success. By the time of his death in 1976, Britten had turned out another half-dozen operas of the first rank; organized the English Opera Group, specifically devoted to the production of chamber-sized operas; and inspired countless other English composers to write for the stage.

To date, American opera has produced one masterpiece, George Gershwin's *Porgy and Bess,* and a number of striking works that have met with varying degrees of public acceptance, among them Samuel Barber's *Vanessa,* Aaron Copland's *The Tender Land,* Carlisle Floyd's *Of Mice and Men,* Gian Carlo Menotti's *The Medium* and *The Consul,* Virgil Thomson's *Four Saints in Three Acts* and *The Mother of Us All,* and, more recently, *A View from the Bridge* and *The Picture of Dorian Gray.* What we have *not* produced is an American Britten, sufficiently gifted and charismatic to serve as a style-setting bellwether for an entire generation of younger opera composers. The newly resurgent appeal of the musical genre Copland wryly called *la forme fatale* is without question a crucial development in the history of American music. Where it will lead is another matter, and an unpredictable one. But one thing is likely: American opera — be it classical or vernacular or some as-yet-unknown hybrid — will not come into its long-delayed maturity until a characteristically American genius leads the way.

Commentary 2000

After Mr. B

How important is ballet? To the balletomane, it is the most important thing in the world, a synthesis of the three arts whose expressive horizons are unlimited. To W. H. Auden, it was a "very, very minor art," undeniably charming but nonetheless trivial by comparison with poetry or painting. No doubt the truth lies somewhere in between — but where? Even though I love ballet passionately, I'm as unsure of the answer today as I was when I first started looking at the dance a decade and a half ago.

That ballet's place among the major art forms is problematic seems to me self-evident. The mere fact that one can even question its importance all but proves the point. (No one would think of asking such a thing about music.) Nor is it reassuring that there have been only two extended periods when ballet was anywhere near the center of Western cultural consciousness. Such was the case in the Twenties, but that was solely because of the spectacular achievements of Serge Diaghilev's Ballets Russes, and Diaghilev's death in 1929 sent ballet into a tailspin that lasted until the founding of American Ballet Theatre in 1940 and the subsequent emergence of George Balanchine as an icon of high culture. For many years after that, few would have seriously thought to question the significance of ballet, of which even the middlebrow media took note. But the death of Balanchine in 1983 marked the beginning of another slow retreat, and now ballet is again on the periphery of the cultural conversation (as any dance critic can tell you from personal experience).

Every art form goes through periods of stasis, but to consider the track record of ballet in the twentieth century is to be struck by how few indisputably major creative figures it has produced. Diaghilev was an impresario, not a choreographer, and next to none of the works for which he served as midwife are still seen on the world's stages. (As Constant Lambert, with whom he briefly collaborated, once suggested, Diaghilev's greatest gift may have been his unrivaled ability to create "a vogue for vogue.") In general, we know more about the Ballets Russes' costumes than its choreography. Mikhail Fokine's *Petrushka* and Vaslav Nijinsky's *L'Après-midi d'un faune* survive more as ideas than actual ballets; Leonide Massine's once-celebrated dances are now revived only as novelties, while Bronislava Nijinska's *Les Biches* and *Les Noces,* though perfectly viable, have never quite succeeded in making their way into ballet's working repertory. For all intents and purposes, the history of modern ballet starts with Balanchine's *Apollo* (1928) and *Prodigal Son* (1929), both acknowledged masterpieces that have been danced more or less regularly ever since their Ballets Russes premieres.

Balanchine's own standing as a major artist is mostly taken for granted, at least by balletomanes. Not only has New York City Ballet, the company he founded, been dancing his work continuously since 1948, but some two dozen Balanchine ballets are also performed by other companies throughout the world. *Apollo, Prodigal Son, Serenade, Concerto Barocco, Ballet Imperial, Symphony in C, The Four Temperaments, Western Symphony, Divertimento No. 15, Agon, Rubies, Stravinsky Violin Concerto:* these are, with *Swan Lake* and *Sleeping Beauty* and *Giselle,* the true "warhorses" of the ballet repertory, the staple items whose presence on a program is a sure sign of artistic seriousness and technical accomplishment. Even such companies as American Ballet Theatre, whose repertory is dominated by full-evening story ballets rather than the plotless one-act dances Balanchine favored, feel obliged to present a few such pieces each season.

But after Balanchine, what? Or, to put it another way, were there any other twentieth-century ballet choreographers of similar stature? If a choreographer's stature can be measured by the frequency with which his work is performed by companies other than his own — and this seems a not-unreasonable standard — then the answer, clearly, is no. Though New York City Ballet continues to perform most of Jerome Robbins's best-known dances side by side with its encyclopedic Balanchine repertory, Robbins was notoriously stingy about making them available to other companies during his lifetime, and it remains to be seen whether more than three or four of the best ones, in particular *Fancy Free, Afternoon of a Faun,* and *Dances at a Gathering,* will achieve wider circulation now that he is gone. Similarly, a mere handful of Frederick Ashton's neoromantic story ballets are danced by companies other than London's Royal Ballet, whose commitment to preserving and protecting its Ashton repertory has in any case been on the wane for years. Antony Tudor, whose "psychological ballets" were once thought to be the last word in modernity, turned out to be a two-hit wonder: only *Jardin aux Lilas* and *Pillar of Fire* are securely entrenched in the international repertory, though a half-dozen of his other dances are revived from time to time. Outside of a sprinkling of lesser efforts by such second- and third-tier figures as Kenneth MacMillan and Agnes de Mille, surprisingly little else survives of the thousands of ballets made between the deaths of Diaghilev and Balanchine. Then as now, the vast majority of the new ballets seen each season were choreographed by the artistic directors of the companies that premiered them, and were never seen anywhere else.

This peculiar state of affairs is taken for granted by dancegoers, perhaps because many of them know comparatively little about other art forms and thus are unaware of just how peculiar it is. But suppose that your entire knowledge of modern art derived from repeated visits to a museum whose permanent collection consisted of two dozen Matisses, ten paintings by Stuart Davis, six by Raoul Dufy, three by Max Beckmann, and one each by, say, Wassily Kandinsky, Chaim Soutine, Walter Sickert, Grant Wood, and Pavel Tchelitchew, plus a rotating exhibit of new work by the museum's own director. What conclusions would you draw about the importance of modern art — or, for that matter, of Matisse?

TO THOSE WHO KNOW LITTLE OR NOTHING OF BALLET, IT WILL surely seem perverse to compare the greatest painter of the modern era with any choreographer, however gifted. Most of my friends regard my own interest in dance as a harmless but mystifying idiosyncrasy, and when I assure them that Balanchine is every bit as important an artist as

Matisse, they look at me as though I'd said that Dawn Powell was as important as Proust.

During Balanchine's lifetime, though, such comparisons were commonplace (though they were more typically made with Picasso, an artist with whom he had far less in common). Back then, it didn't seem so odd for Arlene Croce to declare in the pages of the *New Yorker* that "[i]f George Balanchine were a novelist or a playwright or a movie director instead of a choreographer, his studies of women would be among the most discussed and most influential artistic achievements of our time." For now that dance is largely ignored by the media, it is easy to forget that there was a time when "everyone" in New York went to New York City Ballet — and not just the *beau monde,* either, but poets, painters, playwrights, composers, even intellectuals, all of whom went because they believed Balanchine to be a supremely great artist at the peak of his powers. In his account of the 1958 premiere of *Agon,* Edwin Denby mentioned in passing that "Marcel Duchamp, the painter, said he felt the way he had after the opening of *Le Sacre.*" One need not admire Duchamp to admit the force of the comparison, or of the fact that so pivotal a figure in the history of modern art took the trouble to be present on both occasions.

Agon was, of course, among the most distinguished of the many collaborations between Balanchine and Igor Stravinsky, which reminds us of one of the reasons why Balanchine had such cachet for so long: he was the preferred choreographer of the composer of *The Rite of Spring.* The two men worked together as far back as *Apollo,* and in the year after Stravinsky's death, Balanchine and NYCB put on a week-long Stravinsky Festival at Lincoln Center at which twenty-two new ballets were presented, including three of Balanchine's supreme masterpieces, *Duo Concertant, Stravinsky Violin Concerto,* and *Symphony in Three Movements.* Nor was Balanchine thought to be a mere theatrical valet to the great man, though he was without doubt the junior partner in their collaborations. In most of what was written and said about them between 1948 and 1983, it was assumed that they were peers, and more than enough tastemakers were sufficiently familiar with enough of Balanchine's ballets to make that assumption stick.

Twenty years after George Balanchine's death, the situation has changed, for Balanchine in particular as well as for ballet in general. New York City Ballet is not what it used to be, and has lost its privileged place on the cultural scene. I know few art-conscious New Yorkers who go there more than sporadically — or to any other dance performances, for that matter. Nowadays, there are no longer any "hot tickets" in dance, no events that attract the attention of a truly general audience, and none (except for Mark Morris's eagerly awaited New York seasons) at which artists from other fields are at all likely to be seen. Hence the value of Charles M. Joseph's *Stravinsky and Balanchine: A Journey of Invention,* a book whose purpose is to prove anew what once seemed settled: that George Balanchine was not merely the biggest fish in a very, very small pond, but a theatrical genius fully equal in stature to the musical genius with whom his name will forever be linked.

Joseph's book is of unique interest because he is not a dance critic but a musician. Balanchine's extraordinary musicianship was a byword virtually from the start of his career, but most dance critics, who know next to nothing about music, have had to take it on faith. Only one important dance critic, B. H. Haggin, has been a trained musician, and Haggin, who wrote for a general audience, never attempted to analyze in detail the myriad ways in which Balanchine's ballets reflected their scores. Not only does Joseph supply just such analyses of three Balanchine-Stravinsky collaborations, *Apollo, Agon,* and *Stravinsky Violin Concerto,* but he also provides a detailed discussion of the intensive musical training Balanchine received at the Petrograd Conservatory, where he majored in piano, studied violin, French horn, and trumpet, and learned how to read orchestral scores and prepare his own "exquisitely notated" piano reductions of instrumental works by Stravinsky and Berg. (He was also a competent conductor, dropping into the New York City Ballet pit from time to time to conduct the company orchestra.) Except for Mark Morris, no other choreographer has had anything remotely like this kind of hands-on experience.

Balanchine's knowledge of music was central to his method of making dances. Jean Cocteau remarked of Nijinsky's staging of *The Rite of Spring* that "the ballet failed primarily because the music and movement were parallel. . . . For Cocteau (and Stravinsky, too), the parallelisms of *The*

Rite were, rightly or wrongly, perceived as no more than redundancies." Instead of concocting redundant visual equivalents of the rhythmic details of a piece of music, Balanchine delved deeply into its structure, moving his dancers in counterpoint to its unfolding events:

> Balanchine's sense of movement counterbalanced the music in a way that was neither superficially nor superfluously imitative. His control of motion visually concretized musical relations otherwise likely to have been missed. His choreography didn't offer banal derivatives or garnish the music by adding another layer, nor did he allow the music to function as a subsidiary platform for the dance. In my viewing of *Apollo* and all the subsequent Stravinsky-Balanchine ballets, it seemed to me that the musically astute choreographer possessed the uncanny gift of clarifying what my ears heard through what my eyes saw.

This method of dancemaking was so radically original that it confused many contemporary critics. Raised on Diaghilev's elaborate syntheses of décor, dance, and music (too often in that order of precedence), they found it impossible to appreciate the no-nonsense pieces in which Balanchine placed his simply dressed dancers in front of a plain blue cyclorama and set them in motion without benefit of plot, accompanied not by candy-coated character pieces but large-scale symphonic works like the Bach Two-Violin Concerto (used in *Concerto Barocco*) or Tchaikovsky's Serenade for Strings. Now that Balanchine's stature is universally acknowledged, it is easy to forget how long it took for these dances to win critical acceptance. John Martin, the chief dance critic of the *New York Times* throughout the first half of Balanchine's New York years, wrote with blissful incomprehension of one stunning premiere after another. British dance critics were even worse, believing as they did that Diaghilev was the one true god of modern ballet. When Richard Shead, by no means a stupid or insensitive man, decried the modern tendency toward "decorative abstraction, with music and scenery playing inferior roles," no one doubted that he had George Balanchine in mind.

Balanchine would have been puzzled by such talk had he deigned to take notice of it. For one thing, he never used the word "abstract" to describe his plotless dances. No more than Matisse did he turn his back on the visible world: a Balanchine ballet is a *human* drama in which men and women of flesh and blood, propelled by music, interact with one another in complex ways that, as Mendelssohn once said of his own compositions, are "too *definite*" to be summed up by words. That Balanchine himself thought of at least some of his plotless ballets in highly definite, even literal terms is beyond question, for on rare occasions he let the veil slip. In *Liebeslieder Walzer*, for instance, four couples dance together in a ballroom; the women wear gowns and pumps in the first part, tutus and toe shoes in the second. Asked about the ballet by Bernard Taper, his first biographer, he replied, "In the first act, it's the real people that are dancing. In the second act, it's their souls."

An even more startling "explanation" of a famous Balanchine dance is Alexandra Danilova's little-known description of the last movement of the nominally plotless *Serenade*:

> I danced the first girl, who enters at the beginning. She is a butterfly, having romances with everybody. And then along comes a married man with his wife: they walk, and in their path is this girl. The man has an attraction for her, they dance, but for him it isn't serious, and in the end he continues along the road with his wife. The girl is seeking, suffering, and then she is alone, turning to her friends. I asked Mr. B., and this was his explanation.

Such explanations were rare, though, and Balanchine never publicly endorsed this one. He almost always preferred to let his plotless dances speak for themselves, presumably for the same reason that Henry James left to the reader's horrified imagination the particular evils done by Peter Quint and Miss Jessel to Miles and Flora in "The Turn of the Screw": "Make him *think* the evil, make him think it for himself, and you are released from weak specifications." In much the same way, Balanchine's ballets allow the viewer to think for himself—to see in their music-driven movements whatever occurrences he cares to see—and gain immeasurably in their richness of implication precisely because of their near-complete lack of "weak specifications."

If *Stravinsky and Balanchine: A Journey of Invention* has a defect, it is Joseph's reluctance to fully acknowledge the extent to which some of Balanchine's ballets may have arisen from nonmusical considerations.

Yet this is the defect of a virtue. Dance critics, unable to talk knowledgeably about Balanchine's use of music, prefer as a rule to talk about almost anything else — often, to be sure, quite vividly. But by concentrating primarily on their musical aspects, as in his description of the relationship between Apollo and the three muses in *Apollo,* Joseph restores the necessary balance between both aspects of Balanchine's method that has hitherto been missing in virtually all published criticisms of his work:

> Just as Stravinsky designed an unobtrusive aural accompaniment for the ballet's luminous melodies, so too Balanchine often employed the Muses as a visual accompaniment for Apollo's dancing. The three women function as a cohesive unit without sacrificing their individual identity. . . . Seldom does Balanchine allow the ensemble's collective motion to begin or end in unison. Each Muse usually enters or exits an ensemble passage separately, thus averting a rote duplication of the music. There is almost always some interlocking of gestures, as in a beautifully imbricated visual design.

MERE WORDS, NO MATTER HOW PRECISE OR EVOCATIVE THEY may be, can do no more than suggest the emotional effect of the immediate experience of looking at a Balanchine ballet. Having spent countless hours looking at dozens of them, I have come to believe that Balanchine was not merely the greatest ballet choreographer of the twentieth century, but the only one to have created a body of work that deserves to be remembered in the way we remember the work of Stravinsky — or Matisse. But is it also possible that he was a fluke, a genius who poured his prodigal energies into a pond too small to hold them? And if that is the case, do his dances, no matter how good they were, have a future?

If one goes solely by the past, then Balanchine's future, and the future of ballet as a whole, would appear to be bleak. Only a handful of pre-modern ballets, after all, continue to be danced in their original form, and fewer still can be taken seriously as major works of art. By and large, romantic ballet is remembered more for its music than its steps, just as one inevitably wonders about the extent to which choreography per se was responsible for Diaghilev's success. No other modern ballet choreographer, not even Robbins or Ashton, is comparable in stature to Balanchine. As for the present moment, the only full-time classical choreographer widely acknowledged by critics and audiences as a major artist in the making is New York City Ballet's Christopher Wheeldon, who is much more than promising but still too young to be taken for granted. (A few modern-dance choreographers also work with ballet companies, but only as a sideline.)

Fortunately, there is another way to look at Balanchine, and at the history of ballet as a whole. For it is also possible that we have reached the end of the beginning of the history of dance as a serious expressive medium, and that he will be remembered not as its last giant, but its first. Seen from that perspective, nineteenth-century ballet resembles pre-Renaissance music, or painting before Giotto — by no means insignificant, but mainly of interest to specialists — while Balanchine's absolute primacy among modern ballet choreographers becomes less isolating and more plausible.

To be sure, Balanchine did not make his ballets with an eye on posterity, and affected to believe that they would not long outlive him, at least not in any recognizable form. But he also founded New York City Ballet and the School of American Ballet, which exist to preserve authentic versions of his ballets and teach the techniques necessary to dance them idiomatically, and he left the rights to those ballets not to NYCB but to fourteen individuals — dancers, close friends, and colleagues — who in turn deposited them in the Balanchine Trust, which supervises all authorized productions of the seventy-five-odd surviving ballets it controls. Balanchine was not the first choreographer to start a school or a company. What sets him apart is the existence of a worldwide network of institutions and individuals whose purpose is to disseminate authentic versions of his ballets as widely as possible, and to give them a permanent life in repertory. No other choreographer, whether in ballet or modern dance, has attracted so many followers, and no other choreographic oeuvre has been the subject of so thoroughgoing an attempt at long-term preservation.

It is worth noting in this connection that a steadily growing percentage of the leading dance companies in the United States, among them

San Francisco Ballet, Dance Theatre of Harlem, Pacific Northwest Ballet, Miami City Ballet, Carolina Ballet, and the Kennedy Center's Suzanne Farrell Ballet, are "Balanchine companies" led by NYCB alumni who danced for Balanchine and whose repertories consist in large part of their mentor's work. These are not the only important companies in America, but their common emphasis on Balanchine, and the consistently high quality with which they stage his ballets, seems to me a development of near-unprecedented significance, a sign that the Balanchine style may be evolving into a *lingua franca* for ballet in the twenty-first century, just as the Franco-Russian style of classic ballet provided a firm foundation on which the tradition-steeped Balanchine was able to erect his neoclassical idiom. New York–based balletomanes who view with alarm the continuing decline of New York City Ballet need to start getting used to the notion that the city long known as "the dance capital of the world" may well be on the verge of becoming no more than *primus inter pares* in the increasingly decentralized world of post-Balanchine ballet.

It helps, of course, that most of Balanchine's dances are well suited to the restrictive circumstances under which repertory ballet is normally presented in this country. A piece like *Concerto Barocco,* for example, has no set and no costumes — it is danced in simple practice clothes — making it relatively cheap to produce. Nor does the plotless *Barocco* require elaborate direction to make its theatrical effect: it contains no significant glances, no labyrinthine subtexts, just steps and music. And unlike the myriad dialects of modern dance, the movement vocabulary of classical ballet is for all intents and purposes universal. Thus Balanchine's ballets, radically innovative though they are, can be executed by any reasonably proficient classical company, and the Balanchine Trust readily makes them available to interested companies capable of meeting its technical standards and willing to comply with its rehearsal requirements.

None of this, however, answers the question I posed at the beginning of this essay: how important *is* ballet? That depends on whether New York City Ballet and the other Balanchine companies prove in the long run to have been breeding grounds for a new generation of Balanchine-influenced choreographers capable of producing substantial bodies of major work. To date, the record is mixed. Peter Martins and Helgi Tomasson, who run New York City Ballet and San Francisco Ballet, have been the most prolific of Balanchine's alumni, but their ballets are of strictly minor interest, and have mostly failed to be taken up by other companies. On the other hand, Christopher Wheeldon and Robert Weiss, the artistic director of Carolina Ballet, are making dances that seem to me to have staying power, and Wheeldon's work is already in demand around the world. The same is not yet true of Weiss, but I suspect it is only a matter of time before his full-evening ballets, which resemble Balanchine's *A Midsummer Night's Dream* in their dance-driven storytelling techniques, start to be produced by companies other than his own.

Two choreographers do not a tradition make, and it is too soon to say whether Wheeldon and Weiss will leave behind sizable bodies of work that prove to be of permanent interest. Similarly, I wish I could speak with complete certainty about the future of Balanchine's work, but the jury, once again, is still out. That it *ought* to live and flourish seems to me beyond question, though, and I now think its prospects are quite good, far better than a decade ago, when ballet as a whole seemed to have lost its way. And while I'm sure most balletomanes felt the same way about the Ballets Russes the day Serge Diaghilev died, Balanchine's lean, stripped-down plotless ballets, unlike Diaghilev's evanescent spectacles, were built to last. This is not to say that they can thrive in a vacuum, but the world of dance is full of talented men and women determined to make sure that *Agon, Apollo,* and *The Four Temperaments* last as long as *The Rite of Spring* or *The Red Studio*. If I had to bet, I'd put my money on them, and on George Balanchine.

Yale Review 2003

Going a Lot to the Mark Morris Dance Group

I FIRST SAW THE MARK MORRIS DANCE GROUP SOME EIGHT years after its 1980 debut, by which time every important critic in America had had his or her say about the Bad Boy of Modern Dance. The level of disagreement was high enough to provoke the verbal equivalent of fistfights in print and in lobbies. Some thought Morris was God (or, as he puts it in his programs, god), while others were no less sure he was an overhyped fraud. Nobody appeared to think anything in between. The New York dance scene suffers chronically from this sort of polarization—it's called, appropriately enough, dance politics—but never in my then-brief life as a balletomane had I seen so deep a fissure of opinion.

Determined to make up my own mind, I went to the Brooklyn Academy of Music, where the company was dancing, if memory serves, *Sonata for Clarinet and Piano, Fugue and Fantasy,* and *Strict Songs.* I had my doubts about some of what I saw that night. The range of body types on stage was diverse to the point of comedy—I'd never seen a plumpish dancer before, or a balding one—and the company's manner of moving struck me as puzzlingly loose-limbed. (Later that season, Mikhail Baryshnikov and American Ballet Theatre premiered *Drink to Me Only With Thine Eyes,* and I remember thinking how nice it would be if Morris's dancers looked like *that.*) I thought, too, that Morris was using camp as a way of concealing his emotions, and that there was something unconvincingly ostentatious about the same-sex partnering that at the time was something of a company trademark. Yet for all my reservations, there was no question in my mind about Morris's singular talent. Even then, it was plain to see that he had the rare ability to fill a stage with eye-catching, music-driven movement. I also liked the fact that his pieces were impersonal and unsentimental—the opposite of everything I loathed about the lapel-grabbing school of modern dance drama that Martha Graham had mothered. By that time, I already suspected that Twyla Tharp would not fulfill her youthful promise, and no new choreographer of equal interest had come along since then, which explains why so many of Morris's early fans were inclined to fawn over him. Unlikely as it seemed, this long-haired loud-mouth showed every sign of having the potential to become an artist worthy of comparison with the greatest dancemakers of the twentieth century, George Balanchine very much included.

From then on, I made a point of seeing the Mark Morris Dance Group whenever it came to New York. Unfortunately, there weren't all that many performances to see. The company soon moved to Brussels, and for the next few seasons its American appearances were infrequent. Even after Morris and his dancers returned to this country, they spent most of their time on the road, and their New York seasons tended to be short. In addition, they rarely performed older works—Morris preferred to show new dances—making it impossible to get to know their repertory more than superficially. This lack of familiarity with Morris's work is a greater obstacle to comprehension than is commonly understood. Balanchine was once widely regarded as a "difficult" artist, even by ostensibly knowledgeable critics; not until New York City Ballet began giving extended seasons of repertory at City Center did it become possible for serious dancegoers to become comfortable with such bristlingly complex ballets as *Concerto Barocco* or *Episodes*. Edward Gorey, for instance, attended each and every performance the company gave between 1957 and 1982, later writing a delightfully knowing book called *The Lavender Leotard; or, Going a Lot to the New York City Ballet*. I never went to City Ballet that often, even in my first hot flush of discovery, but within a few seasons I had gone often enough to see most of Balanchine's major ballets a half-dozen times or more, and the more I saw them, the more I saw in them. With Mark Morris, by contrast, what you saw the first time was what you got, and all you got.

By the mid-Nineties, I was regularly covering Morris's New York openings, and my feelings about his work were more or less the same as they had been in 1988. Though he remained the only choreographer under the age of fifty who looked like a major artist in the making, some of his dances I thought successful, others less so, several not good at all, and none unequivocally great. As I wrote in a 1994 essay:

> Those who find Morris irritating also find it impossible to ignore him. I find him extremely irritating, and it would never occur to me to ignore him. There is no young choreographer I admire more. But, then, Morris isn't so young anymore. By the time he was thirty-seven, George Balanchine had made *Apollo* and *Serenade* and *Concerto Barocco*. If the comparison seems unfair—these are, after all, three of the transcendent masterpieces of twentieth-century dance—it is worth remembering that we expect the most out of those we admire the most; they are the only ones who can disappoint us. It is not quite right to say that I have been disappointed by Morris's work to date. What I *have* been disappointed by is its constricted range of emotion, its not-infrequent failure to rise to the highest expressive implications of the music its maker loves so much and understands so well. "Interesting is easy, beautiful is difficult," Gustav Mahler said. I'm ready for Mark Morris to stop being interesting.

This essay was astonishingly presumptuous, given the fact that I had then seen no more than two dozen of Morris's dances, very few of them more than once. But at least I recognized his importance, and though some of his work continued to elude me—I must have been the only critic in America who was left cold by the evening-long *L'Allegro, il Penseroso ed il Moderato,* thought by many to be his masterpiece—I kept on looking, and thinking about what I saw.

With each passing season, I felt more in tune with what Morris was trying to do. For me, the turning point came in 1997 with *Rhymes With Silver,* a forty-minute-long ensemble piece set to a new score by Lou Harrison. The balance between levity and seriousness seemed exactly right, especially in the central pas de deux, which I described in a review written the morning after the New York premiere:

> Kraig Patterson stands stock still while the choreographer flaps and flutters desperately around him. What does Morris want? Why won't Patterson acknowledge his presence? The questions are left wide open

until the end, when Morris clutches his knees (significantly, a dancer's injury), sinks to the floor in apparent agony and crawls away. Then Patterson finally comes to life, walking slowly offstage behind Morris. It is an unforgettable climax to a remarkable dance.

Interestingly, Morris had long been reluctant to choreograph pas de deux. It was almost a matter of principle with him — he preferred ensembles or multiple duets — and I believed that this unwillingness to confront what has traditionally been the expressive focal point of theatrical dance was symbolic of what I still persisted in seeing as an inhibition on his part. Could it be that his sexuality was somehow interfering with his ability to get to the heart of the matter? It wasn't that he was embarrassed about being homosexual (to put it mildly). It was, rather, as if he found the very idea of love embarrassing. Conversely, I saw in *Rhymes With Silver* a new willingness to engage directly with human emotion, and praised it accordingly.

Since then, I have continued to look at Morris's dances as often as I can. What has changed is that I have been able to see more of them, and to see some of them more than once. In 1998, his staging of Henry Purcell's opera *Dido and Aeneas* was presented at the Brooklyn Academy of Music, where I had last seen it in 1989, and American Ballet Theatre finally revived *Drink to Me Only With Thine Eyes*. A year later, Morris's company premiered *The Argument,* a powerful study of three splintered relationships set to Robert Schumann's Five Studies in Folk Style; it was repeated in the summer by Mikhail Baryshnikov's White Oak Dance Project in a slightly different version for a man and three women. The following season, the company performed *The Argument* and four other pieces at the 499-seat New Victory Theater, and prior to that I had the opportunity to spend two weeks watching Morris and his dancers rehearsing in the studio.

Going a lot to the Mark Morris Dance Group has not inspired me to join the ranks of Morris's uncritical admirers, but it has caused me to suspect that when I found some of his earlier work unsatisfactory, the fault was not in the dances or the dancers, but in me. What I once felt to be a "loose, baggy quality" that sometimes came across as "sloppy and unfocused" now looks impeccably right (though I happily stand by my earlier comparison of his idiosyncratic movement vocabulary to "the weird draftsmanship of a Thurber cartoon"). Similarly, greater familiarity has bred keener appreciation of his uncanny musicality, not merely in the large-scale architecture of his dances but also in their point-to-point phrasing. And certain dances that I used to find naggingly campy—especially the party scene from *The Hard Nut,* Morris's comic-book version of *The Nutcracker*—now strike me as funny and touching, just as he meant them to be.

The greatest revelation came from seeing a rehearsal and two performances of *My Party,* a fifteen-minute-long dance for four men and four women set to Jean Françaix's agreeably lightweight C Major String Trio. So far as I know, *My Party* is not generally thought to be a major work (it is mentioned only in passing in Joan Acocella's excellent biography of Morris), though the members of his company claim to love it. "That one always makes people cry," a dancer who took part in the 1984 premiere told me. I found it to be a miniature masterpiece, and one that also sheds light on certain aspects of Morris's style that I once found elusive.

To begin with, *My Party* is a pure ensemble work: all eight dancers are on stage throughout the piece, and they pair off without regard to gender. This, Acocella says, is "the message: no rules, free choice." But according to Morris, *My Party* is not a political statement but a reminiscence of the parties he used to give as a teenager in Seattle in the early Seventies (the decor consists of a single strand of cheap Chinese lanterns), back in the days when he was spending much of his spare time dancing with a Balkan folk ensemble. "I fell in love with the group," he told Acocella. "I fell in love with several individuals in sequence, and they fell in love with each other." Something not unlike this is essentially what happens in *My Party.* While there is one show-stopping moment in the finale when the couples fall to the floor and start rutting—quite amiably, too—the emotional center of the dance is the slow movement, a sweet-and-sour song without words that a more conventional choreographer would have turned into a romantic duet. Instead, Morris's dancers form a circle and embark on a folklike group dance that is at once austere and mysteriously tender. "Isn't it weird?" he says. "It's somehow become sad or poignant, or something. I've no idea how. It's plain. I like plain. And kind of naive." To my eyes, what results is not a sermon on sexual identity (Morris is not given to sermonizing in any case), but an oddly haunting evocation of the awkwardness and uncertainty of adolescence, in which uniformly glamorous bodies and a pas de deux, however beautiful, would have been out of place.

As I watched *My Party* at the New Victory, I recalled with increasing discomfort what I wrote after first seeing *L'Allegro, il Penseroso ed il Moderato:*

> For all its richness, there is a neat, once-over-lightly quality about *L'Allegro* that I find troubling. And Morris's lack of interest in partnering works against him here. To make a full-evening ballet without a single pas de deux is a mark of great ingenuity, but it gives *L'Allegro* a quality of impersonality . . . that leaves a blank at the expressive heart of what ought to be a cathartic experience.

It was around this time that I had occasion to tell another of Morris's dancers that, while I admired his work greatly, I had somehow failed to connect with *L'Allegro.* Instead of bristling, she smiled and replied, "You'll experience it fully in the future, never fear." Time was when *I* might have bristled at so cocky a retort, but by then I already suspected that I was the one at fault—that I had been "seeing" it through the distorting glass of convention instead of looking at the dance itself. In due course, I made my act of contrition. "For some inexplicable reason," I wrote when the Morris company brought *L'Allegro* to the Brooklyn Academy of Music, "I didn't warm to the dance when I saw it at the Lincoln Center Festival six years ago—it struck me as virtuosic but empty. What was I thinking? *L'Allegro* is a whole world of dance in a single evening, everything from childlike pantomime to knockabout comedy to complex groupings reminiscent of George Balanchine in their control and clarity."

I mention this not only because it is a good thing for critics to abase themselves in public, but also because we do it so rarely. As it happens, though, I've changed my mind about art more than once, and in so doing I've learned that I not infrequently start by disliking something and end up liking it. Not always—sometimes I decide on closer acquaintance that a novel or painting isn't as good as I'd thought. (I used to like Picasso's *Guernica* a lot more than I do now.) More often, though, I realize that it was necessary for me to grow into a fuller understanding of a work of art to which my powers of comprehension were not at first equal. The music critic Hans Keller said something shrewd about this phenomenon: "As soon as I detest something I ask myself why I like it." I try to keep that in mind whenever I cover a premiere. I don't mean to say that critics should be wishy-washy—that does nobody any good—but at the same time, we should also remember that strong emotions sometimes masquerade as their opposite.

Most of all, though, I mention it in justice to a great artist whose work I was too quick to judge. Mark Morris may not be perfect, but he is definitely good enough to be given the benefit of the doubt, no matter what unlikely-looking thing he may choose to do next. Whatever it is, I'll be there, the same way I'm there whenever Paul Taylor or Merce Cunningham make a new dance. Like them, he is the real right thing.

Partisan Review 2000

At Full Blast

MARK MORRIS IS MAKING A DANCE — LOUDLY. DANCE studios, with their hardwood floors and mirrored walls, are noisy places even at the calmest of times, and Morris, who is working on a suite of nine dances to the music of Frédéric Chopin, can raise a ruckus sufficient to drown out a medium-size riot. All afternoon, he has been shouting, whistling, singing, and emitting a steady stream of unprintable class-clown wisecracks in his shrill foghorn voice. It's as if John Belushi had decided to take up modern dance, or maybe Ernie Kovacs.

Visitors are often startled by Morris's antics, but his dancers are used to them. "Mark was loud before he was famous," says Tina Fehlandt, a charter member of the Mark Morris Dance Group, not unaffectionately. Meanwhile, Ethan Iverson, the company's music director, clatters away at a finger-twistingly difficult étude on an ill-tuned baby grand in the corner of the studio, while a recording of *The Nutcracker* pas de deux plays irrelevantly somewhere down the hall.

At the center of the hubbub are the five women and four men for whom the dance is being choreographed, and who are doing their best to read its maker's mind. This isn't always easy. "Like" is Morris's second favorite four-letter word, and he has spent the past few minutes piling up increasingly extravagant comparisons in order to get them to do exactly what he wants: "Like a mosh pit. Whatever *that* is." "Like bears and a deer." "Like Pebbles and Bamm-Bamm." "Like you're blacking out." "Like you've just been eviscerated." "Like you're a momerath." (The expressions on the faces of several dancers make it clear that he is not the only Lewis Carroll buff in the room.)

These figures of speech, heavily salted with audible italics and multiple exclamation points, are meant to illuminate the finale of the yet to be named dance, set to the "Winter Wind" Etude, one of Chopin's best-known pieces. (The work will have its premiere at the American Dance Festival later this year.) The tumultuous music has inspired Morris to transform Julie Worden, a handsome young woman who looks like a brainy cheerleader, into a suicidal princess who inexplicably finds herself swept up in some sort of mad Gothic torture fantasy. "Stop!" he screams as Worden sails despondently through the air for the third time in a row. He strikes a great-man pose and yells at no one in particular, "Isn't it *fun* to be the cho-re-o-gra-*pheur*?" The room falls silent as the dancers wait patiently for him to think of something new for them to do. He pokes his head into the musical score that he has been carrying around for the last half-hour.

"This is the only bar where the harmony changes on every beat," Iverson says quietly.

"Well, I'd better make the most of it," Morris replies, screwing his bearded face into a leer, "since it's a well-known fact that I'm the most musical of choreographers." (This last phrase is uttered in a posh grande-dame accent.) He glances at the score again. No one says a word. Finally, he looks at the dancers. "You're over-responding to what seems sentimental in the music," he says, all business. "Nostalgia. And that's what I hate. The reason I'm using this music is because I'm sick of it. It's got too many associations. That's why I never choreographed any Chopin. And it's the most beautiful music in the world! Yes, it's beautiful, but you're not doing what I want. I want . . . I want . . . ANTHRAX!" At which point the studio explodes in laughter, and the world begins to turn again.

What is telling about this vignette is that it hinges on a musical point: the étude has reached its maximum harmonic density, so the dance steps must somehow reflect that event. Some choreographers might well sense this intuitively, though most would probably skate over it without a second thought. But for Morris, who reads music, plays the piano, and almost always makes his dances with a printed score in hand, such subtleties are the heart of the matter.

Though Morris's dances are not about their scores—they are, to paraphrase Igor Stravinsky, about themselves—it is nonetheless true that they arise from the music and are at all times closely attentive to its surface and structure. "You want to make the forms parallel," he explains, a simple sentence that is nonetheless rich in choreographic implications. The parallelism may be as uncomplicated as sending a new dancer skittering across the stage at the first appearance of a new theme, or it may be equal and opposite (as in *Handel Choruses,* an early work in which Morris dances alone, accompanied by a recording of choruses from the oratorios of Handel). More often, though, the sparks struck in Morris's imagination by a musical phrase will fly off in seemingly oblique directions that prove on closer inspection to have been inspired quite directly by the phrase's shape. Bach's C Major Cello Suite begins with a descending scale; in *Falling Down Stairs,* choreographed to the piece, the dancers run down a set of seven steps and splash onstage as the curtain goes up.

Morris's musicality has become such a commonplace that it is almost possible to forget how unusual it once was for an up-and-coming young choreographer, now forty-three, to take so passionate an interest in such matters. By 1980, the year he started his company, music and dance had come unmoored from each other, at least as far as modern dance was concerned. Martha Graham had always used music as a mood-setting backdrop, heedless of its form; Merce Cunningham treated it as a separate event, unrelated to anything his dancers happened to be doing on stage. Postmodern dancemakers like Trisha Brown dispensed with it altogether. But Morris was different, then as now. Not only was he interested in music, but his choice of scores was wildly diverse. The program being performed by his company at the New Victory Theater—one old work, one new work, and three New York premieres—is as representative of his eclectic tastes as any five pieces of music could be. *My Party,* made in 1984, is set to Jean Françaix's String Trio, a good example of what Francis Poulenc liked to call "adorable bad music"; *The Argument,* made last year, uses Robert Schumann's Five Studies in Folk Style, played by the cellist Matt Haimovitz and Iverson. As for the premieres, *Dancing Honeymoon* is accompanied by a medley of popular songs from the Twenties and *Silhouettes* by a group of piano pieces composed in 1993 by Richard Cumming, while *Greek to Me* is a Morris solo set to the microtonal music of the eccentric American composer Harry Partch. The only thing missing is a sample of the baroque vocal music that is the company's trademark.

"I don't *see* dancing," Morris says. "I start with the music. I listen to a lot of music, a lot of the time. Loads of Bach. But for me to want to choreograph a piece, there's got to be some twist to it, something odd. A certain weirdness. It could be rhythmic, or something about the orchestration, or some wrong chord nobody ever notices that makes me crazy. And the concept of 'danceable' music doesn't mean much to me. A lot of music I choose is the opposite of what people would choose to dance to. Partly that's because I think so much music written specifically for dance is bad, or lame in some way. I was thinking about *Coppélia,* but I hadn't heard it in years, so I bought a record, and I thought, 'Eh, too bad—I wish I liked it better.' I've gotten more interested in American music in the past few years—Henry Cowell, Conlon Nancarrow, Lou Harrison. It's not that I'm patriotic. It's that there's something I'm liking about it."

Musicality means different things to different people, and some critics have accused Morris of doing nothing more than "visualizing" the pieces he choreographs, just as a Disney animator might make a pen-and-ink hippopotamus cavort to Tchaikovsky. But his responses to music, though sometimes deliberately obvious, more often have the same uncanny quality found in the ballets of George Balanchine, whose profound understanding of music was also initially questioned by many critics. Tina Fehlandt has spent almost the whole of her career working with Morris, and having watched him evolve, she used to take his methods for granted. "Now that I've staged Mark's dances on other companies," she says, "I realize how differently he does things. I've watched him make stuff up time and time again, but when I saw him make *Sandpaper Ballet* on the San Francisco Ballet last year, I was sort of astounded. I mean, this is someone I've known for twenty years, and I kept saying to myself, 'How did he *think* of that?'"

June Omura, who joined the company in 1988, has a different perspective. She studied classical ballet as a girl ("I cut my teeth on Balanchine"), and it was not until she enrolled in Barnard College, where she majored in English, that she first encountered modern dance. She fell in love with Morris's choreography after seeing him dance *O Rangasayee,* a twenty-three-minute solo set to an Indian raga, and when she is asked about his musicianship, her sharp, amused features shine with a connoisseur's delight: "Music is Mark's foremost passion in life, not dance. He lives with a piece of music. He comes into rehearsal with the score, and he'll understand it phrase by phrase, note by note. He starts choreographing pieces before we've heard them. First he thinks for a second, then he does some strange move. We try to repeat it, he adds to it. *Then* he puts the music on—and it snaps into place. Once I learn a piece of his, I can never forget it. All I have to do is listen to the music and it makes sense."

MORRIS CARES ABOUT MUSIC SO MUCH THAT THE MARK MOR-ris Dance Group, unlike most touring ensembles, no longer performs to taped accompaniments. "Live music isn't a luxury," he says. "It's a necessity. I want the audience quiet and sitting in the dark, and I want the band and the dancers to be presenting something right then, something living and honest. I'd rather have a bad show with real things in it than a good fake show with no blood."

Because of his insistence that the company's wide-ranging repertory be accompanied by live musicians, he requires an unusually versatile music director, and Ethan Iverson fills the bill with room to spare. Most musicians who work with dance companies have classical backgrounds, but Iverson is a highly original jazz pianist whose latest CD, *The Minor Passions,* is astringent, occasionally clamorous, and richly inventive. "I feel like I'm not a strong enough classical player for Mark," he says. "I would never have agreed to do the Chopin two years ago—some of those études are really hard. And I didn't know enough about Baroque music, either, though looking at his dances has taught me to hear it, and to love it. But taking classical pieces on the road and playing them every night with great musicians like Yo-Yo Ma has been incredible for my technique, and now I feel confident that I won't let the dancers down."

A pupil of Fred Hersch, Iverson admits to having been influenced by everyone from Thelonious Monk and Ornette Coleman to such avant-garde classical composers as Frederic Rzewski. Morris revels in his ability to improvise fluently in awkward compound meters, and the two men are forever trying to outwit each other during company class; instead of the usual bland classical fare, Iverson is prone to serve up such startling accompaniments as a piece of faux-Brahms in 5/4 time, or an eerily accurate impression of the boogie-woogie pianist Jimmy Yancey. "Ethan is brilliant," Morris says emphatically. "I'm doing the Chopin for him. I once thought of doing the exact same sequence of pieces as Fokine's *Les Sylphides,* but I found out that Balanchine had already restaged it. Then I heard Ethan practicing one day, and I got interested in Chopin all over again. He's incredibly smart, a fabulous performer, and he's one of those people I value so much because they never try to be sophisticated, or pretend they know something they don't know. He's so guileless, it's shocking!" The dancers are equally fond of Iverson's polystylistic playing, and they turned out in force for a series of four solo recitals he recently gave at the Greenwich House Music School. Julie Worden and Guillermo Resto sat in the front row at one performance, clapping lustily after each number. "We're addicted," Worden said. "We've come to every concert. I think Ethan is a musical genius."

When Iverson joined the company two years ago, Morris was staging Jean-Philippe Rameau's *Platée,* the latest of his controversial operatic productions, which will be given its long-awaited New York premiere by the New York City Opera. Now he is working on Virgil Thomson's *Four Saints in Three Acts,* which the English National Opera will present at the London Coliseum on a double bill with his acclaimed 1989 version of Henry Purcell's *Dido and Aeneas*. "I'd known *Four Saints* a long time ago but forgotten it completely," Morris says. "Then I remembered that I loved it, so I got the old recording and was loving it again. Then I saw Bob Wilson's production and decided I wanted to do the shorter version, which turned out to be perfect for the National Opera." Morris is staging an abridged version of the opera that Thomson had to make for a 1947 recording.

Four Saints and the Chopin dance are being rehearsed simultaneously, and the company switches between them with nonchalant aplomb. Morris's visual renderings of Gertrude Stein's opaque libretto are festive and fanciful, and to watch him sitting behind a music stand, waving his arms like a conductor as Iverson croaks out the vocal lines in his reedy tenor and fills the studio with Thomson's slightly askew hymn-book harmonies, is to suspect that he is presiding over the creation of a masterpiece. But even masterpieces, as Balanchine said, must be made on union time, so Morris is once again all business, spewing similes ("Like an over-the-hill flamenca who's about three feet tall—with a mustache!") and repeating a tricky phrase over and over again as he waits impatiently for the dancers' unfocused movements to coincide with the ones he's imagining. On the next try, the phrase snaps into place with a near-audible click, followed by an unmistakable sigh of collective relief.

"Saint Teresa as a young girl being widowed. Can she sing," Iverson intones shakily, then pounds out an oom-pah-pah as the dancers slip into a giddy waltz.

"Leave later gaily the troubadour plays his guitar," Morris brays in reply, beaming ecstatically.

New York Times 2000

PART FIVE ～ PERSONALS

The Importance of Being Less Earnest

WHATEVER HER OTHER VIRTUES, ISADORA DUNCAN was not exactly the sort of person to whom one would have relished telling a joke. Peter Kurth's new biography, *Isadora: A Sensational Life*, leaves little doubt that the mother of modern dance found few things amusing, least of all herself. "You must all forgive me if I seem somewhat egotistical," she once proclaimed, presumably with a straight face, "but my Life is so tightly bound up with my Art, it is so much one and the same, that I must always refer to it." Not much of her Art has survived the ravages of time (she was never filmed, and we mostly "know" her style from still photographs and reviews), but *My Life,* the personages-I-have-slept-with memoir published shortly after her death in 1927, is the kind of book the critic Guy Davenport had in mind when he remarked, "Sometimes, on reading Goethe, one has the paralyzing suspicion that he thinks he's being funny." While we may not know precisely what her dances looked like, it seems a safe bet that the woman who choreographed "La Marseillaise" and Tchaikovsky's *Pathétique* Symphony never squeezed a stray giggle out of her awestruck audiences — at least not on purpose.

What Duncan sowed was soon reaped by a generation of modern-dance choreographers for whom humor was, to put it mildly, a superfluity. To flip through Edwin Denby's collected reviews of dance in New York in the Thirties and Forties is to be struck by how *dour* he makes their dances sound. Though he made a point of being fair, he also believed deeply in the inestimable value of lightness, and so it is instructive to watch him grapple with Martha Graham, whose clenched-hair psychological dramas did so much to shape the emotional landscape of dance in postwar America. (When Randall Jarrell wanted to spoof modern dance in *Pictures from an Institution,* he made up a perfectly plausible-sounding piece called *The Eye of Anguish,* not realizing that Graham had used that same title four years earlier.) On one occasion Denby described her company as "bold about being earnest, but timid about being lively," which neatly sums up what many balletomanes find unsympathetic about Graham's painfully sincere art.

Perhaps not surprisingly, the Problem of Earnestness in Art, as the capital-happy Isadora might have put it, has been on my mind of late. These are undeniably serious times, and artists are responding to them in undeniably earnest ways. That's the trouble. I haven't seen any dances about September 11 — I've been steering clear of theaters where I might accidentally stumble across one — but I have sat through a half-dozen one-act plays inspired by the destruction of the World Trade Center, most of which go more or less like this:

> SHE: You've got to get over this.
>
> HE: I can't. I never will.
>
> SHE: Your brother would have wanted it that way. *(A beat.)* Besides, I'm pregnant.
>
> HE: Oh, darling, I love you. *(They embrace.)* I guess I'll go back to work today.

Blackout, followed by a critic running up the aisle, stifling inappropriate laughter as he flees to the lobby.

Would that such exercises in timeliness were a mere aberration caused by the intense feelings of the moment. Alas, they have always been with us, especially in wartime and most especially in America, far too many of whose well-meaning citizens are allergic to the exhilarating fizz of high art with a light touch. It seems not to occur to them that life is such an indissoluble mixture of heartbreak and absurdity that it might be more truly portrayed through the refracting lens of comedy. Instead, they prefer what Lord Byron, who knew a thing or two about both life and art, would have crisply dismissed as "sermons and soda-water."

Without getting bogged down in the French-German dichotomy beloved of facile writers on a tight deadline, I think the culprit-in-chief here could well be Richard Wagner, the only man ever to have written a five-hour-long comic opera. German art has always tended to be earnest to a fault, not least at the noontide of romanticism, but Wagner suffered more acutely than any of his contemporaries from the messianic delusion that art—his art—could redeem the world. Compare *Mein Leben,* his comprehensively unfunny autobiography, with the champagne-like *Memoirs* of Hector Berlioz, the most French (and Byronic) of composers, and you will see at once the difference between the seriousness of a world-saver and the seriousness of a melancholic wit who viewed both the world and himself with the same wry detachment. It is no coincidence that Wagner has always been far more popular than Berlioz: he never makes the fatal mistake of inspiring us to laugh at ourselves.

It is also no coincidence that Isadora Duncan went over *way* big with the Wagnerites of her day. As early as 1904, she did the choreography for a Bayreuth Festival revival of *Tannhäuser,* in the process meeting Wagner's widow Cosima, another top-seeded contender for the title of least intentionally amusing person ever. ("I have never met a woman who impressed me with such high intellectual fervour as Cosima Wagner," Duncan wrote, proving the point.) From then on, Wagner's music figured prominently in Duncan's programs—she even danced to the "Liebestod" from *Tristan und Isolde,* a blood-curdling thought—forging a family tie between German romanticism and the swoony pseudo-modernism of first-generation modern dance, which was in point of fact about as "modern" as the waltzes of Brahms to which Duncan also loved dancing.

Small wonder, then, that the children and grandchildren of Isadora, Martha Graham foremost among them, dominated native-born American theatrical dance for so long. They were right at home, particularly during World War II, when American culture, already sick unto death from the political pieties of the Thirties, came close to choking on its own high-mindedness. Dawn Powell, a cruelly funny woman who had no use for such nonsense, skewered the spirit of the age in *A Time to Be Born:* "The poet, disgusted with the flight of skylarks in perfect sonnet form, declaimed the power of song against brutality and raised hollow voice in feeble proof. This was no time for beauty, for love, or private future . . . This was a time when the artists, the intellectuals, sat in cafés and in country homes and accused each other over their brandies or their California vintages of traitorous tendencies."

Small wonder, too, that American popular culture has often appeared more vital, or at least more uninhibited, than its highbrow counterpart. By now it is a dusty cliché, if no less true for being overused, that much of what was characteristic of American art in the twentieth century arose from sources long thought unacceptably plebeian. In any list of artists whose work suggests something quintessential about the American temper, Fred Astaire and Count Basie are as likely to figure prominently as, say, Aaron Copland or Helen Frankenthaler. Nor should we feel uncomfortable about bracketing such superficially dissimilar figures, all of whom know how to say serious things without falling victim to the curse of heaviness.

It took a while for modern-dance choreographers to free themselves from that curse, but Merce Cunningham and Paul Taylor—both, as it happens, alumni of Martha Graham's company—finally turned the trick. It's surprising (well, no, it isn't) how many dance buffs are still suspicious of Taylor, mainly because his work, though serious, is never ponderous. Having seen a lot of art of all kinds since September 11, I'm impressed by how many of the things that spoke to me most strongly, from *Urinetown* to *Ghost World* to the exhibition of Ben Katchor's "picture stories" on display at the Jewish Museum, were either wholly comic or partook of the sweet-and-sourness found in Taylor's best dances. I even saw one very timely play that succeeded in striking the same balance: *After the Storm,* Heather Grayson's richly involving one-woman show about her misadventures in Operation Desert Storm, in which she briefly commanded an Army bomb-disposal unit. Not that defusing land mines is intrinsically funny, but for all the intensity of her play and performance, Grayson went out of her way to make us laugh at the myriad lunacies of military life, thereby throwing the harrowing parts of her experience into still higher relief.

Dancegoers of similar inclination were lucky to get a second look at Mark Morris's *Gong* during American Ballet Theatre's City Center season. A marvelous piece in its own right, *Gong* also contains two parody-flecked pas de deux, both danced without music, which remind us that

Morris, like Taylor, is one of those rare birds who can be serious with a smile. Then, too, there was George Balanchine's *Symphony in C*, which received its long-overdue ABT debut. Few other modern artists working in any medium have had Balanchine's uncanny ability to transport the attentive viewer into a better-ordered universe of romance and grace—and humor. So it was with *Symphony in C*. As the curtain rose for the ten thousandth time on that familiar stageful of women in white tutus poised before a blue backdrop, one felt the world snap back to normal again—just what all the pundits had been assuring us would never happen. It put me in mind of a poem by Edwin Muir, "Reading in Wartime," that makes the case for sonnets about skylarks: "Boswell's turbulent friend / And his deafening verbal strife, / Ivan Ilyich's death / Tell me more about life, / The meaning and the end / Of our familiar breath, / Both being personal, / Than all the carnage can, / Retrieve the shape of man, / Lost and anonymous."

Of course there is a parallel case to be made for earnestness: surely it is people like Isadora Duncan who make the world go round. But who would want to go along for the ride if they also made all the art? Henry James, that wittiest of serious men, underlined the point in an 1893 letter to his friend Edmund Gosse. The occasion was the publication of "A Problem in Modern Ethics," John Addington Symonds's agonizingly earnest pamphlet calling for a change in public attitudes toward homosexuality. "I think," said James, "one ought to wish him more *humour*—it is really *the* saving salt. But the great reformers never have it." No, they don't, but the greatest artists do, and never more than when falling skyscrapers threaten to make us lose sight of the crooked shape of man, absurd and preposterous and—yes—beautiful.

New York Times 2001

I've Got a Crush on You

A FEW YEARS AGO, I FELL IN LOVE—WITH A PROSE style. As I wandered through a Midwestern museum one morning, I saw a painting by Fairfield Porter that spoke to me so strongly that I resolved on the spot to find out more about him. Stopping by the gift shop, I looked for a book about Porter; instead, I found a book he wrote, called *Art in Its Own Terms: Selected Criticism, 1935–1975*. I bought it, went to lunch, and started flipping through the pages, waiting for something to jump out at me. My eye fell on this passage: "Some art has a very open meaning, and can be written about in terms of this meaning; but the chances are that if the meaning is the most interesting thing about it, it does not stand alone, it does not assert itself. It leans on what it means. An implied meaning is richer." I immediately snapped to attention—it was as if an invisible man had clapped his hands next to my ear—and by the time I put the book down, my cheeseburger was stone cold.

What happened that day has happened to me many times before. Sometimes it's only a passing fancy that ebbs in a matter of weeks; sometimes it's far more serious, lasting for a year or more. Sometimes it's with a stranger, sometimes an old friend whom I suddenly come to see in a different light. But no matter who the objects of my literary affection may be, the nature of our relationship is the same: I want not merely to enjoy but to *become* them, to absorb their stylistic essence and be changed by it. Nor are these affairs discreet ones: I invariably blare them from the rooftops, like a teenager who wants nothing better than to walk across the quad at high noon, holding his sweetheart's hand for all to see. Harold Bloom couldn't possibly have had me in mind when he coined the phrase "the anxiety of influence." Within weeks of reading *The Gastronomical Me,* I was babbling to the editor of *Opera News* — over lunch, naturally — about how I wanted to write about opera the way M. F. K. Fisher wrote about food. I rediscovered Raymond Chandler, a writer I've long admired, when the Library of America reissued his novels in an elegant two-volume set, and all at once I broke out in a rash of similes. (In case you haven't noticed, I'm not quite over that one yet.)

As it happens, Fairfield Porter was as compelling an artist as he was a prose stylist. A committed representationalist who never painted an abstract painting in his life, he was nonetheless powerfully influenced by Willem de Kooning, forging an intensely personal style out of de Kooning's Abstract Expressionism and the intimate Post-Impressionist idiom of Edouard Vuillard. He led an equally idiosyncratic private life (he was a bisexual who raised a family of five), as Justin Spring's fine biography, *Fairfield Porter: A Life in Art,* relates. His paintings have yet to attract a wide audience — none have been hanging of late in any major Manhattan museum, though there was a one-man show at the Equitable Gallery — but they are greatly admired by connoisseurs of American art, and his criticism is now widely regarded as among the finest by any American writer.

The particular quality that attracted me to Porter's prose was its compactness. He is not a chatty writer, spinning webs of one-sided conversation in the confiding manner of a familiar essayist; rather, he makes a point, crisply and completely, and then moves on. *Art in Its Own Terms* is full of such points, a dozen of which I have copied into my commonplace book. (Here is another one I especially like: "Discipline is sweetened by compromise.") None of them have the flashy brevity of the self-conscious aphorist, who writes as though he wished to dazzle a drawing room; with Porter, the goal is illumination. "Criticism creates an analogy," he wrote in a piece called, appropriately enough, "The Short Review," "and by examining the analogy you see what the art essentially is. Criticism should tell you what is there." Porter believed this close-packed terseness to be characteristic of painters who write — he claimed that "painters do not have a feeling for words as entities with their own life, but go in for ideas" — but I have also noticed it in a different sort of practitioner turned critic, Edwin Denby, who was a dancer and a poet (and who, interestingly, knew Porter in the Thirties). Denby's dance criticism has the same compact clarity as Porter's art criticism: he tells you what is there, image by image, fixing the successive moments with a dancer's eye and a poet's precision, and then you see what he saw, and partake of his understanding.

Denby, like Porter, is a writer whose influence on me has been considerable, and it was in thinking about what the two men had in common that I made a discovery about the nature of my literary crushes: they are usually on authors whose styles are vastly different from mine. I am a very chatty writer; I've always sought to make my writing sound like a person talking. But when I read Denby or Porter, I feel as if theirs is the only possible way to write, and find myself lusting after a gnomic quality alien to my natural tone. "Ballet," Denby wrote in 1947, "is the one form of theater where nobody speaks a foolish word all evening— nobody on the stage at least. That's why it becomes so popular in any civilized country during a war." When I first read that perfectly balanced pair of sentences, I thought I'd die of envy. Then I started trying to figure out how to write a pair of sentences just like it.

This, at least for me, is how literary influence is like romantic love: desire quickly gives way to disorientation, followed by growing comprehension and, eventually, assimilation. Yet in time I rediscover my own style—transformed by passion, but still recognizably mine. Arlene Croce, with whom I once had a long stylistic fling, had a fling of her own with Edwin Denby: she has wryly described herself as "one who has spent years combing Denbyisms out of her prose." But out of that not-so-brief encounter was born a style that is itself utterly distinctive; it was through submitting freely to Denby's influence that Croce, the finest and most individual dance critic of our time, became herself.

All of this, of course, presupposes that it is a good thing consciously to work on one's style, a notion at which certain austere folk have bridled. "I never knew a writer yet," Samuel Butler wrote, "who took the smallest pains with his style and was at the same time readable." I don't know whether I would have met Butler's standard of readability—probably not—but I do know that for me, style is a project, something at which I am constantly working. Rereading Raymond

Chandler made me feel that my prose was too dry, and so I resolved to fertilize it with metaphor; my encounter with Fairfield Porter, by contrast, has made me want to be more direct (not to mention smarter). And, of course, one can also work on matters that go deeper than style: reading M. F. K. Fisher, for instance, filled me with a parallel longing to write about the place of music in life as it is lived.

DO WRITERS LIKE ME EVER COME TO A STOPPING PLACE, A TIME when we decide that we are, for good or ill, what we are? I suspect not. Surely our lives are permanently unfinished projects: we choose to remain open to new influences so as not to become frozen into our limitations. W. H. Auden, who loved trying on styles, wrote toward the end of his life a couplet that has stuck in my mind: "Blessed be all metrical rules that forbid automatic responses, / force us to have second thoughts, free from the fetters of Self." Coming under the spell of other, better writers is a similar kind of quasi-religious discipline: it is their varied influence that frees us from the fetters of self (which grow tighter as one grows older) and serves as a perpetual source of refreshment and renewal.

That's why I'm not planning to settle down with Fairfield Porter. We're still having a ball, but I'll put him on the shelf sooner or later; somebody else is bound to come along, and I'll be off and running once again. Does that make me promiscuous? No, just a hopeless romantic. Rupert Holmes wrote a wonderfully rueful song about a man who's forever falling in love with women he sees on the street: "And you'll see her on a train that you've just missed / At a bus stop where your bus will never stop / Or in a passing Buick / When you've been pulled over by a traffic cop." That's me, in spades. My bookshelves, like my writings, are haunted by the ghosts of influences past, all remembered with great tenderness, much as one recalls an old flame from college days: Whitney Balliett, Edmund Wilson, William F. Buckley, Jr., A. J. Liebling, Somerset Maugham, Diana Trilling, Randall Jarrell, Otis Ferguson, Joseph Epstein, Neville Cardus. In time, Porter will join them; I hope his spirit is pleased by the company it keeps.

New York Times Book Review 1999

Elegy for the Woodchopper

LEMARS, IOWA, A SMALL FARM TOWN ABOUT THIRTY miles north of Sioux City, is swinging tonight. It is Founder's Day at Westmar College, a United Methodist school with an enrollment of 430, and the college is throwing a Saturday-night dinner dance in honor of the occasion. The picked-over remnants of a hundred platefuls of prime rib have been cleared away. Fifteen men are settling themselves on a folding bandstand, tuning up their instruments, and idly leafing through thick folders of music. Most of them are in their twenties and early thirties. Their leader, who is waiting for his cue in the hall outside the dining room, is seventy-four.

The drummer strikes a crisp roll on his tom-tom, the trombonists wave white plastic mutes in front of their golden bells, and Woody Herman's Thundering Herd swells confidently into the slow, mournful strains of "Blue Flame," the band's theme song. The odds are that I am the only person in the room under the age of fifty who recognizes it. I own two recordings of "Blue Flame." I have heard the Thundering Herd play it in an Independence, Missouri, shopping center, in the auditorium of a suburban high school, and on a warm summer night at an outdoor concert in Kansas City. I have traveled a thousand miles to hear it tonight.

Without further ado, a short, stooped man steps quietly from the wings and begins to make his careful way to the bandstand. He does not smile. He is too tired to smile. I saw him backstage before the dance, bent almost double under the weight of a half-century of one-night stands, and I felt my throat catch at the sight. Every wrinkle on his deeply lined face seemed to stand for another year of bumpy bus rides and cheap motels. Forty years ago, he was a matinee idol who packed movie theaters and ballrooms from coast to coast. The crowds are smaller now, the ballrooms less glamorous, the jumps from job to job longer. LeMars is the Thundering Herd's fourth gig this week, and it seems impossible that this old man will be able to shake off his weariness and face the three hours of hard work that lie before him. But the throaty, growling sounds of "Blue Flame" are working their nightly miracle, and Woody Herman seems to grow more confident with every cautious step. As the room swells with the applause of expectant dancers, the last of the big-band leaders reaches center stage, picks up his clarinet, and begins to play the blues. This is the moment I have waited for. This is the beginning of my dream come true.

THE WORD *NO*, SPOKEN AT THE RIGHT TIME AND IN THE RIGHT place, can change the destined course of a lifetime. I like to think that my father had this in mind when he told me not to touch the old phonograph records in the basement closet. Whatever his intentions, the fact remains that as soon as the back door slammed behind him that Sunday afternoon, I was halfway downstairs, and by the time he was out of the garage, I had pulled the rollaway bed out of the closet and dragged six crumbling cardboard boxes out from behind it.

Had those boxes been full of records by, say, Shep Fields and his Rippling Rhythm, I would have shoved them back behind the bed without a second thought. But my father had been young once, and the music that he favored in his youth was, by and large, the swinging kind. It's true that he loved the music of Glenn Miller, which is perfect for dancing but not very likely to speed up the pulse of a young boy raised on the Rolling Stones. But he had a roving ear, and along with his battered copies of "Moonlight Serenade" and "Perfidia" and "American Patrol," he had preserved dozens of records by Artie Shaw and Stan Kenton and Tommy Dorsey and Claude Thornhill — and Woody Herman.

After he came home from the Philippines at the end of World War II, my father bought many of the records that Woody Herman made in 1945 and 1946 with the band that would later become known as the First Herd: "Laura," "Apple Honey," "The Good Earth," "Your Father's

Mustache," "Caldonia," "Woodchopper's Ball." Once he had danced to them with my mother. Now I held them in my hands, those red-label Columbias, thickly covered with cardboard shavings, unplayed for twenty years and more. I took them over to the basement phonograph, a cast-off Philco portable. I had just read *The Good Earth,* so I put on "The Good Earth" first, wondering what this dusty antique could possibly have to do with Pearl Buck's slow-moving tale of life in China. Curious and mildly expectant, I changed the speed of the turntable from 33 to 78, flipped the needle over, and eased the heavy tone arm onto the record.

Children born in the age of the laser-scanned compact disc will never know the crackle of a steel needle briskly scratching its way through the grooves of a shellac 78, a sound as evocative for the jazz buff as the tuning up of a symphony orchestra is for the lover of classical music. I heard it for the first time that afternoon. Then strange music came crashing out of the speakers, the loud, piercing, joyous strains of a big band in full cry. I heard it plain, unfiltered by nostalgia, unobscured by memories of make-believe ballrooms and the girl you left behind. I turned up the volume as far as it would go, feeling the lift of the rhythms in my bones. I was hooked. The big-band era, decades after its demise, had reached down the corridors of lost time and grabbed a piece of me.

I borrowed a bass from the music room of my junior high school on the first day of summer, carried it home, and played along with my father's records until school started again in the fall. I played every record in the basement a hundred times and memorized all five of the books in the Sikeston Public Library about the big-band era. One of the musicians I read about that summer was Woody Herman. I learned that Herman played clarinet and alto saxophone; that he had survived every change in musical fashion, even the ruthless choke hold of rock and roll; that he was still spending ten months out of the year on the road with his current group, which he now called the Thundering Herd. Hundreds of celebrated musicians had passed through Woody Herman's bands, which thereby acquired a reputation as the great finishing schools of jazz. I learned that he was universally regarded as one of the kindest and most decent men in the business. None of his alumni, I read, ever had a bad word to say about him. The younger ones even had a nickname for him: "Road Father."

I wanted it to be 1945 again, so that I could play bass with Woody Herman. But it was 1975, and so I went off to William Jewell College, played with the college jazz band, and wangled a part-time job writing about jazz for the *Kansas City Star*. I went down to the union hall one afternoon and joined Local 34-627 of the American Federation of Musicians. My first gig was at a bar called the Lucky Penny, which had recently been bought by a bartender who liked jazz and decided to book us without bothering to check with his regular customers, most of whom would have rather gone on listening to country music on the jukebox. The band consisted of a shaky clarinetist whose red face bore the unmistakable signs of hard drinking, an accordion player who spent most nights working in polka bands, a cocktail drummer, and a scared young college kid on bass. All four of us were jammed onto a bandstand the size of my mother's kitchen table. The clarinetist, who knew that this was my first gig, never bothered to call any tunes. He just glared at me through bloodshot eyes, stamped his foot, and started playing.

I must have done all right, for I began to get calls from bandleaders around town, and I started working two or three times a week with a plump, red-faced piano player named Bob Simes. A veteran of the bebop era, Bob knew exactly how to handle kid bass players who thought they knew a thing or two. He liked to sip Scotch and soda between sets, and as we sat together in a quiet bar one night taking five and swapping stories, he started reminiscing. Swirling the Scotch around in his glass, he cocked his head and said, "The first time I played with Charlie Parker . . . " No particular stress was placed on the word *first*, but I got the point anyway. Bob had played with the king of bebop *more than once*. Any questions, kid? I shut up and spent the next two years doing exactly as I was told, and I had the time of my life doing it.

Most of the musicians I met during my two years with the Bob Simes Orchestra had day jobs and played jazz strictly on weekends, though a few of them did nothing but grind out dance dates and wedding receptions night after night. One or two were nasty drunks, but most were intelligent, well-spoken, and honest to a fault. Theirs was a nighttime world of friendship and mutual admiration, of unexpected kindnesses and extraordinary generosity, of hard times and empty pockets and four-in-the-morning courage. I learned a lot from them, about jazz and about other things. I learned to take people as they were, bark and all. I learned what it was like to get home in the middle of the night on a regular basis. I learned how it feels to get blown off the bandstand at a crowded jam session. (In case you're wondering, it feels like hell.) I learned everything except how to drink on the job, something that comes only with age and practice.

It wasn't long before I started to think about trying to play bass for a living. It wouldn't have been very hard to do. I was good enough at what I did and getting better every night. I was being offered twice as many gigs as I had time to play. My colleagues treated me with warmth and tact. But even though I loved playing bass as much as anything I had ever done in my life, I knew in my heart that I didn't quite belong in the world of jazz, that a small-town boy like me could never be truly comfortable living on the after-hours margins of respectability. What turned out to be my last gig was a quartet date with Bob, a hard-driving drummer named Abel Ramirez, and the best tenor saxophonist in Kansas City, a baby-faced lawyer named Mike White, who liked his jazz fast and hot. We were playing for an Oldsmobile dealers' convention, and none of the dealers were sober enough to know what we were doing up on the bandstand, so we played for our own pleasure and ignored the crowd. Had I known for sure that I was quitting music for good that night, I would have called for Horace Silver's "Sister Sadie," Mike's favorite song, at the end of the last set. But I didn't know, so we played "The Party's Over," the tune Bob always played at the end of the last set, and I loaded my bass in the back of my station wagon and drove off to join the middle class.

By the time I came to New York some ten years later, I had learned a lot more about jazz, and about myself. I had played enough lousy gigs to know that I didn't have the true fire in my belly, that I didn't want to play jazz passionately enough to do nothing else. But jazz was in my blood and bones all the same, and I missed it badly. Most of all, I missed the one thing I had not done in my two years as a professional jazzman: I had never gone on the road. The tours I went on in college had given me a taste of what it feels like to live out of a suitcase and play for a different crowd every night. A dozen autobiographies had taught me the miseries of life on the road: broken-down buses charging across rickety bridges, greasy food and crummy pianos and hostile crowds. I could not forget Charlie Barnet's pithy summing-up: *You stay tired, dirty, and drunk.* I had no wish to do any of those things. But I never stopped wondering what else I had missed out on because I had not gone on the road.

One morning, I put my feet up on a desk in an assistant editor's cubicle in lower Manhattan, started sifting through the daily pile of unread magazines, and ran across a short article in the *Atlantic* about Woody Herman. It mentioned in passing that Woody was preparing to celebrate his fiftieth anniversary as a bandleader with a concert at the Hollywood Bowl. I didn't even stop to think twice. I called up a friendly editor at another magazine and started talking very fast. *How about a profile of Woody Herman? Good guy, everybody loves him, fiftieth anniversary, last of the great big-band leaders. I could even spend, oh, a couple of days traveling with the band. . . .*

IT IS FOUR MINUTES AFTER NOON. I AM STANDING IN THE parking lot of a run-down motel on the outskirts of LeMars. Those who eat breakfast have long since boarded the band bus. A handful of stragglers, some of whom have all too clearly just stumbled out of bed, are scrambling on board for the long haul to Kansas City, where the Thundering Herd has a night off. Woody Herman has already left for the Sioux City airport. Too fragile to endure the day-to-day stresses of life on the bus, he will fly to the next gig. No one grumbles about it. Woody paid his dues long before most of the musicians in the band were born.

"This is home, man," one musician says to me as we climb on board. If so, then the Thundering Herd is in desperate need of a housekeeper. The back of the bus, where the rowdier Herdsmen sit, is littered with books, pillows, and old newspapers from various cities. A huge double bass, snugly wrapped in its black canvas case, is balanced gingerly in the seat ahead of me. The overhead luggage racks are crammed with suitcases and overnight bags of every imaginable size and color. Someone has hung a hand-lettered sign on the toilet door: CONTAMINATION! HAZARDOUS WASTE MAY BE HARMFUL TO YOUR HEALTH.

The door hisses shut and the driver pulls out of the parking lot. As the cornfields of southwestern Iowa slip by, the players swap battered paperbacks, play Trivial Pursuit, and trade notes on the restaurants of LeMars. One man is banging away at a pocket calculator, working feverishly on his tax return. A cassette of the rough mix of the band's next record album, taped three weeks ago at a concert in San Francisco, makes its snail-like way from seat to seat; I have brought along my own homemade cassette of Woody Herman's Forties recordings. To my surprise, I discover that most of the people sitting around me have never heard any of Woody's old records. Indeed, my interest in them strikes the tenor saxophonist in the seat across the aisle as somewhat peculiar, perhaps even a mark of squareness. Why should he care about Woody Herman's old stuff? *He* plays with Woody every night. But the other musicians are curious, and my cassette is soon being passed through the bus along with the rough mix of the next Woody Herman album. "Goddamn, man, that stuff holds up *really well,*" the tenor saxophonist says to me a few minutes later, shaking his head as Woody's 1945 trumpet section wails its way through the last chorus of "Northwest Passage."

Sitting behind me is Mark Lewis, a youthful-looking trumpeter who has played with the Thundering Herd since 1980. Cappy Lewis, his father, played with the Herman band more than forty years ago. (He plays the muted trumpet solo on Woody's 1946 recording of "Woodchopper's Ball," one of the tunes on my homemade cassette.) "Dad took me to hear the band one night," Mark tells me. "We went up to meet Woody afterward, and when my father told him that I played trumpet, Woody said, 'So when are you going to play in my band?'"

I ask Mark about the daily grind. "The road," he says, "is the same thing every day. You don't have much time to yourself. You eat bad food a lot of the time. You're stuck on a bus eight hours a day. You wash your underwear in the sink. When you get sick, there's nothing you can do but ride the bus and play the gigs and feel rotten all the time. But I like it. I really do. I know it sounds crazy, but there's a freshness to our work that makes it worthwhile, especially when we get a young crowd. That's what we look forward to. They *make* us want to play. And there's Woody, you know. He lets you be yourself. He keeps things relaxed. You're never afraid to go up on the bandstand with Woody. And he really loves to hear us play. That's why he's there."

Six hours later, the skyline of Kansas City begins to fill the windows of the bus and the members of the band begin to discuss their plans for the evening. A rumor that a convention of beauticians is being held in our hotel ripples through the back of the bus. One group of Herdsmen wants some real Kansas City barbecue. All the musicians with wives or girlfriends at home decide to get together and watch a little television. "Eight o'clock call, guys," says the road manager as the bus pulls into the Downtown Howard Johnson parking lot. A chorus of groans greets his announcement as the Thundering Herd streams off the bus and heads for the front desk in search of room keys.

I leave the bus by myself. I chose this particular weekend to travel with the band because I knew it would be passing through Kansas City, and I have been looking forward to spending a quiet night in my old college town. Italian Gardens, a familiar downtown haunt where I had intended to give myself a good dinner, turns out to be closed on Sundays, so I trudge back to the restaurant of the Downtown Howard Johnson for lack of a better idea. As I chew on a stubborn piece of hotel steak, the words of "Sweet Kentucky Ham," a song by a jazz pianist named Dave Frishberg, flash into my mind, and I realize for the first time that Frishberg wasn't trying to be funny:

> It's six P.M.
> Supper time in South Bend, Indiana
> And you figure, what the hell
> You can eat in your hotel
> So you order up room service on the phone
> And you watch the local news and dine alone
> You got to take what little pleasures you can find
> When you've got sweet Kentucky ham on your mind.

At eight A.M., the same people who barely made it onto the bus in LeMars are barely making it onto the bus in Kansas City. The rumor about the beauticians' convention was true. The married men quiz their bachelor colleagues closely as we pull onto the highway and start our long drive across the prairies of Kansas to El Dorado, an oil town where Butler County Community College is hosting an afternoon clinic and an evening concert. The clinic is for the members of the college jazz band and other student musicians from the area, while the concert is open to the general public.

The afternoon clinic begins with a short performance by the Thundering Herd. About forty students, trumpets and trombones and saxophones in their laps, are scattered around the bleachers of the college gym. Many of them look skeptical. I eavesdrop and learn that a few of them have never even heard of Woody Herman. Dressed in a windbreaker and sneakers, Woody makes his slow way to center stage and offers a few terse words of greeting. The first tune, he says, will be a new arrangement of Duke Ellington's "It Don't Mean a Thing." (How many of these kids, I wonder, know who Duke Ellington was?) The rhythm section pumps out a fast four-bar introduction. The saxophones enter with the theme and the brass fire back a crisp riff. A massive wave of sound rolls off the bandstand and washes over the bleachers. I can see that the students are surprised at how *loud* the Thundering Herd is. It is a special kind of loudness, a kind they have never encountered before. It comes not from tall banks of shrieking amplifiers but from sixteen jazz musicians playing in bold, fat-toned unison, and it quickly sets their feet to tapping.

After the concert, Woody heads for the men's locker room, where a table loaded with cold cuts and soft drinks awaits the band. I have arranged to spend the next hour with him. As he pours himself a glass of orange juice, I ask him about some of his less well known alumni from the Forties and Fifties. This is a gesture of homage, a sign that I have taken the trouble to learn about him, that I am a member of the fraternity of jazzmen, a respectful insider. Woody notices at once. The friendly mask and the polite, unreflective answers of a thousand hurried interviews with general-assignment reporters are promptly laid aside, and his worn face shines with enthusiasm: in his soft, buzzy voice, he begins to tell me elaborate tales of epileptic drummers and heroin-soaked baritone sax players and tough times on the road. "The high-ways are better now," he says with a crooked smile, "so you get to drive even farther every day."

Why, I ask, is he still on the road after fifty years? "There's a reason for the road," Woody tells me. "As long as you're doing one-nighters and moving every day, you have the most freedom for your music. You don't have to answer to the people you worked for yesterday. You're not going to be there tomorrow night. You can play the music *you* want to play. That's why I keep going. Because it's still fun. That's the reason I'm here, and that's why all the guys are here. Sure, they gripe like hell. They go through all the motions of being unhappy people. But then they start playing, and they realize that this is the only thing they want to do. I know I can't think of anything else *I* want to do."

Woody pauses. He is clearly ready to get back to his motel room and rest. I start to trip over my words. Up to this moment, I have been prompting him with ease, but the thing I want to tell him most now will not come out. *My God, Mr. Herman, I want to say, I admire you so much. You can't imagine how hard I schemed to get to where I could sit in this grubby locker room and watch you drink lukewarm orange juice. I called my father last night to tell him about this trip. He used to drive for eight straight hours to come hear me play jazz in Kansas City. He was so proud of me, Mr. Herman, and you did that, you and Stan Kenton and Artie Shaw and Claude Thornhill.*

"Mr. Herman," I say nervously, "do you ever play 'The Good Earth' anymore?"

He shakes his head. "Nope." He rises slowly to his feet. "But I'll see if I can work it in tonight."

That evening the band returns to the gym for a full-length concert. The crowd is a mixture of middle-aged couples and younger fans, in-cluding most of the students who came to the clinic that afternoon. Woody offers them his usual concert program, one I have heard a half-dozen times over the years. There are five numbers from the books of the First and Second Herds: "Blue Flame," "Woodchopper's Ball,"

"Four Brothers," "I've Got the World on a String," and "Early Autumn." There is a rock version of Aaron Copland's *Fanfare for the Common Man* and a jazz version of Gabriel Fauré's *Pavane*. There are a half-dozen numbers from the Thundering Herd's forthcoming record album. The band plays them so beautifully and passionately that even the older members of the audience, the ones who came to touch up their memories, give in happily to the new and unfamiliar sounds.

Woody announces that he will play an old First Herd tune by special request. The players fumble through their music folders. Then he kicks off "The Good Earth." The tempo he sets is a shade too fast for comfort, and the performance is ragged. I know sight-reading when I hear it, and I also know it is unlikely that many of these young players have even heard the tune before, unless they happened to listen to my cassette as we drove to Kansas City. But it is with my forgiving inner ear that I hear Neal Hefti's chart the way it sounded in a New York recording studio on August 10, 1945, at the beginning of the atomic age and the end of the big-band era. I hear Dave Tough's flashing cymbals, Flip Phillips's surging tenor saxophone, Pete Candoli's brazen, slightly acid lead trumpet, Chubby Jackson's springy five-string bass lines. I wonder if Woody can hear them, too.

Nine Herdsmen hang around the gym after the concert to play basketball. The others, too beat to join in, board the bus and return to the motel. I am among them. "Back in the old days," one trumpeter says to me in the lobby, "musicians used to shoot heroin. Now we shoot baskets. Wild life, isn't it?"

AS I FLEW BACK TO NEW YORK THE NEXT DAY, I THOUGHT about the many aging performers I have known who refused to retire. Some of them could not get up in the morning without the certain knowledge that they would hear applause before they went to bed that night. I don't doubt that Woody Herman liked applause, but that wasn't why he stayed on the road. I knew, although I didn't ask him about it, that he toured because he owed the government money. Back in the Sixties, Woody's manager, a fat man named Abe Turchen, spent three straight years gambling away the money for Woody's income tax and the band's withholding. By the time anyone else knew what was going on, Woody owed the IRS $1.6 million in back taxes, penalties, and interest. For the rest of his life, all of his profits and all of his record royalties went straight to the IRS. That was why he kept touring. His choices were limited: he could trade one prison for another.

As the Seventies gave way to the Eighties, Woody's life started to fall apart. Charlotte, his wife, died of breast cancer. Illness caused his clarinet playing to grow shrill and uncertain. He scaled back his solos to the barest possible minimum. Sometimes a critic would knock him in print, leaving a foaming wake of hatred among musicians who read the cold, tactless words and cursed critics, cursed the IRS, cursed the idiot fate that saddled Woody with a merciless financial burden and simultaneously took away his health.

"It's strange," Mark Lewis told me as we drove from LeMars to Kansas City. "I started listening to big bands when I was thirteen. All the old guys were still going strong then, guys like Ellington, Basie, Stan Kenton. Now it's down to Woody. Believe me, there'll be an empty feeling when he quits." But he didn't quit. In fact, he stayed on the road for several months after I returned to New York. As he continued to fly from gig to gig, I tried to write my magazine piece. My first draft was bounced back. *Not enough details,* the editor said. I knew what kind of details he wanted, and I didn't want to put them in. I knew that this story would not have a happy ending.

The fiftieth-anniversary concert at the Hollywood Bowl came and went. Then Woody got really sick, too sick to stay on the road, and he flew back to Hollywood. When the money stopped coming in, the IRS seized his house and put it on the auction block. A real estate speculator bought it for a song and offered to rent it back to Woody. When Woody couldn't make the payments, the speculator hit him with an eviction notice. For the first time in his long life, Woody Herman found himself on the evening news. A band of alumni held a benefit concert in Los Angeles to pay their old leader's rent. He was too far gone to know or care. My editor called me up. "I think that circumstances may have caught up with your piece," he said gently.

Woody Herman died on November 29, 1987. I was sitting in my

office when the news came over the wires. As I read the bulletin, I remembered a scene from my first night on the road with the Thundering Herd. It was twelve-forty in the morning. The dancers were gone, the autographs signed. The pianist and bassist were jamming together on "Willow Weep for Me" as the other musicians, tired and bedraggled from another long night's work, knocked down the music stands and took apart their instruments. Woody was standing alone near the bandstand, listening to the music, idly snapping his fingers to the beat. He picked up his clarinet and tossed off a low, breathy chorus of "Willow Weep for Me." Then he put it down, did a stiff little dance step, and slipped out of the room. Homeless, wifeless, and futureless, Woody Herman was still taking what little pleasures he could find. His music had sustained him for five decades, and it would comfort him until the very end.

I thought about my own youthful dreams of playing bass with the Thundering Herd. Could I possibly have cut it? Now I would never know. My bass had been gathering dust in the bedroom closet for years. I knew I would never play seriously again, that my casual decision to give up jazz had been carved in stone by the passage of time. Most of the time I didn't think about it very much. Sometimes, sitting in a nightclub in Manhattan, I would feel a desperate longing for the life I had so briefly led. That longing gripped me again as I thought about Woody and Bob Simes and the Lucky Penny and a hundred dismal country-club dances. I thought about what I had missed by having been born a couple of decades too late, by having opted for a middle-class job over the constant scuffle of a jazzman's life. I struck a balance in my mind for the ten thousandth time and noted, as usual, that the life I had chosen came out squarely in the black. Then I said a silent farewell to Woody Herman and remembered, not without a touch of rue, the last verse of "Sweet Kentucky Ham":

> It's one A.M.
> They're serving up last call in Cincinnati
> But it's still a nighttime town
> If you know your way around

And despite yourself, you find you're wide awake
And you're staring at your scrambled eggs and steak
And you must admit your heart's about to break
When you think of what you left behind
And you've got sweet Kentucky ham on your mind,
    on your mind
Nothing but sweet Kentucky ham on your mind.

American Scholar 1989

Close to Home

S MALL TOWNS RARELY MAKE THE BIG-CITY PAPERS, AND
are even less likely to turn up in books. I know of just two
biographies that mention Sikeston, the Missouri town where I
grew up. David Maraniss's *First in His Class* records that in 1946, Bill
Clinton's father died in a car crash three miles outside town; nine years
later, according to Peter Guralnick's *Last Train to Memphis,* Elvis Presley
gave a concert there, back when he was young, scared, and thin. Someday the New Madrid Fault will put my hometown on the front pages —
the last major earthquake to hit southeast Missouri was so strong that it
changed the course of the Mississippi River — but until now the only
time Sikeston made news was after an event nobody likes to talk about.
One Sunday morning in the winter of 1942, a man named Cleo Wright
was dragged through the streets by an angry mob, doused with gas-
oline, and burned to death.

Thus it was with considerable interest that I read *The Lynching of Cleo
Wright,* a book by Dominic J. Capeci, Jr., a professor of history at
Southwest Missouri State University. Of course I knew a man was
lynched in Sikeston. It was no secret: my father watched from his
window as Wright's near-naked body bounced over the cobblestones of
Center Street. But it wasn't a tale he relished telling, and I can remember only one other person who brought it up unprompted in all the
time I lived there.

It is a strange experience to learn about one's hometown by reading a
scholarly monograph, especially one written in a style that is two parts
Joe Friday and one part academic lingo. Yet it was only by reading
Capeci's book that I learned of the myriad ways in which Wright's ugly

death overlapped with the idyllic small-town life of my boyhood. To be sure, I had to go searching for some of them, since history almost always rings untrue to the rougher texture of life as it is lived: you would never know from reading Capeci's book what Sikeston looks like or smells like. So I looked, and this is part of what I found.

Early in the morning of January 25, 1942, a black man broke into the home of Grace Sturgeon, a white woman who lived on what was then the east side of town. He spat on her, sliced open her belly with a six-inch folding knife — her intestines fell out — and fled on foot before help could arrive. (Incredibly, she survived, and was still alive in 1993, when Capeci interviewed her for his book.) A half-hour later, Hess Perrigan, a night marshal, and Jesse Whittley, a neighbor, were driving west toward Sunset Addition, Sikeston's black ghetto, searching for the unknown attacker, when they ran across Wright, a twenty-six-year-old oil mill worker, walking down the road, his pants covered with blood. They stopped and searched him, and found the bloodstained knife. Wright pulled a second knife and stabbed Perrigan in the face; Perrigan then shot him four times, and Whittley beat him to the ground.

Word of the arrest spread, and by 11:35 a mob had gathered in front of City Hall, where Wright, who had since confessed his crime, was lying on a cot in the town lockup, near death from his own wounds. David Blanton, the county prosecutor, told the people to go home, but they pushed their way through the doors, breaking one of Blanton's ribs in the process and dragging Wright into the street. The ringleaders commandeered a Ford, hooked his legs over the rear bumper and led a caravan to Sunset, stopping in front of a Baptist church whose terrified congregation looked on as the lynchers poured five gallons of gas over his broken body and set him ablaze; he cried out once, then died. A grand jury was empaneled six weeks later, but no indictments were handed up and no one ever went to trial.

All these things are recounted by Capeci plainly and dryly, with none of the journalist's eye for telling detail. (I doubt it occurred to him, for instance, to point out the ghastly irony that the spot where Wright was executed without trial lies between Lincoln and Fair streets.) But bare facts in dry relation can be enough, especially when they hit close to home. For I never knew that my family doctor was the nephew of

David Blanton, who stood on the steps of City Hall and struggled vainly against the will of seven hundred passionate men, or that my favorite teacher, a Civil War buff whom I loved like an uncle, was the son of one of the grand jurors who let the lynchers go. And though I spent countless hours talking with my best friend about everything under the sun, he never told me that his aunt was the woman Wright had knifed, or that it happened a half-dozen blocks from my childhood home, where my mother lives to this day.

In a small town, past and present stand side by side, almost too close to tell the difference. But there are a thousand differences. I drove up and down the streets of Sikeston on a cloudless day not long ago, looking at the familiar sites Capeci mentions in his book. The old City Hall has been torn down and the cobblestones covered with asphalt, but Grace Sturgeon's battered house is still standing, and it is possible to follow the precise route along which Cleo Wright was dragged to his death. I drove past a pretty park with a white bandstand, and the town bakery, which fills the air with the innocent yeasty smell of Bunny Bread, and stopped at last in the parking lot of a red-brick church whose motto is "The church where no one is a stranger," not ten blocks from the graveyard where my father is buried. As I marveled that green grass could grow on such unhallowed ground, an old black man strolled out of the parsonage. "Would you happen to be the piano tuner?" he asked, smiling broadly. I mentioned at supper that night that I was reading a book about a lynching. "What's a lynching?" asked my ten-year-old niece.

TIMES, THEN, HAVE CHANGED, IF ONLY UP TO A POINT. I HAD no black friends when I lived in Sikeston a quarter-century ago, and there doesn't appear to be much more racial mixing now. And while Dominic Capeci may not be the most graceful of stylists, he knows something I don't know: the names of the twenty men whom FBI agents identified as having taken part in Wright's lynching. I gather he even spoke to some of them, though he identifies them only by pseudonyms. Their median age in 1942 was thirty-five, and most were surely alive when I was a boy, but I knew them not. Did I play with their children? How did their neighbors feel about them? Were they heroes, or pariahs? Or were their identities slowly forgotten?

Those who forget the past, we are told, are doomed to repeat it. I believe this — and yet few things are really neat enough to be folded into an aphorism. Never to forget is sometimes never to forgive. We see on our television screens every night the awful results of historical memory run amok, of ancient irredentist rivalries resolved by shedding rivers of tribal blood. Wright's lynching was awful too, but the fact remains that it was not repeated, at least not in my hometown. Of course his murderers should have been brought to trial, though it is hard to imagine that they would have been convicted, not least because there was no serious question as to Wright's own guilt. (Presumably this is why his name is no longer widely remembered.) But since they were never even indicted, might it be for the best that they were forgotten, their ultimate punishment left to the all-knowing disposition of a higher court? I only know one thing for sure: I feel no temptation to further disturb their unquiet sleep.

New York Times Book Review 1999

My Friend Nancy

"WHAT ONE READS IN THE NEWSPAPER," SAID BIS-marck, "can also be true." I thought of that wry remark as I looked at the obituaries for the cabaret singer Nancy La-Mott that ran in the New York papers. The circumstances of her death made it a newsworthy event, especially in a town with two tabloids: she was married on her bed in a Manhattan hospital, an hour and a half before she died of liver cancer, two weeks short of what would have been her forty-fourth birthday. Yet none of the papers offered a first-hand account of the ceremony, in part because, except for me, no journalists were present, and I wrote nothing about it. It was, I felt, a private matter.

Keeping Nancy's secrets was nothing new for me; I had been doing it since the day we met. She was a blurter: every important thing she ever told me about herself burst out of her without warning, either as soon as we got together or in the middle of a conversation about something else. As a working journalist, I interviewed her twice, and on both occasions she unthinkingly said things that would have been acutely embarrassing, to her and other people, had they been published. Aside from those interviews, the only other time I mentioned Nancy in print was in a piece about Frank Sinatra I published in the *New York Times Book Review,* where I called her the finest cabaret singer of her generation. By then, I knew she was sick and feared she was dying, and I wanted her to see those words before it was too late. I was, of course, biased, but thousands of people who had never met Nancy, or who knew her only slightly, agreed with me. Stephen Holden, who wrote her obituary for the *New York Times,* spoke for them when he said that her "unadorned, heartfelt interpretations of songs epitomized the best of what could be called an all-American style of traditional pop singing."

Her success was a minor miracle of sorts, proof that virtue is sometimes rewarded, at least for a while. Though American popular music has long since turned its back on the traditions Holden invoked, Nancy's unabashedly romantic performances of the old-fashioned songs she loved were nontheless bringing her, after a quarter-century of scuffling, the kind of national exposure no other baby-boom cabaret artist had yet received. When she died, she was on the verge of real fame — not the small-time celebrity of a New York club singer, but something bigger and more far-reaching. That kind of acclaim would inevitably have changed her life, but nothing could have changed her personality. Short (five-foot-one), bottle-blonde, unpretentious, and irrepressibly merry, Nancy was all of a piece, on stage and off. Because she sang without reserve or self-consciousness, her fans felt they knew her, though few of them knew she had spent the whole of her adult life suffering from an incurable intestinal disorder and its various side effects, including arthritis. She did not hide it, but neither did she trade on it, and her courage never failed her, not even at the very end, when, having lost her hair to chemotherapy, she faced her audiences wearing a wig, and, having known both, sang of love and despair.

I CAN'T REMEMBER EXACTLY WHEN I FIRST HEARD NANCY sing, or what the occasion was, though I think my curiosity must have been piqued in 1993 by an issue of *New York* magazine in which the editors of that trend-happy journal dubbed her "the best cabaret singer in New York." Not that the honor would necessarily have impressed me. In the Fifties, cabaret was a recherché alternative to the mainstream pop of singers like Sinatra and Tony Bennett; by the Nineties, four decades after Elvis Presley turned American popular music inside out, it had become a black-tie life-support system for the show tunes of yesteryear. But early or late, it had always been a haven for singers with uninteresting voices and interchangeable styles: arch, overdramatic, brittle around the edges. The infectious brio of a Bobby Short, or the emotional directness of a Mabel Mercer, merely served to make far too many of their colleagues seem pale and gray by contrast. And the cabaret repertoire, with its relentless emphasis on Cole Porter and Stephen Sondheim, seemed to me as suffocatingly narrow as its manner.

Whatever the reason, I found myself one afternoon in an Upper West Side record store, holding a copy of Nancy's second CD, *Come Rain or Come Shine: The Songs of Johnny Mercer,* trying to decide whether or not to buy it. I was intrigued by the uncabaret-like choice of material—"Moon River," "Hit the Road to Dreamland," "The Days of Wine and Roses"—but it was the cover photo that tipped the scales. Though dressed glamorously enough, the woman in the picture seemed on closer inspection anything but glamorous: with her long blonde hair, tightly shut eyes, and blissful half-smile, she looked like a precocious child playing dress-up on a rainy afternoon. Charmed by the incongruity, I bought the disc, brought it home, and put it on. An hour later, I went back and bought Nancy's two other CDs, *Beautiful Baby* and *My Foolish Heart,* and spent the next few days playing all three of them over and over again. What I heard on those discs was a warm, husky mezzo-soprano voice that seemed twice as big as the woman in whom it was housed; a vivid yet unaffected way with lyrics; and a quality at once sensuous and achingly idealistic. Later, after I had met Nancy, I would write that her singing sounded "as if the girl next door had snuck out at two A.M. to make a little whoopee with her steady boyfriend," a description that delighted her no end.

Viewed from one angle, Nancy's albums fit more or less comfortably into a cabaret mold. Though she had a wonderfully sure sense of what jazz musicians call "time" (she swings with impressive ease, for example, on the title track of *Come Rain or Come Shine*), she was not a jazz singer. Her vocal routines were carefully worked out in advance, and she never improvised. And though her voice was unexpectedly large, most of her singing was intimate in approach, as befit the modest size of the rooms in which cabaret artists usually appear. (The Oak Room of the Algonquin Hotel, where Nancy performed regularly in the last few years of her life, seats eighty.) Her recording of "Surrey with the Fringe on Top," which appears on *Beautiful Baby,* was in this sense a *locus classicus* of her art. The singing is delicate and airy, the reading of Oscar Hammerstein's faux-naïf lyrics precisely detailed, and the overall effect strikingly similar in scale and style to classical art-song.

But Nancy's singing contained no trace of the affectation that is the blight of the cabaret style. It was, rather, firmly rooted in the tradition of such full-voiced, full-hearted women singers of the Fifties as Jo Stafford and Rosemary Clooney. Even when she sang Sondheim (*My Foolish Heart* contains a medley of two songs from *Merrily We Roll Along*), she did so with passion and honesty. The blasé disengagement that nowadays passes for irony formed no part of her musical vocabulary. For her, popular singing was serious business.

THAT WINTER, I WENT TO THE CHESTNUT ROOM OF TAVERN ON the Green, a restaurant on the western edge of Central Park, to hear Nancy in person. The Chestnut Room, whose lavishly mirrored decor is a bizarre blend of high camp and early-American tourist trap, is the last place one would expect to find a classy singer, and I wondered how she would fit in. The answer came quickly: she marched onto the bandstand, looked around, and announced, with an enormous grin, "This place looks like a gay hunting lodge." After a split-second pause, the crowd exploded with laughter.

Nancy sang a canny mixture of material from her three albums and various other songs, some familiar and some obscure. Her patter sounded spontaneous, though it was in fact as carefully rehearsed as her singing (I would hear her use the hunting-lodge line a half-dozen times, fracturing the audience every time), and she seemed relaxed and confident. But the thing that impressed me most was her ability to project herself so fully that you came away feeling you had had a personal encounter. This was what made audiences fall for Nancy. There was nothing either self-indulgent or exploitative about it: her sincerity was real, and it was irresistible.

Were it not for the fact that she also had a beautiful voice that she used with exceptional skill, one might have been tempted to say that Nancy's art was more theatrical than musical: she approached each song as if it were a one-act play, with herself as the main character. The theater critic John Simon, who admired her greatly, wrote of one of her performances that "she fully fathoms what a song is about, and then, rather than merely singing it, lives it." Singers who can do this, be they popular or classical, are the rarest and most precious of birds.

One evening in the spring of 1994, representing the features section of the *Daily News,* I showed up for an interview with Nancy at an inexpensive restaurant in the theater district of New York, wondering what I had let myself in for. Singers are notoriously temperamental as a breed, and even for experienced reporters, interviews are almost always awkward: both parties bring unrelated agendas to the table, and mutual manipulation is often the order of the day. I was prepared to be disappointed.

Nancy was already there when I arrived, and I was struck by her pleasant, plain-spoken manner. We ordered dinner, she with a gusto unexpected in so petite a woman. (I learned soon enough that she loved food almost as much as music.) After an ice-breaking fiasco with the miniature tape recorder I had purchased for the occasion, I pulled out a notebook and started asking questions about her early days. She came from a medium-sized town in Michigan. Her father had been a part-time trumpeter, and she had gotten her start with his band. "My family visited New York when I was twelve," she said, "and I was already the kind of kid who read Earl Wilson's column and wanted to go to Sardi's and a Broadway show." Laughing, I confessed that I, too, had read Wilson's Broadway column as a child in Missouri. Indeed, the longer we talked, the more we found we had in common. Both of us had cut our teeth on jazz, longed to see the lights of Broadway, and traveled to New York to seek our fortunes.

What started off as an interview imperceptibly became a conversation. She spoke frankly of her struggle with Crohn's disease, of the ileostomy she had undergone the year before in order to relieve the condition, of the hard times she had known and the hopes she had. After dinner, I walked her to the Lunt-Fontanne Theater, where she was singing anonymously in the pit of an ill-fated musical called *The Best Little Whorehouse Goes Public,* a thankless chore she had taken on in order to pay her medical bills. She was so tiny that I had to stoop to hear her over the roar of traffic in Times Square.

Once the interview was published, I sent Nancy a copy of a book I had written about growing up in the Midwest. She called a few days later to tell me she had liked both book and interview, and I invited her to the ballet. It took a month to find a night on which we were both free, but we finally settled on George Balanchine's dance version of *A*

Midsummer Night's Dream, which she had never seen. Afterward we ate at O'Neal's, a dancers' haunt across the street from Lincoln Center, and talked until closing time. I mentioned at one point that my favorite popular song was Leonard Bernstein's "Some Other Time," and sitting there in the near-empty restaurant, she sang it for me: *Where has the time all gone to? / Haven't done half the things we want to / Oh, well, we'll catch up / Some other time.*

We felt from the first as though we had known each other for years. After her funeral, Nancy's brother would ask me how long we had been friends. Seventeen months, I told him, and he shook his head. "From the way she talked," he said, "I figured you guys went *way* back."

I STARTED GOING TO HEAR NANCY WHENEVER SHE SANG IN New York, sometimes at Tavern on the Green and sometimes at the Oak Room. I continued taking her to the ballet occasionally, and we had dinner together whenever we could find the time. But like most friendships between busy people, ours was conducted more often than not over the telephone. Nancy's messages all began the same way: "Hi, LaMottski here." Then she would talk until the answering machine cut her off. When I called back, we would chat for an hour or so.

Many of our conversations were about music. Nancy had thought hard about her art, and had the clearest possible understanding of what worked for her as a singer. It had little to do with received ideas about cabaret: she preferred wistfulness to rue, and hope to high tragedy. "I'm a major-chord singer," she liked to say, and certainly she was the only cabaret singer in New York, if not the world, who preferred Rodgers and Hammerstein to Rodgers and Hart. Her repertoire ranged from Irving Berlin to James Taylor, with plenty of room in between for new songs by younger writers. But she also had a special liking for certain moss-covered standards thought to be dead beyond recall. "I try to take songs that everybody gave up on, and rethink them," she once said.

I find a point of view that works for me and sing them in a way that makes people love them. Take a song like "Moon River." Sure, it's a really good song, but you know what people think about it: "Who wants to hear *that* again?" And that's when I start to get interested. I love it when people come up to me and say, "I really hated that song until I heard you sing it."

Nancy knew how good she was, and was not shy about saying so. Neither of us had much use for the "classic" cabaret style, and while she was quick to praise other women singers she liked—she was unstinting, for example, in her admiration of Wesla Whitfield, a jazz-inclined cabaret singer from San Francisco—these were few and far between. I laughed at what we called her "thou-shalt-have-no-other-gods-before-me" moods, but never teased her about them. Success was important to her: she had started out as a chubby, awkward teenager with a promising but raw style, and by sheer force of will had turned herself into a beauty whose taste and musicality were respected by every professional who ever heard her. "I've sung a lot of Holiday Inns," she once told me. "Anything I get, I deserve."

Nancy's toughness was born of a life filled with suffering, both physical and emotional. Illness had kept her from working regularly—there were long stretches when she could not perform at all—and now that surgery had made it possible for her to take a serious crack at the big time, she was determined to reach the top. She had also been repeatedly unlucky in love (though, characteristically, two of her broken engagements ended in friendships so strong and enduring that both ex-fiancés were present at her marriage, jointly serving as best men). All this was spun off into her singing, which grew steadily deeper and more intense, even during the brief time I knew her.

But there was more to Nancy than her art. Perhaps because there had been so much pain in her own life, she had a genius for friendship. A booklet given out at her memorial service contained letters of remembrance from more than seventy people, all of whom were plainly devastated by her death. No doubt for the same reason, she was an easy touch for charity, though she made light of her frequent appearances at fund-raising events. People who knew Nancy longer and better than I swore she could be lazy, demanding, and willful (though never, so far as I know, malicious—there was no spite in her). But these were mere surface flaws, not outward marks of a divided soul—a condition that affects some artists so profoundly it becomes impossible for the people who know them to reconcile who they are with what they do. With Nancy, there was no difference, and that was part of the reason why listeners responded so strongly to her singing. For all the sophistication of her art, she was a small-town girl at heart, kind and generous and uncomplicated, and she knew how to be happy.

IN MARCH 1995, I WENT TO HEAR NANCY SING AT TAVERN ON the Green. It was a midweek performance, and she had made me promise to catch the last set and then join her as she ate her free dinner (one of the coveted prerogatives of a singer who performs in a club with a good chef). I saw as soon as she mounted the bandstand that something was wrong. When the set ended, she came straight to my table, sat down, and blurted, "I have cancer." Over the next nine months, she underwent hormone therapy, a hysterectomy, and a grueling course of chemotherapy. But she also planned, rehearsed, and recorded her last and most ambitious album, *Listen to My Heart;* made her debut at Carnegie Hall; sang at the Algonquin and, again, at Tavern on the Green; and met the man whom, when her time was up at last, she chose to marry.

Peter Zapp was an actor Nancy had met while singing in San Francisco. When she told me about him on the phone, she added that she had also seen him perform on stage, but was untypically reluctant to supply further details. I pressed her: what show? what part? She paused, probably for effect. "Well," she finally said, before giggling, "he was playing Roy Cohn in *Angels in America.*" Nancy had gotten lucky, and just in time. Pete soon came to New York to care for her after the hysterectomy, but the cancer, it turned out, had metastasized. She canceled her engagements for the rest of the year, except for a week-long run in October at Tavern on the Green. By then, the disease had reached her liver, her hair had fallen out, and her weight was down to 104. Somehow she got through the week, and gave a radiant closing-night performance, during which she did, surprisingly, a Rodgers and Hart song. Many in the audience were close friends and knew what she was singing about: *I didn't know what year it was / Life was no prize / I wanted love and here it was / Shining out of your eyes / I'm wise, and I know what time it is now.*

A week or so later, she called up and asked me to come over for Thanksgiving dinner, as I had done the year before. But when she opened the door to her apartment, she looked shrunken and weak. Then Pete appeared. In a crazily romantic gesture, he had shaved his own head. And frail as Nancy was, she pulled herself together sufficiently to cook dinner while we heard *Listen to My Heart,* a first copy of which had arrived a few days earlier.

Listen to My Heart is a collection of Nancy's most frequently requested numbers, including a show-stopping pairing of the Johnny Mercer–Harold Arlen ballad "Out of This World" and Cole Porter's "So in Love" (the only Porter song I ever heard her sing). It was her first album with a large studio orchestra, and she had had the good fortune to work with Peter Matz, a veteran arranger from Los Angeles. I had watched her record the vocal tracks in the studio in July, but this was my first hearing of the finished product. It was clear that if this was to be her final album, her career would be ending on its highest note.

Nancy sang in public for the last time on December 4, at a party celebrating the anniversary of the opening of WQEW, the all-standards radio station in New York whose disc jockeys had done much to promote her career. When I called her the following Saturday, she was still groggy from chemotherapy, so I merely asked if there was anything she needed. "Not today," she said, "but maybe I'm going to need something from you early next week."

Three nights later, I learned that she was back in the hospital. Her liver had been eaten away by the cancer, and her kidneys had shut down. There was no hope. In her room the next day I held her hand, startled by how warm it was, and told her I loved her. It was all she could do to draw breath. When I came back that evening, a handful of her closest friends and relatives had gathered in the corridor, telling stories and pretending to be calm. Then a doctor arrived, to say the only way to make her comfortable was to give her a dose of morphine that might send her into a coma. Pete thought it right that she decide for herself, so he shouted in her ear until she clawed her way back from the edge of oblivion. Pete had proposed the day before, and now she told him that she wanted the morphine — but that she wanted to marry him first.

The rest I remember only in flashes, ending with the arrival of a priest and the hurried exchange of vows. For weeks afterward, I would close my eyes and see Nancy lying in her death and marriage bed, gasping for air through the blackened scab that was her mouth, visibly exalted by the ceremony, shouting "Yes, yes, *yes!*" to the priest. Only a handful of days had passed since I had last seen her, bald and thin but recognizably herself. Now she was already resident in another kingdom, yet somewhere deep within there still lay the power to receive this ultimate sacrament of life and love.

Nancy died that night, with Pete at her side. Two months later, a memorial service was held at the Church of Saint Paul the Apostle in Manhattan, and people lined up halfway around the block to say farewell. The *New York Times* had published a long story about her in January, accompanied by a Thanksgiving snapshot of her sitting on a couch with Pete, the two of them bald as a pair of peaches, smiling happily; a few weeks later, *People* ran an enthusiastic review of *Listen to My Heart*. At long last, she was a star.

"LIVE ALL YOU CAN," HENRY JAMES WROTE TOWARD THE END of his own long life, "it's a mistake not to. It doesn't so much matter what you do in particular, so long as you have your life. If you haven't had that what *have* you had?" Unlike James, Nancy LaMott had only half a life, but she lived all she could, and with even greater passion as she knew it was drawing to a close. She was that most uncommon of artists, one whose life was worthy of her work. I listen to her records often, and whenever I do I think of her goodness and bravery, which ennobled every note she sang, and miss her more than I can say.

Commentary 1996

About the Author

Terry Teachout is the music critic of *Commentary*, the drama critic of the *Wall Street Journal*, and a contributor to the *Washington Post*, for which he writes "Second City," a column about the arts in New York City. He also writes about books, dance, film, music, television, theater, and the visual arts for the *New York Times*, the *Wall Street Journal*, *National Review*, *Crisis*, and other magazines and newspapers. He was previously a senior editor of *Harper's*, an editorial writer for the *New York Daily News*, and the *News*'s classical music and dance critic.

Teachout is the author of *The Skeptic: A Life of H. L. Mencken* and *City Limits: Memories of a Small-Town Boy* and the editor of *Beyond the Boom: New Voices on American Life, Culture, and Politics* and *Ghosts on the Roof: Selected Journalism of Whittaker Chambers, 1931–1959*. He wrote the foreword to Paul Taylor's *Private Domain: An Autobiography* and contributed to *The Oxford Companion to Jazz*. In 1992, he rediscovered the manuscript of *A Second Mencken Chrestomathy* among H. L. Mencken's private papers, subsequently editing it for publication by Alfred A. Knopf.

Born in Cape Girardeau, Missouri, in 1956, Teachout attended St. John's College, William Jewell College, and the University of Illinois at Urbana-Champaign. From 1975 to 1983 he lived in Kansas City, where he worked as a jazz bassist and as a music critic for the *Kansas City Star*. He now lives in New York City.

Index